CESAR MAJUL
MUSLIMS IN THE   1973
PHILIPPINES

Muslim Rulers and Rebels

+ THE CONTEMPORARY
MUSLIM MOVEMENT IN
THE
PH.

U.S. ANTI-COLONIAL LOBBY LIMITED PLANTATION COLONY

PURCHASES IN MINDINAO.

16 HECTARES / INDIV. 1024 / PER CORP.

1985

+ BECAME SETTLER COLONY INSTEAD (90)

SULTAN OF SULU SIGNED BATES AGREEMENT

1899 ACKNOWLEDGING U.S. SOVEREIGNTY —

SIMILAR AGREEMENT W/ COTABATO — SO AMERICANS

COULD RESIST NATIONALIST FORCES IN NORTH.

BUT BY 1903 — GEN. LEONARD WOOD MOVED TO

DIRECT RULE. (TO SUBVERT "PETTY CHIEFTAINS" +

ENCOURAGE INDIVIDUALISM.   p 91

1914 = TOTAL DIRECT RULE + ABANDONMENT OF

RECOGNITION OF ADAT = CUSTOMARY LAW.

3 DATUS WHO WORKED W/ AMERICANS HAD FEW LINKS

TO TRADITIONAL AUTHORITIES —   p 101

TENUOUS TIES TO SULTANATES

SYRIAN XIAN SCHOLAR + ADVISOR OF U.S. POLICY ON

MOORS — NAJEEB SALEEBY = RECOMMENDED UNITY OF

MOROS THROUGH ISLAM = THEY WERE NOT UNIFIED +

DID NOT PRACTICE ISLAM. —

DATUS + MORO COURTS SHOULD BE RE-ESTABLISHED.

FUTILE TO TRY CONVERSION. 107.

EDWARD KUDER, SUPERINT. OF SCHOOLS 1924 — TRIED TO

FOSTER ETHNO-LINGUISTIC UNITY AMONG MOROS —

INFLUENCED BY SALEEBY

Comparative Studies on Muslim Societies
General Editor, Barbara D. Metcalf

1.   *Islam and the Political Economy of Meaning,*
     edited by William R. Roff

2.   *Libyan Politics: Tribe and Revolution,* by John Davis

3.   *Prophecy Continuous: Aspects of Aḥmadi Religious Thought
     and Its Medieval Background,* by Yohanan Friedmann

4.   *Sharīʿat and Ambiguity in South Asian Islam,*
     edited by Katherine P. Ewing

5.   *Islam, Politics, and Social Movements,* edited by
     Edmund Burke, III, and Ira M. Lapidus

6.   *Roots of North Indian Shīʿism in Iran and Iraq: Religion and
     State in Awadh, 1722–1859,* by J. R. I. Cole

7.   *Empire and Islam: Punjab and the Making of Pakistan,*
     by David Gilmartin

8.   *Islam and the Russian Empire: Reform and Revolution
     in Central Asia,* by Hélène Carrère d'Encausse

9.   *Muslim Travellers: Pilgrimage, Migration, and the Religious
     Imagination,* edited by Dale F. Eickelman and James Piscatori

10. *The Dervish Lodge: Architecture, Art, and Sufism in Ottoman
     Turkey,* edited by Raymond Lifchez

11. *The Seed and the Soil: Gender and Cosmology in Turkish Village
     Society,* by Carol Delaney

12. *Displaying the Orient: Architecture of Islam at Nineteenth-
     Century World's Fairs,* by Zeynep Çelik

13. *Arab Voices: The Human Rights Debate in the Middle East,*
     by Kevin Dwyer

14. *Disorienting Encounters: Travels of a Moroccan Scholar in
     France in 1845–1846, The Voyage of Muḥammad aṣ–Ṣāffar,*
     translated and edited by Susan Gilson Miller

15. *Beyond the Stream: Islam and Society in a West African Town,*
     by Robert Launay

16. *The Calligraphic State: Textual Domination and History in a
     Muslim Society,* by Brinkley Messick

17. *The Rise of Islam and the Bengal Frontier, 1204–1760,*
    by Richard Eaton

18. *Rebel and Saint: Muslim Notables, Populist Protest, Colonial
    Encounters (Algeria and Tunisia, 1800–1904),* by Julia A.
    Clancy-Smith

19. *The Vanguard of the Islamic Revolution: The Jamaʿat-i Islami of
    Pakistan,* by Seyyed Vali Reza Nasr

20. *The Prophet's Pulpit: Islamic Preaching in Contemporary Egypt,*
    by Patrick D. Gaffney

21. *Heroes of the Age: Moral Faultlines on the Afghan Frontier,*
    by David B. Edwards

22. *Making Muslim Space in North America and Europe,* edited by
    Barbara D. Metcalf

23. *Nationalism and the Genealogical Imagination: Oral History
    and Textual Authority in Tribal Jordan,* by Andrew Shryock

24. *Between Marriage and the Market: Intimate Politics and Survival
    in Cairo,* by Homa Hoodfar

25. *Putting Islam to Work: Education, Politics, and Religious
    Transformation in Egypt,* by Gregory Starrett

26. *Muslim Rulers and Rebels: Everyday Politics and Armed
    Separatism in the Southern Philippines,* by Thomas M. McKenna

Muslim Rulers and Rebels

Everyday Politics and Armed Separatism
in the Southern Philippines

Thomas M. McKenna

UNIVERSITY OF CALIFORNIA PRESS
Berkeley · Los Angeles · London

University of California Press
Berkeley and Los Angeles, California

University of California Press, Ltd.
London, England

1998 by
The Regents of the University of California

Library of Congress Cataloging-in-Publication Data

McKenna, Thomas M., 1952–
    Muslim rulers and rebels : everyday politics and armed separatism
in the southern Philippines / Thomas M. McKenna.
        p.   cm. — (Comparative studies on Muslim societies ; 26)
    Includes bibliographical references (p.   ) and index.
    ISBN 0-520-21015-8 (alk. paper). — ISBN 0-520-21016-6 (pbk. :
alk. paper)
        1. Cotabato City Region (Philippines)—Politics and government.
    2. Muslims—Philippines—Cotabato City Region.   3. Mindanao Island
    (Philippines)—History—Autonomy and independence movements.
    4. Muslims—Philippines—Mindanao Island—Politics and government.
    5. Moro National Liberation Front.   I. Title.   II. Series.
    DS689.C67M35   1998
    959.9'7—dc21   97-49422
                                                                                CIP

Printed in the United States of America
9 8 7 6 5 4 3 2 1

The paper used in this publication meets the
minimum requirements of American National
Standards for Information Sciences—Permanence of
Paper for Printed Library Materials,
ANSI Z39.48-1984.

To the memory of my father

Contents

List of Illustrations and Tables   XI

Acknowledgments   XIII

Introduction: Extraordinary and Everyday
Politics in the Muslim Philippines   I

  1. The Politics of Heritage   11
  2. People and Territory in Cotabato   25
  3. Islamic Rule in Cotabato   45
  4. European Impositions and the Myth
     of Morohood   69
  5. America's Moros   86
  6. Postcolonial Transitions   113
  7. Muslim Separatism
     and the Bangsamoro Rebellion   138
  8. Regarding the War from Campo Muslim   170
  9. Unarmed Struggle   197
 10. Muslim Nationalism after Marcos   234
 11. Resistance and Rule in Cotabato   269

Notes   291

Glossary   337

Bibliography   339

Index   355

Illustrations and Tables

FIGURES

1. Muslim street vendor selling tobacco
   in Cotabato City   38
2. Interior view of Campo Muslim   42
3. Datu Utu with his wife, Rajah Putri,
   and retinue, circa 1890   93
4. Datu Piang with attendants, 1914   95
5. Edward Kuder with his student
   Salipada Pendatun, 1927   111
6. Laborers unloading cargo at riverside landing   126
7. Cotabato MNLF fighters, circa 1975   159
8. Photograph commemorating the 1951 visit
   of Maulana Mohammad Abdul Aleem
   Siddiqui to Cotabato   201
9. Wedding Procession near Campo Muslim   224
10. Dayunday performance in Campo Muslim   225

MAPS

1. Cotabato and the Pulangi River System   26
2. Physiography of southwestern Mindanao   28
3. Three Present-Day Provinces
   of the Cotabato Basin   34
4. Campo Muslim   198

TABLES

1. Muslim and Non-Muslim Populations
   of Cotabato   116
2. Top Eight Vote-Getters for Mayor
   in Six Campo Muslim Precincts,
   1988 Municipal Election   265

Acknowledgments

This is a book about Islamic solidarity and social disparity in the Muslim Philippines. It chronicles both an extraordinary Muslim nationalist struggle and everyday political relations between rich and poor Muslims in the Cotabato region of the southern Philippines. Based on field research in an urban Muslim community, this study combines political ethnography and historical interpretation to investigate the rhetoric and practice of Philippine Muslim politics.

I have spent more than a decade on the research and writing presented in this work and incurred a great many debts of gratitude along the way. Two extraordinary teachers, William G. Davis and John Walton, have provided unstinting guidance and support from the very outset of the project. I thank them and would hope they find something of what they taught me reflected in this work. A number of scholars of the southern Philippines generously offered valuable advice and encouragement very early on. Most I have never thanked properly, and I wish to do so here. My (belated) thanks to Carter Bentley, Eric Fleischman, Thomas Keifer, Cesar Majul, Lela Noble, Stuart Schlegel, and James Stewart.

The following institutions made my research in the Philippines possible in 1985–86, in 1988, and in the summer of 1995: the National Science Foundation, the University of California, and the University of Alabama at Birmingham. Archival research in the United States was underwritten by a Faculty Research Grant from the University of Alabama at Birmingham and an Academic Sharing Grant from the Center for South and Southeast Asian Studies at the University of Michigan. I am indebted to a great many individuals for smoothing my path in the Philippines, only a few of whom may be mentioned here. Joel Rocamora provided valuable contacts in Manila and Cotabato. In Manila, Dr. Jesus Peralta, the curator of the Anthropology Division of the National Museum as well as a scholar of the southern Philippines arranged my affiliation with the museum and generously shared his knowledge with me. Of my friends and acquaintances among the Christians of Cotabato City, I am most deeply indebted to Patricio Diaz, the Bravo family, and to Fr. Jun Mercado, who first brought me to Campo Muslim.

My most enduring debt of gratitude is to the people of Campo Muslim for their generosity and patience toward an itinerant scholar who had little to offer in return other than the promise to tell their story. I am especially grateful for the hospitality shown me by the family of Imam Akmad. Though far from the first lost soul that the imam and his wife had welcomed into their home, I was certainly the most exotic. Five individuals in the Muslim community made extraordinary contributions to my research, for which I want to express my sincere appreciation. My three research assistants, Nur Miskin, Abdul Karim, and Zamin Unti, were not only careful workers but involved advisors and valued friends. Kasan Kamid was my principal consultant and confidant in Campo Muslim and I treasure his friendship. I am also deeply indebted to Sultan Mohammad H. Adil—soldier, scholar, Magindanaon nobleman, and Moro nationalist—for allowing me to record his remembrances.

I am grateful to the following people for reading and providing valuable comments on various drafts of this book—some of them more than once: John Bowen, Colin Davis, William G. Davis, Dale Eickelman, Brian Hesse, Cynthia Mahmood, Michael Peletz, Jennifer St. John, John Walton, and an anonymous reviewer for the University of California Press. I thank all of them for their suggestions, which prompted me always to rethink and very often to rewrite.

Zamin Unti painstakingly, and lovingly, constructed the map of his community, Campo Muslim. Ken Thompson added his talent as an illustrator to that map and the others, and transformed them into the professional looking products included here. Wilma Nappier has assisted me in numerous ways in the preparation of this manuscript. My thanks to each of them.

This long list of benefactors ends appropriately with those closest to me. I choose to thank them in few words so as not to dilute the message. I am forever grateful to my wife, Patti, for making it all possible and to my son, Matthew, for making it all worthwhile.

Extraordinary and Everyday Politics in the Muslim Philippines

That ordinary men and women spill their own blood and the blood of others in armed nationalist struggles seems an intractable reality of the modern world. We attempt to make sense of such conflagrations by identifying their propellants; yet this is frequently the most difficult puzzle to solve about any instance of armed ethnonationalism: whence the willingness of the rank and file to fight and die in the cause of a would-be nation? This book investigates the meanings and motivations of one such struggle—the movement for Muslim separatism in the Philippines. It traces the development of a Muslim nationalist identity in the Philippines, the origins of the Muslim insurgency against the Republic of the Philippines, and the mobilization of popular support for the separatist movement in both its armed and unarmed phases.

The present study, it should be noted, is neither a report from the "front lines" nor a depiction of the political command centers of the Muslim nationalist movement in the Philippines. This ethnography portrays the view from a community of urban poor Muslims, many of them made refugees by the armed rebellion. There are two principal reasons for my choice of perspective. First, when I began my research in 1985, there already existed a number of journalistic reports and one excellent scholarly work (Majul 1985) on the leadership of the Muslim separatist movement. There had also been some careful ground-level reportage of the armed rebellion (see, e.g., Ahmad 1982) but nothing at all about Muslim civilians other than unanalyzed accounts of military atrocities against Muslims or unadorned statistics on Muslim refugees. It was my opinion that an account of the separatist movement from the point of view of "ordinary Muslims" was most needed, especially as separatist leaders had just begun to rely on unarmed mass politics as a new tactic in the separatist struggle.

The second reason relates to more practical and ethical concerns. In 1985 when I began my fieldwork, the Muslim regions of the Philippines were under de facto martial law rule and military occupation. Habeus corpus remained suspended until the end of the Marcos regime and membership in a Muslim separatist organization was an activity punishable by both legal and extralegal measures. The effective reach of the Philippine military did not extend to rebel camps in the hills but did to urban communities. Under such circumstances it was not possible for me to study both rebels under arms and urban Muslims without the risk of endangering my urban informants. As a result, I did not spend any time in rebel camps while conducting my urban research. Philippine and Western reporters did regularly travel to rebel camps, mostly, it seemed, for photo opportunities. That was another source of my hesitancy about making trips to rebel camps. I did not want to be viewed by rebel commanders (who were very well aware of my research in the city) as yet another Western writer come to Cotabato looking for Muslims with guns. While conducting my research among Muslim civilians I also never inquired directly about an individual's separatist affiliations and only interviewed community residents about previous or current separatist activities after the subject had been broached by an interviewee. Despite those self-imposed restrictions, I held conversations with, and obtained significant information from, a considerable number of current and former separatist insurgents, both midlevel commanders and rank-and-file fighters.[1]

There are approximately 3 million Muslims in the Philippines, the only majority Christian country in Southeast Asia. Though they represent only a small percentage of the Philippine population (about 5 percent), Muslims are geographically concentrated in the south of the country and are distinguished from Christian Filipinos not only by their profession of Islam but also by their evasion of three hundred years of Spanish colonial domination. Although Spanish colonizers had consolidated their hold on the northern tier of the Philippine archipelago by 1600, they never accomplished the complete subjugation of the Muslim South. Philippine Muslims are also separated from one another in this archipelagic nation by very significant linguistic and geo-

graphic distance. They are divided into three major and ten minor ethnolinguistic groups and are dispersed across the southern islands.
Cotabato, a traditionally Muslim region on the large southern island
of Mindanao, is the general setting for this study, and home to the second largest Muslim ethnolinguistic group, the Magindanaon. It has
also been the site for many of the key events of the Muslim separatist
rebellion.

The modern movement for Muslim separatism originated among a
small set of Philippine Muslim students and intellectuals in the late
1960s. It gained popular support after the eruption of sectarian violence in Cotabato in 1970 and emerged as an armed secessionist front
in response to the declaration of martial law by Philippines President
Ferdinand Marcos in 1972. Muslim separatist rebels, numbering as
many as thirty thousand armed insurgents, fought the Philippine military to a stalemate, obliging the Philippine government to negotiate a
cease-fire and peace treaty in 1977. Muslim civilians overwhelmingly
supported the separatist insurgents and suffered cruelly at the hands of
the Philippine military.

The peace settlement, which called for the establishment of a "Muslim autonomous region" in the southern Philippines, was never genuinely implemented by the Marcos administration. As a consequence,
fighting broke out once more before the end of 1977, but it did not
again approach the level of intensity experienced prior to the cease-
fire. The Muslim separatist movement entered a period of disarray
marked by factional infighting and a weakening of popular support.
By the early 1980s it had refashioned itself in Cotabato into a mass-
based and self-consciously Islamic movement guided by Islamic clerics.
With the fall of the Marcos regime in 1985, movement leaders (with
the now-modified aim of genuine political autonomy for Philippine
Muslims) fully adopted the practices of popular politics, organizing
mass demonstrations to petition the government for political autonomy and forming an Islamic political party to contest provincial elections. In most of those endeavors they received substantial support
from ordinary Muslims.

My investigation into the origins and meanings of the struggle for
Philippine Muslim separatism as it occurred in Cotabato uncovered
two intriguing paradoxes. The first was revealed by historical evidence
suggesting that the Muslim nationalist identity that undergirds the
separatist movement—a movement that describes itself as Islamic and
anticolonial—originated only during the American colonial period

(1899–1946) with the active encouragement of American colonial authorities. My interpretation of that evidence contradicts the prevailing view among scholars of the Muslim Philippines that Philippine Muslim (or Moro) identity was forged over the course of three hundred years of resistance to Spanish aggression against the Muslim polities of the South and tempered by Muslim resistance to American colonial rule.

A second paradox was presented by ethnographic evidence indicating that the central symbol of the Muslim separatist movement—the notion of a Philippine Muslim nation (Bangsamoro) had little or no resonance among the movement's rank-and-file adherents. Most ordinary followers neither denominated themselves as "Moro" (the term chosen by their leaders to denote the citizens of the new nation) nor proclaimed that they were fighting primarily for the sake of the new nation. This finding challenges the core assumption contained in almost all contemporary theories of nationalism that ordinary adherents of nationalist movements are principally motivated by the resonant force of elite-generated nationalist ideas.[2]

My aim in this study is to explain these (and other) paradoxes of the Muslim nationalist struggle in Cotabato by questioning prevailing anthropological analyses of nationalism as well as the understandings of culture and power that underlie them. The pervasiveness of ethnic strife and nationalist yearnings in the contemporary world has prompted a great deal of theorizing about ethnonational movements such as the one found in the Muslim Philippines. A number of recent anthropological studies have concentrated on the production of nationalist ideologies by intellectuals and political elites (see, e.g., Dominguez 1989; Handler 1988; Spencer 1990; Verdery 1991). Others have examined the various ways by which those ideologies have captured the imaginations of ordinary citizens (see, e.g., Brow 1988, 1990; Crain 1990; Kapferer 1988; Swedenburg 1990, 1991; Spencer 1990; Woost 1993). Surprisingly few anthropological works (see, e.g., Bendix 1992; Bowman 1993; Sluka 1989) have regarded that process as problematic and looked for reinterpretations of, indifference toward, and sometimes outright resistance to nationalist ideologies by those who comprise their primary intended audience. This work treats both sides of the nationalist equation, tracking official nationalist discourse as well as the knowledge, concerns, and experiences of ordinary adherents of the Muslim separatist movement.

My thesis is that the struggle for Muslim separatism in the Philippines (or for that matter any separatist struggle) may only be adequately understood by means of a wide-ranging and multilayered analysis of domination, accommodation, and resistance. To make sense of the American colonial genesis of Moro identity requires a thorough reassessment of the character of political relations between Muslim leaders and external powers—not only American colonial agents but also Spanish intruders, as well as the Christian Filipinos who have dominated the Philippine national state since its inception. To understand why it is that rank-and-file Muslim separatists fight for or otherwise support the movement yet remain unmoved by their leaders' appeals to the Philippine Muslim nation requires the reexamination of widely held assumptions about the nature of political relations between Muslim leaders and followers, not only within the separatist movement but in Cotabato as a whole, and from the precolonial era to the present.

Explaining the paradoxes of Muslim separatism in Cotabato thus demands the analysis of power relations operating in two political arenas—the external state and the local domain. It is insufficient, however, simply to "toggle" between them, examining now external domination and indigenous response, now indigenous rule and local resistance. We need also to fix on those actors and activities that link the two arenas. An essential but understudied feature of separatist movements is their complex conjuncture of power relations. Separatist movements defy the modern states in which they are found, disavowing their authority and, almost inevitably, confronting their armed forces. The leaders of such movements present themselves as rulers as well as rebels and at the earliest opportunity attempt to supplant the jurisdiction of the alienized state with their own more localized version. Muslim rebel leaders in Cotabato, who defy the Philippine state in order to command Cotabato Muslims, clearly straddle the two political arenas. But so do ordinary Muslims, who may simultaneously resist both external domination and local manifestations of power.

While political arenas are always interlinked to some degree, in separatist movements those linkages are intensified and expressed in complex forms. The struggle for Muslim separatism in the Philippines exemplifies the political complexities found in similar political movements formed in postcolonial situations. The remote causes of Muslim separatism in the Philippines may be traced to Western colonizers. The Spaniards created two distinct populations in the archipelago—the colonized and Christianized peoples of the North and the unsubjugated and mostly Muslim peoples of the South. American colonizers yoked those two populations unevenly together in a colonial and then national state. A more proximate cause may be found in the policies and practices of the postcolonial, Christian-dominated Philippine state.

That causal sequence is complicated by various considerations. Although individual Muslim polities offered sporadic armed resistance to Spanish attempts to conquer the South, no significant concerted opposition to Spanish aggression ever developed among the separate Muslim peoples of the archipelago. During the American period, and especially in Cotabato, accommodation was the most frequent response of Muslim leaders to the colonial subjugation of Philippine Muslims. The development of a transcendent and self-conscious Philippine Muslim ethnic identity occurred for the first time during the American period and was encouraged and facilitated by colonial authorities for their own purposes. The content of that identity was significantly influenced by a global process described by Richard Fox as "a world-systemic orientalism," a process whereby colonized populations "come to define their own culture according to the 'indigenations' asserted in Western Orientalism" (1989, 98, 92).

After the establishment of the Philippine republic in 1946, most members of the Muslim political elite aligned themselves with the new state and its policies, including state sponsorship of large-scale Christian migration to the Muslim South. The principal leaders of the separatist movement that began in the late 1960s were young men from non-elite Muslim families who had attended universities in Manila on government scholarships expressly intended to integrate Muslims into the Philippine nation. In Cotabato, those separatist leaders were eventually able to attract popular support because established Muslim leaders had done nothing to protect ordinary Muslims[3] from the severe disruptions wrought by massive Christian in-migration.

The nationalist project of the separatist leaders, rooted in a politics of heritage, reaffirmed "traditional" forms of governance and unintentionally strengthened the positions of established Muslim elites, most of whom were opposed to the separatist rebellion and actively collaborating with the martial law state. When the separatist rebellion seemed likely to achieve some success, certain of those established elites joined the rebel leaders in overseas exile and attempted to gain control of the movement. At the same time, the Philippine government was able to persuade some prominent rebel commanders to defect from the cause with the promise of official positions allowing them to govern large numbers of Muslims. In their new positions, some of those defectors protected

Muslim civilians from the predations of the Philippine military. As a result they were viewed as heroes by many ordinary Muslims who remained nonetheless committed to the separatist rebellion. Following a cease-fire agreement in 1976 the separatist struggle in Cotabato gradually transformed itself into a mass-based, mostly unarmed movement. This was accompanied by an ideological shift away from traditionalism and toward Islamic renewal. That cultural project, however, received a mixed reception from ordinary Muslims, who resisted many of the social and ritual modifications promoted by movement leaders.

The shifting power relations just described may best be imaged as two conjoined fields of force.[4] The first, an exterior field, concerns external domination and local response in Cotabato. It is a dynamic and complexly structured social field exhibiting quite varied historical and regional configurations. Relations between the various external forces striving to control Cotabato and individual Muslim leaders seeking to secure or maintain positions of dominance within local social orders have, in different times and places, been characterized by confrontation, avoidance, armistice, collaboration, tutelage, and dependency. A second, interior, field of force pertains to power relations between ruling and subaltern groups within Cotabato. This is an equally dynamic and multidimensional social field, encompassing production relations, exchanges, and political tensions among classes, estates, kinship groups, and ethnic entities, as well as interactions among variously situated Muslim rulers.

While these two fields of force have always been closely articulated, with power relations within Cotabato continually reshaped in response to external perturbations, the contemporary Muslim separatist movement provides a striking instance of the concurrence of everyday and extraordinary resistance to power by Muslim subordinates. When antagonisms between the Philippine state and Muslim nationalists erupted into armed rebellion in the early 1970s, fighters rallied to the separatist cause, and the insurgency eventually received broad popular support. Muslim subordinates nevertheless evaluated the pronouncements of movement leaders based on their separate shared experience. Those evaluations were symbolized independently of authorized discourse and led at times to actions that not only deviated from the official aims of the separatist movement but effectively thwarted them. Ordinary Muslims were equally skeptical of the hegemonic project of the martial law state and its Muslim elite collaborators, measuring those dominant representations against their own lived experience.

This study supplements ethnography with historical materials to trace the political economy of Cotabato from the precolonial period to the present day. Knowledge of the development of "traditional" arrangements is, of course, essential for an understanding of contemporary political relations. The nature of relations between those of superordinate and subordinate status in Muslim Cotabato (as well as the meanings of those statuses themselves) has undergone several alterations in the past four hundred years, most often in response to externally induced economic and political transformations.

I trace the complex configurations of power and resistance in contemporary Cotabato by means of an ethnography of a specific urban community. Campo Muslim is a shantytown in a riverside marsh at the edge of Cotabato City. It is a community that typifies the peripheralization of many of the indigenous inhabitants of Cotabato. As a Muslim encampment constructed on the fringe of a Christian-dominated city and populated in large part by political and economic refugees, Campo Muslim is a product of ethnic strains and social upheaval in the region. As the site of a concentrated, self-consciously Muslim population, it is considered by separatist leaders to be a vital resource for waging the Muslim nationalist struggle. I provide an ethnographic account of economic survival and political mobilization in Campo Muslim based on fourteen months of continuous residence and research in that community. Ethnographic material from Campo Muslim provides the basis for examining the attitudes and actions of community residents in relation to those who seek their adherence. The latter include underground separatist leaders, Islamic clerics who publicly advance the moral and political program of the rebels, and Muslim politicians allied with the separatist front. Opposed to this coalition is another set of Muslim leaders aligned with the Philippine state. The two competing elite alignments control separate kinds of political resources and make different sorts of appeals to the Muslim urban poor. Faced with those alternatives, Campo Muslim residents search cautiously for the response that best balances economic necessities, political realities, and Islamic ideals.

My analysis of power and resistance in Cotabato is indebted to Benedict Kerkvliet's pathbreaking 1990 study of everyday politics in Central Luzon. In that work, Kerkvliet pushes beyond the conventional approach to politics that for so long dominated Philippine studies—one limited to the investigation of "election campaigns, government activity, and rebellions"—to focus on the debates and conflicts among individuals and groups regarding the control of material and nonmaterial resources (1990, 8). While I devote a good deal of attention in this work to both elections and armed rebellion, it is the everyday politics observed in Campo Muslim that anchors my analysis of power relations in Cotabato.

Chapter 1, "The Politics of Heritage," introduces the analytical approach taken in subsequent chapters—one which argues against the regnant view that nationalist mobilization is accomplished primarily by means of the hegemonic effect of nationalist ideas. It examines the core concept guiding many anthropological analyses of culture and power—cultural hegemony—and finds it wanting. The hegemony concept, with its central assertion that political subordinates are dependent upon the symbols issuing from a dominant ideological formation firmly rooted in everyday life, fails to capture the dynamic and imaginative responses to power made by Cotabato subordinates.

Chapter 2, "People and Territory in Cotabato," profiles the land, people, and contemporary political economy of Cotabato. The following three chapters consider the precolonial and colonial past in Cotabato and trace the derivation of a shared Muslim nationalist identity. Chapter 3, "Islamic Rule in Cotabato," evaluates various idealized versions of the precolonial past in Cotabato against evidence found in the historical record and unauthorized oral narratives. Chapter 4, "European Impositions and the Myth of Morohood," describes how political and economic relations within Cotabato were transformed by European contact and evaluates assertions that an oppositional identity as Philippine Muslims (Moros) is ancient, deep, and broadly shared. Chapter 5, "America's Moros," depicts the incorporation of the Cotabato sultanates into the Philippine colonial state and argues that the origins of Muslim nationalism are to be found not, as so many have imagined, in the anti-Spanish struggle but in the practices of American colonialism.

Chapter 6, "Postcolonial Transitions," chronicles the political and demographic transformations of the early postcolonial period and the creation of self-consciously ethnic Muslims in Cotabato. The subsequent two chapters consider the armed separatist struggle in Cotabato. Chapter 7, "Muslim Separatism and the Bangsamoro Rebellion," describes the watershed decade of 1968 to 1979 in Cotabato, a period of sectarian violence and armed rebellion, and one of economic devastation for many Muslims. In Chapter 8, "Regarding the War from Campo Muslim," I consider the armed separatist rebellion and its immediate aftermath from the perspective of its rank-and-file insurgents and their supporters.

The next two chapters offer ethnographic material from Campo Muslim to examine the movement for Muslim autonomy in its more recent unarmed form. The emergence of a new group of well-educated and politically active Islamic clerics, and the reaction of urban Muslims to their teachings, forms the subject of Chapter 9, "Unarmed Struggle." Chapter 10, "Muslim Nationalism after Marcos," describes the reinvigoration of electoral politics in Cotabato with the removal of the martial law regime and the unprecedented employment of Islamic and Muslim nationalist discourse in electoral campaigns in Cotabato.

In Chapter 11, "Resistance and Rule in Cotabato," I return to the theoretical issues surrounding the politics of heritage and examine them in light of the various configurations of culture and power evidenced in Cotabato from the precolonial period to the present. I conclude by proposing an alternative approach for analyzing both ordinary and extraordinary resistance—one based on a radically reformulated notion of hegemony as *public* accommodation to power.

CHAPTER I

The Politics of Heritage

My sense memories of the Muslim quarter of Cotabato City are vivid and abundant. They include colors and patterns—bright designs of red, orange, and green—unfamiliar or long forgotten elsewhere in the Philippines. I recall the scent of wet goats and wood smoke and other reassuring aromas of rural life transposed to an urban setting. But the most insistent sensations, those leaving the deepest traces, are the sounds, and especially the melodies heard there. My days in the city were saturated with music, and an interior sound track accompanies almost every recollection. Most ubiquitous was Western (typically American) popular music, heard almost everywhere on radios and cassette tape players. More than once the sound of rock and roll standards roaring from a portable radio in an especially unlikely setting would induce that peculiar shock of the familiar in an exotic context.

There were, however, other popular musics more local and much-listened-to, and often, as I walked the main road of Campo Muslim in the early evening, the sounds of three or four musical genres emanating from as many houses competed for my attention. There were the traditional musics of Cotabato, bright tunes played on the *kulintang* (gongs), or ballads (*bayuk*) sung unaccompanied by instruments, or, most popular, *dayunday*—romantic song duels between men and women sung in an archaic upriver dialect but accompanied by modern guitars. Rebel songs were another immensely popular musical form. These were composed by ordinary rebel fighters during the armed insurgency and sung in Magindanaon, usually to the tunes of popular Filipino or American songs. They had been locally recorded and were played on jukeboxes in coffeehouses throughout the Muslim district. Increasingly, one could also hear popular Islamic songs from the Middle East or Malaysia played on the nightly Islamic radio program and available on cassettes.

These musics, like musical forms everywhere, tend to be associated with particular social identities. Western pop music, for example, is a central component of Philippine popular culture, arguably the most Western-oriented mass culture of any Southeast Asian nation. Muslims who listen to Western pop (or who engage in a number of other activities) participate in the dominant culture of the Philippine republic, that of Christian Filipinos. The sound of indigenous music induces listeners to identify as Magindanaons, or often more particularly as "upriver" or "downriver" people. Rebel songs are the music of the proponents of a Philippine Muslim nation even though, as shall be seen, they also include many distinctly local associations; and those who listen to Islamic songs are partaking in a form of revitalized Islamic identity as self-consciously "true Muslims" (in Magindanaon, *tidtu-tidtu a Muslim*).

Unsurprisingly, most residents of Campo Muslim prefer more than one music, and some listen to them all. The musics (and their associated identities) occasionally jostle one another but mainly coexist, both in Muslim communities and in individual Muslim selves. That coexistence is facilitated by the existence of one additional music, composed of sacred words and sounds, that transcends the other musics (not only because it issues from the largest loudspeakers) and betokens a more inclusive social identity. The sound of the call to prayer defines the limits of the Muslim quarter of Cotabato City. Those who recognize that call (including those not moved by it to pray) identify themselves as members of an established community of Muslims joined to the world of Islam (*dar al-Islam*).

The inclusivity of the everyday Muslim identity articulated by the call to prayer is such that virtually every activity contained within its purview—even enjoying the latest hit song by Madonna—is in some sense a distinctively "Muslim" activity simply by the fact of its occurrence in a Muslim community. There is nothing uniquely Islamic about this phenomenon. The church bells that pealed majestically each noonday of my childhood announced an urban Catholic neighborhood and rang just as meaningfully for local street toughs, "bad girls," and bar patrons as they did for clergy and churchgoers. All who recognized the Angelus were equivalently identified by its daily declaration of bounds.

Appreciation for the inclusive nature of the everyday Islamic identity of Cotabato Muslims compels the realization that it is a privileged identity but not, as some have imagined, a primordial and determining one (one that transcends time and space). While it encompasses numerous cultural and social distinctions it by no means extinguishes them; and although it references a universal and scriptural Islam, it is grounded in localized and informally transmitted understandings of historical experience. The most inclusive collective identity available to Cotabato Muslims—their self-recognition as a *Muslim* people—is, no less than their other social identities, specifically situated and historically contingent.

Problems arise when such complexly constructed identities become targets for intense politicization. The politics of heritage (see below) is a politics of exclusivity. The leaders of the Muslim separatist movement in Cotabato have attempted to advance a new, objectified, Philippine Muslim identity cleansed of complexities. Local allegiances have been de-emphasized in favor of Muslim national sentiment; well-loved customs have been disapproved as un-Islamic and unfamiliar ones encouraged. Ordinary Muslims have cautiously but firmly resisted these attempts to dictate identity while, at the same time, they have provided strong support to the separatist cause.

This book tracks the historical construction of both the everyday Islamic identity of Cotabato Muslims and the Muslim nationalist identity prescribed for them by separatist leaders. It chronicles the extraordinary contemporary struggle for Muslim autonomy from the Philippine state as well as the subtle everyday contests between ordinary Muslims and those who would lead them. The remainder of this chapter examines various attempts to theorize the attempted politicization of transcendent identities, especially in the context of armed separatism.

NATIONAL SENTIMENT, SOCIAL DISTANCE,
AND THE PROBLEM OF ADHERENCE

The proliferation of separatist struggles in the postcolonial world in the past decades has prompted a surge of scholarly interest since 1980 in nations and nationalisms (see, e.g., Anderson 1983; Fox 1990; Handler 1988; Hobsbawm and Ranger 1983; Kapferer 1988). In his singularly influential essay, "Imagined Communities," Benedict Anderson offers an "anthropological" definition of the nation as "an imagined political community—[one] imagined as both inherently limited and sovereign" (1983, 15). Anderson's nations imagine themselves as sovereign entities even though they may find it impossible to achieve or maintain genuine political independence. In its current anthropological formulation, "nationalism" refers to shared "conceptions of peoplehood" or of a "common ('national') culture" (Fox 1990, 3). By that measure, all nationalisms are *ethno*nationalisms in that all are concerned with peoplehood and with "cultural productions of public identity" (Fox 1990, 4). Nations do differ from certain other imagined or ascribed ethnic entities—Irish Catholics, for instance, or Asian Americans, or "people of color"—in that they are almost always bounded territorially as well as conceptually, with territoriality a matter of utmost significance even in those cases where a considerable proportion of a nation's citizens reside outside its enunciated boundaries. Nations (or nationalist political movements) are also distinguished by their possession of official nationalist ideologies. Nationalist elites produce particular conceptions of peoplehood and create "citizens" by means of formal discourses, representations, and rituals.

Nationalism constitutes a politics of shared heritage in that nationalist ideologies invariably assert a collective birthright of sovereignty over a particular territory. Nationalism is also a politics of heritage in the less literal sense in that nationalist ideologies prominently feature self-conscious attempts to identify and preserve a posited cultural heritage (see, e.g., Handler 1988; Bendix 1992; Spencer 1990). Nations, or "nation[s]-in-waiting" (Bowman 1993, 451), are self-regarding social collectivities with specific political goals, the most important of which is the control of the core territories claimed as their rightful heritage. Separatist struggles feature attempts by aspiring nations to wrest control of a proclaimed national territory from the illegal grasp of an alien state.

The Bangsamoro Rebellion—the armed endeavor by supporters of a proclaimed Philippine Muslim nation (Bangsamoro) to reclaim the "traditional" lands of the Muslim peoples of the Philippines—typifies such a separatist struggle. Its examination also points up a characteristic complexity when one attempts to understand the process by which symbolic appeals to a particular shared heritage are used to mobilize populations for nationalist action. As is the case with most other envisioned nations, the social collectivity imagined as the Philippine Muslim nation contains substantial disparities in social power—disparities that generate conflicting interests and centrifugal tensions. Insofar as social collectivities constituted (or in the process of constituting themselves) as nations tend overwhelmingly to be crosscut by structurally opposed positions and interests, analyses of nationalism must face squarely the problem of the mobilization of national sentiment across class, caste, and other structural divides. To assert in response that nationalist mobilization in such cases is accomplished by means of nationalist ideologies merely begs the question. One must confront first an accumulation of inharmonious data concerned with political relations within modern states. On the one hand, we find a good deal of evidence that appears to support Benedict Anderson's characterization of nations as imagined *communities:* "The nation is imagined as a *community,* because, regardless of the actual inequality and exploitation that may prevail in each, the nation is always conceived as a deep, horizontal comradeship. Ultimately, it is this fraternity that makes it possible, over the past two centuries, for so many millions of people, not so much to kill, as willingly to die for such limited imaginings" (1983, 16). Various historical and journalistic accounts exist of collective national action that seems to express the broad-based communalism noted by Anderson.

Counterpoised to such evidence for the potency of national sentiment is a second body of research examining everyday resistance by political subordinates to local power or local expressions of supralocal domination. This analytical project, whose preeminent practitioner has been James Scott (1985, 1990), chronicles the omnipresent though often hidden existence of divergent interpretations and subversive discourses. Writes Scott in portraying everyday forms of ideological struggle: "The process by which any system of political or religious beliefs emanating from above is reinterpreted, blended with pre-existing beliefs, penetrated and transformed is characteristic of any stratified society ... Deviant interpretations—ideological heterodoxy—are hardly astonishing when they arise among subordinate classes which, by definition, have the least stake in the official description of reality" (1985, 319).

These separate projects prompt one to ask how it is possible that members of subordinate classes, on the one hand, respond readily to nationalist calls to action and, on the other, routinely manage to penetrate elite rhetoric and subvert domination. Recent anthropological analyses of nations as imagined communities have sought to overcome this problem by various means, very often by recourse to a concept that has been broadly employed to understand power relations in complex societies—that of "cultural hegemony."

INTERROGATING HEGEMONY

For the past decade, anthropological analyses of power relations in colonial and postcolonial societies have sought to transcend the antipodal notions of domination and resistance by detailing the complexity of social power and advancing a view of social order as a dynamic and uneven process.[1] While applying insights about discursive and nondiscursive practice from Michel Foucault (1978) and Pierre Bourdieu (1977), these efforts have often drawn prime inspiration from an earlier continental source: Antonio Gramsci's (1971) concept of hegemony, usually by way of the reading given it by Raymond Williams (1977). It is this notion of hegemony that has undergirded a number of recent anthropological investigations of nationalism (see, e.g., Brow 1988, 1990; Crain 1990; Fox 1989, 1990; B. Williams 1991; Swedenburg 1990, 1991; Toland 1993; Woost 1993). In the view of these analysts, nationalisms operate hegemonically to channel sentiment and mobilize antagonisms; or to state it the other way around, it is hegemony that constructs Anderson's "imagined communities." While subordinates are never merely passive recipients of nationalist ideas (they may reinterpret them in various ways to incorporate their specific political concerns), the dialogue between nationalist elites and ordinary adherents is distinctly asymmetric, with elites ultimately controlling both the production of nationalist ideas and the vehicles of their transmission.

The concept of cultural hegemony has acquired a range of utilization in social thought well beyond the immediate analytical intentions of the political theorist and activist credited with introducing it. Antonio Gramsci, writing from prison in the years between 1929 and his death in 1935, developed the concept of hegemony chiefly to explain why capitalism in the industrialized West had not yet collapsed as a result of its own inner contradictions (Gramsci 1971; see also Perry Anderson 1976; Laclau 1977). Despite Gramsci's concern with the peculiar characteristics of capitalist ideology in the liberal democracies of the industrialized West, his notion of hegemony began to be applied to dissimilar settings soon after his writings became available in English.[2] Cultural anthropologists came relatively late to the topic of cultural hegemony but in recent years have embraced the concept in their analyses of social relations (see, e.g., Comaroff and Comaroff 1992; Contursi 1989; Fox 1985, 1989; Lagos 1993; Linger 1993; Rebel 1989; Roseberry 1989, 1991, 1994), often with specific reference to nationalism (see, e.g., Brow 1988, 1990; Crain 1990; Fox 1989, 1990; B. Williams 1991; Swedenburg 1990, 1991; Woost 1993).

Despite hegemony's broad popularity in the social sciences, analysts have disagreed when interpreting its essential meaning. Definitions vary because, for one, Gramsci himself, as numerous commentators have noted, used the term inconsistently (see, e.g., Perry Anderson 1976; Abercrombie et al. 1980; Lears 1985).[3] If anything approaching an interpretive mainstream does exist, it may be found among those scholars who accent Gramsci's writings on the complexity of working-class consciousness. That interpretive emphasis has been demonstrated most famously by Raymond Williams, first in a 1973 essay entitled *Base and Superstructure in Marxist Cultural Theory,* and later in his 1977 *Marxism and Literature.*[4] In that first work, Williams offers his reading of hegemony as . . . "the central, effective and dominant system of meanings and values, which are not merely abstract but which are organized and lived . . . [Hegemony] thus constitutes . . . a sense of absolute because experienced reality beyond which it is very difficult for most members of [a] society to move, in most areas of their lives . . ." ([1973] 1980, 38). The "dominant culture," however, is neither monolithic nor univocal: ". . . alternative meanings and values, . . . alternative opinions and attitudes, even some alternative senses of the world . . . can be accommodated and tolerated within a particular effective and dominant culture" (1980, 39).[5]

This eloquent formulation incorporates an apparent contradiction. For Williams, hegemony shapes the experience of subordinates to such an extent that it constitutes a sense of absolute reality for them; yet in some unspecified manner, the dominant culture also allows subordinates the opportunity to devise "alternative senses of the world."[6]

Williams's explication of hegemony in terms of a dominant culture has been quite influential among anthropologists, and most who employ the concept follow closely his usage.[7] Williams's reading of cultural hegemony has also guided various anthropological analyses of nationalism (see, e.g., Brow 1988, 1990; Crain 1990; Fox 1990; Swedenburg 1990, 1991; Toland 1993; Woost 1993).[8] These analysts tend to agree that subordinate classes are incorporated into the imagined community of the nation through nationalist discourses that work by "articulating . . . the insecurities, preoccupations, hopes and fears of everyday consciousness" (Wright 1985, 175). Nationalist hegemony remains nonetheless vulnerable to challenges, primarily in the form of active assessments by subordinates of the claims and promises of nationalist leaders. In response, nationalist leaders make rhetorical and material concessions; however, these concessions never imperil the nationalist project itself. In the end, the dialogue of nationalist discourse is always a profoundly unequal one. Nationalist ideologies powerfully constitute individuals as subjects, with subordinates experiencing "a powerful reorganization of their common sense" as "these ideologies . . . become part of meaningful life" (Woost 1993, 516–17).

Before considering hegemony's relevance to nationalism, the concept itself requires closer examination. The notion of cultural hegemony depicts a dynamic process whereby systems of domination maintain themselves not only by means of rules and other coercions but by their profoundly formative effect on ordinary understandings of the social world. This depiction provokes a question: how do coercion and cultural hegemony interact to maintain a system of domination? Or, more to the point, how do we know when one or the other is operative? While Gramsci's writings are again inconsistent on this point, most anthropologists who employ the concept seem confident in their ability to discern hegemony at work.

James Scott, however, counsels utmost caution when attempting to disentangle the presumed ideological effects of cultural hegemony from the impositions of economic necessity and physical coercion. Domination, he notes, "produces an official transcript that provides convincing evidence of willing, even enthusiastic complicity" (1990, 86). Moreover, underclasses, for strategic purposes, avoid open defiance or the public discrediting of the official transcript's account of social relations. Most public events are thus available to researchers only in their official versions, as aspects of an elite-produced transcript in which exploitation appears natural and domination legitimate. Scott, for more than a decade the most energetic and articulate critic of the concept of hegemony, has drawn attention to the ubiquity of everyday resistance by subordinate classes. Such resistance includes a subtle but authentic ideological struggle in which "official descriptions of reality" are routinely "penetrated and transformed" (1985, 319) by subordinates who at the same time produce their own unauthorized "hidden transcript" of power relations (1990, 4).

Various anthropologist advocates of the hegemony concept have directly criticized Scott's views, arguing that by posing a dichotomy between domination and resistance he has failed to grasp "the complex dynamic nature of the hegemonic process" (Lagos 1993, 53).[9] In their formulations, cultural hegemony is said to encompass *both* domination and resistance. But what, precisely, is meant by that claim? The consensus opinion seems to be that while hegemony accommodates— even "thrives on"—discontent, it "makes revolution hard to think" (Linger 1993, 3, 4). Resistance and even rebellion can be accommodated within a system of domination because "webs of domination,"woven mainly through discursive practice, encompass subordinates even as they try to resist (Lazarus-Black and Hirsch 1994, 9). The result is "the experiential starvation of the political imagination," with most resisters co-opted from the start by their use of the dominant political rhetoric (Linger 1993, 18).

Scott, however, rejects the central assumption of his anthropological critics that hegemony inhibits the political imagination of subordinates, citing abundant local versions of "the world turned upside down" to support his assertion (1990, 80). He has argued that subordinates generally limit the scope of their resistance and couch their protests in the language of the dominant ideology for strategic reasons, not as a result of the cognitive constraints imposed by cultural hegemony. Those strategic considerations primarily concern the personal safety and economic survival of members of subordinate groups. Before looking to discursive practice to explain the relative quiescence of subalterns, due notice should first be given to the coercive force ready to be applied against them, their experiences of past failures of open opposition, and "their daily struggle for subsistence and the surveillance it entails" (Scott 1990, 86).[10]

Nothing in my reading of the Cotabato case supports a view of hegemony as encompassing both domination and resistance. As we shall see, Muslim subordinates in Cotabato have not depended on elite-generated language and images to make sense of power relations. Rank-and-file adherents of the Muslim separatist movement have routinely resisted official interpretations of events, often by means of imaginative narratives that served as charters for political decisions directly at odds with the directions of movement leaders. While it is prudent to approach dichotomous categories of social analysis such as domination/resistance with caution, overnuanced analyses of power

relations carry their own analytical distortions and produce mostly in-
determinacy. To declare that hegemony comprises both domination
and resistance removes an unwanted binary but reveals nothing about
the sources and consequences of unroutinized insubordinations. In
such a formulation, hegemony is incongruously imagined as an encap-
sulating dominant culture that is ever vulnerable to challenge yet ultimately imperishable, both constantly becoming and always already accomplished.

As this is the interpretation of hegemony most often employed to
counter Scott's strong criticisms of the entire notion, there is good reason to remain unimpressed by claims made for hegemony as "a potent
concept for the analysis of cultural order" (Woost 1993, 503). As
noted, hegemony has been rather widely applied in anthropological investigations of nationalism. It remains to examine its performance in
that analytical realm.

HEGEMONY, NATIONALISM, AND THE
INVESTIGATION OF ARMED SEPARATISM

Nationalist projects, and especially armed separatist movements,
would seem particularly useful cases for evaluating the conflicting
claims for the analytical utility of the concept of hegemony. After all,
nationalist projects are, unavoidably, popular undertakings—projects
that involve "inviting the masses into history" (Nairn 1977, 340).
Though conceived from above by elites, armed nationalisms are incar-
nated on the ground by rank-and-file fighters and adherents struggling
to replace one set of state-level elites with another, more familiar one.[11]
In the absence of direct physical coercion, what motivates such per-
ilous endeavors on the part of subordinates? How serviceable is the
hegemony concept for understanding mobilization for armed separatism?

Armed secession is almost always an exceedingly hazardous undertaking, defying as it does an established state whose military might is
usually far superior and whose reaction to attempted secession nearly
always vengeful. Armed separatist struggles demand mortal sacrifices,
requiring individual adherents "not so much to kill, as willingly to die"
for the nationalist cause (Anderson 1983, 16).[12] That elite appeals to
the "nation-as-community" (Foster 1991, 241) appear to move so
many ordinary actors to collective and often costly action invites reliance on cultural hegemony as an analytical tool. The voluntary par-

ticipation of rank-and-file adherents in armed nationalist movements would seem to provide prima facie evidence for the motive force of resonant nationalist ideas.

Employing hegemony to understand armed nationalism is not, however, free of complications. For one, the notion of hegemony was originally devised to explain the political inertia of subordinate classes (those who had yet to launch a proletarian revolution in Gramsci's Western Europe), not their mobilization for collective action. Analyses of nationalist mobilization keyed to hegemony (or to kindred concepts—see, e.g., Bentley 1987; Kapferer 1988) do not of course employ it to explain political immobility on the part of subordinates but rather their engagement in "concerted, directed action" (Kapferer 1988, 83). Explaining collective action and accounting for social stasis are quite dissimilar undertakings. Successful collective action requires, in addition to an initial propellant, direction, containment, and continual remotivation. Adequate explanation of such action requires making sense of motion—of how political movements surge and subside and change course.

There are more practical problems as well when applying hegemony to the explanation of separatist movements. Separatist insurgencies in particular present certain methodological difficulties for ethnographers attempting to gain subordinate perspectives on ethnonational movements. Direct interviews of ordinary adherents tend to draw political statements exhibiting self-conscious attempts at correctness ranging from self-censorship to psittacism (see, e.g., Swedenburg 1991; Bowman 1993, 457, n. 19). That is to say, the likelihood is great that, under conditions of armed struggle, political questions posed to fighters and supporters will elicit only authorized answers—only the "official transcript" of political relations and events (Scott 1990).[13] There is, in addition, the problem of obtaining official permission to conduct ethnographic fieldwork in regions where the authority of the central state is actively contested. Such difficulties may account for the relative scarcity of ground-level ethnographic accounts of separatist insurgencies.[14]

It is a central irony of modern ethnonationalist movements that, though fashioned to disengage from totalizing, centralizing states, they invariably advance ideological projects mandating cultural and political homogenization within their own declared territories.[15] The personal costs of one such hegemonic project have been powerfully described by the Croatian journalist Slavenka Drakulic, who describes herself as "pinned to the wall of nationhood—not only by outside pressure from Serbia and the Federal Army but by national homogenization within Croatia itself" (1993, 51): "The trouble with this nationhood . . . is that whereas before, I was defined by my education, my job, my ideas, my character—and, yes, my nationality too—now I feel stripped of all that. I am nobody because I am not a person any more. I am one of 4.5 million Croats." (1993, 51).

The formative and inhibitive effects of ethnonationalist movements on their ordinary adherents are evidenced most dramatically and coinstantaneously in armed secessionist struggles. The vindictive responses of state authorities to separatist movements, and the ferocious hostility of their militaries toward civilians suspected of seditionist leanings, substantiate separatist rhetoric and provide significant impetus for the creation of a transcendent national identity constituted in large measure on the possession of a common enemy (see Bowman 1993). At the same time, such struggles tend to create political environments comparable to that described by Drakulic in her observation that today "in Croatia it is difficult to be the kind of person who says, 'Yes, I am Croat, but . . .'"(1993, 51). That double-edged character of armed separatism—opening a new discursive space for imagining a transcendental (and oppositional) community while severely restricting the space for expressing other identities and concerns—suggests that listening for voiced dissension about the location of the crucial community should be a primary task for ethnographers attempting to assess the hegemonic force of nationalist ideas on such movements. It also, of course, renders the elicitation of dissident rank-and-file perspectives on armed nationalist movements through direct discourse especially problematic.

Such problems are prominently evidenced in Ted Swedenburg's study of popular memory among Palestinian peasants (1991, 1995). Swedenburg observes that in response to Israeli "repression of all manifestations of Palestinian identity," and in accord with official Palestinian nationalism's efforts to "marginalize the dissonant strands" of popular memory, his informants "couched popular-democratic statements in nationalist language, as divergent rather than oppositional versions of a national past" (1991, 165, 175). He also remarks that his informants felt that, through him, "they were addressing a U.S. audience, which they recognize as a powerful determinant of their situation . . . Accordingly, and in line with official discourse, informants often practiced self-censorship, presenting an image of the revolt suitable for both national and foreign consumption" (1991, 172). Swedenburg's attempts to solicit "dissident strands" of popular memory among Palestinian peasants were thus effectively blocked by both the repressive context of his fieldwork environment and his own identification as a conduit to an American audience. When attempting to analyze his methodological difficulties, however, he turns to a version of cultural hegemony, noting, "Whereas I previously tended to regard nationalism as a discourse imposed from above, I have come to conceive of it as a joint construction of the popular classes and the leadership . . . *All parties* agree that [the] internal struggle [between Palestinian leaders and followers over various social issues] is secondary to the fight for national liberation" (emphasis mine, 1990, 28). One wonders exactly how Swedenburg is able to ascertain what "all parties" agree upon when those whose opinions most concern him are (as he has just informed us) practicing self-censorship.[16]

While the notion of cultural hegemony appears at first regard to hold promise for understanding ethnonational mobilization, the problems attendant on its application generally—how to disentangle the operation of coercion from that of hegemony, how to determine the political authenticity of the authorized narratives of power relations told by (and to) subordinates—are actually intensified in situations of armed separatism. One route around those problems is to seek out the equivalent of James Scott's "hidden transcript," the unauthorized, "offstage" discourse of subordinates (1990, 4). While not necessarily contradicting the official account of power relations, "a hidden transcript is produced for a different audience and under different constraints of power than the public transcript. By assessing the discrepancy between the hidden transcript and the public transcript [it becomes possible] to judge the impact of domination on public discourse" (Scott 1990, 5). The informal ways in which Campo Muslim residents speak to one another about the Muslim separatist movement constitute a discursive practice (a form of hidden transcript) that, while not fundamentally subversive of Muslim nationalist interests, does articulate a collateral view—one that includes, and often privileges, goals and identities different from those authorized by movement leaders. In particular, the unofficial songs and stories of the separatist rebellion have been discursive vehicles for independent evaluations of the separatist project and have sanctioned subordinate actions that, in some cases, have directly contravened the edicts of movement leaders. Songs composed by rank-and-file fighters proclaimed that they were "fighting for the *inged*"—the local, face-to-face community—and made no mention of the Bangsamoro, or Philippine Muslim nation. Popular narratives of supernatural assistance provided to those fighting to defend Muslims from aggression spoke, in some cases, of divine mercy bestowed on individuals shunned by the rebel leadership and in others of the denial of divine assistance to officially approved rebels.

Analyses of nationalism have taken notice of the fact that the keywords of nationalist ideologies may be significantly altered in meaning while being absorbed by subordinate classes (see, e.g., Chatterjee 1993; Wright 1985). Unauthorized narratives of the Bangsamoro Rebellion spoken in Campo Muslim reveal not only the alteration of official descriptions of the separatist movement but the use of independent language as well—language expressing distance from the authorized aims of Muslim nationalism. The critical assessments made of the rebellion by ordinary adherents questioned not only the claims and promises of movement leaders but also their fundamental aims and assumptions.

The view from the ranks in Cotabato poses a direct challenge to the prevalent assumption that successful nationalist mobilization requires the ideological incorporation of ordinary adherents. Despite the notable misalignment between the official discourse of the rebellion and the language, perceptions, and intentions of its ordinary adherents, the Muslim separatist struggle in Cotabato has had considerable success. The practical compliance of subordinates is at least as consequential for successful mobilization. As we shall see, the practical compliance of ordinary adherents is based importantly on their possession of a common enemy but also on a host of collateral intentions: self-defense, defense of community, social pressure, armed coercion, revenge, and personal ambition, among others. The Cotabato material bolsters Scott's critique by questioning the utility of the concept of hegemony (as presented in most current usages) both for the analysis of ethnonationalism and for relations of domination in general. Even so, I am not so inclined as Scott to reject the notion entirely. There remains the need for a vocabulary for speaking about the *relationship* between physical coercion (broadly defined) and public political culture. Appropriately refashioned—by emphasizing, for example, its grounding in "everyday fear" (Sayer 1994, 374)—hegemony may usefully serve that purpose.[17]

CHAPTER 2

People and Territory in Cotabato

Aden maulad a lupa
a gadung a pedsandengan

Behold in the distance
a wide green land.

THE LAND

The wide green land evoked in the first line of a popular song of the Muslim separatist rebellion is a metaphorical reference to the territory known as Cotabato and a description of the Cotabato River Basin, the broadest expanse of lowland on the island of Mindanao and the most densely settled. Mindanao is the second largest island in the Philippines, and "Cotabato" (see map 1) is the term used to refer to the entire southwestern quadrant of Mindanao, which is divided into roughly half lowland and half upland areas. That region formed the domain of the two principal sultanates of Mindanao. With colonialism it was incorporated as a single political subunit—the District of Cotabato—under the Spanish and Americans, and the Province of Cotabato under the Philippine republic. It is presently divided into four separate provinces but still considered collectively as Cotabato. The hydraulic, demographic, and political hub of Cotabato has always been the Cotabato River Basin.

The Cotabato Basin is drained by the Pulangi River, referred to respectfully by the Spaniards as the Rio Grande de Mindanao. The Pulangi has its source in the Central Mindanao Highlands near the northern coast of the island and flows southward across the Bukidnon Plateau. It then emerges onto the Cotabato plains, depositing fertile mountain silt as it widens and arcs westward through the 1,000-square-mile Cotabato River Basin, and finally empties into Ilana Bay.

Map 1. Cotabato and the Pulangi River system

Where the river makes its wide turn to the west, two large marsh-lands—the Libungan and Liguasan Marshes—have been created. To-gether they cover an area of 450 square miles during normal water lev-els, with each marsh expanding dramatically when the river overflows its banks during seasonal rains. This periodic inundation of much of the valley floor is the source of the name for the principal ethnolinguis-tic group of the Cotabato Basin—the Magindanaon. The word "danao" refers to inundation by water, and "magindanao" is likely a shortened form of "mag inged sa danao" or "those residing at a flooded place" (Llamzon 1978, 131). The Magindanaon, or "people of the flood plain" (Stewart 1977) lent their name, in its shortened form, to the entire 36,000-square-mile island, called Mindanao by the Spaniards in apparent acknowledgment of the extensive territorial in-fluence of the Magindanao Sultanate, the foremost principality of the island.

The term "Cotabato" is a hispanicized version of the Magindanaon "Kuta Watu," or fort of stone. That Spanish appellation for the city and region (formerly identified on maps as Magindanao or Mindanao) was said by Najeeb Saleeby, writing early in the twentieth century, to be "very modern" (Saleeby 1905, 13). The name "Cotabato" was taken from an actual stone fort that stood on Tantawan Hill in the middle of present-day Cotabato City (Mastura 1979; Millan 1952). About twenty miles before reaching the sea the Pulangi splits into two branches. The narrower southern fork is known as the Tamontaka River. The wider north fork of the Pulangi flows past Cotabato City, which is located on its southern bank about four miles above the river mouth. The Pulangi also collects water from several large tributaries along its lower course.

The Cotabato Basin (see map 2) is bounded on the southwest by the Tiruray Highlands. These uplands extend for more than 125 miles along the Moro Gulf and Celebes Sea and descend sharply to the west, dividing a slender coastal plain from the long and narrow Alah Valley. To the north lie the Bukidnon-Lanao Highlands, which encompass nearly all the northern portion of the island. The Lanao Plateau and Lake Lanao Basin lie at the southwestern corner of these highlands, closest to the Cotabato Valley. The densely populated basin of Lake Lanao is the single exception to the general pattern of sparse settle-ment in the highlands. To the east lie the Central Mindanao Highlands, a succession of mountain ranges that separate the Cotabato Basin from the lowlands facing the Davao Gulf.

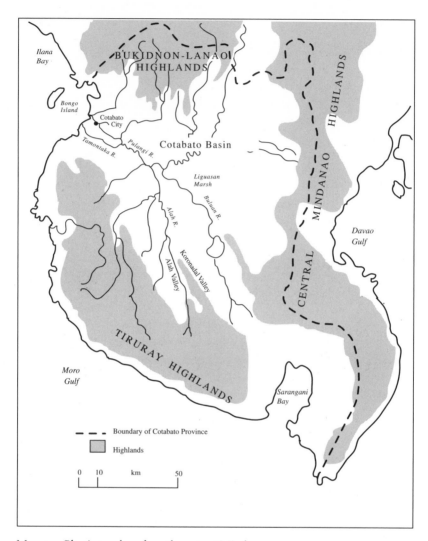

Map 2. Physiography of southwestern Mindanao

THE PEOPLE

The indigenous inhabitants of the Cotabato Basin are divided into three principal language groups. While Magindanaon speakers far outnumber speakers of the other two languages and figure most prominently in the present study, knowledge of all three groups is essential for comprehending past and present political relations.

THE MAGINDANAON

The largest indigenous ethnolinguistic group in the Cotabato River Basin are the Magindanaon.[1] For most of the recorded past they have also been the politically dominant population. The 1980 Philippine census estimated their number at 644,548 persons, or 25.7 percent of the total Philippine Muslim population. This figure places them as the second largest of the thirteen Philippine Muslim ethnolinguistic groups (IBON Databank 1981; Abbahil 1984).[2] Two major dialects of the Magindanaon language are spoken in the Cotabato Basin.[3] The terms for these two dialects—*tau sa Laya* (upriver people) and *tau sa Ilud* (downriver people)—are place-names indexing the fluvial orientation of a people living along a great river. This dialectal separation reflects demographic, cultural, and political polarization between the two major historical population centers on the Pulangi, one at its mouth in what is now Cotabato City and the other thirty-five miles upstream near the present-day Datu Piang. These two settlements were, respectively, the traditional seats of the Magindanao Sultanate and the Buayan Sultanate—interdependent but dueling realms for most of their histories.[4]

The distinction between downstream (ilud) people and upstream (laya) people has as much subjective as objective import. Downriver people tend to view themselves as the "true" Magindanaon, citing their "purer" dialect, their (somewhat) earlier exposure to Islam, and their connections to the Magindanao Sultanate, the first and hence noblest Magindanaon royal house. They hold this view in spite of (perhaps because of) the fact that the Magindanaon of the interior have dominated indigenous cultural and political life in the valley for the past 150 years. Many continue to distinguish tau sa laya (upriver people) from "Magindanaons" in the same manner as my downriver neighbor in Cotabato City, who remarked of tau sa laya immigrants to the city: "How can they call themselves 'Magindanaon' when they cannot even speak our language?"

Despite some dialectal and cultural differences, the upriver and downriver Magindanaon in the historical period have shared social and political institutions, a profession of Islam, certain symbols of collective identity in dress and ornamentation, and similar means of subsistence. Traditional Magindanaon communities tended to be dispersed along the banks of the numerous waterways of the Cotabato Basin. Thomas Forrest, writing in 1775, describes the pattern:

> In a country thinly inhabited, and where ground is of no value, Mahometans especially choose not to crowd together; each desiring a house on the bank of a river. Peculiarly is this visible here, where upon the winding [river] banks . . . and the sides of the many creeks that intersect the ground between . . . rivers, at the distance of almost every three hundred yards, sometimes we see a single house, sometimes a group of houses, with gardens of coconut, mango, and plantain trees, sugar canes, and rice fields, for many miles up those rivers . . . Wherever is a house, there is a small portion of the river sufficient for bathing, railed in, against alligators. (Forrest 1969)

For the Magindanaon, the Pulangi River system, with its tributaries, channels, and estuaries, has been a source of food and water, a principal thoroughfare, and the means of trade and communication with the outside world. Control of the Pulangi has thus been crucial for the acquisition and maintenance of political power by the rulers of the Cotabato Valley throughout the historical period. The traditional Magindanaon were horticulturists, growing either dry rice in upland fields or wet rice in lowland paddies. In the modern period many Magindanaon have shifted to plow and harrow methods of wet rice cultivation (Stewart 1977).[5]

THE IRANUN

Writing in the mid-nineteenth century, the Spanish chronicler Francisco Gainza described a population of skilled and fiercely independent sea raiders living along the eastern shore of Ilana Bay who called themselves "Iranun."

> [T]his large population, designated by some geographers with the name of the Illana [Iranun] Confederation, in reality does not form a single political body except to defend its independence when it is found threatened . . . They live loaded with weapons; they reside in dwellings artfully encircled by barricades . . . and they maintain their bellicose spirit by continuously engaging in robbery and theft. Through piracy they strive to gather slaves for aggrandizement and to provide their subsistence . . .

In short, this particular society can only be considered a great lair of
robbers, or a nursery for destructive and ferocious men. (Quoted in
Bernaldez 1857, 46–47)

The Iranun today are a population whose size has never been accu-
rately estimated by a government agency but who probably number
somewhere between 50,000 and 150,000 individuals.[6] Most Iranun
continue to reside along the eastern shore of Ilana Bay, although some
have also long inhabited the hill country lying between the coast and
the southern edge of the Lanao Plateau. The Iranun language is closely
related to the languages spoken by the Iranun's more populous Muslim
neighbors, the Magindanaon and the Maranao of the Lanao Plateau.[7]
The Iranun share with their neighbors the profession of Islam, as well
as a number of other cultural institutions. There has long been intermarriage between the Iranun, Magindanaon, and Maranao, and the
percentage of intergroup marriages has increased since midcentury.

As Gainza's account indicates, the Iranun living at the coast once
practiced a distinctive maritime adaptation. For at least 150 years
prior to the inception of American colonial rule at the turn of the century, they specialized as seagoing marauders. The Iranun raided
throughout island Southeast Asia, from the Celebes in the south to Luzon in the north and as far west as the Straits of Malacca, attacking
merchant shipping and coastal settlements in search of slaves and plunder.[8] They continue their seafaring ways today, but now as fishermen
and long-distance traders.[9]

THE TIRURAY

The Tiruray are non-Muslim[10] upland horticulturalists who inhabit the
northern portion of the Tiruray Highlands. In 1980, the Tiruray were
estimated to number about 30,000 persons (Schlegel 1977). The Tiruray have made their living as shifting cultivators in the densely forested
mountains and valleys of the highlands, growing rice, corn, tobacco,
and other crops in upland fields and foraging in the surrounding
forests.

For centuries the Tiruray have maintained significant trade relationships with Magindanaon communities in the lowlands. Similar to the
pattern found throughout Southeast Asia, this upland-lowland trade
involved exchanges of forest and swidden products for iron tools,
cloth, and salt, and took place within unequal and often coercive clientage arrangements. Since the beginning of the American occupation at

the turn of the century, the Tiruray have been experiencing rapid social change. Today they are divided approximately in half between those more accessible communities that have been drawn into plow agriculture and all its attendant sociocultural transformations, and those communities of still-traditional people in the remote forests of the Tiruray Highlands (Schlegel 1979). As a result of the extensive and detailed ethnographic fieldwork of Stuart Schlegel, more is known about traditional Tiruray subsistence and social life than about any of the other indigenous populations of Cotabato (see, e.g., Schlegel 1970, 1972, 1979).

CONTEMPORARY COTABATO: THE REGION AND CITY

The daily Philippine Airlines flight from Manila to Cotabato City wings south over the Sulu Sea to Mindanao, then veers east across the Zamboanga Peninsula and Moro Gulf to approach the Cotabato coast from the west. As the coast and airport come into view the initial peaks of the Tiruray Highlands are visible on the right to the south of the city. This is the territory of the Tiruray, now increasingly denuded by loggers and occupied by Christian settlers. To the left, north of the city across the Pulangi River, are the last reaches of the Bukidnon-Lanao plateau, and the principal mountain stronghold of Cotabato's Muslim separatist insurgents. On the coast below, near the mouth of the river, stands the lone mesa known as Timako Hill, and offshore, the dark crescent of Bongo Island. Looking east and inland, the Cotabato Basin widens and reaches to the horizon. The broad Pulangi River may be seen above its fork at Kabuntalan, stretching as far east as Datu Piang, the old capital of the upriver sultanate.

Directly ahead, Cotabato City extends for about three miles along the southern bank of the north fork of the Pulangi River. As is typical of cities in the southern Philippines, the officially designated perimeter of Cotabato City encloses an area much larger than the city proper. The political boundaries of Cotabato City encompass all of the territory that lies between the forks of the Pulangi, from their common origin at Kabuntalan to Ilana Bay, an area of about 176 square kilometers. Large areas of land above and below the urban area are semiflooded and roadless. The city proper is also encircled by water, almost all of it lying within the area circumscribed by the Pulangi, Manday, Matampay, and Esteros Rivers. For most of its history as the downriver capital, water transport was the most reliable means of travel in and around the city, and the Pulangi River was its main thoroughfare. Today, the Pulangi continues to carry significant traffic, comprised primarily of the Muslim inhabitants of the city. A traveler's account from the early 1960s (a period of relative prosperity for many Muslims in the city) captures the contemporary atmosphere of urban life along the Pulangi: "At Cotobato [*sic*] it is life on the water for everyone. There are hundreds of motor-boats, steam vessels, launches, outrigger canoes (some without outboards) and large, ponderous, box-like barges with brightly clothed people sitting on or clinging to every available perch ... There is a feeling of eighteenth-century Venice, of Canaletto and Guardi, in the intimacies of daily life observed along this waterway ..." (Kirkup 1967).

A cutoff channel, dug in the early 1960s, begins at the western edge of the city and slices an unnaturally straight route to the sea, facilitating access from Ilana Bay and lessening the occurrence of serious floods in the city caused by the Pulangi overrunning its banks. Cotabato City now relies on roads and bridges for most of its transportation, and a major road bisects the city, running perpendicular to the Pulangi.

Cotabato City remains today the principal commercial center for Cotabato, although the original province has been divided into four separate provinces.[11] That division is directly related to the most significant political and economic development of the modern era—the mass migration of Christian homesteaders from the northern and central Philippines to Cotabato. Magindanao Province (see map 3), which encompasses somewhat more than half of the Cotabato Basin (that closest to the Pulangi River) as well as the northern portion of the Tiruray Highlands, is the only one of the four provinces in which indigenous inhabitants comprise the majority population.[12]

The Cotabato Basin's long-recognized promise as the future "rice granary" of the Philippines appears to be approaching fulfillment. Rice production in the basin has increased steadily since 1982,[13] although yields per hectare continue to vary significantly from area to area.[14] Corn and coconuts (the latter yielding the export commodities copra and coconut oil) are the other two principal agricultural products of the basin.

As the primary agricultural service center for the Cotabato Basin, Cotabato City is the site of large hardware, machinery, and chemical supply stores; the head offices of rural banks; rice and corn mills; and copra and rice dealers. As the principal city of southwestern

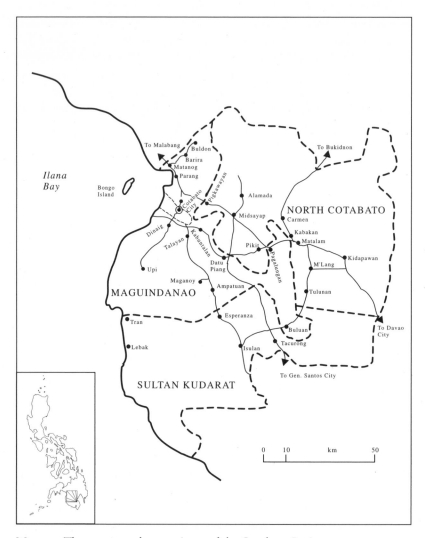

Map 3. Three present-day provinces of the Cotabato Basin

Ilana
Bay

Bongo
Island

To Malabang
Buldon
Barira
Matanog
Parang

Pigkawayan
Alamada

Cotabato
City
Midsayap

To Bukidnon

NORTH COTABATO
Carmen

Dinaig
Talayan
Kabuntalan
Piki
Kabakan
Matalam

Pagalungan
Datu
Piang
M'Lang
Kidapawan

Upi
Maganoy
Ampatuan

MAGUINDANAO
Tulunan

Tran
Esperanza

Buluan
To Davao
City

Lebak
Isulan
Tacurong

SULTAN KUDARAT
To Gen. Santos City

0   10   km   50

Mindanao, Cotabato is also a center for transportation, communications, postsecondary education, and government services.[15] There are no large industrial enterprises in the city, although six fairly large agro-processing firms are located in the near vicinity.[16] For most of its colonial and postcolonial history, Cotabato Town was the *poblacion,* or capital of the Province of Cotabato. In 1959, the capital town of Cotabato was converted into a chartered city and granted administrative and fiscal autonomy from the province.

Cotabato City has an estimated 1990 population of 127,000 persons, of whom about 48 percent are Muslims (NEDA 1992). It exhibits many of the characteristics of a secondary city of substantial size. The city contains bars, nightclubs, restaurants, and movie theaters. It boasts private schools and colleges, civic groups, radio and television stations, and two weekly newspapers. It accommodates beggars, fugitives, prostitutes, and transvestites; and it is the scene of violent crimes, security guards, and profound disparities in wealth and status. At the same time, Cotabato City retains some features associated with much smaller communities. Important information is communicated broadly and with remarkable swiftness by word of mouth; and the city elite, comprising both Christians and Muslims, tends to be quite well-integrated.

One of the most noted features of Cotabato City is its ethnic diversity.[17] In addition to indigenous Magindanaon and Iranun inhabitants, who comprise about 46 percent of the population, the city is composed of immigrants from other regions of the Philippines, the vast majority of them Christians.[18] Cebuanos and Illongos from the central Philippines together make up about 25 percent of the city's population, and Tagalogs and Ilocanos from Luzon in the northern Philippines comprise another 22 percent. About 2 percent of the city's population are immigrant Muslims, mostly Maranao from Lake Lanao just to the north. Most of the Chinese residents of the city are also non-Christians. Though they are also immigrants to the region, ethnic Chinese have resided in Cotabato for at least four hundred years, centuries longer than any other immigrant group. In sharp contrast to virtually every other city in Mindanao, in Cotabato City Tagalog (the national language of the Philippines) is the lingua franca.[19] This is likely a result of the ethnic diversity of immigrants but also the fact that many of the earliest Christian immigrants to the city were Tagalog speakers who came as civil servants under Spanish and American colonial administrations. A fairly distinct ethnic division of labor has obtained in the city for some time, altered only somewhat in the past twenty years. The ethnic Chinese tend to control both retail trade and the processing of agricultural commodities. As evidenced elsewhere in the Philippines and throughout Southeast Asia, the significance of their economic role is far out of proportion to their numbers. Tagalogs have tended to be heavily represented in government service as administrators, clerks, and teachers. Visayan migrants (Cebuano and Ilonggo speakers) are generally found in the professions, in agriculture, and in commercial establishments such as barbershops and drugstores. The Magindanaon and Iranun comprise a large percentage of the fish-sellers, street vendors, and stevedores in the city. Other Muslims are farmers, fishermen, or goldsmiths, and some own and operate inter-island vessels or small rice mills.

By far the most subjectively significant ethnic division in Cotabato City is that between Christians and Muslims—between indigenous Muslim inhabitants and Christian immigrants. The topic of Muslim-Christian relations in Cotabato has been addressed in a number of written works (see, e.g., Hunt 1957; Schlegel 1978; Gowing 1979; Rodil 1986), and Muslim-Christian conflict remains the most typical framework for discussing ethnic politics in Cotabato and all of the Philippine South.[20] I have chosen to approach the politics of group identity in Cotabato from a somewhat different direction—focusing principally on the internal dynamics of Muslim politics in the region. Nevertheless, Muslim politics are inexplicable without some knowledge of the nature of Muslim-Christian relations in Cotabato City.

Cotabato City Christians are possessed of an ethnoreligious chauvinism that stems from their identification with a dominant national culture—that of Christian Filipinos (who comprise more than 90 percent of the population of the Philippines). Voiced attitudes of local Christians toward indigenous Muslims tend to oscillate between paternalism and apprehension, either expressing condescending tolerance for a benighted folk or betraying anxiety about "uncivilized" (and thus unpredictable) neighbors. Ordinary Christians appear to be accepting of, and comfortable with, particular Muslims in direct proportion to the extent to which those Muslims exhibit the cultural markers of Christian Filipinos. Such markers include speaking Tagalog or English, wearing completely Westernized dress, and, in the case of men, drinking alcohol. Although a few Christians vaunt their ability to speak "Muslim" (Magindanaon), the great majority, even those who have lived in Cotabato all their lives, neither speak any indigenous language nor possess any appreciable knowledge of Muslim customs. This does not seem to be the result of a lack of regular ethnic interaction. Although the local economy is structured in such a way that Christians do not ordinarily employ Muslims, Christians do regularly engage in commercial transactions with Muslims, attend school with them, and, today, work side by side with Muslims in government offices. That local Christians who have studied and worked with Muslims nevertheless express unfamiliarity with their most basic cultural beliefs and practices indicates that Christian ignorance of Muslim customs results from lack of effort rather than insufficient contact.

One illustration of the publicly expressed attitudes of Christians toward Muslims is found in the remarkably persistent pattern of editorial comment in the local newspaper disapproving of Muslim street vendors. During a three-year period from 1985 through 1988—the years covering my first two visits to Cotabato—the Cotabato City newspaper ran regular front-page editorials accompanied by photographs (often on a monthly basis), complaining that Muslim street vendors were a hygienic hazard because they sold fruits or vegetables on the ground and a public nuisance because they blocked walkways. Street vending is engaged in by both Christians and Muslims but is a particularly significant source of income for poor Muslims, many of them women, who sell fruit, vegetables, tobacco, or cigarettes in various parts of the city. Given that pedestrian paths in the city are frequently blocked by a wide variety of commercial and noncommercial activities, and that poor sewage disposal and sanitation have been intractable problems in the Christian-dominated public market, the underlying complaint in these editorials appears to be not that Muslim street vendors are especially unsanitary or obtrusive, but that they appear prominently out of order in Christians' comprehension of the city in which they predominate.

As citizens, albeit mostly reluctant ones, of a predominantly Christian city and state, the Muslims of Cotabato City are generally much more conversant with the cultural beliefs and practices of Christian Filipinos than Christians are with local Muslim culture. Virtually all Muslims under the age of forty speak Tagalog, and a number of younger Muslims, as well as some older men who attended school during the American period, speak English. Local Muslims are regularly exposed to the dominant national culture through popular films, radio, and comic books. Their most protracted exposure to the national culture, however, comes during their education at state-sponsored

1. Muslim street vendor selling tobacco in Cotabato City. The great majority of Muslim street vendors are women, many of them older women, who support their families selling fruits and vegetables, betel, tobacco, and other items on the street corners of the city.

schools.[21] The great majority of Muslim children in the city attend state schools for a minimum of six years, most continue for an additional four years, and a fair number carry on for a further four years of postsecondary education. Most young Muslims have Christian school acquaintances, and a few have Christian friends. Muslim-Christian marriages, most commonly between Muslim men and Christian women, are not at all uncommon in the city. Many younger Muslims also tend to join, at least indirectly, in the celebration of Christian holidays such as Christmas, New Year's Eve, and Saint Valentine's Day.

Cotabato City possesses a reputation, justified by the available evidence, for maintaining harmonious Muslim-Christian relations. Residents point out that, even during periods of violent conflict between Muslims and Christians in the region, armed sectarian clashes were virtually absent in the city. For most of the past thirty years Christians have supported Muslim politicians for city offices and Muslims have voted for Christian candidates. At the same time, Muslims are aware that Christians have been better able to advance their own interests in the city because of their greatly superior economic and political power. Finally, we sharpen our focus to examine a particular urban Muslim community—Campo Muslim.

THE COMMUNITY OF CAMPO MUSLIM

As a poor Muslim community constructed on the fringes of a city now dominated by Christians, Campo Muslim stands as an architectural testament to the peripheralization of Cotabato's Muslims under the Philippine republic. Campo Muslim is a shantytown assembled in a riverside marsh. In 1985 it consisted of 520 houses with more than forty-two hundred residents. Campo Muslim faces the Pulangi River and is bordered by two older and more prosperous communities. Just upriver and closer to the center of the city is the community of Manday. Manday has a majority Christian population, paved roads, and a large Catholic church. Adjoining Campo Muslim on the west is Lugay-lugay. The residents of Lugay-lugay are primarily Muslim and middle class. Formerly, they consisted mostly of successful smugglers or Muslim Chinese-mestizo merchants.[22] Today it is also composed of supervisory-level civil servants employed by the regional government. Lugay-lugay features paved roads, a large public elementary school, and an impressive mosque.

As its name suggests, Campo Muslim is a self-consciously Muslim community with 99 percent of residents identifying themselves as Muslims. The community contains two simply constructed mosques and two Islamic schools. Although its residents are not uniformly poor (a few households would be considered relatively wealthy by Cotabato City standards), Campo Muslim is the poorest community of its size in the city. There are no paved roads and no sewage or drainage systems of any kind. More than 70 percent of households are without toilets and three-quarters lack running water. Less than half of the households in the community have electricity hookups.[23]

The average Campo Muslim dwelling covers ninety square feet of ground (roughly the size of a child's bedroom in a typical American house) and houses eight persons. Nearly 20 percent of the houses in the community are less than sixty square feet in size. Most of these are extremely rudimentary shelters with partially open sides. Because of the community's location on the outskirts of the city, natural building materials tend to be inexpensive or, as with coconut fronds, freely available. As a consequence, relatively few houses in Campo Muslim resemble the *barong-barong* shanties found in Manila and other large cities, dwellings constructed of cardboard, paper, plastic sheeting, and other discarded industrial materials. Most Campo Muslim dwellings are assembled from some combination of wood (either used or flawed pieces bought cheaply at a nearby lumberyard), nipa palm, and split bamboo. About half of the houses have corrugated metal roofs. The simplest dwellings are constructed of nipa and coconut fronds. In sharp contrast to the two neighboring communities, relatively few houses (15 percent) incorporate any concrete in their construction. Most of the approximately sixteen-hectare area of Campo Muslim is owned by two individuals; the largest portion by a Chinese-mestizo Muslim who lives in Campo Muslim, and a smaller section by a Christian businessman who lives in neighboring Manday. Campo Muslim residents are not squatters. They pay monthly land rents to one of the two owners.

As a community composed largely of urban migrants, Campo Muslim exhibits considerable diversity in dialect and place of origin. In 1985, when I conducted my community census, about 30 percent of household heads hailed from upriver (sa laya) municipalities. Another 58 percent had birthplaces in downriver (sa ilud) municipalities. The remaining 12 percent included those with birthplaces in localities south of Cotabato City along the coast (*taga-biwangan*) and to the north across Ilana Bay (*taga-kawanan*). Magindanaons constituted the largest ethnic category in Campo Muslim, with 58.8 percent of household heads identifying themselves as Magindanaon. Those who identified themselves as Iranun comprised the next largest category, at 34 percent. Maranaos made up only 3.5 percent of community residents. Thus, three separate languages are spoken in Campo Muslim, as well as at least four distinct dialects of Magindanaon.

The urban diversity and poverty encountered every day by Campo Muslim residents cannot be satisfactorily conveyed in quantitative terms. Enumerations alone fail to evoke the texture of daily life in a crowded community of mostly impoverished migrants. The most severe poverty in Campo Muslim is hidden away from casual observers or passersby. The community is segmented by three or four dirt roads (built using soil brought from outside) bordered by houses. The interior portions of the community, those that lie behind the roadside houses, remain at least partially flooded throughout the year. Here in the interior (*sa lusud*) live most of the poorest community members in simple shelters crowded closely together. The following passage from my field notes describes a typical dwelling sa lusud:

> Babu Ensay's house is two-storied and covers about 70 square feet of ground. The walls are of ragged nipa [woven palm] panels, cardboard, and paper. The house stands on very low ground and the first floor often floods. The floor is constructed of coconut fronds laid across a wooden frame. A tiny hearth sits just inside the entranceway. Other than one or two cooking pots there are very few belongings and no furniture of any kind on the ground floor.
>
> A crude ladder leads to the second floor, which has a nipa roof and a floor of split bamboo. Upstairs are a few mats and some cardboard boxes for storing clothes and other items. At the time I was there, Babu's husband, Bapa Akub, who works as a laborer at the pier, was repairing damage to the roof from the previous night's storm. Virtually all their belongings had been soaked by the rain.[24]

Sa lusud residents enter and exit by way of narrow passageways, over ever-wet stepping stones and precariously balanced planks. It is here, inside, that one finds the highest incidence of infant mortality, malnutrition, and tuberculosis. Life is only somewhat less difficult for most of the residents *sa liyu* (of the exterior) bordering the roads. For the great majority of community members, Campo Muslim is a demanding and often disheartening place. Closely built houses and narrow paths offer no privacy, and the lack of toilets for most makes defecation an uncomfortably public act at the nearby Pulangi River.[25] The rapid rate

2. A view of the interior (*sa lusud*) of Campo Muslim after a heavy rain.

of movement into and out of the community means that neighbors are often neither relatives nor friends and sometimes are scarcely acquainted. The threat of fire hangs over the crowded community and residents suffer repeated infections because of poor living conditions. No regular police force provides protection in the community, and burglars regularly steal clothes and cooking pots from families who own little else of value.

Residents often experience their deprivation as a sense of marginality. Christian city dwellers very rarely enter Campo Muslim. Most have never been near it. In the eyes of city Christians, Campo Muslim is a far-off place lying outside the Christian pale and harboring Muslim bandits.[26] Many Campo Muslim residents have accepted this characterization and self-consciously view their community as remote and separate from the city, even though they can walk to the city plaza in less than fifteen minutes, and despite the fact that community members play an integral part in the city economy as laborers, fish and vegetable vendors, and drivers of the motorized pedicabs that serve as the main form of public transportation in the city.

Just the same, Campo Muslim is a vibrant locality, one suffused at times with an almost buoyant energy. Each morning the main road fills with traffic as residents make their way to work or school. Every evening the same road becomes a meeting place where adults gather to share news and teenagers joke and sing, while children absorbed in exuberant street games swirl among them. A variety of musics played on scores of radios and tape players continuously enlivens the surroundings, and colorful flowers in coconut shell planters brighten the poorest dwelling sa lusud. And community residents, despite their differences and deprivations, share a strong sense of being members of a Muslim community—the largest in the city. That sense of solidarity is most evident during ritual suspensions of normal social life, in particular the *puasa*, or annual fast of Ramadan. But it is also apparent, in less dramatic form, in many small but significant aspects of ordinary activity in the community.

As noted, most community members are acutely conscious of being poor Muslims in a city dominated by Christians. That awareness has induced a tempered resentment toward city Christians that may occasionally be agitated into intense anger by a perceived offense.

I witnessed one such infuriation in Campo Muslim on the morning of the most important Muslim holiday of the year in Cotabato, Buka, or Eid al-Fitr, the celebration that marks the end of the month of fasting. It is customary to bathe on the morning of Buka before dressing in one's best new clothes to attend congregational prayers at the local mosque. As households awoke just before dawn that day, and members prepared to bathe, they found that the taps that supplied them with city water were dry. The unannounced shutoff of city-supplied water was not a rare event, but neither was it a regular occurrence. This shutoff was especially inopportune for community residents, as they were forced to use the available stored rainwater or bathe in the dirty Pulangi River. Young men voiced their outrage throughout the early morning, declaring that the lack of city water was a work of "sabotage" by *kafirs* (disbelievers—referring, in this case, to the Christians who control the city). But community frustration gradually evaporated as bathing was accomplished despite the lack of city water and residents commenced a long-awaited day of festivities. Community anger at the shutoff of water was not simply aimed at city Christians as infidels, but as immigrants, who today dominate a city and region once ruled by indigenous Muslims.

The anger of Campo Muslim residents on this occasion was unmistakably an ethnic anger, one directed at any and all non-Muslim outlanders. At other times, however, community or individual ire sparked by living conditions in Campo Muslim has been aimed at other, more specific targets—Ferdinand Marcos, the city mayor, the Muslim barrio captain, even at Islamic clerics.

We turn now to consider the history of power relations both within Cotabato and between Muslim rulers and various outsiders. The three chapters that follow survey power relations in Cotabato in the precolonial and colonial periods. The external aggression and colonial subjugation experienced by the Muslim polities of the South constitute the root causes for the marginalization of Cotabato Muslims in their traditional homeland and for the Muslim separatist movement. In addition, investigating the history of political and economic relations among Muslim overlords, their subordinates, and various agents of external powers provides the essential foundation for evaluating both the mythic representations of Muslim nationalist ideologues and the responses of rank-and-file followers to them.

CHAPTER 3

Islamic Rule in Cotabato

REPRESENTATIONS OF THE PRECOLONIAL ORDER

Two origin myths animate Muslim nationalist politics in Cotabato. The first is an ancient myth that explains social disparity (past and present) among Cotabato Muslims by sanctifying it. This myth of sanctified inequality delineates an aristocracy entitled to rule Cotabato Muslims on the basis of their ancestral ties to the legendary figure who first brought Islam to Cotabato and, through him, to the Prophet Muhammad.[1] The second is a modern myth about ancient origins. The myth of Morohood is shared widely by Muslim nationalists throughout the Philippines and states that a transcendent Philippine Muslim (or "Moro") identity was uniquely forged among the various Muslim ethnolinguistic groups of the southern Philippines in the course of their struggle (begun more than four hundred years ago) against Spanish attempts to subjugate them. That shared oppositional Islamic identity, together with the tradition of aristocratic rule, is considered to constitute the primordial foundation for the contemporary Muslim separatist movement.

In this chapter and the two that follow I will consider these two myths in their historical contexts. While they tend to be complementary and mutually reinforcing (the anti-Spanish resistance posited in the second myth was inspired and organized by the Muslim nobility constituted by the first), they have not had equal motivational force in the struggle for Muslim separatism. The myth of Morohood is universally embraced by Muslim nationalist ideologues. The myth of sanctified inequality, on the other hand, has been at least indirectly challenged by some separatists. It has also been appropriated by prominent Muslim opponents of the separatist cause. Nevertheless, the two myths remain securely coupled in nationalist ideology and so will be analyzed in tandem.

The revanchist or revitalistic spirit that publicly motivates most ethnonational movements almost always includes assertions of the preferability of traditional governance. The Muslim separatist movement in the Philippines is no exception to this tendency. While depictions by Muslim nationalist ideologues of the precolonial past have been mostly vague, they invariably extol the moral and material advantages of the premodern order.[2] Assessing such claims, and the responses of ordinary movement adherents to them, requires the investigation of past political and economic relations. This chapter examines the ideological expression and practical operation of the system of Islamic governance in precolonial Cotabato.[3]

PRECOLONIAL GOVERNANCE AND ITS IDEALIZATION IN COTABATO

In contemporary Muslim politics in Cotabato, the past inhabits the present in a manner insufficiently expressed by the term "traditionalism." Various idealized versions of the precolonial past are used as models for present-day political action by a wide range of Muslim political actors, from separatist insurgents to Philippine government officials. Recourse to an imagined past for present political guidance is, of course, a common element in contemporary nationalist movements. The extraordinary aspect of its occurrence in Cotabato is the extent to which not only various Muslim separatist factions but also Christian politicians and state functionaries share the perception that the political fate of Cotabato Muslims is tied to their traditional nobility as a result of ancient and immutable bonds. Both proponents and opponents of Muslim separatism tend to assume that ordinary Muslims reverence their highborn leaders (or *datus*) for their sacred ancestry and could not imagine politics without them. In this view, any political arrangement to enhance Muslim self-determination in Cotabato must include prominent consideration of the role of the traditional nobility. It is considered preferable to attempt to reform the unsuitable practices of contemporary datus rather than to try to undermine their influence, because the bond between traditional leaders and followers is the epitome of Muslim political culture in Cotabato.[4]

Little historical scholarship exists by which to evaluate the validity of these perceptions. Although a number of the available scholarly works are quite astute in their political observations (see Ileto 1971; Stewart 1977; Beckett 1982; Adil 1955), none has provided a comprehensive analysis of traditional sociopolitical relations. I offer such an analysis here in order to provide a historical standard by which to measure contemporary political relations between Muslim leaders and followers.

My depiction of political relations in the Cotabato sultanates relies on ethnographic information garnered from interviews I conducted in and around Cotabato City in the mid-1980s. My primary consultants in this matter were four individuals, three of them elders, who were unusually knowledgeable about traditional arrangements.[5] Two—Datu Mohammad Adil and Datu Kasim—are descendants of the Magindanaon high nobility.[6] Imam Akmad, an Iranun speaker, is the imam (prayer leader) of the Campo Muslim mosque, and Hadji Abbas is a descendent of the *dumatus,* a special status group in the Magindanao Sultanate (see below). Each of these informants shared with me oral traditions learned from their elders, as well as their own inferences about the nature of traditional governance in Cotabato.[7]

I supplement ethnographic material from Cotabato with primary indigenous historical sources from the Muslim Philippines and works based upon them (Saleeby 1905; Adil 1955; Glang 1969; Majul 1973; Hooker 1983; Mastura 1984; Loyre 1991). I rely as well on historical evidence from Western sources (Blumentritt 1893; Combes 1903–19; Saleeby 1905; Dampier 1906; Forrest 1969; Arcilla 1990) and on scholarly works based on those sources (Ileto 1971; Majul 1973; W. H. Scott 1982, 1984, 1994). In addition to information pertaining peculiarly to Cotabato, I also use European source materials and scholarly works that describe precolonial polities in other parts of the Muslim Philippines (Mednick 1965, 1974; Warren 1981; W. H. Scott 1994), the non-Muslim Philippines (W. H. Scott 1982, 1984, 1994), and elsewhere in Islamic Southeast Asia (Gullick 1958, 1987; Milner 1982; Sullivan 1982; Andaya 1993).

FROM HETERARCHY TO HIERARCHY: THE DECLINE OF LOCAL DESCENT GROUPS

Pre-Islamic Magindanaon social organization consisted of a number of localized cognatic descent groups, or *bangsa,*[8] that were associated with particular autonomous or semiautonomous ingeds, or localities.

The Magindanaon bangsa were most likely similar to those of the Maranao, the neighboring Muslim ethnolinguistic group of the Lanao Plateau. As described by Mednick (1965), membership in a Maranao bangsa provided access to rights in a specified area—most importantly, usufruct rights in land, or the right to exploit a certain natural resource—as a result of an ancestral association.

In pre-Islamic Cotabato, these large, localized descent groups produced chiefs who, under certain conditions, were able to extend their power beyond their own bangsa and become chieftains or, in exceptional cases, rulers of harbor principalities. With the coming of Islam, however, the bangsa were crosscut, and eventually attenuated, by a separate, societywide aristocracy whose members claimed descent from a common ancestor, Sarip Kabungsuwan, an émigré nobleman. With the establishment of the Cotabato sultanates,[9] local chieftains became principally interested in establishing the maximum number of descent links to Sarip Kabungsuwan, the prime ancestor. Their new status aspiration was to establish their rank positions in respect to the paramount rulers of the sultanates, who ruled by right of their membership in the aristocratic lineage (*barabangsa*) founded by Kabungsuwan. With increased status delineation and relative political centralization, the significance of local ancestors and the power of local corporate descent groups were greatly diminished. While local identity remained strong, local ancestry retained only secondary importance as a criterion for local rule.[10]

Magindanaon bangsa survived as *tupus,* or local descent lines. Informants report the existence of forty-two Magindanaon tupus, although none could name more than twenty of them.[11] It appears likely that while localities (ingeds) remained largely independent entities under the sultanates, local descent lines gradually lost both depth and meaning. The descent line of Sarip Kabungsuwan, the point of reference for ruling datus, became not only the paramount descent line but the only significant one. Tupus seem to have been insubstantial categories that did little more than focus loyalty to place. Bilateral kindreds replaced bangsa as the largest effective kinship units for ordinary Muslims.

ISLAMIZATION AND THE MYTH OF SANCTIFIED INEQUALITY

The coming of Sarip Kabungsuwan to Cotabato is the charter event for the claims of the rulers of Cotabato in the historical period to nobility and moral authority. The story of the arrival of Sarip Kabungsuwan is told in the *tarsilas,* the written genealogies that link the royal houses of Cotabato with their progenitor. The term "tarsila" is derived from the Arabic "silsila," meaning name-chain, and the genealogical accounts in the Magindanaon tarsilas not only linked living datus with Sarip Kabungsuwan, their apical ancestor, but also contained supplementary sections tracing the ancestry of Sarip Kabungsuwan to the Prophet Muhammad. The tarsilas were written on paper in Magindanaon or Malay in Arabic script and were possessed by the sultans and all leading datus. Individual tarsilas were frequently recopied for updating or to replace worn copies.

According to the tarsilas, Sarip Kabungsuwan was the son of Jusul Asikin, the daughter of the Sultan of Johore, and Sarip Ali Zain-ul Abiden from Mecca. Thus, Kabungsuwan was the offspring of a princess of the Melaka royal family and, more significantly, the son of a *sharif* (the original Arabic form of "Sarip"), and hence a direct descendent of the Prophet Muhammad. Majul (1973) suggests that the historic Kabungsuwan must have sailed to Mindanao some time after 1511, when the Melaka royal family, to which his mother belonged, was driven from Melaka by the Portuguese and established a sultanate in Johore.

The tarsilas relate how Kabungsuwan arrived by chance at the mouth of the Pulangi River and began to convert local chieftains and their followers to Islam. He married the daughters of some of these chieftains, thus establishing in Mindanao a barabangsa, or royal lineage, whose members claimed a sacred genealogy, tracing their origins to the Prophet Muhammad. The tarsilas report that the first wife married by Sarip Kabungsuwan in Cotabato (Putri Tunina) was found in a bamboo stalk. Kabungsuwan's son, Sarip Makaalang, married a woman who emerged from a crow's egg. The existence of these supernatural children raised the status of the female descent line, thus further distinguishing the barabangsa line from autochthonous lineages.[12]

Sarip Kabungsuwan founded the Magindanao Sultanate at the coast and his rule passed to his son, Sarip Makaalang. The upstream Buayan Sultanate originated, according to the tarsilas, from a union between the daughter of Sarip Kabungsuwan and a Buayan chieftain. Because the male descent line carries more genealogical weight than the female, the Magindanao Sultanate was able to designate itself the premier royal house of Cotabato, while the rulers of Buayan for most of its history used the title raja (prince) rather than sultan.[13] The traditional system of hereditary ranked statuses is also traced to the arrival of Kabungsuwan. This system, in its most general configuration, comprised four tiers. At the apex were the datus—rulers or descendants of rulers. Their ascendant status stemmed from Sarip Kabungsuwan's assumption of sovereignty over Muslim Mindanao (and its dependencies) and from their ability to trace descent from Kabungsuwan and, through him, to the first ruler of Muslims, the prophet Muhammad.[14]

Passing over, for a moment, the second level, we find on the third tier the *endatuan,* meaning literally "those who are ruled." The endatuan were the subjects of datus rather than of the realm; they were considered residents of particular ingeds (settlements) and subordinate to specific datus. The status of the endatuan seems to have been negatively defined. They were the followers of (and likely bore some kinship relation to) local chieftains. But unlike their rulers, they were unable to demonstrate sufficient kinship links with Sarip Kabungsuwan, the prime datu ancestor, to qualify as datus.

The second tier was occupied by the dumatus. This intermediate status has not been reported for other Philippine Muslim populations. The dumatus, as they describe themselves today, were neither datu nor endatuan—neither rulers nor ruled. The dumatus are the descendants of Tabunaway, a legendary Magindanaon chieftain who welcomed Sarip Kabungsuwan to Cotabato. The tarsilas record that Tabunaway acknowledged the sovereignty of Sarip Kabungsuwan and his descendants in exchange for certain privileges. The first entitlement was that neither he nor his descendants would pay tribute to any datu. Hadji Abbas expressed the distinction between endatuan and dumatu in his inged this way: "At harvest time the datu sent sacks to the endatuan who were obliged to fill all the sacks the datu gave them. The dumatus were not sent sacks and did not have to provide rice to the datu." The second dumatu entitlement was that no datu could be proclaimed as sultan without the participation of a Tabunaway descendent.[15] The dumatus have kept their own genealogical records of the Tabunaway descent line, principally to preserve their privileges vis-à-vis the Magindanaon aristocracy. Theirs is the only tarsila in Cotabato that does not trace descent from Sarip Kabungsuwan. The special status of Tabunaway descendants has allowed them to maintain, more so than any other group, their separate bangsa by remaining ancestor focused, self-ruled, and relatively corporate.

The fourth and lowest tier comprised the *ulipun*, or "disfranchised" (W. H. Scott 1982, 142) persons.[16] Ulipun were debt-bondsmen whose unfree status resulted from punishment for a legal offense, from failure to pay tribute or repay a debt, or from being sold by relatives (or occasionally by self-sale) into servitude in times of economic crisis. Ulipun status, unlike the other three estates, was, in general, neither ascribed nor permanent. It could, however, be inherited and, in practice, the system inhibited self-redemption by debt-bondsmen, probably because datus favored maintaining a high proportion of bound followers. As Warren (1981) describes the system of debt slavery in another Philippine Muslim polity—the Sulu Sultanate—the debt-bondsman's service to his creditor "did not generally count towards repayment of his debt" (1981, 216). Ulipun status was likely similar in most respects to the position of debt-bondsman described by Warren. Despite their inferior status, the ulipun, as Magindanaons and Muslims, were societal insiders and possessed certain rights, including the right to own chattel slaves (*banyaga*). Those ulipun who were members of a datu's retinue were treated as household dependents and were occasionally able to rise to positions of significant responsibility. Banyaga, on the other hand, were despised outlanders who were not included in the system of social rank. They were captives acquired for the most part outside the territory of the sultanates, were usually not Muslims, and had no recognized rights and no social status other than as acquired persons— the property of others.[17]

The central organizing principle of this system of ranked statuses was *maratabat* (from the Arabic "martabat," or "rank"). Among the Magindanaon, "maratabat" primarily connotes rank and secondarily the honor due to rank. Maratabat is the quantifiable essence of status rank and is measured most commonly as a monetary valuation when determining the proper amount of bridewealth (*bantingan*) to be exchanged at marriage or the amount of wergild (*bangun*) required to avert a feud. It is expressed generally as a gradation of four standard sums required for bridewealth within each of the four ranked estates; datu maratabat is valued at one thousand units, that of dumatus at seven hundred, the maratabat of the endatuan at five hundred, and that of ulipun at three hundred units. These quantities were expressed to me in Philippine pesos by informants but almost certainly referred originally to Mexican silver dollars, used as media of interregional exchange in Southeast Asia as recently as the early American period (Forrest 1969, 279; Gullick 1958, 20 n. 1; Miller 1913, 341).[18]

IDEOLOGICAL INCORPORATION AND RANK
COMPETITION WITHIN THE ARISTOCRACY

In precolonial Magindanaon society, a close correspondence obtained between datu status and political and economic predominance. As detailed in the chapter that follows, the Magindanaon nobility composed a ruling class that extracted tribute in various forms from ordinary Muslims and other subject peoples. Many aristocrats also invested the wealth so obtained in trading or raiding expeditions and further enriched themselves. Ideological instruments existed that promoted ruling class closure and authorized existing social arrangements. The foremost of these were the tarsilas themselves. With the single exception of the tarsila of the descendants of Tabunaway (which does not trace descent from Sarip Kabungsuwan), the Magindanaon tarsilas provide a charter for an aristocratic ruling class. They provide "proofs of legitimacy" (Majul 1973, 3) for a tribute-taking elite, most importantly by asserting descent from the Prophet Muhammad through a sharif line and thus justifying the role of datus as political and religious leaders.

In addition to the written genealogical accounts, there were formal and informal oral traditions that advanced an ideology of aristocracy. *Taritib* (from the Arabic "tartib," meaning "order" or "sequence") refers to a body of oral guidelines or regulations concerning the proper criteria for the choice of a sultan and the procedure for his installation and, generally, to the protocol governing relations between the sultan, datus, and subordinate classes. Taritib may still occasionally be heard in Cotabato orated by elder members of the royal houses on Magindanaon radio programs.

Aside from taritib, there were a number of anecdotes, adages, and precepts concerning the Magindanaon nobility that circulated within the ruling class. The highest-ranking members of the aristocracy were perceived to have "Arab" features, that is, relatively light skin and aquiline noses. Datu Kasim told me that the phrase "Watu na Ulu" (head of stone) referred to the conviction that every Magindanaon community required a strong leader identified with the nobility. The precedence of highborn status over acquired wealth was affirmed in various narratives (compare Gullick 1958, 65). Hadji Abbas related one such narrative told to him by his parents. It concerns a well-dressed young man of modest rank who attended a celebration at the house of the datu and sat in a prominent place. An elder relative of the datu could only afford poor clothes and so sat far from the datu. When the datu noticed this, he had his armed retainers remove the well-dressed man and seat the datu's poor relation in his place. A proverb accompanied the story: "You wear a rich garment and I only a poor one; but when we arrive at the court of the datu, there we shall see which of us shines with the golden radiance of nobility."[19]

Other cautionary proverbs were sung by bayuk performers—praise singers who performed at special ceremonial occasions of the nobility. The familiar metaphor used in these proverbs was that of the small bird who endeavors to fly very high but in the end falls back to his old nest. The admonition was to young men of questionable status who wished to marry high-ranking women but lacked proper genealogical qualifications.

The principal impulse for the status-related behavior of individual members of the traditional Magindanaon ruling class was rank competition. Gullick's observation for the Malay states, that "the concept of differential status was one of the main interests and values of the ruling class" (1958, 66), is equally accurate for the Cotabato sultanates. The sultan was the apex of the ruling class in each state and the point of reference by which members of the aristocracy determined their relative status. Sultans, ideally, were distinguished by their *pulna* status; those individuals designated as pulna were able to trace direct ancestry from Sarip Kabungsuwan through both parents.[20]

Within the datu estate as a whole, claims to status rank were predicated upon the quality and quantity of descent lines linking an individual to Sarip Kabungsuwan. The quality of a descent line was determined by its association with an inherited, ranked title. These titles originally corresponded with specific offices conferred by a sultan upon particular individuals. Such titles were inherited and often lost any direct connection with a functional administrative position while remaining significant status markers.[21]

Judicious marriages were vital for maintaining or increasing family status among the Magindanaon nobility. The rule of hypergamy—mandating that a woman could only be given in marriage to a man of equal or higher rank—ensured, for instance, that the offspring of a woman of pulna status would always remain pulna. However, it also meant that women flowed up through the ranking system as parents endeavored to contract marriages for their daughters that would increase the status of their grandchildren's line. Because tribute-takers were also wife-takers, the rule of hypergamy also encouraged particular forms of class exogamy as datus obtained junior wives from among

their non-elite followers. With descent figured cognatically, so that kinship links through females mattered, a formally straightforward status
system was, in practice, quite complex.[22]

Because of the rule of hypergamy and the practice of polygyny, a
sultan or other titleholder would likely have numerous recognized offspring whose status ranks ranged from pulna to the lowest status levels
of the datu estate (through unions with endatuan or ulipun wives).
This was advantageous for a ruler, who was thus possessed of a number of daughters of differing ranks whom he could bestow on various
datu allies without violating the rule of hypergamy (Beckett 1982).[23]
Because the Cotabato sultanates lacked a rule of primogeniture, succession to a title was open to competition. Potential conflict was limited, however, by taking into account the status of the mother as well
as the father of the claimant. In this way, the inheritance rights of rival
claimants—half brothers, for instance—might be decided on the basis
of fine distinctions in their relative maratabat, or rank (Beckett 1982).

The effect of the combination of rank gradations within the datu estate, cognatic descent reckoning, and status group exogamy was to
render the ideal of discrete valuations of maratabat based on social
categories impractical and largely irrelevant. With the children of differently ranked parents allocated to a rank intermediate between those
of their parents, the system of prestige stratification generated an "in-
tergraded spectrum of rank" (Stewart 1977, 290) rather than sharply
defined status groups. Just as marriage was the major vehicle for rank
enhancement, bridewealth determination was the primary occasion for
the public evaluation of a family's maratabat. Bridewealth negotiations
were complex and delicate affairs necessitated by the status refine-
ments produced by almost every marriage union (compare W. H. Scott
1982).

As instruments for the determination of relative status, tarsilas were
considered private warrants rather than public documents. Although
they served to define and delimit the aristocracy, their principal purpose was to assign rank within it. A tarsila, in other words, was possessed primarily to substantiate the rank of its holder, but it might also
be employed to ascertain the rank of other individuals in specific situations for the purpose of assessing—in an ad hoc manner—one's
maratabat relative to a particular other.[24] Titleholders employed tarsilas to seat guests at ceremonial occasions according to rank. Hadji Abbas related the following story about the use of tarsilas by individual

datus to assess relative rank: "When boats passed by the house of a datu, their passengers were required to fold or lower their umbrellas unless they were of higher rank. If a passenger did not do so, the datu immediately had his expert check the tarsila. If the man was found to be of lower rank the datu would order his men to sink the boat." Tarsilas were also used by datus individually to enforce the status privilege of the aristocracy as a whole. As described by Datu Adil, certain garments and dress styles were reserved for the nobility: "Women of high status and those of lower status wore their *malongs* (sarongs) differently and carried themselves in different ways. High status women would carry their malongs over one arm. Lower status women would wear theirs more in the manner of men. If a woman of questionable status was found wearing her malong in the style of a high status woman the tarsila was examined. If she was found to be a commoner she would be fined forty pesos by the local datu. If she was unable to pay she would be made to work for the datu for one or two years."

The myth of sanctified inequality was the basis for an ideology of nobility embraced by a ruling class that nonetheless regularly contradicted some of its basic doctrines: aristocratic endogamy, the association of paramount rule with the purest bloodlines, and the indelibility of the lines separating social strata. As in other political belief systems, rather than provoking confutations these irregularities generated mechanisms (such as genealogical manipulation or special appointment) for the "post hoc ennoblement of the powerful" (Beckett 1982, 398).[25]

The "struggle for status" (Geertz 1980, 116) within the Magindanaon aristocracy fostered coherence among the ruling class by mitigating the many centrifugal tendencies inherent in a political field where local leaders competed for followers and slaves in an underpopulated region. The notion of a common noble ancestor provided a mechanism that bridged the gap between various ingeds (localities) so that individuals were motivated to marry and otherwise relate to one another in order to maintain their positions within the status group. The spatially dispersed members of the datu stratum were integrated by ties of supposed shared ancestry that crosscut local descent lines. As the source of all aristocratic titles and the focal point for the system of prestige stratification, the office of sultan (if not always the current officeholder) was treated with deep respect by members of the datu stratum. Ruling class coherence even extended between sultanates (whose elites shared the ruling ideology) and probably helped to

smooth intersultanate trade relationships and temper the level of en-
demic intraregional hostilities.

RULING IDEAS AND THE INCORPORATION OF SUBORDINATES

The post-Althusserian social theory of the past twenty years offers a
broad range of analyses of the reproduction of social disparity within
complex political structures. While analysts, as we have seen, disagree
sharply on many of the basic issues, general accord is evident on at
least one point. It is agreed that it is inaccurate to measure the incorporation of political subordinates merely by assessing their belief or dis-
belief in the legitimizing myths of a ruling class. Political structures are
significantly reproduced by other means (and here there is disagreement): by nondiscursive practices, by coercions, by compensatory beliefs or the "common sense" consciousness generated as part of the
everyday operation of systems of domination (see, e.g., Bourdieu 1977;
Foucault 1978; Abercrombie et al. 1980; Williams 1980; Corrigan and
Sayer 1985; Elster 1985; J. Scott 1985, 1990).

The contemporary descendants of the Magindanaon aristocracy favor the view (shared by a range of political actors) that Magindanaon
subordinates have perfectly shared (and continue to share) the dominant myth of sanctified inequality. Datu Alunan Glang notes that
"down to this day, many of them still hold the datus in characteristic
religious awe and adulation" (1969, 33). Datu Michael Mastura sec-
onds this sentiment when he writes that "much of Magindanao's sociopolitical history can be evaluated in terms of the tradition for loyalty to the datus or at least in the veneration of descent groups
belonging to the Magindanao core lineage" (1984, 40). Bai Rebecca D.
Buan ("Bai" is the form of reference for a female member of the nobility), in a 1978 letter to the editor of a Cotabato newspaper, takes a peculiar pre-Islamic slant when she comments that "the datus of olden
days . . . were the living gods of their people" (*Mindanao Cross*, April
7, 1978).

An examination of the historical evidence and oral traditions from
Cotabato suggests that ideological adherence was more fragmentary
and symbolic power relations more complex than imagined by contemporary datus. Looking first at the more formal constructs of the myth
of sanctified inequality, we find that the tarsilas had little relevance for
subordinates except on the occasions when they were used to restrain
the behavior of a social-climbing commoner. As essentially private doc-

uments, the tarsilas were viewed rarely, if ever by subordinates (Majul 1973, 3). Commoners were more likely to hear tales of nobles past and present performed by professional reciters and praise-singers at weddings and other celebrations. The primary audience for these performances was aristocrats, and their first purpose was rank competition rather than the edification of commoners.

A second official forum for the transmission of the dominant ideology would have been the mosque, particularly at Friday community prayers. As putative sharifs, sultans and ruling datus were religious as well as political leaders. Imams (prayer leaders), themselves datus, were appointed by rulers, and they paid customary obeisance to those rulers before beginning public prayers in the mosque. In their Friday orations, imams asked special blessings for the sultan, his family, and his royal predecessors (Saleeby 1905; Loyre 1991). Accounts of public religious practice suggest, however, that the mosque was not a primary arena for interclass instruction. William Dampier visited Cotabato for seven months as an officer aboard a British privateering vessel, the *Cygnet*. His 1697 account, *New Voyage Round the World*, provides the best ethnographic description of Cotabato in the seventeenth century. It includes the following description of mosque attendance: "Friday is their Sabbath; but I never did see any difference that they make between this Day and any other Day, only the Sultan himself goes to the Mosque twice . . . The meaner sort of people have little Devotion: I did never see any of them at their Prayers, or go into a Mosque" (1906, 344–45).

The entire community did gather for such ceremonial events as royal weddings, installations, or lustrations. These were certainly (as elsewhere in Southeast Asia) occasions for displaying the power and splendor of the ruler, but they offered limited opportunity for the direct inculcation of dominant beliefs.[26]

The ideology of sanctified inequality was tracked by more elemental (and more indigenous) representations of rule. These were symbolizations of individually exercised power rather than sanctions for collectively claimed authority. Jeremy Beckett notes that the term "datu" had two meanings: "ruler" and "one entitled to rule on account of his descent from datus" (1982, 396). The ideology of nobility emphasized the latter meaning. In practice though, the regular occurrence of feuds, wars, and succession struggles ensured that the personal attributes of a datu, especially his ability to command fear and deference, remained a key factor in his political successes.[27] Datu Adil informed me that the ideal datu acquired recognition without demanding it and obtained tribute without exacting it—not because of his elevated rank but as a result of his personal force. That regard for personal power and its projection was often represented in the names of prominent datus, three of which—Mangelen, Makapuges, and Dilangalen—may be glossed as "the Controller," "the Enforcer," and "He Who Cannot Be Moved." It was also evident in some inherited titles. The full title of one of the highest offices in the Magindanao Sultanate, "Amirul Umra a Tibpud a Bangias a Dimakudak u Pagilidan," translates as "Commander of Decisive Power Who Treads upon the Seashore."

The substantial power of a ruling datu was projected symbolically through his supernatural abilities. As with the political skills that secured his position, those abilities were individually acquired, not innately possessed. The single exception to the pattern of intentional acquisition of supernatural abilities was the supernatural potency that inhered in the person of the sultan. That endowment of potency was equally capable of benefaction or injury. As related by Imam Akmad, "The sultan would bathe ceremonially in the Pulangi River to drive away the three evil spirits of Satan [Saytan]. Ordinary people were careful never to bathe downstream from the sultan. It was believed that the sultan was toxic, that the water that flowed past his body would make a person ill."[28] All other aristocrats, I was told, acquired their supernatural abilities through the study of esoteric arts known collectively in Magindanaon as *kamal* or *ilmu* ("special power" or "special knowledge"). Kamal was taught by special masters and was effectively limited to members of the aristocracy. Kamal arts included the abilities to repel blades and bullets, leap great distances, and disappear at will.

Ethnographic evidence suggests that these symbolizations of power were appreciated, and often embellished, by Magindanaon subordinates. When asked about the supernatural powers exercised by past rulers, contemporary datus had few stories to offer, and those they did tell usually emphasized how the powers were acquired from specific teachers rather than relating how such powers were used to secure or maintain political power.[29] By contrast, Magindanaon commoners related numerous narratives of supernatural power—stories that diverged from those of datus in interesting ways.

I often heard stories of datus of old (and a few in living memory) possessed of extraordinary physiognomies: terrible visages, monstrous bodies, extra eyes and fingers. Rulers also exhibited various marvelous powers—those directly related to the kamal arts but others as well: prognostication, remote vision, and the ability to strike a man dead without touching him. In these stories, neither extraordinary appearance nor exceptional powers was explicitly linked to noble descent. They were attributed only to prominent and powerful members of the nobility and served as both metaphors for and explanations of the personal power of individual rulers. The narratives related by non-elite Muslims tend to be unclear about, or indifferent to, the ways in which kamal powers were acquired by rulers. They focus instead on linking the power of command with the command of supernatural powers. Taken as a whole they form a subordinate mythology of power analogous to but distinct from the dominant mythology of nobility.

While the myth of sanctified inequality is advanced by many in Cotabato today as the fundamental axiom of traditional governance, it is more likely that symbolic representations of power, some of them generated endogenously out of the experiences of subordinates, were more significant for social reproduction.

INTERPRETING POLITICAL RELATIONS
IN PRECOLONIAL COTABATO

How are we to characterize the political relations represented by the myth of sanctified inequality? In recent years, the most favored interpretive stance for reconstructing the precolonial polities of Southeast Asia has been to privilege local epistemologies and search self-consciously for authenticity (see, e.g., Geertz 1980; O. W. Wolters 1982; Milner 1982; Errington 1989; Bentley 1986).[30] Proponents of this approach tend to focus interpretive attention on sacred texts, courtly ceremony, and the formal schemata of social hierarchy as crucial bases of traditional political order. These phenomena are analyzed not as instances of symbolic power relations but rather as expressions of broadly shared "structures of experience" (Milner 1982, 113) signifying that "political systems are expressions of culture" (O. W. Wolters 1982, 9).

The works cited above—and particularly those by Clifford Geertz and Shelly Errington—present evocative and finely detailed portraits of traditional Southeast Asian polities and demonstrate the value of an anthropological perspective for illuminating Southeast Asia's precolonial past. Nevertheless, their aversion to exploring linkages between political culture, material relations of domination, and the reproduction of disparities in social power raises the suspicion that they don't provide the full picture. That impression is reinforced by the fact that these works nearly always present an exclusively elite view of traditional arrangements. What anthropologists should also be able to offer as a complement to Southeast Asian historical sources is a village-level view of the traditional social world; yet ethnography in these works is not employed to examine possibly divergent viewpoints from the peasant periphery, but relied upon only for oral description of the "exemplary center" (Geertz 1980, 11; see also Errington 1989).[31]

The works by Milner and O. W. Wolters mentioned above share this top-down perspective and its limitations. Concern with shared "structures of experience" tends to overlook the fact that traditional nobilities and their mostly rural subjects had very different life experiences, and that, as Pierre Bourdieu reminds us, those occupying disparate economic and political positions in a social configuration tend to produce distinct "practical interpretations" of objective conditions (1977, 116). It is precisely those sorts of divergent practical interpretations that I have attempted to draw out and analyze in my own reconstruction of the precolonial social order in Cotabato.

In contrast to the emphasis on the unifying effect of shared culture found in the works just cited, various depictions of political relations in the precolonial sultanates of the Philippines have emphasized material remuneration and dyadic negotiation between leaders and followers as the principal bases for political adherence (see, e.g., Mednick 1974; Gowing 1979; W. H. Scott 1982). The writers of these works have been tempted to view precolonial political relations through the same "dyadic alliance" (Lande 1965) lens so prominently utilized to analyze contemporary political activity in the Philippines (see, e.g., Lande 1965; Lynch 1984; Hollnsteiner 1963). Exclusive attention to "rational actors" and personalized relationships obscures the profoundly constraining effect of political-economic structures on the negotiation of vertical dyadic ties.[32] As we shall see, the larger political context in precolonial Cotabato—one marked by armed coercion and legal insecurity—diminished much of the negotiating advantage of subordinates, despite the fact that land was plentiful and followers were a relatively scarce, and thus highly valued, resource.

William Henry Scott (1982) characterizes the tacit agreements binding datus and subordinates in the Philippine sultanates as follows:

> The datu's power stems from the willingness of his followers to render him respect and material support, to accept and implement his decisions, and to obey and enforce his orders, and is limited by the consensus of his

peers. Followers give their support in response to his ability and willingness to use his power on their behalf, to make material gifts or loans in
time of crisis, and to provide legal or police protection and support
against opponents. . . . Failure to discharge such duties may result in the
quiet withdrawal of cooperation and support, so that autocratic behavior on the part of any datu is the result rather than the cause of sub-
servience on the part of others. (W. H. Scott 1982, 139–40)

Scott's depiction of the sultanates as virtual free markets for the negotiation of political linkages between individual datus and followers is
not well-supported by the evidence from Cotabato and elsewhere.

Relations of subjection in the Philippine sultanates exemplify what
Orlando Patterson (1982, 18) has termed the "personalistic idiom" of
power. In such social settings power relations are humanized, often
employing the principle of kinship, but not mystified. Domination is
direct and discernible. "No dependent in such societies ever loses sight
of the stark and obvious fact that he or she is directly dependent on a
more powerful party" (Patterson 1982, 19).

In the Philippine sultanates, as elsewhere in such systems, dependency was often euphemized as the receipt of protection. An alternate
term for Magindanaon "endatuan" (one who is ruled) was "sakup,"
meaning one who is protected. While commoners had a genuine need
for protection, the search for a powerful datu protector was driven less
by the benefits to be gained from dependency than by the hazards associated with freedom from it. The social context for the protection offered by datus is outlined in Charles Wilkes's 1842 depiction of the
predicament of subordinates in the Sulu Sultanate:

> the untitled freemen . . . are at all times the prey of the hereditary datus,
> even those who hold no official status. By all accounts these constitute a
> large proportion of the population, and it being treason for any low-
> born freeman to injure or maltreat a datu, the latter, who are of a
> haughty, overbearing, and tyrannical disposition, seldom keep them-
> selves within bounds in their treatment of their inferiors. The conse-
> quence is that some lower class of freemen are obliged to put themselves
> under the protection of some particular datu, who guards them from the
> encroachment of others. The chief to whom they thus attach themselves
> is induced to treat them well in order to retain their services, and attach
> them to his person, that he may, in case of need, be enabled to defend
> himself from depredations, and the violence of his neighbors. (Wilkes
> 1842 quoted in Mednick 1974, 21)

Wilkes's observation indicates that some of the commoners compelled
to bind themselves to a datu for their own defense might be utilized to

protect that datu against his enemies. Similar arrangements pertained in the Cotabato sultanates, according to my Magindanaon consultants. Although the officers of the armed forces of a datu or sultan were usually members of the nobility, the soldiers were principally drawn from the endatuan. In an unpublished paper, Muhammad Adil, who holds the title of "Sultan of Kutawatu," describes the traditional protective relationship this way: "Usually the nucleus of an 'inged' is the house of the ruler who in the early days was both ruler and protector but later on, when the caste system was fully developed, was only a ruler, protected and defended by the people" (Adil 1955).

Another benefit cited by W. H. Scott is the datu's redistribution of food or goods in the form of gifts or loans in times of crisis. None of my elder Magindanaon consultants could recall accounts of datus redistributing food in periods of shortage, although all could remember the details of tribute collection and some remembered stories of droughts, epidemics, or other natural calamities so severe that families were forced to sell their children.[33]

I heard only one story, told by Hadji Abbas, of gifts provided to followers by datus, and those coincided with debts incurred to other followers: "In previous times in our inged the datu would sometimes donate the remainder of the bantingan [bridewealth] of young men who were unable to raise the entire amount. However, he never actually paid any money to the family of the bride but only promised it as a debt owed by him."

The most frequent service performed by datus, according to W. H. Scott, was adjudication and the provision of legal protection. Adjudication was the principal official function of Magindanaon datus, but, according to published sources and Magindanaon memories, it was almost always performed for immediate compensation and very rarely conducted impartially.[34]

The Cotabato sultanates employed a set of written legal codes known as the *Luwaran* ("selection"). The Luwaran consisted of selections from the Shafi'i school of Islamic law combined with customary (*adat*) law. Saleeby (1905), who first translated these codes into English, estimated that the Luwaran was compiled in the mid-eighteenth century. He also had the following to say about Magindanaon jurisprudence: "The Moros are not strict nor just in the execution of the law. The laws relating to murder, adultery, and inheritance are seldom strictly complied with . . . [and] Moro law is not applied equally to all classes. Great preference is shown to the datu class"(1905, 66).

Stories told me by various Magindanaon elders tend to concur with this assessment. After detailing the various customary fines assessed by a datu for murder or adultery, Hadji Abbas related with some hesitation the "real situation" in his inged in former times: "The elders [*mga lukes*] told secret stories of the datu in our place. He was one of the highest officials of the Sultan of Magindanao. That datu was very harsh with the common people but he showed great leniency when passing judgment on his relatives, some of whom were notorious rustlers of water buffalo. Those water buffalo often found their way to the land of the datu. I was also told that troublesome wives brought to the datu by their husbands for judgment were sometimes raped by the datu or his men."

Datu Adil, in detailing the misdeeds of "bad" datus provided similar stories. According to him, the justice administered by these datus was inequitable and their fines oppressive. He also recalled stories of datus raping young unmarried women accused of unlawful (usually premarital) sexual activity or elopement. A young man caught thus would be fined for seduction and elopement. The punishment prescribed in the Luwaran is one hundred lashes each for the man and woman and mandatory marriage (Saleeby 1905, 71, article XL). These accounts suggest that partiality and inequity may have been the rule rather than the exception in datu adjudication.[35]

Finally, Scott suggests that followers were able to withdraw support from datus who failed to discharge their obligations. Mednick concurs when remarking that "about the only choice a freeman seems to have had was the right to attach himself to a leader and to abandon him if he chose" (1974, 21). Other evidence indicates that even this choice was very narrowly constrained. It seems likely that the open competition among datus for followers both moderated the behavior of datus toward their followers and encouraged followers to look for better arrangements if unsatisfied with their present situation. All the same, the actual ability of followers to change leaders was probably severely limited. Both leaving one's current datu and joining another were risky undertakings because of the advantages and interests held by datus collectively. A datu could convert his follower into a debt-bondsman (ulipun) practically at will and without warning; and, because all notable datus had debt-slaves, members of the ruling class respected each other's property rights in acquired persons and tended to honor requests for the return of escaped debt-bondsmen (Ileto 1971; Gullick 1958). Followers were undoubtedly aware of these possibilities and presumably avoided behavior (including obvious dissatisfaction with their situation) that would raise the suspicions of the datu or his lieutenants as to their constancy. That followers occasionally deserted their datus for new ones is certain. Nevertheless, switching datus was not nearly as commonplace and unproblematic as envisioned by W. H. Scott. The exchange of one leader for another probably occurred most commonly en masse, under conditions where a datu was so severely weakened that followers were certain he could neither protect them against other datus nor retaliate against them if they abandoned him.

ALTERNATIVE SOURCES OF POLITICAL CONTROL

It is worth noting that in both historical accounts and oral traditions of precolonial politics, the most consistent theme concerns the notably autocratic and arbitrary nature of traditional rule. Dampier (1906) explains the "laziness" of seventeenth-century Magindanaons by suggesting that it ". . . seems to proceed not so much from their natural Inclinations, as from the severity of their Prince of whom they stand in awe: For he dealing with them very arbitrarily, and taking from them what they get, this damps their Industry, so they never strive to have anything but from Hand to Mouth" (1906, 334).

Dampier provides several examples, including one of the Sultan's ploys to extort money from subjects: "Sometimes he will send to sell one thing or another that he hath to dispose of, to such whom he knows to have Money, and they must buy it, and give him his price; and if afterward he hath occasion for the same thing, he must have it if he sends for it" (1906, 342).[36] Thomas Forrest, in his 1775 journal of his visit to Cotabato, also notes the capriciousness of the Magindanao sultan (Forrest 1969, 278).[37] Both Dampier (1906, 370) and Forrest (1969, 289, 291) describe swift and harsh punishments for disobedient followers.

Oral traditions primarily concern Datu Utu, the nineteenth-century Sultan of Buayan. Ordinary Muslims continue to tell stories of Datu Utu as the man who reduced recalcitrant followers to "human ducks" (itik a tau) by crushing their knees and depositing them to live in the mud beneath his house.[38] Beckett also reports folk memories depicting Utu as a "monster" (1982, 399) and remarks that he held his dominion together by terror; yet the many examples of the severity of traditional rule suggest that Datu Utu's tyranny was exceptional only in its heinousness.

Those examples also suggest that, while datus might rely upon en-datuan to defend against external threats, a local ruler's control of the means of destruction was a fundamentally important mechanism for dominating followers and suppressing dissent. Datu Adil (1955) de-scribes political relations within a typical inged in precolonial Cota-bato: "To express one's opinion unasked on any question invites not only dire consequences but almost certain condemnation or even death. One who expresses his opinion, especially if in protest against any despotic act of the ruling tyrant usually brings death upon the hap-less one and slavery to his family. In extreme cases the offending sub-ject may be publicly executed to give an example to the whole people. If however, he is a member of the ruling family or the 'barabangsa' class, he may only be banished from the kingdom."[39]

All ruling datus maintained core groups of armed retainers. At least two paramount officeholders in precolonial Cotabato (Forrest 1969; Ileto 1971) possessed personal retinues of thirty or more armed war-riors composed entirely of banyaga slaves. These troops—the Southeast Asian equivalent of Ottoman janissaries—were fed, clothed, and pro-vided with wives by the officeholders.[40] They formed a force of trusted and privileged soldiers whose reliability derived from their status as outsiders with no rights or relatives within Magindanaon society.

There was an additional social factor, noted by Beckett (1982), that may have significantly promoted compliance to datu rule. That was the fact that, in general, the most exploited groups in precolonial Cota-bato lived, or originated from, outside Magindanaon society. These were the upland client groups such as the Tiruray and the banyaga slaves acquired from Christian settlements and the more distant high-lands. Beckett (1982, 398) implies that the existence of exploitable ex-ternal groups functioned as an indirect form of remuneration, whereby the commoner followers of a powerful datu were able to share in the tribute, plunder, or captives taken from outsiders. Followers undoubt-edly gained some direct or indirect material benefits from the exploita-tion of outsiders, but the way in which that exploitation functioned to foster the compliance of commoners may have been as much psycho-logical as material.

The evidence for the material benefits to commoners from tribute and captives seized abroad is lacking. Although commoners were legally able to own slaves there are no historical records to indicate what percentage of them actually did. Neither is it known to what ex-tent commoners shared in plunder or tribute (although in the case of tribute it is highly unlikely that they partook at all). Furthermore, it is important to remember that the boundary that separated commoners from chattel slaves was a status divide and not one of class. Multiple commentators on the Philippine sultanates have pointed out that the material conditions of life for banyaga slaves were not appreciably worse, and were in some cases better (the banyaga bodyguards of the sultan are a case in point), than for the average commoner (Ileto 1971; Mednick 1974; Warren 1981). The presence of disdained aliens may have worked to sustain the stratification system largely through its psychological effect on subordinates, who were inclined to draw the most meaningful social dividing line below rather than above themselves and identify with insider Muslims as opposed to outsider pagans and Christians.

SUMMARY: THE BASES OF TRADITIONAL RULE

In synthesis, there existed in the Cotabato sultanates, from at least the mid-sixteenth century, a distinct ruling class that, although often absorbed in internal status competition, was nevertheless integrated by a well-developed ideology of nobility—one that entitled its members to exercise authority over, and extract tribute from, the Cotabato populace.

The fundamental basis of power of datus was their control over subordinates, both those legally free as well as unfree ones. Individual datus strove to acquire the greatest possible number of endatuan, ulipun, banyaga, and client Tiruray from whom to extract surplus directly. On this foundation they were able to build impressive personal retinues of armed and unarmed dependents. An ambitious datu with a large force of followers could further expand the scope of his power and wealth by subduing or sufficiently impressing lesser datus so as to convert them into vassals; by leading or financing large-scale external raiding and trading expeditions; or by entering into strategic alliances with other powerful datus in order to influence state-level or even regional politics.

What was the social cement that kept the Magindanaon political order intact? It was undoubtedly an amalgam of armed force, material remuneration, and cultural commitment. Datus effectively controlled armed violence, and the use or threat of physical coercion was a consequential source of social control in the Cotabato sultanates, even though it is the least acknowledged in written indigenous records. The precolonial lords of Cotabato were, on the whole, capricious and, in some cases, ruthless autocrats. Domination was exercised directly and overtly; and if it was not openly acknowledged by subordinates, or only expressed metaphorically (with atrocious actions denoted by ogreish appearance), it was because obvious dissatisfaction would likely have invited additional repression.

Remuneration was also a significant source of political compliance in the Cotabato sultanates. However it did not play the key integrative role envisioned by W. H. Scott (1982) and others. Goods controlled by a datu were very unevenly distributed, with those closest members of his retinue receiving by far the greatest share. Neither were relations of redistribution between traditional leaders and followers simply a premodern version of the political clientelism found in the modern Philippine state. While followers were as essential to precolonial datus as they are to present-day politicians, datus had more means at their disposal to acquire clients and forcibly retain them once they had them. Subordinates were unable to attach themselves to more than one datu at a time and their ability to change datus was severely limited. In addition, despite the claim for such in the ruling ideology, the provision of legal and armed protection by datus was mostly illusory.

Finally, cultural commitment was an important factor for sociopolitical cohesion in precolonial Cotabato. Commoners (endatuan) and even debt-slaves (ulipun) presumably identified themselves, if only nominally, as Muslims. They felt themselves to be insiders—members of the dominant sociocultural category in the Cotabato Basin—and thus superior to Christian or pagan banyaga slaves or Tiruray clients. They were attuned to the symbolic role of the sultan and acquainted with the rudiments of the ideology of nobility. Evidence suggests, however, that ruling ideas were not shared nearly as well, nor as completely, by Cotabato subordinates as is imagined by those anthropologists who have been principally concerned with political culture in precolonial polities in Southeast Asia.

There is evidence also for the existence of independent perceptions and representations of the social order by Cotabato subordinates. In this unofficial transcript, power relations were not naturalized as the product of a self-evident hierarchical order. Instead, social power was *denaturalized* by according it a supernatural essence. Such images portrayed a profoundly unequal distribution of social force, vividly illustrating the belief, based on direct experience, in the power of certain rulers "to prevail in any encounter" (J. Scott 1990, 73). While such beliefs may have had considerable ideological effect, they bear scant resemblance to the products of the hegemonic process posited by most analysts of cultural domination. In particular, subordinate images of datu rule were applied not only independently, but selectively, as only some ruling datus were endowed by Muslim subordinates with supernatural attributes. Moreover, as we shall see for contemporary Cotabato, such endogenous symbolizations of power also contain a large measure of counterhegemonic potential in that what has been endowed independently may be unilaterally withdrawn.

CHAPTER 4

European Impositions
and the Myth of Morohood

The predominant theme enunciated in the official discourse of Muslim nationalism in the Philippines is that of Morohood—the postulated existence of a single, deeply rooted, Philippine Muslim (Moro) cultural identity. Morohood is said to have developed principally as the result of more than three hundred years of religious warfare against Spanish invaders. This chapter examines the modern myth of Morohood in light of the historical evidence from Cotabato concerning the nature of armed resistance to Spanish aggression in the Muslim Philippines. I begin by investigating the political economy of the precolonial Cotabato Basin, tracing how political and economic relations within and between its indigenous polities were shaped and transformed by external perturbations in international trade and European conquest.

While a significant number of Southeast Asian sultanates were founded or dramatically expanded as the direct or indirect consequence of the initial European invasion of Southeast Asia at the opening of the sixteenth century, none have had their histories more thoroughly entangled with that of European penetration of the region than the Cotabato sultanates.[1] The rise and fall of the Cotabato sultanates is bracketed by two separate conquests—that of the first Western colonial power in the region and that of the final. Sarip Kabungsuwan, the legendary founder of the Cotabato sultanates, was a refugee from the Portuguese seizure of Melaka in 1511. Datu Ali, the last independent Cotabato ruler, was captured and killed by the American colonizers of the Philippines in 1905. In the intervening centuries the Cotabato sultanates were inflected and eventually deranged as the result of encounters with various agents of European expansion. The most frequent and intense engagements—economic and military—were with the Spaniards, who from the outset of their occupation of the northern Philippines in 1571 sought the political subjugation of, as well as expanded trade with, the southern sultanates.

A TRIBUTARY MODE OF PRODUCTION

The three main indigenous populations of the Cotabato Basin—the Magindanaon, Iranun, and Tiruray—were linked together from the earliest historic period in a single political-economic system based on the external acquisition of plunder and slave labor and the internal production of commodities for external trade. It was a system propelled by the direct extraction of surpluses from primary producers by political or military means, and the circulation of that surplus "through the transactions of commercial intermediaries" (Wolf 1982, 82), what has been called a tributary mode of production (Amin 1973; Wolf 1982).

That system comprised two principal socioeconomic categories that crosscut ethnolinguistic boundaries: tribute-takers and tribute-providers.[2] Tribute-providers were predominantly direct producers, either freemen or slaves.[3] Tribute-takers consisted primarily of local overlords (datus) linked with one another through intermarriage, through patronage arrangements, and by means of the ideology of nobility related in the previous chapter.

Chinese sources from the Ming period and earlier suggest that, by at least A.D. 1300, there existed in Cotabato a harbor principality engaged in substantial direct trade with China.[4] Early Spanish accounts of Cotabato from the mid-sixteenth century are the first to report the existence of two rival power centers in the Cotabato Valley. These adjacent sultanates had areas of influence corresponding to the dialect boundaries between Tau Sa Ilud and Tau Sa Laya, with the seat of the Magindanao Sultanate in present-day Cotabato City at the mouth of the Pulangi River, and that of the Buayan Sultanate upstream near what is now Datu Piang. However, at different points in the history of their rivalry, each one was controlled for significant lengths of time by the other.

The upriver and downriver sultanates were similarly structured, and they conformed to a general sociopolitical type that has been characterized as a "segmentary state" (Southall 1965) or "contest state" (Adas 1981). They were loose confederations of local overlords, or datus. Datus formed a tribute-taking aristocracy with hereditary claims to allegiance from followers. While a ruling datu was almost always associated with a specific district, or inged,[5] the index of relative political potency was command of people rather than control of territory. In accord with the pattern that pertained throughout precolonial Southeast Asia, where arable land was more abundant and thus less valuable than human resources (Reid 1988), the wealth of a ruling datu was secured through rights over persons rather than rights in land. The land under cultivation in a particular domain was held in usufruct by individuals, but the datu had the final right of disposition (see W. H. Scott 1982).

Datus usually held large tracts of land for their own use that were worked by slave labor. The nonslave followers (endatuan) of a datu were obliged to provide him support in the form of scheduled payments of a portion of their crops and unscheduled contributions for prestige feasts or bridewealth payments. They were also required to perform military and nonmilitary labor service. Datus used surplus wealth to support themselves and the armed followings that were the basis of their power (compare Gullick 1958). Wealth also was used as capital to engage in or finance trading or slave-raiding expeditions. Chattel slaves (banyaga), taken in raids or warfare or purchased, were a common form for storing (and investing) surplus wealth (compare W. H. Scott 1982; Warren 1981). Banyaga were exchanged as part of bridewealth payments and were also a medium of commercial exchange (Forrest (1969 [1779]).[6] Other nonfree subjects of datus were debt-slaves (ulipun). Endatuan could be reduced to ulipun for a number of causes, the rate of reduction often being related to the availability and cost of banyaga at a given time (Warren 1981, 216). New debt-slaves were either added to a datu's personal following or put to work to produce food or provide menial services to the datu's household. Typically, a significant portion of a datu's debt-slaves were utilized as personal retinue or armed retainers and were supported by banyaga or other debt-slaves.[7]

The Magindanaon tribute-taking elite recognized the hereditary claim of one among them to allegiance from all other members of the aristocracy. Because of the existence of a royal (barabangsa) bloodline, the sultan was not simply a primus inter pares ruler. He was, nonetheless, a datu who, as a result of a combination of pedigree and political savvy, commanded the allegiance of other datus. That allegiance was accomplished and maintained primarily through the creation of dyadic alliances between the sultan and individual datus—arrangements commonly sealed either by his bestowal of a daughter in marriage or his marriage to a daughter of another datu. Because datus ruling ingeds were the basic components of a sultanate, the authority of a sultan was exerted not over a royal domain as such but over his datu supporters, linked together in a network of dyadic alliances.

A reigning sultan had the formal right to collect taxes and tariffs, render legal decisions, and make various administrative appointments. He did not hold a monopoly on the means of violence, and, despite his capability to apply substantial coercive force, military power was widely diffused (W. H. Scott 1982).[8] In addition to the taxes collected by the sultan (primarily tolls on commercial river traffic) and the tribute he received in various forms from datu supporters, the sultan had his own inged and tribute-providing commoners. A significant portion of a sultan's wealth, however, probably came from his privileged access to sources of wealth external to his realm, derived from wars conducted on his enemies, slave raids on (or tribute-collecting visits to) non-Muslim neighbors, and his privileged access to trade with external powers.[9] Much of a sultan's wealth was also held in the form of slaves, the number of which was "the most important index of prestige and power" (Ileto 1971, 50).

EXTERNAL ACQUISITIONS
AND THE FLOW OF TRIBUTE

Despite their development as rival power centers, the two principal Cotabato sultanates were linked throughout most of their history in a single economic system based on the commercial production of rice and the collection of forest products, and the external exchange of those commodities for prestige goods, firearms, and bullion.[10]

The upriver Buayan Sultanate was located in the fertile upper valley of the Pulangi. Rice was one of the primary exports from Cotabato and it is likely that the major portion of all rice exported from Cotabato was grown in the upper valley. Slave labor was centrally important to the economy of the Buayan Sultanate and much of it was probably utilized in commercial rice production. In the mid-nineteenth century, Datu Utu, the effective Sultan of Buayan and the most powerful man in the Cotabato Valley for much of his rule, was reported to have four to five thousand slaves (Gayangos cited in Ileto 1971). Lesser datus usually held fewer than one hundred slaves (Ileto 1971).

While debt-slaves almost always originated from within the domain of the sultanate, chattel slaves (banyaga) were originally acquired from outside. It is probable, because of the proximity of the Buayan Sultanate to upland areas and its relative distance from the seacoasts that were the source of slaves seized from Spanish-held territories, that most of the banyaga of the Buayan Sultanate were obtained in raids on non-Muslim upland groups.

For most of its history, however, the Buayan Sultanate did not raid its closest upland neighbors, the Tiruray, for banyaga slaves. Instead, slave hunters went farther afield to raid the Manobo of the central Cordillera or the Bilaan or T'boli of the southern Tiruray Highlands (Ileto 1971). This was because Tiruray communities had been incorporated as client groups into both sultanates. Tiruray communities entered into unequal, ritually reinforced trade relationships with individual Magindanaon datus. In exchange for Tiruray products, the datu provided salt, iron, cloth and other manufactured goods, and, just as important, protection from other datus. During his stay in Cotabato, Forrest observed profoundly unequal exchanges between Tirurays and Magindanaons. He reported loans forced on Tirurays to create permanent indebtedness and described Tirurays in their own communities being abused and treated like "slaves" by visiting Magindanaons (1969 [1779], 266).[11]

The incentive for incorporating the Tiruray into the Buayan Sultanate as clients was the value of the products the Tiruray could provide. In their upland fields the Tiruray grew tobacco, an important item for external trade, and upland rice valued by the Magindanaon for domestic consumption. Equally important were the forest products collected by the Tiruray. The mainstays of the forest product trade were beeswax, rattan, and hardwoods.[12] The Tiruray were thus critically important to datus as collectors (or, in the case of tobacco, producers) of products that could be traded externally at great profit for highly valued Chinese goods.[13] Consequently, they were not enslaved but instead incorporated into the economic system as clients to perform this specialized role. Tiruray communities were compelled to collect forest products to meet the trade and tribute demands of

Magindanaon datus, as well as to satisfy their own consumption needs. The terms of exchange probably shifted according to changes in the external market and were constrained, on the one hand, by datus needing to avoid exploitation so extreme as to drive Tiruray communities beyond their effective reach, and, on the other, by the awareness on the part of those communities of their need for externally derived goods and the long-range capabilities of Magindanaon slave raiders.

Relations between the upriver and downriver sultanates were also centered on internal and external trade. The upriver Magindanaon were in need of the very same salt, metals, and cloth that they provided to the Tiruray. They obtained these, as well as prestige goods and bullion, in trade with the downriver sultanate. In exchange they provided rice, tobacco, forest products and, occasionally, upland banyaga slaves for domestic markets and further trading. Although external trade was sometimes carried on directly, it was more commonly channeled through the downriver sultanate. Despite periods of political tension and warfare, trade relations were always maintained, even when the downriver sultanate was occupied by the Spanish. After 1755, the river trade between the sultanates was increasingly facilitated by Chinese traders (see below).

While the upriver and downriver sultanates were similarly structured, the Magindanao Sultanate, because of its location at the river mouth, exhibited certain important differences. The Sultan of Magindanao probably had no more success than his upriver counterpart at collecting all the taxes and tribute due him from his client datus—especially those from outlying ingeds (compare Gullick 1958, 127). However, he did possess a greater number of alternative sources of revenue than did the Buayan sultan. In addition to collecting river tolls on vessels engaged in internal trade, the Sultan of Magindanao levied customs duty on arriving merchant ships and collected anchorage fees from warships.

The capital of the Magindanao Sultanate was wealthier and more cosmopolitan than that of the interior sultanate. William Dampier described the capital (located then in Simuay, just across the Pulangi River and downstream from present-day Cotabato City) in 1686 as "the chiefest City on [the] Island . . . of Mindanao" (1906, 335) and reported that Malay, the trade language of insular Southeast Asia, was spoken widely and well there.[14]

A key element in the maritime orientation of the Magindanao Sultanate was its relationship with the Iranun populations that resided within its territory. European accounts beginning in the mid-eighteenth century identify the Iranun as specialized maritime raiders who channeled large amounts of externally acquired wealth—in the form of slaves, plunder, and occasionally external tribute—back into the sultanate (Warren 1981).[15] Swift Iranun warships set out south from Ilana Bay to harry coastal villages, merchant vessels, and Dutch settlements in Sulawesi (the Celebes) and Maluku (the Moluccas) (Warren 1981).[16] Larger Iranun raids were directed against Spanish territories in the Philippines. The coastal towns of southern Luzon and the Visayas were the victims of persistent, large-scale attacks from "Moro" sea raiders. Captives were sold externally, usually to Bugis or Brunei slave traders, or internally along the Pulangi River.[17] Spaniards or other prominent captives were usually allowed to redeem themselves by ransom immediately after their seizure (Warren 1981, 229).[18]

The Iranun occupied an important niche in the socioeconomic system of the precolonial Cotabato Basin. They formed autonomous coastal communities headed by datus or petty sultans. Although living in close proximity to the Magindanao Sultanate and often aligned with it, the Iranun were never incorporated into the sultanate as subjects, and they assiduously guarded their political independence.[19] When allied with the downriver sultan, the Iranun provided him with very significant economic and political support. The internal circulation of the wealth seized externally by Iranun raiders was also a vital component of the economic prosperity of the Magindanao Sultanate.

One nonindigenous population played a significant role in the commercial life of the precolonial Cotabato Basin. The Chinese have lived continuously in Cotabato longer than any other non-Muslim immigrant group. Chinese permanent presence in the Magindanao Sultanate almost certainly predates the Spanish occupation of the northern Philippines. Dampier found an established Chinese community in Cotabato in 1686, some of whose members worked as accountants for the sultan (1906, 364).[20] In 1755, the expulsion of most of the Chinese in the Spanish-held Philippines was carried out by colonial authorities. Some of those expelled settled in the Magindanao Sultanate (Wickberg 1965). That resettlement would account in part for the larger and more visible Chinese community described by Forrest in 1775. He reports Chinese in Cotabato working as carpenters and herbalists and operating commercial rice mills and palm wine distilleries (1969 [1779], 183, 216, 224). They were also apparently well-engaged in the intersultanate trade in local products for Chinese goods. According to

Forrest, the Chinese settled in the Magindanao Sultanate were not permitted to trade farther upriver than Buayan, the upriver capital, because the Magindanaons were "jealous of their superior abilities in
trade" (1969 [1779], 185).

Despite their commercial success, the social and legal status of the
Chinese in the Cotabato was precarious and certainly no better than
that of the Chinese of Manila.[21] While the Chinese possessed skills and
provided economic benefits to the Magindanao Sultanate comparable
to those of the Iranun, their lack of political and military power tended
to relegate them to the status of the Tiruray or other upland client
groups.

PRECOLONIAL COTABATO
AND EUROPEAN MERCANTILE EXPANSION

In his watershed work, *Europe and the People without History,* Eric
Wolf cautions that the operation of a tributary mode of production in
any particular state is "at least in part determined by whether that
state is weak or strong in relation to other polities . . . Successful surplus extraction cannot be understood in terms of an isolated society
alone; rather, it is a function of the changing organization of the wider
field of power within which the particular tributary constellation is located" (1982, 82). The proposition that power relations between societies have a determining influence on local political-economic orders is
nowhere more clearly illustrated than in the Cotabato sultanates.
Within decades of their establishment (which occurred most probably
in the first half of the sixteenth century), the Cotabato sultanates began to feel the severe effects of the intrusion of European powers into
the region. The most intense collisions were with the Spaniards, who
occupied the northern Philippines in 1571 and almost immediately
sought to subdue the Muslim South. The first three Spanish military
expeditions against Cotabato were failures. On the third, in 1596, the
commander of the expedition was slain and the Spaniards forced eventually to abandon the fort that had been their foothold in Cotabato.
Before doing so, the acting commander reportedly "cut down or set
fire to all the coconut and sago palms within reach of his patrols, to
the number of 50,000 trees" (de la Costa 1961, 279), a tactic fore-
shadowing the economic strangulation to be applied to Cotabato in
place of direct armed assault.[22]

The Spaniards withdrew to Zamboanga where they established a garrison at the tip of the Zamboanga Peninsula in order to control the sea lanes leading to and from Cotabato. The Spanish fort commanded the channel between the peninsula and the island of Basilan, the normal route of sea travel between Cotabato and the rest of the archipelago. Patrol boats based at the fort rerouted Chinese junks coming from the north bound for Cotabato. When manned, the fort was quite effective in impeding the direct China-Cotabato trade. It was much less successful at curtailing maritime raiding. Iranun marauders easily eluded Spanish patrol boats in the Basilan Straits to raid throughout insular Southeast Asia, with the Spanish Philippines becoming their preferred destination. By the mid-eighteenth century, Spanish colonial authorities had largely disarmed the Philippine populations subject to Spanish rule but had not provided them with adequate coastal defense forces. The Iranun responded to those changed circumstances opportunistically, launching annual slave raids against the Spanish North that rarely met with significant armed resistance.

The power and prestige of the Cotabato sultanates intensified during the periods when the Zamboanga garrison was abandoned (1599–1635, 1663–1718) and subsided when the blockade was reestablished. In the first part of the seventeenth century the China trade flourished in Cotabato and the political and economic might of the downriver polity—the Magindanao Sultanate—reached its peak under Sultan Kudarat. By 1775, however, Forrest was able to describe economic conditions in the Magindanao Sultanate as follows: "Spaniards have long hindered Chinese junks, bound from Amoy to Magindanao, to pass Samboangan [Zamboanga]. This is the cause of so little trade at Magindanao, no vessels sailing from Indostan thither; and the little trade is confined to a few Country Chinese . . . and a few Soolooans [Tausug] who come hither to buy rice and paly [*palay*, or unhusked rice], bringing with them Chinese articles: for the crop of rice at Sooloo can never be depended on" (1969 [1779], 280).

By 1800, the Magindanao Sultanate had begun an inexorable economic decline that coincided with the expansion of another Muslim polity of the South. The Sulu Sultanate encompassed the islands of the Sulu archipelago, which forms the boundary between the Sulu Sea and the Celebes Sea. Its favorable location at the juncture of several trade routes ensured its continuation as a maritime entrepôt. The Magindanao Sultanate, no longer able to obtain trade goods directly, was now reduced to providing rice to the expanding Sulu Sultanate in exchange for Chinese goods formerly obtained directly at much more advantageous rates of exchange (Forrest 1969 [1779]). On the basis of evidence from Forrest and others, Warren (1981) suggests that, after 1780, Iranun raiders, who formerly had sailed as economic allies of Magindanao datus, began to raid independently or shift their allegiance to the Sulu Sultanate.

Spanish economic and military pressure also impinged on relations between the upriver and coastal sultanates of the Cotabato Basin. The two rival power centers alternately aligned with the Spaniards against one another as their fortunes waxed and waned. In 1605 and 1635, the Spaniards signed treaties with the reigning upriver (Buayan) sultan recognizing him as the paramount ruler of Mindanao. In 1645 and 1719, similar agreements were made acknowledging the paramountcy of the Sultan of Magindanao. In 1734, the successor to the Magindanao throne was crowned sultan by the Spaniards, and by 1837 the downriver sultanate was a virtual protectorate of the Spanish colonial domain, with the government in Manila controlling trade and choosing the successor to the sultan (Ileto 1971). The Buayan Sultanate, on the other hand, was increasing its influence during this period and annexing tributaries who had abandoned the Magindanao Sultan.

With the introduction by the Spaniards of steam-powered gunboats in 1846 to patrol the Basilan Straits, Iranun raids against the northern Philippines from Ilana Bay were, for the first time, effectively curtailed. This was the final blow to the economic viability of the Magindanao Sultanate. In 1861, the Spanish flag was raised without resistance over the palace of the Sultan of Magindanao, and the downstream sultanate became a colonial possession of Spain. The occupation of the Magindanao Sultanate was accomplished without bloodshed, and plans were soon underway to force the submission of the upstream polity.

The suppression of Iranun slave raiding in the Spanish Philippines coincided with an increased demand for slaves in the Sulu Sultanate to meet the labor needs associated with its recent position as a powerful commercial link in the European trade with China. In the late eighteenth century, the British East India Company was looking for a way to redress its adverse trade balance with China. In particular, it sought a means to stem the flow of silver from British India to China in exchange for the tea so highly desired in Britain. British merchants discovered the long-established Sino-Sulu trade—wherein marine and forest products were exchanged for Chinese goods—and interposed themselves to the commercial benefit of both the Company and the Sulu Sultanate. The British provided textiles, guns, and other manufactured goods in exchange for the marine and forest products valued in China. The greatly expanded demand for these products led to the rapid growth of the Sulu Sultanate and an increased need for the recruitment of a large labor force to do the work of procurement of trade produce. This need had been met by the seasonal slave raiding conducted by the Iranun and other seagoing raiders (Warren 1981).

With slave raiding in the Spanish Philippines greatly diminished after 1846, the gap in the supply to Sulu was filled through increased raids by Cotabato Muslims on upland groups in eastern Mindanao. The Cotabato Chinese became active intermediaries in the expanded slave trade from Mindanao to Sulu (see Warren 1981; Wickberg 1965). During the 1872 smallpox epidemic and famine in Cotabato, Jesuit missionaries bought for redemption children from Chinese middlemen, who had purchased them from their Muslim owners or parents with the intention of reselling them in Sulu (Bernad 1984). An 1890 Jesuit report describes Chinese traders on the upper Pulangi purchasing slaves from slave raiders. Cotabato Chinese merchants were also involved in the gutta-percha boom of the 1880s. They exported this forest product (used as insulation in the building of the transatlantic cable) to Singapore via Sulu (Wickberg 1965). These late nineteenth-century export opportunities gave impetus to Chinese enterprise in Cotabato, and by the turn of the century the external trade of Cotabato as well as Sulu was controlled by Chinese merchants (Warren 1981).

His need for firearms to resist the Spaniards, along with his recognition of the shortage of marketable slaves for Sulu, provided Datu Utu, the last independent Sultan of Buayan, with an irresistible incentive. He and his datus ignored the centuries-old clientage arrangement between the Magindanaon and the Tiruray and began to raid them to acquire slaves to exchange for firearms. Hundreds of Tiruray were enslaved and taken to Sarangani Bay at the southern tip of Mindanao to be sold (along with rice, cacao, coffee, and forest products) to Chinese, Bornean, and European traders in return for the supplies needed to resist the Spaniards who were pushing upriver (Ileto 1971). Responding to new political exigencies and new economic opportunities, upriver datus, in the final decades of precolonial Cotabato, sold their Tiruray clients into slavery in the distant Sulu Sultanate. A combination of Spanish military pressure and British-impelled economic incentives had produced a dramatic (if predictable) alteration of production relations between Magindanaon datus and the Tiruray, whereby collectors of commodities became themselves commodities as datus reduced former clients to chattel slaves.

SPANISH AGGRESSION AND THE MYTH
OF A UNIFIED "MORO" RESISTANCE

Having traced the contours of Spanish aggression against the Cotabato sultanates and the various local responses made to that aggression, we may turn now to examine the modern myth of Morohood that under-girds the official ideology of Philippine Muslim nationalism. That myth, in its most fundamental rendering, refers to the conviction that a transcendent Philippine Muslim (or "Moro") identity was fashioned among the various Muslim peoples of the southern Philippines in the course of more than three hundred years of Spanish offensives against the Muslim polities of Mindanao and Sulu. It is a view advanced not only by Muslim nationalists or nationalist-oriented historians (e.g., Majul 1973) but also by various other scholars of the Muslim Philippines (e.g., George 1980; Gowing 1979; Molloy 1988; Bauzon 1991). A representative capsule expression of the myth of Morohood is found in a recent piece concerned with the contemporary politics of Muslim separatism in the Philippines.

> For over 400 years, the Moros perceived their struggle as a fight to pro-tect their religion, cultural identity and homeland against foreign in-vaders. They have fought many wars for political independence against the Spanish, the Americans and lastly, the Christian Filipino govern-ments in Manila. With their strong sense of Islamic nationalism, the ma-jority of the Muslims regard themselves simply as Moros and not Fil-ipinos at all. Over the centuries Islam has been important to the Muslim people in the Philippines not only in forging the basis of their self-identity, but also in acting as the cement between deep ethnic divisions that exist among the many cultural-linguistic groups that make up the Moro people. (Molloy 1988, 61)

As the passage demonstrates, "Moro" is the term used to designate the shared identity postulated for Philippine Muslims. "Moro" (or "Moor") was the appellation applied to all the Muslim populations of Southeast Asia by the Portuguese who seized Melaka in 1511. It was the same label used by the Spanish conquerors of the northern Philip-pines. With their Reconquista of Muslim Spain a recent collective memory, the Spaniards in Manila regarded the Southern sultanates and beheld Moros—familiar Muslim enemies. "Moro" denoted a Muslim inhabitant of the unsubjugated southern islands. It was applied categorically and pejoratively with scant attention paid to linguistic or political distinctions among various "Moro" societies. While, for instance, eighteenth-century British and Dutch chroniclers most often refer to sea raiders from Cotabato as "Iranun" or "Illano" (see, e.g., Forrest 1969 [1779]; Hunt 1957), contemporaneous Spanish reports virtually always denominate them as "Moros" (Warren 1981, 165 ff).

The Spaniards referred to the non-Muslim inhabitants of the Philippines as "indios," a term that eventually came to designate the subjugated and Christianized populace. For indios—the principal victims of "Moro" marauders—the term "Moro" connoted savage and treacherous pirates. A folk-theater form known as the *moro-moro* survived into the postcolonial period. It enacted the defeat of pillaging Muslim villains by Christian heroes (Majul 1985).

Beginning in the late 1960s, Philippine Muslim nationalists attempted to appropriate the epithetic "Moro" and transform it into a positive symbol of collective identity. The "Moro National Liberation Front" was formed to direct the struggle for an independent political entity proclaimed to be the "Bangsa Moro," or Moro Nation. Muslim nationalist ideologues have proposed, with the support of certain historians, that the Spanish ascription "Moro" reflected an actual social entity—a self-conscious collectivity of Philippine Muslims engaged in a unified, Islamic-inspired, anticolonial resistance. More specifically, it is proposed that Spanish aggression against the southern sultanates generated an oppositional Islamic identity (or intensified an already existing one) that transcended linguistic and geographic boundaries and motivated steadfast and widespread armed opposition. The individual skirmishes, engagements, and campaigns are referenced cumulatively as the "Moro Wars" (Majul 1973).

These suppositions are confected from meager historical evidence. My reading of this material suggests, to the contrary, that Spanish aggression against the Muslim polities of the archipelago did not, to any significant degree, stimulate the development of an overarching ethnoreligious identity self-consciously shared by members of various Muslim ethnolinguistic groups.

Consider first the claim that the "Moro Wars" were "fundamentally religious in character" (George 1980, 44). This view is advanced by the foremost historian of Muslims in the Philippines, Cesar Majul, who notes that "the motivating force behind the [Moro] wars was religious difference" (1985, 18). The discourse of Spanish offensives against the Muslim South was undeniably religious in tone. Spanish attempts to reduce the southern sultanates to submission were voiced through an ideology of aggressive Christianization. Official documents, beginning with those from the earliest Spanish expeditions against the sultanates in 1578 and continuing up to those associated with the military campaigns of the last decades of the nineteenth century, order or advocate the destruction of mosques, the suppression of Islamic teaching, and the coercive conversion of Muslims to Christianity (see, e.g., Blair and Robertson 1903–19, 4: 174–81; de la Torre quoted in Saleeby 1908, 252–53). Nevertheless, this religious rhetoric is most often inlaid in texts that also announce more mercenary objectives related to monopolizing trade, controlling resources, and collecting tribute.[23]

Related to the first claim is the supposition that Spanish hostility provoked the development of a transcendent and oppositional Islamic consciousness among the Muslim peoples of the archipelago. While it is reasonable to assume that Islamic appeals were occasionally employed to mobilize opposition to Spanish aggression in the southern sultanates, there is little historical evidence to suggest that indigenous resistance to the Spanish threat led to a heightened Islamic identity among the Muslim populace, or that such elevated consciousness "stiffen[ed] the resistance of the Muslims" (Majul 1973, 343). When considering the frequency and importance of Islamic appeals, it may be noted that the two most famous anti-Spanish appeals on record—the 1603 address by Datu Buisan (the father of Sultan Kudarat) to the Leyte chiefs and Sultan Kudarat's 1639 exhortation to the Iranun datus (see above)—contain no reference to Islam nor any mention of religion whatsoever (quoted in Majul 1973, 118, 141). Those speeches were reported by the Spanish Jesuits who witnessed them, and one presumes those diarists to have scrupulously recorded any religious references they may have heard. The evidence available for later in the Spanish period is fragmentary and inconclusive. While there exist several accounts of religious observance by the high nobility of various sultanates, descriptions of the level of religiosity of Muslim subordinates are quite scarce. As we saw for Cotabato in chapter 3, one of the most complete of those accounts—that of William Dampier (1906)—remarks upon the lack of apparent religious devotion observed among ordinary Magindanaons. Prior to the late nineteenth century (see Arcilla 1990, Blumentritt 1893; Ileto 1971), there is also no direct evidence for Islamic clerics preaching anti-Spanish resistance to the general populace.[24]

Finally, there is the assertion that this postulated Islamic consciousness motivated a sustained and broad-based armed resistance. Available evidence suggests that if Philippine Muslims shared a self-regarding Islamic identity in opposition to the Spaniards, it was hardly ever manifested in concerted action against them. The term "Moro Wars" has been employed to describe an assortment of armed collisions, occurring over more than three hundred years, between Muslim polities in the southern archipelago and Spanish colonial forces. It has also been used to refer to the great number of slave raids made by various Muslim seafaring marauders—most notably the Iranun of the Cotabato coast—against Spanish-held territories in the North. While often closely connected economically with one or more sultanates, the Iranun and other raiders usually had no formal political ties to any large sultanate. They were, in European parlance, freebooters—those engaged in plundering without the authority of national warfare.[25] If we exempt the private Muslim raids against the North, which occurred almost yearly between 1768 and 1846 (Warren 1981), the three hundred–year conflict was primarily a cold war consisting of extended periods of mostly peaceful coexistence with the Spanish colonial intruders in the North coinciding with intersultanate rivalry in the South. That relative calm was only occasionally punctuated by armed confrontations between the Spaniards and particular sultanates, clashes that tended to be isolated events of relatively brief duration.

We need look no further than Cotabato for illustration. For the first few years following the initial abandonment of the Zamboanga garrison by the Spaniards in 1599, the two Cotabato sultanates jointly sponsored annual slave-raiding forays against Spanish-held territories in the Visayas and as far north as southern Luzon. Those raids were state-sponsored military expeditions, some with as many as three thousand warriors, and were always led by the highest officeholders of the sultanates (de la Costa 1961). The discontinuation of major state raiding expeditions after 1605 was due in part to the growth of intersultanate rivalry in Cotabato (motivating the Buayan sultan to enter into a peace treaty with Spain that year) and a consequence of the expansion of the China trade during periods when the Zamboanga fort was not garrisoned. The lucrative trade made the rulers of the sultanates both less interested in leading raids themselves and more concerned with controlling piracy in general (Ileto 1971). The 1719 agreement

between Spain and the Magindanao Sultanate occurred as the result of
a plea by the downriver sultan to the Spaniards to aid him in his war
with the Sultan of Sulu; the same sultan later requested Spanish assistance in suppressing an internal rebellion (Ileto 1971). Despite occasional armed clashes, Cotabato trade with the Spaniards increased
steadily over the centuries. The Spaniards attempted to block the direct
China-Cotabato trade not only to force the subjugation of the sultanates but to interpose themselves in the trade network. As a result,
for the greatest portion of the Spanish period, the Spanish colonial
capital of Manila was a major trading partner of the Cotabato sultanates. The largest portion of the beeswax collected in Cotabato was
shipped by local Chinese intermediaries to Manila in exchange for Chinese goods (Laarhoven 1989, 147).[26]

Cotabato's history of sultanate-Spanish relations indicates that depictions of the Philippine Muslim response to Spanish intrusions as a
three hundred–year-long religious struggle fail utterly to capture the
complexities and contradictions of that period. Muslim nationalist ideologues are not, of course, interested in unearthing discrepancies or
discontinuities. As with all nationalist discourses, their narratives en-
tail "the subjugation of a threateningly unruly history" (Spencer 1990,
287) in support of their ideological stance that a self-conscious oppositional identity as Philippine Muslims is ancient, deep, and broadly
shared.[27]

I shall return in a later chapter to the official discourse of Muslim
nationalism; my principal purpose in taking up the myth of Morohood
here is to draw attention to its uncritical acceptance by certain scholars
of the Muslim Philippines, and to the theoretical and methodological
consequences of their endorsements. The analytical significance of political myths in general lies less in the details of their formulation and
dissemination than in how they are received and what they obscure. It
is interesting to note in this regard that the myth of Morohood has
been professed as historical fact by various scholars who are not
avowedly Muslim nationalists (see, especially, Gowing 1979; George
1980; Molloy 1988; Bauzon 1991). Their receptivity to this myth suggests that these scholars, for reasons of their own, elect to believe (despite the ample existence of disconfirming evidence) in the ancient existence of a distinctive Moro culture, in a consolidated Moro history.
Their retellings of the myth of Morohood obscure for their readers the
historical complexity and cultural diversity I have outlined here.

More important for our purposes, these historical narratives share the core premise that a deeply rooted cultural homogeneity among Philippine Muslims has not only surmounted geographic and linguistic barriers but bridged social distance as well. Leaders and followers, aristocrats and commoners, are bound to one another by enduring Islamic bonds forged in the flames of jihad against infidel invaders. The presumption in these writings of a particular shared structure of historical experience precludes notice (in a manner similar to those culturological depictions of the precolonial history of other Southeast Asian polities) of divergent interpretations of relations of power by political subordinates. It also obviates any need for the social analysis of present-day political mobilization for Muslim separatism; ordinary adherents of Philippine Muslim nationalism are simply reenacting the precolonial past—driven by similar impulses and commanded by comparable leaders. It is the reason that most accounts of Muslim nationalism in the Philippines neglect the questions that compose the core basis of this study: What were ordinary Muslims fighting for? What precipitated their involvement in the separatist rebellion? How did they respond to the appeals of movement leaders? What did they hope to obtain from their participation?

One other matter has been obscured by the myth of Morohood, a topic that requires our attention before we turn to examine popular participation in the Muslim nationalist movement in Cotabato. Morohood—the self-conscious ethnoreligious identity as a Philippine Muslim—is evidenced among many Muslim citizens of the Philippines today and plainly predates the contemporary struggle for Muslim separatism. If not the consequence of a coordinated "Moro" resistance against Spanish aggression, what is its source? When and under what circumstances did it develop? I will argue in chapter 5 that Moro identity was first developed and nurtured during the American colonial period with the active encouragement of representatives of the colonial state.

CHAPTER 5

America's Moros

In his 1983 work on early American colonial rule in the Muslim Philippines, Peter Gowing cites a passage from a 1909 report to General Tasker Bliss, the second governor of the "Moro Province": "I find that the Moros who attended the St. Louis Exposition bought and brought in, apparently without question, no less than fifty rifles and revolvers of the very latest models . . . [M]any of them have changed hands, thus making it a very profitable business for the Moros who were lucky enough to have visited the United States" (Lt. Jesse Gaston to Bliss, January 8, 1909, cited in Gowing 1983, 177). While not remarked upon by Gowing, this short passage says much about the responses of Philippine Muslims to the early American occupation of the southern Philippines. It refers to the one hundred "Moros" (certainly many datus among them) who, with representatives of other subject groups of the American-held Philippines (one thousand individuals in all), were brought to the 1904 St. Louis World's Fair and placed on exhibit. The report complains of the behavior of the Moros, who apparently did not content themselves with their assigned roles in a "living ethnological display" but also spent their time shopping for the most sophisticated firearms that American industry had to offer (Rydell 1984, 162). It is tempting to imagine them making their way from their "ethnological village" in the "Philippine Reservation" to the Palace of Manufactures, there to regard those gleaming, high-calibered benefits of Western technological progress (1984, 167).

This depiction of subjugated Philippine Muslims as both objects of colonial intentions (quite literally so in this instance) and strategizing subjects is characteristic of political relations in Cotabato throughout the American period, especially those between Muslim notables and colonial agents. The most successful Cotabato datus of the colonial period publicly collaborated with American colonial authorities and used American resources to consolidate both their economic bases and their political control over the Muslim populace. This chapter examines Cotabato datus as both colonial subjects and local rulers—as points of articulation between two conjoined fields of force. It depicts the complex power relations of colonial Cotabato and the construction during the colonial period of a transcendent Philippine Muslim identity.

The story of the incorporation of the Cotabato sultanates into the Philippine colonial state has been told from the perspective of the colonizers as part of broader studies of American colonial policy toward Philippine Muslims, by Peter Gowing (1983) and Benjamin Thomas (1971). It has been related in a more specific, ethnohistorical form by Reynaldo Ileto (1971) and Jeremy Beckett (1982). I have chosen to tell the story primarily by means of political biographies of four twentieth-century datus. I do so to avoid retreading previously explored historical terrain and for more substantive reasons as well.

First, in Cotabato, more than in any other Muslim province, colonial pacification and assimilation were expedited by the strategic actions of particular datus, with the result that there was less concerted armed resistance to American colonialism there than anywhere else in the Philippine South. Second, despite the context of profound socioeconomic changes—including the formal abolition of slavery and the introduction of private property in land—the basic character of political relations between Magindanaon datus and subordinates changed hardly at all between 1890 and 1968. Accordingly, even those datus most closely associated with the colonial regime were able to maintain traditionally based followings and exercise control over followers in much the same way as they had in precolonial times. Magindanaon datus—in sharp contrast to the collaborating traditional elites (*uleebelang*) of the same period in Aceh (Siegel 1969) but similar to contemporary Christian Filipino elites (Beckett 1982)—were not socially isolated by their connections to alien authority and remained soundly at the center of regional politics during the colonial period. An examination of the careers of selected twentieth century datus thus offers a fruitful approach for comprehending the political dynamics of the period.

Third, as we shall see, American colonial authorities, especially in the first years of their occupation, ruled indirectly through cooperating datus, concerning themselves little with the Muslim populace but rather intensely with those who claimed to be their leaders. In the case of colonial Cotabato in particular, reports concerning local elites comprise the great majority of primary source materials in colonial archives.[1]

Fourth and most significant, the investigation of the political careers of selected Cotabato datus during the colonial period provides additional insight into the twin myths of Philippine Muslim nationalism introduced in the foregoing chapters. These colonial lives chronicle, on the one hand, the remarkable persistence of precolonial relations of domination—including the justificatory myth of sanctified inequality—despite the virtual dissolution of the core nobility and the formal transformation of local political structures. On the other hand, they reveal the gradual development, with the active encouragement of colonial agents, of a new transcendent ethnoreligious identity as "Moros."[2]

COTABATO UNDER SPANISH AND AMERICAN RULE: THE EMERGENCE OF A COLLABORATIONIST ELITE

Effective Spanish political control of the Cotabato Basin was short-lived and lightly felt. Although the Spaniards occupied the delta in 1861, it was not until 1888 that they were able, with the help of some early datu collaborators, to splinter the powerful alliance constructed by Datu Utu, the de facto Sultan of Buayan, and pressure him into retirement in 1890, thus finally attaining military supremacy of the entire region (Ileto 1971). Spanish colonial control consisted almost exclusively of the establishment and maintenance of military garrisons, with little attempt made to administer the native population. By 1899, the Spaniards were withdrawing from Cotabato, leaving it, after a brief independent interlude, to a new colonial power.

Early rule by Americans in the Muslim Philippines followed a pattern quite similar to their governance of the rest of the colony—pious paternalism punctuated by often brutal pacification operations. In the Muslim South, however, pacification took longer to achieve, requiring even harsher methods, while paternalism was also more pronounced. Military government gave way to civil rule in the Visayas and Luzon in 1901, but continued in Muslim areas until 1913. In 1906 in Sulu, more than six hundred men, women, and children were killed by

American forces in the battle of Bud Dajo, prompting American journalists to decry the carnage (Gowing 1983, 164).[3] Gowing observes that the slaughter at Bud Dajo—the consequence of a local rebellion against the imposition of a head tax—"was simply the last, most dramatic and most publicized of a long list of military operations" authorized by General Leonard Wood, the first military governor of the Muslim Philippines (1983, 164). In all, at least three thousand Philippine Muslims were killed by American forces between 1903 and 1906 (Gowing 1983, 164).[4] Violent repression was supplemented by an administrative paternalism grounded in the colonial perception that, as non-Christians, Muslim Filipinos were among the most benighted members of a backward people and required additional tutelage and protection to bring about "their advancement into civilization and material prosperity" (Philippine Commission Act No 253, Oct. 2, 1901, quoted in Thomas 1971, 9).

That Mindanao did not became an American planter colony, despite the wishes of a considerable number of colonial administrators and businessmen (and notwithstanding its demonstrated suitability for rubber cultivation—see Pelzer 1945, 105), is attributable to the same complex of causes that saw America's Philippine colony persist for more than forty-five years while purportedly on the verge of decolonization virtually since its inception. The peculiar policy that undergirded American colonial rule in the Philippines is termed by David Steinberg "self-liquidating imperialism" (1987, 276). That policy was originally shaped and periodically reconfigured as the result of contention between two domestic political blocs divided along party and sectoral lines. Arrayed around the Republican Party were interest groups in favor of American imperialist expansion: industrialists searching for markets and cheap sources of raw materials, and military analysts mindful of the strategic advantages of Far Eastern naval bases. Aligned against them were interests associated with the Democratic Party: a powerful lobby consisting principally of domestic beet- and cane-sugar producers (but also tobacco, hemp, and fruit growers, fearing competition from foreign crops), and the considerable political influence of the Anti-Imperialist League, headquartered in Boston (Pelzer 1945; Wernstedt and Simkins 1965; Constantino 1975; May 1987; Walton 1984).

With its dual doctrines of "free trade (especially sugar for manufacturers) and scheduled decolonization (at least in its formal trappings)," American colonial policy reflected a compromise between those opposed domestic interests (Walton 1984, 49). The anticolonial political bloc strongly opposed the large-scale entry of plantation capital into the Philippines and succeeded in limiting the maximum amount of public land that could legally be acquired to 16 hectares per individual and 1,024 hectares for corporations and associations. Philippine nationalist politicians (with the help of a reluctant American Congress) resisted all later attempts (including strong lobbying by American administrators of Muslim areas) to relax limits on the size of private landholdings (Pelzer 1945; Thomas 1971). Those limits effectively foreclosed the development of plantation agriculture on any significant scale in Mindanao until the end of the American period. Instead, Mindanao was developed as a settler colony. The homestead system instituted under the Americans had little impact on Muslim areas during the colonial period, but its successor programs under the Philippine Commonwealth and Republic were to have profound consequences for the indigenous inhabitants of the Cotabato Basin.

COLONIAL POLICY AND THE COTABATO TRIUMVIRATE

The course of colonial policy in the region that the Americans termed "Moroland" (Gowing 1983) was altered abruptly more than once as American aims in the rest of the archipelago (and Philippine nationalist opposition to those aims) evolved. The earliest American governance in the Muslim South was an indirect rule similar to that found at the time in British Malaya and the Dutch East Indies. It was a strategy intended to neutralize Muslim groups in the South in order to concentrate on overpowering Philippine independence forces in the North. In 1899, a formal treaty, the Bates Agreement, was signed with the Sultan of Sulu in which the Americans promised not to interfere in Sulu religion, law, and commerce (and to pay the sultan and his datus monthly stipends) in exchange for the sultan's acknowledgment of United States sovereignty. Informal agreements of a similar nature were made during that period with Muslim leaders in the rest of the Muslim South, including Cotabato (Gowing 1983).

The colonial policy of indirect rule was soon modified and not long thereafter abandoned. In 1903, a tribal ward system was established in the newly constituted Moro Province wherein local headmen were placed under the direct supervision of a district governor (Gowing 1983). The rationale for the administrative shift toward direct rule was given by General Leonard Wood, the first governor of the Moro

Province, in a 1904 letter to an English friend: "You are quite content to maintain rajahs and sultans and other species of royalty, but we, with our plain ideas of doing things, find these gentlemen outside of our scheme of government, and so have to start at this kind of proposition a little differently. Our policy is to develop individualism among these people and, little by little, to teach them to stand on their own two feet independent of petty chieftains. In order to do this the chief or headman has to be given some position of more or less authority under the government, but he ceases to have any divine rights" (Wood quoted in Gowing 1983, 115).[5] The Bates Agreement was unilaterally abrogated by the United States in 1905 with the Sultan of Sulu retaining only colonial recognition as the "religious head" of Sulu Muslims (Wood quoted in Gowing 1983, 119). The policy of indirect rule was entirely abandoned in 1914 when the administrative act that inaugurated civilian colonial governance in Mindanao and Sulu also explicitly repealed the previous official recognition of the customary (adat) law of Muslim populations.

In what follows I illuminate the earlier colonial period in Cotabato by means of biographies of the three principal collaborating datus of the early twentieth century. These three datus have been called the "triumvirate" of Cotabato (Millan 1952, 9). While they lived contemporaneously and their careers overlapped, their major contributions to the transition from sultanate to colony occurred at different periods. I will therefore introduce them chronologically.

DATU PIANG

The first and most influential of the colonial datus of Cotabato was Datu Piang. According to the hagiographic biography of Piang contained in the 1952 Cotabato Guidebook (Millan 1952), he was born circa 1850, the son of a Chinese trader from Amoy named Tuya Tan and a Magindanaon mother. Datu Adil relates the following story about the birth and boyhood of Datu Piang: "The trader Tan came to Dulawan [the capital of the Buayan Sultanate] selling China goods. He presented silks and perfumes to Datu Utu and they became friends. Datu Utu gave one of his concubines to Tan and called a pandita [religious practitioner] to marry them. The girl became pregnant but Tan went off trading and never returned. The child that was born was unique—it had fair skin, so it was believed he was the child of Tan. He was named Piang and was an industrious child. He cultivated the friendship of the officers of the Spanish garrison at Bakat by running errands for them." Throughout his life Piang was unashamedly aware that he had little or no noble blood in his veins. The 1952 biography notes that he never used the honorific "datu," instead calling himself "Ama ni Mingka" (or its shortened form "Amai Mingka"), or father of Mingka, the name by which he is still best known among the Magindanaon.[6]

Piang became a fast-rising protégé of Datu Utu, the Sultan of Buayan, who made him his "Minister of Lands" (Ileto 1971, 63). By 1890, however, the Spanish tactic of establishing forts in Cotabato to dissolve local lines of communication had proved successful and Datu Utu's inged was encircled, cutting him off from all sources of slaves and firearms (Ileto 1971). Piang as well as other of his lieutenants broke with Datu Utu when he was no longer able to provide them with firearms (Ileto 1971). Oral tradition relates that Utu's other followers deserted him in favor of Datu Piang because they could no longer tolerate his cruelty (see also Millan 1952). Piang very quickly replaced Datu Utu as the most powerful datu in the upper valley by forming an impressive alliance that included Utu's most forceful former confederates. Utu retired downriver to "spend his last years under Spanish protection" (Beckett 1982, 399).

Piang also quickly allied himself with Spain and sought the goodwill of Spanish authorities. His *turugan* (palace or stronghold; literally "sleeping place") was a short distance from the new Spanish fort at Reina Regente (just south of present-day Datu Piang). The fort provided him a shield from his Magindanaon enemies while he supplied its garrison with foodstuffs in exchange for cash (Ileto 1971; Beckett 1982). Equally important were Datu Piang's downriver ties in Cotabato town, particularly with Chinese traders. Beckett cites a 1901 American dispatch reporting 204 Chinese in the town of Cotabato, primarily engaged in the export of rice, beeswax, coffee, almaciga, and gutta-percha, the aggregate value of which was estimated at 150,000 Mexican dollars (1982, 402). Most of these products originated in upriver areas under the command of Piang, who apparently controlled both their production or collection as well as the terms of their export via Chinese merchants. Another contemporary American chronicler, Najeeb Saleeby (see below) reported that by "the time of the Spanish evacuation [Piang] had become the richest Moro in Mindanao and the most influential chief in the island" (Saleeby 1908, 292).

3. Datu Utu (seated center) with his wife, Rajah Putri, and retinue, circa 1890. This photograph was probably taken on the occasion of the elderly Utu's move downriver to live under Spanish protection in Cotabato town in 1890. Datu Utu's severely crossed eyes may be the source for some of the stories told about his fierce appearance. Courtesy of the U.S. National Archives.

Piang's loyalty to Spain lasted just as long as the physical presence of Spanish soldiers. With the Spanish evacuation of Cotabato in 1899, the men of Piang and his allies sacked Cotabato town, and a number of Christian Filipinos were killed or forced to flee. The Cotabato Chinese remained under Piang's protection and were spared. Ileto (1971) reports that Piang also declared himself Sultan of Mindanao in spite of his lack of genealogical precedent. Whether or not Piang made such a formal declaration it appears clear that at that point he was the effective ruler of Cotabato.

Piang's independent leadership of Cotabato lasted only a few months. The American occupying forces arrived in late 1899, and within a short time Piang was on his way to becoming—as described in his 1952 biography—"America's Great Friend" (Millan 1952, 292). One of the early significant services rendered by Piang to the

Americans was his assistance in eliminating the threat to American policies posed by his son-in-law, Datu Ali, the highborn nephew of Datu Utu. Between 1903 and 1905, Datu Ali led the only large-scale armed resistance to American rule in Cotabato.[7] Ali commanded a large number of armed followers, was skilled in guerrilla warfare, and, as heir apparent to the sultanate of Buayan, seemed capable of mobilizing the entire upper valley in revolt against the Americans. Datu Piang provided the intelligence that allowed Ali, stricken with malaria, to be surprised and slain by American soldiers. Oral tradition asserts that the Americans obtained Piang's assistance only by torturing him. Nevertheless, as Beckett points out, "Ali's death saw [Piang] on the winning side, the authorities in his debt, and his aristocratic rival out of the way" (Beckett 1982, 401).

By 1908, Cotabato was reported to be the most peaceful district in the Muslim Philippines, due in large part to the influence of Piang (Mastura 1979; Beckett 1982). Piang was also exceptionally responsive to American programs. The great majority of high-ranking datus were deeply distrustful of Western education and, when told they must have their sons educated at colonial schools, sent slaves in their place.[8] Piang, however, sent his own sons all the way to Manila to study (Beckett 1982). He also supported the settlement of Christian immigrants from northern islands and the establishment of agricultural colonies, which began in 1913 (Thomas 1971).

In 1915, with the end of the tribal ward system and the establishment of colonial administration in the South similar to that in the rest of the colony, Datu Piang was appointed as the only Muslim provincial board member for what was now the province of Cotabato. In the following year he was appointed to the National Assembly by the American governor general. These two positions had few formal responsibilities and conferred virtually no legal authority. They were, however, emblems of official American recognition of Piang as the preeminent leader of Cotabato Muslims as well as incentives to assure his continued cooperation with the now expressly stated colonial policy of integrating Muslims into the national political structure.

The political potency achieved by Datu Piang through his association with the armed might of the Americans, and before them the Spaniards, was symbolized by Magindanaons in their representations of Piang's index finger as supernaturally efficacious. According to Datu Adil: "It is said that the index finger of Piang was magical. If he pointed it and said 'enemigo,' people were killed; if he said 'amigo'

4. Datu Piang (front row, second from right, with cane) and his officials and
attendants, circa 1914. Despite his quite considerable wealth and power, Datu
Piang is reported always to have dressed quite simply, in contrast to the more
elaborate attire worn by most Magindanaon datus of the period (see, for example, the dress of Datu Utu in Figure 1). The datu's attendants include two
kris bearers, a *kampilan* (long sword) bearer (second from left, rear), and two
men carrying brass containers for betel nut. Courtesy of the U.S. National
Archives.

they were saved. He was feared because of that."[9] Piang's economic
achievements under American rule were comparably impressive. He
continued his lucrative connections in the Chinese-controlled export
trade while expanding into rice-milling and lumber (Beckett 1982). He
also maintained his base in the upper valley and by 1926 was reported
to have accumulated massive wealth that included "42,000 coconut
trees (they are good for $1 per tree each year) thousands of carabao
[water buffalo] [and] thousands of hectares of rice land . . . to say
nothing of the tithe paid him by his loyal subjects."[10]
    Evidence from various sources suggests that Datu Piang was an ex-
ceptionally shrewd and independent-minded collaborator, ever mindful
of the opportunities for personal gain made available through his

gatekeeper role. A 1906 letter from the American governor of the Moro Province to the district governor of Cotabato expresses anger and exasperation at Datu Piang's attempt to collect rent from the superintendent of schools for the use of a school building that Piang had constructed in his inged at Dulawan. The letter states in part: "You will tell him, furthermore, that if he and his people cheerfully paid the cedula [head tax] and other taxes due from them to the government, we would ask from him no such assistance, but that in view of their dereliction in this and in view of the further reasons set forth above, it is believed to be a fair proposition that he should give the free use of this building for school purposes" (Bliss to the district governor of Cotabato, August 14, 1906, quoted in Gowing 1983, 198). Datu Adil tells of a road that Datu Piang contracted to build for the Americans across a swampy tract in the upper valley for twenty thousand pesos: "Piang called on his [client] datus to assist him. They arrived with their followers and enough food to feed them. The road took more than two months to build but Piang never shared any of the money he received with his datus."

These stories illustrate how collaborating datus were often able, relying on traditional power relations, to call out corvée labor in order to avail themselves of new opportunities to enrich themselves during the early colonial period. Datu Piang seems to have been more successful at this strategy than any of his contemporaries. He died in 1933 at the approximate age of eighty-four (Millan 1952). Five of his sons became either politicians or professionals.

In 1918, Piang's niece, Bai Bagungan of Buluan, became the first female municipal district president (a colonial-era post comparable to mayor) in the Philippines. Though her late husband preceded her in the post, she did not automatically succeed him. Shortly after her husband's death she married a younger man of much lower status who had served in his household. Datu Piang was furious that he had not been consulted in the matter and ordered the couple confined in the provincial jail to force Bagungan to change her mind. She remained steadfast and Piang eventually gave way and sanctioned the marriage. When the datu appointed by Piang to fill the municipal post resigned, Bai Bagungan was appointed municipal district president after receiving an overwhelming vote of confidence from the male electors of the district. Bai Bagungan was an active official who, in the words of Philippine Governor General Cameron Forbes, "became a vigorous partisan of public schools, especially for girls, and in other ways a

valuable influence in the extension of American administration in Mindanao" (Forbes 1928).[11]

DATU IGNACIO ORTUOSTE

Datu Ignacio Ortuoste was the most extraordinary member of the
Cotabato triumvirate in that he was entirely a product of colonialism.
His career, which spans the years between 1904 and 1935, illustrates
most dramatically the disjunctions wrought by colonialism in Cotabato. There is very little written information available on Datu Ortuoste. Beckett (1982) does not mention him and Gowing (1983)
assumes him to be a Christian Filipino. According to Datu Adil, Ortuoste was neither a Christian Filipino nor a Magindanaon nor originally
from Cotabato. He was a Maranao from the Lanao Plateau who was
captured as a child in a skirmish between Spanish soldiers and
Maranao warriors. He was brought to the Jesuit mission at Tamontaka, on the south fork of the Pulangi River. There he was reared and
educated, baptized and given a Christian name.[12]

Like his contemporary Datu Piang, Ortuoste made a very successful
transition from Spanish to American rule. Unlike Piang, his main assets
were his ability to read, write, and speak Spanish as well as local languages, and his familiarity with colonial as well as local culture. Utiliz-
ing these attributes, Ortuoste became a highly effective intermediary
between the local representatives of colonial authority and those who
militantly resisted that authority. His singular personal background
made him an ideal cultural and political broker, negotiating the subjugation of defiant local leaders to an occupying foreign power.

The first reported occasion for Ortuoste's mediation occurred in
1904 when he reportedly played a prominent role in dissuading Datu
Ali from attacking the American military garrison in what was then
the town of Cotabato (Millan 1952). Ortuoste's next recorded assignment for the Americans was in 1914, when he assisted in negotiating
the surrender of Datu Alamada, an Iranun insurgent who had fought
the successive colonial regimes for twenty years in the mountainous
area between Cotabato and Lanao with a force of more than five hundred men (Gowing 1983).

American administrators again sought the assistance of Ortuoste in
1923 as a mediator in the surrender of another Iranun insurgent, Datu
Santiago, the last leader of resistance to American rule in Cotabato.
Santiago had rebelled against the imposition by the Americans of a

head tax (*cedula*), the compelling of Muslim girls to attend Christian schools, and the practice by school authorities of using forced labor without compensation to construct and repair school buildings (Hurley 1936; Tan 1982). Datu Adil remembers stories told by Ortuoste that, in this instance at least, he played a double role, simultaneously assuring colonial authorities of Santiago's imminent surrender and advising Santiago on the concessions he should demand from the Americans in return for his submission.

At some point after this, Datu Ortuoste was accorded the title Datu sa Kutawatu (Datu of Cotabato) by Sultan Mastura, who was installed as Sultan of Magindanao in 1926. Sometime after helping secure the surrender of Datu Alamada he was also appointed assistant to the governor of Cotabato.[13] In his political career, Datu Ortuoste enjoyed considerable influence among colonial administrators and gained the recognition of the Muslim elite of Cotabato. He accumulated large tracts of property in and around Cotabato City before he died, sometime before 1952. Two of his sons became civil servants in Cotabato.

That Datu Ortuoste was, in all important respects, a colonial creation is evidenced in the exceptional title bestowed upon him by the reigning Sultan of Magindanao. The office of Datu sa Kutawatu was unusual not only in that it was newly created—the creation of new royal offices was uncommon but not unheard of (see below). It was also the first traditional title that in its very nomenclature acknowledged colonial domination. "Cotabato," after all, was the Spanish and American term for the territory locally known as Magindanao. As the ceremonial Datu sa Kutawatu, Datu Ortuoste personified the new colonial construct called Cotabato. He was the first purely colonial datu.

DATU SINSUAT BALABARAN

After Datu Piang, Datu Sinsuat Balabaran was the most influential indigenous ruler of the American period. He was the central consolidating figure in a three-generation dynastic line that began with his uncle, the nineteenth-century Datu Ayunan—described in a contemporary account as belonging "body and soul" to the Spaniards (Rincon 1894 quoted in Ileto 1971, 92)—and extends to his sons, three of whom at various times in the past thirty years have held the most powerful political positions in Cotabato.

Datu Sinsuat was the son of Balabaran, the younger brother of Datu Ayunan. Ayunan led the pro-Spanish, anti-Utu faction in the mid-1880s. Saleeby (1908) suggests that because Ayunan was much lower in rank than Datu Utu he intended to use an alliance with Spain to strengthen his own position. Datu Ayunan died in 1898, just at the close of the Spanish period. Before he died he passed on to his brother Balabaran the title *gobernadorcillo del delta* (petty governor of the delta), an office conferred on him by the Spaniards and one that he dearly prized (Ileto 1971; Beckett 1982).

There is little historical information on Balabaran. Datu Adil recalled a story about his demise: "There is a legend that Datu Balabaran was devoured by crocodiles because he tried to proclaim himself sultan. Balabaran had gathered his datus and told them to assemble at Dimapatoy for his proclamation. The crocodiles overheard this and ate him. They knew he had insufficient maratabat to rule as sultan, so they punished him for his brashness. Only one forearm was found. It was taken to his inged at Taviran [near Dinaig] and buried."[14]

Datu Sinsuat was born in 1864 and his political career spanned the entire American colonial period. His official biography states that as a boy he was adopted by Datu Piang and that as a young man he served as "a *delegado* of the Spanish Military Governor" (Millan 1952, 296). In 1916 he was appointed municipal district president of Dinaig, his home territory. Between 1923 and 1931 he served as special adviser to the governor of Cotabato Province.

Datu Sinsuat's ascent to power was due almost entirely to his close cooperation with colonial authorities. His prominence among Cotabato Muslims was achieved in part by strategic marriages designed to cement relationships with influential allies and elevate the status of his children.[15] He did not attain a preeminent position among Cotabato Muslims until the death of Datu Piang, a man in whose shadow he had long remained (Beckett 1977).

Sinsuat was also engaged in economic endeavors that included control of smuggling and gambling operations in his municipality and the acquisition of large tracts of land for cattle raising and coconut farming. Having secured his economic and political base in Dinaig, Sinsuat moved to Cotabato town, the seat of provincial government, during his tenure as assistant to the governor. As a colonial center since the late nineteenth century, the former capital of the Magindanao Sultanate had been without effective traditional rule for some time. The current sultan and high nobility of Magindanao lived, most of them in much-reduced circumstances, either north of town across the river in Nuling or even farther away across Ilana Bay in Sibugay. Datu Sinsuat used his affinity with colonial authorities to expand his sphere of influence from the neighboring municipality of Dinaig and fill that void.[16]

While in Cotabato town, Sinsuat reportedly derived a considerable proportion of his income from the levying of traditional fines. Such practices had apparently become so widespread among datus who had been appointed as local officials in the colonial government that they were specifically prohibited in a 1935 directive from the Director of Non-Christian tribes: "It has come to our attention that in certain districts inhabited by Mohammedans, provincial and district officials and employees . . . taking advantage of their official positions, try and adjudicate the so-called religious cases. Such officials, it has been reported to us, when trying those cases impose fines upon the persons involved, collect those fines which they keep and appropriate for themselves and in those cases where the fines cannot be satisfied, the persons concerned are imprisoned and required to work for their personal benefit. This practice is not sanctioned by any of our laws."[17]

Datu Sinsuat was the first of the colonial datus to develop considerable political connections at the national level. In 1934 he was appointed to the Philippine Senate. That appointment was likely the result of his acquaintance with Senator Manuel Quezon, soon to be the first president of the Philippine Commonwealth. For some time, Quezon had cultivated the support of a few datus whom he could reasonably rely on to be supportive of Philippine independence, a position opposed by most Philippine Muslims, who feared (with good reason) the prospect of direct rule by Philippine Christians (Thomas 1971). Datu Sinsuat, in his political career, pursued a strategy that resembled that of his uncle Ayunan, who consolidated a strong traditional following and local base before moving on to expand his political power "within the framework of submission to the colonial master" (Ileto 1971, 92). However, Sinsuat far surpassed Ayunan in his success at advancing the myth of his own nobility and that of his descendants and antecedents. It was a myth directed at both Cotabato Muslims and Christians as well as at the colonial rulers. We find evidence for it in an excerpt, entitled "A Man of Royalty," from a ceremonial volume presented to Elpidio Quirino, the second president of the Philippine republic, shortly after Datu Sinsuat's death in 1949:

> The name Sinsuat in Cotabato and for that matter the whole length and breadth of Mindanao is more than the mere inference of a family name . . . For the fact is that the brand Sinsuat is a family dynasty that conjures in the trained mind a nobility, a well-guarded family tradition encased in honor and fame, imbedded in illustrious and amazing achievements, silkened in the tender and luminous carpet of distinction and treasured by the glorious and exemplary exhilarating breeze and potency of fame and honor . . . And the history of this family name is as old as the history of Mindanao itself. To speak of a Sinsuat is almost a temptation to call it Mindanao in rabid generalization.

Beneath the breathless hyperbole may be found an unmistakable instance of nobility by assertion, a modern variant of what Beckett has described for the precolonial period as the "*post hoc* ennoblement of the powerful" (1982, 398).

COLONIAL-ERA DATUS AND THE CONTINUATION OF "TRADITIONAL" RULE

The careers of the "Cotabato triumvirate" provide the basis for assessing the effect of American colonialism on indigenous political and economic relations in the Cotabato Basin. The biographies indicate, first, that the colonial datus generally had only tenuous ties to the high nobility of the Cotabato sultanates, and some had none at all. While the old high nobility was permanently devitalized by the colonial order—surviving only as dignitaries—the "new datus . . . created their own *maratabat* [rank honor]," as well as purchased it for their children through intermarriages with noble families, often facilitated by extraordinarily high bridewealth payments (Beckett 1982, 408). This process is clearly evident in the dynasty-building careers of Piang and Sinsuat.

The new datus of the colonial period were able to enhance their traditional status because of the power and wealth they had obtained through collaboration with American colonial authorities.[18] With the early abandonment of the policy of indirect rule, their political positions were not predicated on any official American recognition of their traditional right to rule Cotabato Muslims. Instead, they were bestowed with new ceremonial offices—as municipal district president, assemblyman, or (occasionally) senator—as tokens of their political ability to mediate between ordinary Magindanaons and an alien colonial authority, and as rewards for their political willingness to ensure

Muslim compliance with colonial aims. In return for these services they received, besides the trappings and privileges of office, the opportunity to exploit new potential sources of wealth. They also retained control over the agrarian sector during the colonial period. They were none the less a dependent and sectional elite. Commerce was almost entirely controlled by the Chinese, and public administration remained exclusively in the hands of Christian Filipinos (Beckett 1982).

Despite their diminished political autonomy the new datus were able to amass significant wealth. We have seen that Datu Piang greatly increased his wealth under the Americans and that Datus Ortuoste and Sinsuat gained theirs. Some of this wealth, such as that derived from the imposition of fines and the drafting of corvée labor for colonial projects, resulted from the extension of traditional relations to new contexts. Other sources were novel, such as datus' advantaged opportunities to create or acquire private property. Another source, neither traditional nor entirely new, was the intensification of agriculture. In 1908, exports from Cotabato were reported at 21,246 pesos. In 1911 they were 311,043 pesos, and in 1919, 760,428 pesos (Forbes 1928, 28; Beckett 1982, 403). Rice was the most important item in this dramatic expansion of exports, followed by copra and corn. Between 1920 and 1935, the area under rice cultivation increased from 1,864 hectares to 24,630 hectares (Beckett 1982, 403).[19]

It seems unlikely that the expansion of rice production in colonial Cotabato followed the pattern that occurred either earlier in the mainland deltas of Southeast Asia or simultaneously on the Central Luzon Plain. In those cases expansion was accomplished by rural smallholders or tenants with capital advanced by landlords, mill owners, or middlemen (the latter two often Chinese) and involved the restructuring of traditional production relations. Because commercial rice production had existed for some time in Cotabato, and because private property in land was not well established until after 1930, it is more likely that the expansion of rice production in the early American period occurred within the traditional production relations established between datus and their subordinates. Despite the abolition of slavery, many datus of this period retained their existing banyaga slaves and continued to acquire debt-bondsmen (Beckett 1982). Datus also maintained control over the endatuan subordinates who comprised their ingeds. It seems reasonable to imagine that datus responded to the new commercial opportunities of the American period in the same way they reacted to the earlier demand for foodstuffs to supply Spanish garrisons—by intensifying agricultural production to the extent of their capabilities.[20] Although the exact outlines of the intensification process are not known (Chinese merchants did own rice mills and may have made crop loans directly to producers), it is likely that datus were the major beneficiaries of the agricultural expansion of the early American period.

The wealth and political connections of the new datus were used to launch family dynasties. Generally, this was accomplished by their acquisition of a mix of old and new durable resources. They secured new resources such as tracts of land and other productive property, new commercial connections, new extralocal political patrons, and new colonial educations for at least some of their sons. They were also careful to secure more traditional sorts of resources: political allies and subordinates and, just as important, maratabat (rank honor) for their children and grandchildren by obtaining high-ranking wives for themselves and their sons.

One of Datu Piang's sons became the first Magindanaon attorney. Two others obtained college educations and became politicians. However, with the death of the most dynamic of these sons, Congressman Gumbay Piang, in 1949, the dynasty was irreversibly weakened, and the Piangs are no longer a powerful political force outside their home municipality. The Sinsuat family dynasty has exhibited the most political endurance. The sons of Datu Sinsuat have held positions as congressman, governor, and mayor (of Cotabato City and Dinaig), and continue to be powerful players in regional politics. The sons of the non-Magindanaon Datu Ortuoste were, predictably, an exception. They chose Philippine Christian culture (their mother was almost certainly a Christian), were educated in Manila, and became local civil servants. The family dynasty founded by Datu Ortuoste thus became a Christian one and the title of Datu sa Kutawatu lapsed with his death.

As the colonial-era datus established their names and consolidated their local political domains they invariably embraced the myth of sanctified inequality. They came to regard themselves as a traditional nobility, as the legitimate successors of the precolonial rulers of Cotabato. This accentuation of ancient roots and illustrious bloodlines was not only (or even primarily) for the benefit of Magindanaon subordinates. As illustrated colorfully in the portrayal of Datu Sinsuat as "A Man of Royalty," it was also intended to impress American colonial agents and Christian Filipino nationalists by confirming their preconceptions about the continued importance of a potent and exotic Muslim nobility.

COLONIAL AGENTS AND THE
CONSTITUTION OF MORO IDENTITY

An inconsistency may be evidenced in American colonial policy toward
Philippine Muslims that was at least partly occasioned by the "self-
liquidating imperialism" that formed the basis of America's overall
Philippine colonial policy. After their brief experiment with indirect
rule, American colonial authorities explicitly refused any formal recognition of the aristocracies of the Philippine sultanates or of indigenous
legal systems. Muslims were not to be excepted from direct colonial
rule; close American supervision was required in order for Philippine
Muslims to achieve a level of "civilization" sufficient to allow their integration with their Christian counterparts in an eventual Philippine
republic. Despite the official denial of traditional rights of rule, however, American colonial agents came to place great emphasis on the
Muslim nobility as implementers of colonial policies intended specifically for Philippine Muslims.

The throughout the course of American rule in the Philippines, a particular set of policies was formulated in reference to a category of colonial subjects denominated as "Moros." Although official American attitudes toward Philippine Muslims lacked the holy war complex that
prompted the Spanish use of that designation (and despite the fact that
the term was well established as a pejorative among Philippine Christians), American authorities adopted the usage "Moro," with all of its
conglomerating and epithetic connotations, as the exclusive term of
reference for the entire thirteen Muslim ethnolinguistic groups of the
Philippines. It is nearly impossible to find in official documents, even
among the writings of the most sensitive American observers, any clear
indication of the distinct histories and cultures possessed by the various subject peoples designated as "Moros."[21]

One of the most influential agents in the early American colonial
administration of Philippine Muslims was Najeeb Saleeby, a Syrian-
born physician who came to the Philippines as a U.S. Army doctor in
1900 (Thomas 1971). Saleeby was assigned to Mindanao and became
fascinated with its Muslim inhabitants. He made the acquaintance of
numerous prominent Muslims and learned two local languages—Magindanaon and Tausug. He used his knowledge of those languages, and
of Arabic, to translate entitling genealogies (tarsila, *salsilah*) and law
codes (Luwaran) for the main sultanates of the region, including the
Magindanaon and Buayan Sultanates. Saleeby was quickly recognized

by colonial authorities as the resident American specialist on Philippine Muslims and in 1903 was appointed Agent for Moro Affairs. In 1905, the same year he published his *Studies in Moro History, Law, and Religion* (the first scholarly work on Muslim Filipinos published in English), he became the first superintendent of schools of the Moro Province.

Saleeby opposed the move to direct administration of the Muslim regions of the South and, though overruled, he was instrumental in conditioning official attitudes about the governance of Philippine Muslims, and particularly about the utilization of traditional Muslim elites to implement colonial policy. Saleeby's views on the "development" of the Muslims of the Philippines were expressed most cogently in a 1913 essay entitled *The Moro Problem*.[22] In that work he disputes the popular perception of Moros as savages and religious fanatics. Moros, he observes, "have so little religion at heart that it is impossible for them to get enthusiastic and fanatic on this ground" (1913, 24). Moros do, however, possess relatively sophisticated, if "feudal," political communities ruled by datus. "The datu is God's viceregent on earth. He is of noble birth and the Prophet's blood runs through his veins. The people owe him allegiance and tribute" (1913, 17). He notes further that, for the most part, the datus had not been actively opposed to American aims and that "religion has never been a cause of conflict between Americans and Moros"(1913, 24). Moreover, "the Moros are greatly disunited . . . [E]ach district is inhabited by a different tribe and these tribes have never been united" (1913, 15). It is in the Americans' interest, in fact, to unite the Moros under their traditional leaders in order to initiate a "process of gradual development" (1913, 17). In furtherance of such a goal Saleeby, himself a Christian, declares that "religion" (meaning Islam) "can be encouraged and promoted" for the benefit of both the colonial government and the Moro people (1913, 24). As envisioned by Saleeby, with the reestablishment of "datuships" and "Moro courts," "the individual Moro would find himself well protected and would become more thrifty and intelligent. Moved by a natural tendency to imitate superior civilization, he would unconsciously reform his customs and home life and gradually acquire American ideas and new ambitions. An enlightened Moro community, wisely guided by efficient American officials, would undoubtedly work out its own destiny, and following the natural law of growth and development would gradually rise in wealth and culture to the level of a democratic [meaning Philippine Christian] municipality" (1913, 30).

In these remarkable passages, Saleeby outlines nothing less than the colonial genesis of Morohood. Saleeby was more knowledgeable about the history, culture, and contemporary political culture of the separate Muslim peoples of the Philippines than any other colonial administrator. He knew that the various Muslim ethnolinguistic groups were in no sense united, nor did they possess—jointly or individually—a politically potent oppositional Islamic consciousness. He urges the promotion of Muslim unity, not through the preservation or restoration of individual traditional polities (i.e., by means of straightforward indirect rule), but through the formation of a new transcendent Philippine Muslim identity: through the development of Morohood.

In his essay, Saleeby proposes the creation of Muslim unity for the sole purpose of propelling Philippine Muslims along a path of development parallel to that of Christian Filipinos in order to prepare their eventual integration into an inevitable postcolonial Philippine nation. They should be led on that path by members of their traditional nobility because, regardless of American attitudes toward aristocracies, the Muslim populace affirms their indefeasible right to rule by fact of their hallowed ancestry.[23] Saleeby's account of Muslim political culture accentuates the myth of sanctified inequality and couples it with Morohood. Islam should be encouraged by colonial authorities because it is that which binds the Muslim populace most indelibly to their leaders—leaders who for the most part have been inclined toward cooperation rather than confrontation with the American regime. Moro religion, law, and customs do, of course, require rationalization by imitation of "superior" culture. Through that process of rationalization by imitation, American principles working on this distinct Philippine population—unique primarily because it had not experienced three hundred years of Spanish colonial rule—would achieve an outcome analogous to that devised for Christian Filipinos.

Although Saleeby's specific proposals were never formally incorporated into colonial policy toward Filipino Muslims, many of his recommendations substantially influenced the attitudes and practices of key colonial administrators.[24] Among those was Frank Carpenter, the first governor of the Department of Mindanao and Sulu, who took office in 1914 shortly after the publication of Saleeby's essay. Carpenter expressed his views in a 1919 letter to the colonial secretary of the interior requesting that Princess Tarhata Kiram, the adopted daughter of the Sultan of Sulu, be sent to the United States as a government student. After reporting the "generally accepted" conclusion that it is "practically futile to attempt the conversion of "a Mohammedan people as such to Christianity," Carpenter restates Saleeby's suggestions about guided development through the agency of Muslim notables.

> [It] is essential to the efficiency, commercially as well as politically, of the Filipino people that all elements of population have uniform standards and ideals constituting what may well be termed "civilization"; and as the type of civilization of the Filipino people in greatest part is that characteristic of the Christian nations of the world, the bringing of the Sulu people from their primitive type of civilization to the general Philippine type may be stated as the objective of the undertaking of the Government in its constructive work among them. No more effective and probably successful instrumentality appears for this undertaking than the young woman who is the subject of this communication.

In suggesting particular arrangements for the American education of the princess, Carpenter goes on to list two considerations of "fundamental importance":

> That she be not encouraged nor permitted to abandon her at least nominal profession of the Mohammedan religion, as she would become outcast among the Sulu people and consequently her special education purposeless were she to become Christian or otherwise renounce the religious faith of her fathers. . . .
>
> That she be qualified to discuss intelligently and to compel respect from the Mohammedan clergy she should be encouraged to read extensively and thoroughly inform herself, so far as possible from the favorable point of view, not only the Koran itself and other books held to be sacred by Mohammedans, but also the political history of Mohammedanism.[25]

James R. Fugate, the American governor of Sulu from 1928 to 1936, also acted upon Saleeby's suggestions by implementing colonial policies through individual Sulu datus (Thomas 1971, 189). No colonial administrator was more apparently influenced by the views of Saleeby than Edward M. Kuder, who, beginning in 1924, spent seventeen years as superintendent of schools in the three Muslim provinces of Cotabato, Lanao, and Sulu. Like Saleeby, Kuder endeavored to learn local languages and eventually gained proficiency in Magindanaon, Maranao, and Tausug, the languages of the three main Muslim ethnolinguistic groups of the Philippines.

Kuder expressed his views on the education of Philippine Muslims in a 1935 report to the Educational Survey Committee on "the present education of the non-Christian Filipinos," observing that "[t]he chief value . . . of education among the non-Christians has been the establishment of a linking element among them, very close in thought, feeling and national identity with the country as a whole, while still conscious of the good things in its own cultural background."[26] Writing as the Philippines were about to be granted partial independence (see below) and amid growing Western concerns about Japanese aggression in Asia, Kuder proposes an additional potential political benefit (one not articulated by Saleeby) to be obtained from the education of Muslims. "Through the proper treatment and education" of Philippine Muslims, valuable ties may be established with neighboring Malay nations (all still under Western colonial tutelage), forging a regional compact able to withstand "alien" (i.e., Japanese and Chinese) forces: "And here lies the hope of the Philippines for survival—coalition into eventual Malay solidarity . . . And here lies the value of . . . maintaining . . . by means of education, that linking element of non-Christian Filipinos . . . [F]or this Non-christian Filipino element is largely Mohammedan and the great Malay races . . . are overwhelmingly Mohammedan—not the gloomy and fanatic faith of Arabia, but tempered and moderated by the genial Malay hospitality and courtesy and hence compatible, through a proper and common education, with the Christian Philippine civilization."[27]

Kuder put Saleeby's ideas about datu-led development into practice by undertaking personally the training of a generation of Philippine Muslim leaders. In his travels throughout the Muslim provinces he sought out honors students (all of them boys) from various Muslim groups, most usually the sons of datu families, and fostered them, bringing some of them to live under his roof to be tutored by him. In this manner, Kuder personally educated a considerable number of the second generation of Philippine Muslim leaders of the twentieth century. Datu Adil, who had a distinguished career as an officer in the Philippine Constabulary, was one of Kuder's students. He recalled with fondness his time spent as Kuder's "foster son" fifty years earlier, recollecting that he was "strengthened by Mr. Kuder's discipline." In the course of one of our conversations Datu Adil produced a treasured keepsake, a beautifully bound volume of Burton's translation of *The Thousand and One Nights*. Mr. Kuder had presented the complete set to him when he left the University of the Philippines, telling him it was important that he appreciate his religion.

In a scholarly paper (entitled *The Moros in the Philippines*) published in 1945 on the eve of full formal independence, Kuder looked back on his accomplishments. He observes initially that the term "Moro" is an exotic label affixed by Europeans to Philippine Muslims in general and one not used among them. He also notes, echoing Saleeby, that more than three centuries of Spanish hostility had failed to bring about an overall alliance among the separate Muslim societies of the Philippines. There follows a revelatory passage: "Within the decade and a half preceding the Japanese invasion of the Philippines increasing numbers of young Moros educated in the public schools and collegiate institutions of the Philippines and employed in the professions and activities of modern democratic culture had taken to referring to themselves as Mohammedan Filipinos" (Kuder 1945, 119). Kuder is here referring indirectly, but with detectable pride, to his protégés, the Muslim students he brought together and personally trained in his seventeen-year career prior to World War II. These young men, he avers, are the very first generation of Muslims in the Philippines to possess a shared and self-conscious ethnoreligious identity that transcends ethnolinguistic and geographical boundaries. Kuder's statement is an oblique assertion that he had accomplished in less than two decades what Spanish aggression was unable to provoke in more than three centuries. He had developed a core group of "Mohammedan" Filipinos. The use of that most emblematic of Orientalist terms suggests that the content of this new shared identity had been at least partly formed by his instruction.

It is apparent that Kuder, following Carpenter's lead, not only educated his students in the arts of "modern democratic culture" but also encouraged them to approach Islam (in Carpenter's words) "from the favorable point of view"—that is to say, through the eyes of Western arts and sciences. That at least some of Kuder's students referred to themselves as Mohammedans is attested to by the formation in 1932 of the "Mindanao and Sulu Mohammedan Students' Association," a small organization composed of Philippine Muslim students at the University of the Philippines in Manila, many of them former students of Edward Kuder. In a 1935 letter to Joseph Ralston Hayden, the then vice-governor general of the Philippines, Salipada Pendatun, Kuder's star pupil (see below) and a principal organizer of the association, described its aims: "Our primary purpose in view is to act as the unofficial representative of our people at home; in order to protect their rights and interests, to help them realize the value of education; to inculcate in them the value of cooperating with the leaders of Christian Filipinos in working for the common welfare of the country."[28]

Kuder's aim was to create an educated Muslim elite trained in Western law and government and able to represent their people in a single Philippine state—a cohort ready to direct Muslim affairs through enlightened forms of traditional rule. That goal was realized in great measure in the careers of Kuder's students. Most became lawyers, civil servants, and politicians; married Christians; and remained formally monogamous. At the same time, they conserved their traditional roles as Islamic adjudicators in what were now nongovernmental tribunals and as sources of moral authority.

DATU SALIPADA K. PENDATUN

The most prominent of Kuder's former students in Cotabato, and one of the most successful of any of his "foster sons," was Salipada K. Pendatun.[29] Datu Pendatun (more commonly known as Congressman Pendatun) became one of the most nationally prominent and influential of the postcolonial datus of Cotabato. Pendatun was born in 1912 at Pikit, Cotabato, of noble parentage. His father, the Sultan of Barongis, a small upriver sultanate, died when he was still a boy and Pendatun was brought to live with Edward Kuder, becoming one of his first students. Pendatun retained a close relationship with his former teacher until Kuder's death in the early 1970s.

After leaving Kuder's tutelage, Pendatun studied law at the University of the Philippines in Manila. In 1935, the Philippine Islands were granted partial independence under Commonwealth status by the United States, with the promise of independence in ten years' time. In that year, Pendatun, still a law student, wrote another letter to Vice-Governor General Hayden noting the rush of immigrants to Cotabato induced by the Commonwealth's new road-building policy and the increasingly disadvantaged position of Muslims vis-à-vis Christian settlers in attempting to acquire public lands. He urged (unsuccessfully) that a special agent be appointed to help Muslims with the registration process (Thomas 1971). Datu Pendatun graduated from the University of the Philippines in 1938 (the first Magindanaon to do so) and was appointed by Philippines President Quezon to the Cotabato Provincial Board to replace Datu Sinsuat, recently elected to the National Assembly. Pendatun was elected to the same post in 1940 (Glang 1969).

The transitional Commonwealth period of American sovereignty in the Philippines was profoundly disrupted in 1941 by the Japanese invasion and occupation. During the war against the Japanese, Pendatun led one of the most active guerrilla units in Mindanao, a group that included Americans and Christian Filipinos as well as Magindanaons. In 1942, his fellow guerrilla leaders selected him as their "General"

5. Edward Kuder (seated) with the young Salipada Pendatun, 1927. Pendatun, shown here in the simple garb of a Muslim schoolboy, was the son of
the Sultan of Barongis, as well as Kuder's foster son and star pupil. He went
on to become the most prominent and influential Philippine Muslim politician
in the postindependence period. Courtesy of *Phillipines Free Press.*

(Thomas 1971, 301). In recognition for his war efforts, Pendatun was appointed governor of Cotabato in 1945 by President Sergio Osmena.

Datu Pendatun's early career was one of the most successful of any of the second-generation colonial datus. He is representative, however, of a number of other Philippine Muslim political figures of his generation (some of them also former students of Edward Kuder). By the founding of the Philippine republic in 1946 they were politically well established with ties to the apparatus of national rule in Manila and able to command local allegiance on the basis of traditional social relations. This new Western-educated Muslim elite had also begun to develop a self-conscious transcendent identity as Philippine Muslims. That consciousness derived not from opposition to American rule but rather from studied adherence to its objectives.

The peculiar form of direct colonial rule established by the Americans for Philippine Muslims—combining official repudiation of the authority of traditional rulers with a wardship system for certain Muslim elites specifically designed to enhance their abilities as "Mohammedan" leaders—produced effects inverse to those found in another Southeast Asian colonial system attempting to rule Muslims. The Dutch development of *adatrecht* for colonial Indonesia was intended to de-emphasize Islam by "constituting local particularisms in customary law [and] favoring the traditional authority structures linked to them."(Roff 1985, 14). While Dutch policies fostered (indeed created) ethnic divisions among Indonesian Muslims, the attempts by various American colonial agents to rationalize and objectify the Islamic identities of a generation of Muslim leaders provided the basis for ethnicizing Islam in the Muslim Philippines. As we shall see, that newly cultivated Muslim ethnic identity acquired particular saliency when Muslim political leaders found themselves representing a small and suspect religious minority in an independent nation dominated by Christian Filipinos.

CHAPTER 6

Postcolonial Transitions

On July 4, 1946, a severely war-damaged Philippines received its formal independence. A number of scholars have observed that the most notable feature of the newly created Philippine republic was its continued economic and military dependence on the United States (see, e.g., Constantino 1975; Walton 1984; Wolters 1984). Independence did significantly alter the structure of local and provincial politics in the Philippines. The electorate was expanded,[1] campaigns grew more expensive (at least partly because vote-buying became more common), and politicians became more dependent on the top-down distribution of funds through one or the other national political parties. Those funds flowed primarily through the party that controlled the state, much of them originally acquired from the national treasury or directly from American aid and international funds (Wolters 1984; compare Lande 1965).

In this chapter I relate how these nationwide trends in electoral politics—a larger electorate, more expensive campaigns, and an increased reliance on extralocal resources—took on a peculiar cast in postindependence Cotabato. In Cotabato, the immediate postcolonial period saw both a surge in Christian immigration to the region and the continuation of autocratic rule by colonial-era datus. The expanded electorate in Cotabato was composed overwhelmingly of Christians, many of whom voted for datu candidates for prominent offices based on the perception that Muslim officeholders could best supervise indigenous

Muslims and thereby protect Christians. While datu politicians received significant national party funds, their political expenses did not measurably increase because their armed domination of their districts precluded the need for extensive campaigning or vote-buying. Datu politicians instead invested in various emblems of Islamic identity—pilgrimages, mosques, and Islamic schools and organizations. I argue that those investments in identity represented both the continued development of the transcendent Muslim ethnic identity first nurtured in the late colonial period and an effort on the part of particular Muslim politicians to project the image of a unified and revitalized Muslim populace in order to gain purchase in a nation-state controlled by Christian Filipinos.

The most significant change in postcolonial Cotabato was a demographic one. Independence brought a tremendous expansion of Christian immigration from northern provinces to the South and particularly to the Cotabato Basin.[2] I begin by telling the story of that postcolonial migration, then go on to describe a second, related one—the movement of Cotabato Muslims in significant numbers, for the first time, to Cotabato City. Next I examine the continuation of "traditional" datu rule in postcolonial Cotabato despite political and economic changes far greater than those seen in the colonial period. Finally, I consider the ethnicization of Islam in the new Philippine republic by examining the evidence for an Islamic resurgence in the Muslim Philippines in the early postcolonial period.

CHRISTIAN IMMIGRANTS AND THE PERIPHERALIZATION OF RURAL MUSLIMS

Government-assisted migration to Mindanao on a large scale began with the establishment of the Philippine Commonwealth in 1935. While the American colonial government had sponsored agricultural colonies in Muslim Mindanao as early as 1913, those settlements remained limited and experimental.[3] American efforts to encourage Christian immigration to Muslim Mindanao were motivated in large part by the intention to "civilize" Muslims by contagion. That intention was articulated by Governor Frank Carpenter in a 1917 report: "The problem of civilization of Mindanao and Sulu according to modern standards, or as it may be termed, 'the Philippinization' of the Mohammedan and pagan regions which comprise almost the entire territory of Mindanao-Sulu, has its most expeditious and positive solution in the movement under Government direction to that territory of sufficient numbers of the Christian inhabitants of Visayas and Luzon" (Carpenter quoted in Gowing 1983, 294).

The Commonwealth administration was principally interested in developing Mindanao economically for the benefit of the nation as a whole and, particularly, in providing an outlet for tenant farmers in the population centers of the North who had become further impoverished (and increasingly embittered) by the global depression. Christian political leaders at the national level neither anticipated nor encouraged any significant Muslim participation in their development schemes (Thomas 1971). In 1939, the National Land Settlement Administration (NLSA) was established and given the task of creating and administering a larger and better integrated system of settler colonies in Mindanao. By early 1941 the NLSA had established two large colonies, both in Cotabato Province—in the Koronadal and Alah Valleys (see map 2)—that accommodated approximately thirty-seven hundred families, all of them immigrants from the North (Pelzer 1945). Unlike the earlier American-sponsored agricultural colonies, no effort was made to include Muslim families among the settlers (Thomas 1971).

After the wartime hiatus, government-sponsored and subsidized immigration resumed at an accelerated pace under a succession of new government agencies. One of those programs was specifically intended to relieve severe political as well as population pressures. On the eve of formal political independence in 1946, the fledgling Philippine state was faced with a rapidly expanding armed rebellion in Central Luzon, the most populous and agriculturally productive area of the country. By 1950, the Hukbalahap Rebellion—a popular insurgency seeking agrarian reform as well as complete economic independence from the United States—had an estimated fifteen thousand armed fighters and a half million sympathizers and was posing a severe challenge to the postindependence state[4] (Kerkvliet 1977; Walton 1984).

The Hukbalahap Rebellion was subdued in 1953 with the application of immense amounts of military aid and development expenditures by the United States (Walton 1984). Foremost in the government's policy of attraction—and the only element of its agrarian reform program that was effectively implemented—was a resettlement program for "Huk" fighters and supporters in Mindanao. The army-administered Economic Development Corps (EDCOR) established

TABLE I

MUSLIM AND NON-MUSLIM POPULATIONS
OF COTABATO

	1918	1939	1948	1960	1970
Non-Muslims	61,052	135,939	284,507	672,659	711,430
Muslims	110,926	162,996	155,162	356,460	424,577
Muslims, percent	64.53%	54.53%	35.29%	34.64%	37.37%

SOURCE: O'Shaughnessy 1975, 377.

settlement projects primarily in Cotabato (in Buldun and Alamada), but its first project, in 1951, was in the fertile Kapatagan Basin in neighboring Lanao Province (Scaff 1955). Demographic data are available only for Kapatagan, but they illustrate the scale of the postwar influx of Christian migrants. There were about 24 Christian settlers in the Kapatagan area in 1918. By 1941 their number had risen to 8,000 and by 1960 there were a total of 93,000 immigrants, many of whom had arrived under the EDCOR program. By 1960, Christian immigrants vastly outnumbered the 7,000 Maranao Muslims still living in the area (Hausherr 1968–69 quoted in Thomas 1971, 317).

The demographic shift throughout Muslim Mindanao in the postwar years, while not as dramatic as in Kapatagan, was equally momentous. The population of Central Mindanao (comprising the pre-1968 provinces of Cotabato, Lanao, and Bukidnon) soared from .7 million persons in 1948 to an estimated 2.3 million persons in 1970; representing a growth rate of 229 percent, as compared with the national figure of just under 100 percent (Burley 1973). Cotabato received the bulk of the postwar migrants. Net migration to Cotabato province in the period between 1939 and 1960 totaled 523,037 persons compared with 231,445 persons for the rest of the region (Burley 1973). During the twelve years prior to the 1960 census, the population of Cotabato Province grew at a rate of 8.48 percent per year, the highest population growth rate of any province in the Philippines (Wernstedt and Spencer 1967). Table 1 displays figures (reported by O'Shaughnessy 1975) showing that, while Muslims comprised 54.5 percent of the population of Cotabato Province in 1939, by 1960 Christian in-migration had caused the Muslim share of the population to slip to 34.6 percent.

While the scale of Christian immigration to Cotabato caused inevitable dislocations, the manner of its occurrence also produced glaring disparities between Christian settlers and Muslim farmers. As early as 1935, prominent Muslims such as Salipada Pendatun were complaining about the inherent disadvantages faced by Muslims who tried to compete with Christians in acquiring legal title to lands (see chapter 5). From 1935 onward, the successive administrations of the Philippine Commonwealth and Republic provided steadily more opportunities and assistance to settlers from the North. By contrast, the government services available to Muslims were not only meager compared to those obtained by immigrant Christians but were also fewer than they had received under the colonial regime. The land laws of the postcolonial government defined all unregistered lands in Mindanao to be public land or military reservations (Gowing 1979). Unfamiliar with the procedures or deterred by the years of uncertainty, the steep processing fees, and the requirement to pay taxes during the interim, many Muslims neither applied for the new lands opened up by road construction nor filed for the land they currently occupied (Thomas 1971). For their part, officials and employees of the Bureau of Lands (virtually all of them Christians) were at best indifferent to Muslims. Christian settlers, on the other hand, regularly obtained ownership of the best new lands as well as crop loans and other forms of government assistance. The new Christian communities became linked to trade centers and to one another by networks of roads while Muslim communities remained relatively isolated.

By 1970, this differential access had produced a profound economic gap between Muslim and Christian communities throughout Mindanao. In 1971 the Philippine Senate Committee on National Minorities reported that until that year there were no irrigation projects in any municipality in Mindanao where Muslims were a majority (Gowing 1979). A 1972 survey of three communities in Pigkawayan, a municipality adjacent to Cotabato City and one of the leading rice-producing districts in central Mindanao, revealed circumstances symptomatic of Cotabato as a whole. Muslims, who comprised 20 percent of the population of the municipality, occupied a remote, swampy portion of one of the villages in the three-village sample and did not possess legal title to the land they farmed. They had adopted new rice varieties but, unlike Christian farmers, did not use fertilizer, herbicides, or tractors and threshers. In sharp contrast to Christian farmers, no Muslims had received government aid, although all Muslims polled cited government aid as the most important way that farming could be improved (E. K. Tan 1974).

The fact of differential access to state resources for Christians and Muslims despite an official policy of equal access was exacerbated by the purposeful thwarting of the intentions of the government policy by bureaucrats and speculators. Both ordinary Muslims and Christians were disadvantaged by these manipulations, but the most obvious abuses of the system often favored Christians over indigenous Muslims.

Pelzer (1945, 12) notes that during the Commonwealth period it was common for homesteaders to rush to a road construction site to find that "influential persons who had been privately informed of the construction even before it was begun had taken up the choice land on both sides of the road. These people then held the land for speculative purposes, using hired labor to meet the bare minimum requirement for improvements."

Such collusions between speculators and bureaucrats were still common in Cotabato in the 1950s and 1960s. Speculators received information on roads to be constructed through undeveloped sections and gained title to the best adjoining lots for later resale. Legal limitations on the size of landholdings were circumvented by, among other means, titling lots in the names of fictitious persons or absent relatives and hiring children to simulate (by using their big toes) the required thumbprints on application forms. Philippine Constabulary officers were reportedly able to obtain large and valuable tracts of land for themselves. Also common was the practice by employees of the Bureau of Lands to apply for title to parcels of land in recently surveyed areas in the names of their absent relatives in Luzon or the Visayas. Their applications would be given priority treatment and relatives would then be notified to come to claim their lots.

Most rural Muslims (as exemplified by the indigenous inhabitants of Pigkawayan) found themselves peripheralized in place as a result of the maneuverings of Christian settlers and speculators. Others, however, were physically dispossessed of their lands. The Bureau of Lands recognized land rights on the basis of priority of claim filed, not priority of occupation. It was not unusual for individuals to obtain legal titles, either intentionally or unintentionally, to already occupied lands.[5] In such cases, the legal owners were mostly (but not always) Christians and the previous occupants ordinary Muslims. Poor Muslim "squatters" would usually be offered small amounts of money to vacate the land and would often accept it and leave. If the occupants refused to move and the titled owner was sufficiently wealthy or influential, he or she would gain possession of the land by use of armed might, most often supplied (in the case of Christian titleholders) by local units of the Philippine Constabulary.

MUSLIM MIGRATION TO COTABATO CITY

The dislocations wrought by the massive migration of Christian settlers into Cotabato in the postwar period provided a major stimulus for an internal migration of Cotabato Muslims into Cotabato City. The migration of large numbers of Muslims within Cotabato was not in itself a novel phenomenon. The indigenous inhabitants of the region had long responded to perceived external threats by moving en masse out of harm's way. Laarhoven (1989) reports the 1693 migration of five thousand families upriver and away from the coastal capital because of the fear of a Dutch-English invasion. Another massive upriver migration followed the occupation of the Pulangi Delta by the Spaniards in 1861 (Ileto 1971). The postcolonial movements differed from previous internal migrations in two important ways. First, the direction of movement was reversed, with migrants transferring downriver rather than up. Second, this was a rural-to-urban migration, with most Muslims relocating to Cotabato City and taking up urban occupations. Those who arrived prior to 1970 were overwhelmingly economic migrants. While many were pushed into the city as the result of the rural disruption caused by Christian immigration, others were pulled there by the new economic opportunities made available by that in-migration and more generally by developments in the postcolonial economy.

The movement of rural Muslims into Cotabato City in the postwar period may be seen as one component of a gradual rehabitation of the traditional downriver capital after the withdrawal of its Spanish occupiers in 1899. That process began with Datu Piang's attack on Cotabato town in the wake of the Spanish evacuation and was advanced with Datu Sinsuat's move to Cotabato town in the 1920s. Regrettably, hardly any information exists about ordinary Muslims in the city proper prior to the 1950s. Chester Hunt, who conducted a survey in the *población* (provincial town) of Cotabato in 1953, reported a "considerable representation" of Muslims there ([1957] 1974, 194). He found a majority of Muslims in the city working as fishermen or stevedores, with a small number operating small businesses such as goldsmithing and a few in river transportation, a business of somewhat larger scale.

The ethnic geography of Cotabato City has changed hardly at all from the way Hunt found it in 1953. Muslims still tend to live and work close by the Pulangi River or along tributary streams on the outskirts of the city. All three major mosques in the city are located on riverbanks. Christians, on the other hand, generally reside in neighborhoods on the higher ground south of the city center or along the main highway running south.[6] The Chinese still typically "occupy flats located above stores in the business district" in the center of the city (Hunt [1957] 1974, 197). The continued riverine orientation of city Muslims is most strikingly apparent on the banks of the Pulangi at the northern edge of the city. Virtually all of the economic enterprises and activities found here—water taxis, coffee shops, goldsmithing, furniture-making, fish-selling, vegetable-vending, cargo handling—represent uniquely Muslim occupations. Christians, by contrast, rarely travel on the river and hardly ever venture into the Muslim areas along its banks.[7]

In 1963, ten years after Hunt's survey, the *Mindanao Cross,* a weekly newspaper published in the city, reported more than 750 "landless families" living in Cotabato City (August 24, 1963). In 1966, in a newspaper article by a local social worker, it was noted that there were about 1,000 families "living in slum conditions" in Cotabato City, most of them along the riverfront road that forms the core of the Muslim sector of the city (*Mindanao Cross,* December 10, 1966). Hunt's 1953 survey makes no mention of urban shantytowns or squatters. While some of these families may have been composed of destitute Christian immigrants, it is most likely that the great majority of them were Muslim urban migrants arrived since the mid-1950s.

In the early 1960s a new community of Muslim urban poor was created in the middle of the Pulangi River. This was Bird Island (also known simply as *Punul,* or "The Island"). Bird Island was originally a small, low-lying island in the Pulangi River directly across from the main city pier. The Spaniards had built a brick armory there in the late nineteenth century and the Americans had used it as a garbage-dumping site during their short occupation of Cotabato City after World War II. After a disastrous flood in the city in 1960 caused by unusually heavy rains and the progressive silting of the Pulangi River bed, city fathers, with the help of Congressman Pendatun, successfully petitioned the national government to dredge a cutoff channel. The channel straightened the lowest portion of the river, from Cotabato

City to the sea. Part of the sand from that dredging operation was placed on Bird Island, creating five hectares of relatively high, dry land. Within a very short time a community of more than two hundred dwellings emerged in the middle of the river.

At the height of its occupation in the mid- to late 1960s, Bird Island was a vibrant multiethnic Muslim community with two mosques. The eastern, or upriver, half of the island was occupied by Tau sa Laya (up-river) Magindanaons, many of whom worked as laborers at the main city pier. Most of the residents of the western, or downriver, side of the island were Iranun from the coast, and they worked as fish vendors in the riverside neighborhood of Mabini. Bird Island was a convenient refuge for Muslim urban migrants. There they could live without the cost of land rent in a secure Muslim community only a few hundred yards from their work sites.

When asked today to recall life in Cotabato City in the 1950s and 1960s, Muslim residents invariably recollect a cleaner, safer, and more prosperous city. One lifelong resident offered a typical remembrance: "When I was a boy I could dive for five-centavo pieces in the Pulangi River at Matampay bridge, the water was so clear. The river was filled with large shrimp, clams, and fish. Fishermen would give fish away. One peso would buy a string of large *dalag* [mudfish]. [Muslim] Women wore nothing but gold jewelry, and they were ashamed if they had only one piece. They wore heavy wrist and ankle bracelets, hairpins, necklaces, earrings, and brooches—all gold." Even allowing for the soft focus of reminiscence, such memories suggest that life for ordinary Muslims in the city then was appreciably less difficult than today. The remembered abundance was due in large part to a relatively thriving provincial economy stimulated by at least three new sources of external revenue. First, the immediate postindependence period saw an influx of wealth into the province in the form of war-damage payments, back pay awards, and reconstruction aid received directly or indirectly from the United States. We shall consider the political effects of that new source of wealth shortly but may presume for now that some significant proportion of it benefited Cotabato Muslims. Second, the 1950s and 1960s brought not only a flood of new people into the province but also large amounts of government resources to pay for road building and other infrastructural improvements and as loans and other forms of aid to Christian migrants. Muslim urban dwellers benefited indirectly in that virtually all Christian migrants to the province passed through Cotabato City, thus making more work available for cargo handlers, fish vendors, and transport workers—all occupations where Muslims predominated.

The third novel source of external wealth was largely the result of Muslim enterprise and most directly benefited significant numbers of ordinary Muslims in the city. Beginning in the mid-1950s, a lucrative Philippine-wide trade in contraband American cigarettes became centered in Cotabato City as a group of Muslim entrepreneurs—mostly Iranun speakers—began to take advantage of a newly opened economic niche: an enormous, unfilled demand for low-cost, high-quality cigarettes. Until the outbreak of World War II, the Philippines had exported significant quantities of high-quality cigars and cigar tobacco. While much of the productive capacity of the tobacco industry was destroyed during the war (Reed 1963, 351), equally damaging to the national industry was a shift in domestic and world market demand away from cigars (which the Philippines produced) to cigarettes (which it did not). American cigarettes flooded Philippine markets in the immediate postwar period and, for the first time, the country became a net importer of tobacco products.

The government passed legislation in 1954 intended to revitalize domestic production through a combination of government price supports, high tariffs, and import restrictions (Hartendorp 1961; Golay 1961). The price supports discouraged, however unintentionally, the production of higher grades of tobacco, and by the mid-1950s the combination of high demand for quality cigarettes, severe import controls, and continued low quality of domestically produced cigarettes led to large-scale smuggling of American cigarettes into the country (Reed 1963). The so-called back door to the Philippines from Sabah in Borneo through Sulu to Mindanao was the ideal entry route for illegally imported cigarettes, and Jolo (the capital city of Sulu) and Cotabato quickly became the two key points in a very substantial contraband trade.[8]

The Iranun residents of the Cotabato coast were perfectly situated to participate in the cigarette trade with Borneo. As seafarers, fisherfolk, or fish traders, they were familiar with the sea routes and maintained long-distance ties (including kinship connections) with partners in Zamboanga and Jolo. Iranun smugglers, usually working with partners from Sulu (who were sometimes also Iranun speakers), captained *kumpits*—large motorized boats with a loading capacity of thirty tons—manned with an armed Iranun crew. The kumpits would sail to a port in Sabah where they took on cartons of American cigarettes (actually produced in Hong Kong under American license) as well as umbrellas, perfumes, and enameled goods. They would then proceed to Cotabato, attempting to avoid government anti-smuggling patrols.

On their arrival in Cotabato, the boats put in at isolated moorings in the river delta west of Cotabato City. New Muslim communities grew up at the river mouth whose residents ferried cargo from the boats at night to the city and other distribution points. From Cotabato City, cigarettes were shipped by truck throughout Mindanao and by interisland ferry to Manila and other northern cities where they were readily available for sale on most street corners. I found no evidence of non-Muslims participating in or funding smuggling ventures and only very limited involvement by the Cotabato Muslim political elite. The smuggling economy did, however, have wide-reaching effects among Muslim residents of Cotabato City. It not only provided direct employment for a significant number of ordinary Muslims in various stages of the smuggling operation but also infused money into Muslim urban communities by stimulating the growth of numerous secondary enterprises ranging from boat building to the fabrication of nipa-palm panels for simple urban housing. The two main Muslim riverfront communities in the city, which today are noted primarily for their poverty and high unemployment, were both economically vigorous in the mid-1960s at the height of the smuggling economy.

By 1970, cigarette smuggling had been largely curtailed due to an anti-smuggling pact negotiated by Ferdinand Marcos with Malaysia, to more efficient antismuggling patrols in Cotabato, and to a drop in demand for imported cigarettes as better quality cigarettes came on the Philippine market.[9] The most successful smugglers invested in legitimate business ventures in and around the city, but the widespread prosperity of the smuggling economy was not restored.

The relative prosperity enjoyed by urban Muslims in the postcolonial city was also on the wane by 1970. Early in that year Bird Island was ordered demolished by the Christian city mayor as an eyesore and a hindrance to shipping in the river. The Pulangi had silted up once again and it was decided to remove Bird Island entirely to facilitate the free movement of river traffic.[10] By June of 1970 the dismantling of Bird Island had begun, with no relocation sites provided for its residents. They dispersed to various Muslim areas in or near the city, and

some went to the low-lying, swampy area on the edge of the city that
came to be known as Campo Muslim. It was a far less desirable location than Bird Island and, as we shall see, a more difficult place to live.

POSTCOLONIAL DATUS AND THE
PERSISTENCE OF AUTOCRATIC RULE

How was Muslim politics in Cotabato affected by the changes, demographic and otherwise, introduced under the Philippine republic? Here
I will examine the political and economic strategies employed by various postcolonial datus, both in Cotabato City and at the provincial
level.

For the first twenty years of the Philippine republic—from 1947 to
1967—the mayorship of Cotabato City was held by Datu Mando Sinsuat, a son of Datu Sinsuat Balabaran. His tenure in office represented
the continuation of Sinsuat control in the city. Unlike his father, however, Datu Mando officially governed *all* the residents of Cotabato
City, not solely its Muslim inhabitants. He required the votes of a large
percentage of the Christian electorate to remain in office and received
them without difficulty, according to the Christian editor of the city's
weekly newspaper. The editor, who by 1986 had observed Cotabato
City's political scene for almost twenty-five years, related that among
Christians in the city prior to the late 1960s, "there was an idea that a
Muslim mayor could control Muslims," and that many Christians
opted to vote for Datu Mando "because of his personal appeal."

Additional indirect evidence exists to support this view. In Cotabato
City electoral politics from 1946 to 1968, ethnic political coalitions
were virtually absent. The slates of city council candidates that campaigned in conjunction with a particular mayoral candidate were
almost always composed of both Muslims and Christians. Muslim
mayoral candidates invariably had Christian running mates, while
Christian candidates paired themselves with Muslims. Every city council in each of Mando Sinsuat's administrations had a large majority
(and in one instance, a totality) of Christian members. Moreover, despite Datu Mando's continued electoral successes, the Sinsuat political
clan neither monopolized Muslim politics in the city nor, for that matter, did it form a united front. In every one of his campaigns for office,
Mando Sinsuat was opposed by another Muslim candidate for mayor,
very often one of his half-brothers.[11] Given this relatively free market
for votes in city elections, it seems likely that Christian voters or, more

to the point, Christian political brokers, would support the mayoral candidate most able to protect their interests.

Another son of Datu Sinsuat, Datu Blah, exploited a new urban niche using methods reminiscent of his father's. One of the primary urban occupations for poor Muslim males in the postwar city was that of dockworker, or *kargador* (from the Spanish, *cargador*). Cargo handling at Cotabato City piers was (and remains) strenuous and dangerous work for very little pay. It was also viewed as demeaning labor associated traditionally with banyaga (chattel slaves). From the early 1950s, most Cotabato City dockworkers were organized into associations referred to euphemistically as "labor unions" (see Hunt [1957] 1974). Those organizations determined the piece rate charged to shippers, provided workers to handle cargo, and guaranteed against damage to cargo that occurred during handling. Two of these organizations were established in Cotabato City in the early 1950s by two Magindanaon commoners, one of whom made his way from labor gang foreman to controller of the largest share of riverfront cargo handling. This was the peak period for immigration to Cotabato and a time of rapid growth in the amount of goods shipped to and from the province.

By 1957, the scale of expansion on the waterfront (and the potential profits to be gained there) attracted the participation of Datu Blah Sinsuat (a former Congressman—see below), who began an organization of his own, the Progressive Labor Union. Because of his name, and the force he was able to exert, he soon succeeded in taking control of most of the riverfront by establishing new contracts with shippers and bodega owners and drawing laborers away from the established organizations through intimidation. While one of the commoner labor bosses succumbed rather quickly to the offensive mounted by Datu Blah, the other boss—Makabalang, who wielded unprecedented power for a Muslim commoner in those days—resisted him vigorously and effectively for some time. His defiance led to his eventual death by ambush in the city at the hands of Philippine Constabulary troops loyal to Datu Blah.

In 1986, all dockworkers at the main city pier were members of the Progressive Labor Union (PLU), now headed by the daughter of Datu Blah, Bai Fatima Sinsuat. According to the laborers I interviewed, the PLU appropriates 20 percent of the daily earnings of member laborers by withholding that amount from the handling fees earned by each labor gang. In addition, each worker pays an annual membership fee of

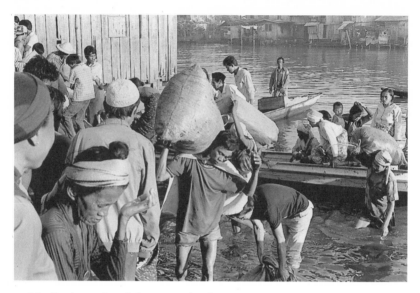

6. Muslim *kargadors* (laborers) unloading cargo at a riverside landing at the main city market.

fifteen pesos. In return, members receive identity cards and little else in the way of regular benefits. They are not insured against accidental breakage and must pay for the goods they damage from their earnings share. Workers have no job security and no guarantee of daily earnings. They typically work seven days per week and earn twenty to thirty pesos (approximately $1.00 to $1.50) per day, but there are also days with no work and no earnings. On those days, they may ask their foreman for a cash advance. PLU members also report that Bai Fatima has given members money in times of family emergencies and has also bailed laborers out of jail. This organization of work relations on the city's main pier, first consolidated by Datu Blah, demonstrates a combination of exploitation and protection (from economic calamities or governmental authorities) that duplicates to a remarkable degree the structure of traditional relations between datus and their subordinates.

To consider the fortunes of the postcolonial datus at the provincial level we may first examine the postwar career of Datu Salipada Pendatun, the most prominent former student of Edward Kuder. Pendatun was appointed governor of Cotabato in 1945 by Philippines President Sergio Osmena and was the first Muslim to serve in that post. He was subsequently elected to the Philippine Senate in 1946. His Senate term ended in 1949 with the election of Elpidio Quirino to the Philippines presidency. During the Quirino administration, Cotabato province was controlled by Pendatun's political rivals, the Sinsuats. Quirino appointed Datu Duma Sinsuat (another son of Datu Sinsuat Balabaran) governor of the province. His half-brother, Datu Blah, was elected congressman while Datu Mando, also a half-brother, served as mayor of the capital.

Pendatun returned to practice law in Cotabato City until winning election to the House of Representatives in 1957, where he served without interruption until the declaration of martial law in 1972. During his tenure in Congress, Pendatun (having apparently learned from his experience in the Senate) changed his party allegiance more than once in order to remain aligned with the party of the man who held the presidency—such allegiance securing access to the primary font of political funds.

In 1966, Pendatun ushered a bill through Congress to divide Cotabato into two provinces: North Cotabato and South Cotabato. Political leaders in southern Cotabato, virtually all of them Christian, had been agitating for a division since 1956. Because of the rapid increase in population, there had been twenty-six new municipalities created in the province since independence; most of them offshoots of the two large settler colonies established in the Alah and Koronadal Valleys in 1941 (Wernstedt and Spencer 1967). Pendatun championed the bill after losing the southern Cotabato vote in a previous Congressional election by a two-to-one margin to a Christian former protégé. As a result of Pendatun's efforts, the old Empire Province of Cotabato was divided in two on the first day of 1968. With an eye to the continued preservation of his political position, Pendatun was, as early as 1966, planning the further subdivision of the province (*Mindanao Cross*, July 16, 1966).

Congressman Pendatun was a respected but somewhat remote figure to most Cotabato Muslims. That detachment was due in large measure to his absence from the province for a good part of any year. It was also, however, a cultural distance. Pendatun was very highly educated by provincial standards, had married a Christian wife, and moved in social and political circles far removed from the traditional Muslim politics of Cotabato. When non-elite Muslims remember Pendatun today, they occasionally refer to the supernatural powers he must have possessed to survive a Manila assassination attempt in 1972, but are more likely to remark on the presence of Catholic statuary in his Cotabato City mansion.

DATU UDTUG MATALAM

A far less remote figure, who was also considerably more "traditional" than Pendatun and almost equally powerful, was Datu Udtug Matalam, who held the post of governor of Cotabato Province from 1946 to 1949 and from 1955 to 1968. Datu Udtug was a lifelong comrade of Salipada Pendatun and in most ways his political opposite. Whereas Pendatun was Westernized, cosmopolitan, and relatively aloof, Matalam was traditional, provincial, and personally popular among ordinary Muslims. Together, they controlled Cotabato politics for the first twenty years of the Philippine republic.

Datu Udtug was the son of the Sultan of Pagalungan, another small upriver sultanate aligned with the larger Buayan Sultanate. He was born in the last decade of the nineteenth century and spent his life under nominal American or Philippine hegemony. Nevertheless, an anecdote related by Datu Adil (a close associate of Matalam's) concerning Datu Udtug's childhood establishes Udtug's ties with a heroic precolonial past.

> When Udtug was just four years old his father was defeated in battle and beheaded by Datu Mantawil, the Sultan of Kabuntalan. The place where he was beheaded is still called *Pagagawan* [the Battlefield]. One day not long after his father's death, Udtug was playing with other children beside the Pulangi River. Datu Mantawil passed by with his men in a *vinta* [longboat] beautifully decorated with mirrors. The children heard the rhythmic paddling and then the datu's caller announcing, "Datu Mantawil is passing." Young Udtug found a piece of wood, threw it, and hit the old datu. Datu Mantawil unsheathed his *kris* and demanded to know the culprit. He was told that it was Udtug, the son of his slain enemy. Years later, the family of Datu Mantawil submitted to Datu Udtug. He vanquished them but did not kill them.

In 1914, while still a young man, Datu Udtug was appointed assistant colony superintendent of the American-sponsored agricultural colony established in his district of Pagalungan. He was charged with managing the affairs of the Muslim colonists, who comprised approximately half the total number (Gowing 1983). Later, he became the district school inspector and saw to Muslim school attendance, persuading Muslim parents to send their children to colonial schools. Datu Udtug's early career was thus spent cooperating with colonial authorities by facilitating the incorporation of Muslims into the new American order.[12]

With the Japanese occupation of Mindanao during World War II, Pagalungan became a central assembly point for the anti-Japanese guerrillas of Cotabato. Datu Udtug fought at the side of his brother-in-law Salipada Pendatun and was given the rank of major. His arms, men, and supplies were a key factor in the successes of the guerrillas.

In 1946 Datu Udtug was appointed governor of Cotabato Province at the behest of Pendatun, who had just been elected to the Philippine Senate. Within three years, ten new municipalities had been created in the province and Udtug, despite his lack of formal education, had gained a reputation as an able administrator. He resigned the governorship in 1949 with the installation of a new national administration but was elected to the same office in 1955, the first year of full suffrage, and served four consecutive terms until his retirement in 1968.[13] The provincial leadership of Udtug is remembered as strong and efficient and his administration is noted for its fiscal soundness. In a parallel to political arrangements in Cotabato City, many Christians in the province were apparently of the opinion that a Muslim governor could better keep Muslims in line and were specifically in favor of the governorship of Udtug Matalam. According to the newspaper editor quoted above, "Christians really trusted Matalam." They also reportedly felt their interests adequately represented by his "formula" for administrative power-sharing—a Christian vice-governor and a Christian majority on the three-man provincial board (*Mindanao Cross*, January 1, 1983).[14]

Those who knew him recount that Datu Udtug was an indifferent campaigner and infrequent speechmaker by comparison with other Muslim political figures.[15] His political staying-power seems to have been a direct consequence of his continued access to external resources. That access, first acquired through his personal political skills, allowed him to attract followers and create political allies. The possession of such resources and skills was a particularly critical factor in the Muslim politics of postwar Cotabato because the indigenous political arena had been significantly altered as a result of the war. The absence of American colonial authority during the Japanese interlude and the infusion of firearms and ammunition into the region during that period allowed reinvigoration of the political power of local datus in Cotabato and throughout the Muslim South and the resurgence of precolonial patterns of feuding and adjudication (Gowing 1979; Mednick 1965; Thomas 1971). The influx of wealth into the province after the war, in the form of war-damage payments, back pay awards, and reconstruction aid amplified this process. Local datus spent a good deal of the newly obtained cash on bridewealth payments, pilgrimages to

Mecca, mosque building (see below), ceremonial feasts, and other means to increase their prestige and followings (Mednick 1965). Violent intra-elite conflict among datu families was also common in the early postindependence period.[16]

It was the talent of Datu Udtug to be able to forge a number of these revitalized local datus, as well as a growing number of Christian politicians, into a political bloc. That was accomplished in part by providing local leaders with official political bases as the mayors of newly created municipalities. Udtug granted local datus officially sanctioned local power as well as a certain amount of public and party funds. In return, the mayors guaranteed the votes of their constituents. In municipalities with populations that were overwhelmingly Muslim, voting typically did not occur at all. Mayors merely delivered tally sheets indicating 100 percent support to the provincial center and local subordinates dared not protest their disenfranchisement. In mixed Muslim-Christian municipalities with datu mayors, voting might take place but results were altered if unacceptable. According to Datu Adil, Datu Udtug regarded this, and most other datu larcenies, as "a necessary evil."

Throughout the postindependence Philippines, the possibilities for self-enrichment through election to office at the provincial or municipal level were greater than ever before due to the increased importance of the state as a provider of capital and the absolute reliance of central state politicians on the votes delivered by local officeholders (Wolters 1984).[17] In Muslim Cotabato, however, in contrast to most other provinces in the Philippines, the costs of attaining political office did not rise concomitantly because the local capabilities of autocratic datus precluded the need for the expense of extensive campaigning and/or vote-buying.[18] Connections at the national level were of course important, and these were provided by Salipada Pendatun. Pendatun and Udtug ruled Cotabato in tandem: Pendatun furnished the high-level associations in Manila, while Udtug cultivated the provincial alliances and generally followed Pendatun's lead in party affiliation.[19]

As the effective owner of provincial votes, Udtug was courted by representatives of both national political parties and provided with significant amounts of party campaign funds.[20] As Datu Adil remembers: "Liberalista Party and Nacionalista Party leaders would come to Udtug and ask him for his support. They would give him money even though he would never promise them anything. That money was the single largest source of his income despite the fact that he never asked for any of it." There is a sense in which Datu Udtug approximated the

cultural ideal for datus envisioned in the precolonial ideology of aristocratic rule: he was regularly presented with tribute without having to
demand it. Of course the greatest portion of Udtug's revenue came not
from subordinates but from powerful outsiders, and a more accurate
analogy is available from the colonial period. Datu Udtug was the true
political successor of Datu Piang of Buayan, who enriched himself by
selling supplies and services to Spanish and American colonial occupiers. Datu Udtug brokered votes, the new political currency of the
postindependence Philippines and, like Piang before him, was adept at
obtaining favorable terms in his dealings with external political forces.

Datu Udtug was a popular and impressive figure for Cotabato Muslims. As the first Magindanaon governor of the province, he represented the assumption by indigenous Muslims of modern political authority and the end of colonialism. As the heir, in body and spirit, of
the Sultan of Pagalungan, he personified a cultural continuity with the
precolonial past.[21] Most important for ordinary Muslims, however, he
embodied the characteristics of a "good datu" (*mapia a datu*)—one
who protected his subjects without exploiting them. Datu Udtug's inclination to behave in such a manner was certainly encouraged by his
ready access to externally derived resources. Like Congressman Pendatun, Datu Udtug is said to have accumulated significant wealth during his career, much of it in the form of productive land. However, unlike many other colonial and postcolonial datus, his wealth seems not
to have been gained primarily at the expense of his subordinates.

The careers of Datus Pendatun and Udtug illustrate one of the most
interesting features of the postcolonial datus in general: a distinct dis-
continuity among them that correlates with a greater or lesser degree
of incorporation into the dominant culture of the Philippine state.
Congressman Pendatun is a notable example of the more culturally incorporated type. These postcolonial datus had some college education
(often having attended Manila universities) and were usually professionals (most often lawyers or educators). They tended to be familiar
with, and comfortable in, Manila, the national capital, often having
lived there for a number of years. They were versed in national party
politics and personally acquainted with national political figures. In
addition, they exhibited a pronounced tendency to marry Christian
wives and often to remain (or become) monogamous as a result of
those marriages. Hunt ([1957] 1974) cites evidence that as many as
forty prominent Magindanaon men (most of them presumably datus)
had Christian wives in 1953.

Because of the relative acculturation of these datus, as well as their
tendency to be physically absent from Cotabato for significant lengths
of time, they risked alienating themselves, socially and politically, from
Magindanaon followers and allies. That danger tended to be averted
by the maintenance of special relationships with representatives of the
other general type of postwar datu. The partnership between Congressman Pendatun and Datu Udtug exemplifies that sort of relationship, and Datu Udtug epitomizes the second variety of postcolonial
datu. Those datus (much more numerous than the former type) tended
not to be well-educated. Many were effectively illiterate and most, like
Datu Udtug, neither spoke nor read English, the language of national
politics. They were local leaders—in the case of Datu Udtug a metalo-
cal leader—and national politics held little interest for them. In most
essential aspects, in fact, they were datus ruling ingeds and no different
from their precolonial counterparts. Those with mayoral offices governed traditionally and autocratically, with little regard for official
rules or administrative procedures. In most areas they continued to adjudicate traditional cases and impose fines. They usually completely
controlled the armed force and electoral outcomes in their municipalities. They tended to be polygynous, maintained relatively large personal followings, and in general were tradition oriented in most of
their practices.[22]

ISLAMIC IDENTITY IN THE NEW REPUBLIC

It remains to inquire about the further development, in the early postcolonial period, of the transcendent Philippine Muslim identity fostered under American colonial rule. As argued in the preceding chapter, American colonial policies had the effect of ethnicizing Muslim
identity in the Philippines. By "ethnicizing" Islam I mean to say that
American colonial rulers encouraged the development of a self-
conscious Philippine Muslim identity among a generation of educated
Muslim elites who were otherwise divided by significant linguistic,
geographic, and, to some extent, cultural barriers. It was an identity
founded upon the Spanish ascription "Moro" (or Philippine Muslim),
but, as the term "Moro" remained a pejorative among Philippine
Christians, the most common alternative denomination became "Muslim Filipino," connoting a Muslim citizen of the new (or soon-to-be)
Philippine nation (see, e.g., Glang 1969 and below).[23] As with so many
other ethnic identities in the colonial and postcolonial world, Muslim

Filipino identity was as much negatively as positively defined; Muslim Filipinos were *non*hispanicized Filipinos who shared the profession of Islam. The Islamic content of that identity was, as we have seen, rationalized—even sanitized—to conform with Western assessments of Islam's "favorable" aspects.

How was the new ethnic identity engendered among Muslim elites in the late colonial period employed and expanded in the new Philippine nation? The standard account of the postcolonial history of Muslim identity in the Philippines (in simplified form) is that, beginning circa 1950, an Islamic resurgence began to manifest itself throughout the Muslim areas of the Philippines (see, e.g., Bauzon 1991; Majul 1985; Hunt [1957] 1974; Gowing 1979), and that this Islamic consciousness intensified and eventually culminated in an Islamic insurgency against the Philippine state (Madale 1986; Gowing 1979; George 1980; Majul 1979). A critical review of the available evidence suggests to the contrary that, rather than witnessing the widespread development of a heightened Islamic consciousness, the early postcolonial period saw a strengthening of ethnoreligious identity on the part of prominent Muslims. What is evidenced, in other words, is not an expansion of Islamic observance among Philippine Muslims as a whole but rather an amplification among political elites of an ethnic identity as Muslim Filipinos. That ethnic assertion represented not a reversal of the tendencies of the colonial period but their logical extension.

More than one chronicler of the postwar Muslim Philippines has commented that American war-damage payments and back-pay awards at the end of the Japanese War stimulated, among other things, a surge in mosque-building, the establishment of *madrasahs* (Islamic schools; the Arabic plural, *madari,* is also sometimes used by Philippine Muslims) and pilgrimages to Mecca (see, e.g., Thomas 1971; Ravenholt 1956; Gowing 1979; Madale 1986). That link between the final American expenditures of the colonial period and an increase in Islamic-related investments by certain Muslims suggests something about the nature of the postwar Islamic resurgence in the Philippines. The major share of American reparation payments was monopolized by established Muslim elites, especially those (such as Salipada Pendatun or Udtug Matalam) most closely aligned with the Americans before and during the war. The financial boon allowed many more of these individuals than ever before to make the pilgrimage to Mecca and to enjoy the prestige that attached to *hadji* status.[24] The most prominent among them invested in more elaborate status enhancements, building mosques and opening madrasahs. Muslim congressmen especially endeavored to become patrons of Islamic schools (Mastura 1984; Ravenholt 1956). The competitive character of such sponsorships is revealed in a passage from Ravenholt relating the short history of a madrasah established in 1951 by a Maranao congressman: "For a time some 600 Moro students were enrolled in Mindalano's 'college' . . . The school, however, was located too far from the main centers of Moro population on the Lanao Plateau, and when several competing Muslim 'colleges' were started in and around Dansalan by his political enemies Mindalano's enterprise foundered" (1956, 8).

The stated purpose of this and other enterprises in religious education was to promote a specifically Muslim contribution to the new Philippine nation. Ravenholt reports that "it is the conviction of Mindalano and the group working with him that if they are to bring constructive order to their people and make them full-fledged participating citizens in the [Philippine] Republic, this can only be accomplished by making them better Muslims" (1956, 11).

Similar sentiments may be found in the writing of postwar Muslim intellectuals such as Alunan Glang. In a representative piece entitled "Modernizing the Muslims" (1969), Glang, a Magindanaon datu, first restates the sine qua non of Philippine Muslim identity previously pronounced by Saleeby—the moral authority of datus: "The system of datuship has long kept the Muslims united and spiritually bound together. So deeply ingrained into the fabric of Muslim life is this institution that the faith and loyalty of the Muslims have withstood the severe vicissitudes of time and change. Down to this day, many of them still hold the datus in characteristic religious awe and adulation" (1969, 33). Glang then proposes a prescription for "modernization" remarkably resonant with that proposed by Saleeby more than fifty years earlier: "One of the biggest single factors that may bring about the orchestration of the Muslim Filipino into the fabric of Filipino national life appears to be the Muslim leaders themselves whose pervasive influence had for centuries dominated and dictated much of the Muslim Filipino thinking and psychology" (1969, 33). Taken together, the statements reported for Mindalano and written by Glang indicate an effort to undergird datu leadership in the Muslim regions of the new Philippine nation by reemphasizing its Islamic nexus.

While it is difficult to assess with any accuracy the socioreligious effects of the heightened Islamic activity among Muslim elites in the postindependence period prior to 1968, that activity does not seem to have resulted in an Islamic resurgence as the term is normally understood (see, e.g., Denny 1987; Hunter 1988). There is, for example, no evidence for any significant increase in attendance at communal prayers or of an enhanced political role for clerics.[25] The newly established madrasahs had minimal results in heightening the Islamic consciousness or religiosity of ordinary Muslims (Hassoubah 1983). Of the Islamic organizations created in the early postcolonial period—organizations often cited as tangible evidence for Islamic resurgence (see Gowing 1979; Mastura 1984; Majul 1979)—most seem to have been little more than paper entities with no genuine existence apart from an organizational name and set of bylaws.[26]

An important exception was the Muslim Association of the Philippines, the oldest, largest, and most vigorous of the new Muslim organizations. The composition and activities of the Muslim Association of the Philippines (MAP) tell us much about the nature of the postcolonial Islamic resurgence. The association was headquartered in Manila, the national capital, and had as its forerunner the Society of Indian Muslims, an organization established in 1926 to look after the needs of immigrant Muslims. By the mid-1930s, the society had reached out to include Philippine Muslims living in Manila, mostly politicians and students (among them Salipada Pendatun), and changed its name accordingly. The association fell dormant with the Japanese occupation but was revived in late 1949 by Congressman Ombra Amilbangsa of Sulu.

By the time MAP sponsored its first National Muslim Filipino Conference, held in Cotabato City in 1955, its membership was primarily indigenous Muslims who were nearly always also Western-educated politicians, professionals, or university students. A featured speaker at the first conference was Edward Kuder, now an official with the United States Veterans Affairs Office in Manila and occasional consultant for the Philippine government on matters pertaining to Philippine Muslims. Kuder's chosen subject was "Education—A means of Improving Conditions in Muslim Communities." In his speech he noted with understandable satisfaction (given his key role as superintendent of public schools in the Muslim South) that "it is mostly due to increased literacy among Muslims, and to the rise of a highly educated articulately literate class among them, all because of the Philippine Public School system, that such nation-wide conferences of Muslims [as this] are now not merely a possibility, but a reality. I thank God I have lived to see it" (Muslim Association of the Philippines 1956, 42). Kuder also

reviewed once again the benefits for the Philippine nation of an appropriate Islamic education for Philippine Muslims, remarking that "the
Muslim parents and children who are acquainted with the precepts of
their religion are more peaceful and better citizens" (1956, 43).

It is hardly overstatement to describe the annual Muslim Filipino
conferences sponsored by MAP in the 1950s (the national conferences
were its primary formal undertaking) as the postcolonial product of
Edward Kuder's tutelage.[27] The conferences brought together members
of the "articulately literate class" of Muslims from throughout the
Philippines to acclaim their newfound ethnic identity as Muslim Filipinos, advocate Muslim self-improvement, and deliberate the place of
Muslims in the fledgling Philippine nation.

The emblems of Islamic resurgence in the two decades following independence were primarily signs rather than practices. Rather than
spawning a religious revival in the Muslim Philippines they signaled a
deepening ethnic self-recognition (found primarily among elites) as
Muslim Filipinos. The ethnic affirmations initiated by Muslim political
elites were the logical extension of the process of Muslim Filipino identity formation begun in the late colonial period. Western-educated
Muslim elites such as Pendatun and Mindalano underscored their
shared hyphenated identity as Muslim-Filipinos rather than their separate ethnolinguistic designations as Magindanaon or Maranao. The Islamic content of that shared identity was affirmed largely by rational-
izing it through the establishment of various Islamic "colleges" and
organizations. The expressed intention of molding individuals into
"better Muslims" referred fundamentally to creating self-consciously
ethnic Muslims. Such efforts and intentions were expressive of the
Muslim elite's contradictory position (established during the American
colonial period) as modernizing traditional leaders. While intent on retaining and reinforcing their customary positions as Islamic authority
figures, they nevertheless remained the most Westernized (and Filip-
inized) of Philippine Muslims. Unsurprisingly, none of the public Islamic assertions of Muslim elites during this period directly challenged
the legitimacy of the new Philippine state to rule Muslims.

While the Islamic affirmations of Muslim elites in the postindependence period are largely understandable as the natural progression of
forces set in motion during the colonial period, they should also be examined in light of the disjunctions brought about by the establishment
of the Philippine republic. As we have seen, the most consequential of
those was large-scale Christian migration to the Muslim South. As il-

lustrated by the postwar careers of Congressman Pendatun and Datu
Udtug, the responses of Muslim political leaders to the influx of Christians tended to be quite pragmatic. While the demographic balance remained favorable to them they readily formed coalitions with Christian politicians and appealed to Christian voters. Implicit in those
appeals was their claim to be able to "control" Muslims, which presumably included the assurance of Muslim acquiescence to continued
Christian immigration.

When the demographic tide shifted against them, Pendatun and Udtug did not hesitate to cede large portions of their political territory in
order to retain a secure hold on power. That consolidation of Muslim
territory in response to rising Christian political power in Cotabato
suggests an additional motivation for the activation by Muslim elites
of rationalized emblems of a single Muslim ethnic identity. Such signs
of Muslim solidarity may also be seen as a defensive response to Christian ascendancy in Mindanao. To Christian politicians and agents of
the central state, they projected the image of a unified and energized
(though manageable) Muslim populace—a populace that would tolerate large numbers of new arrivals but would countenance neither official disregard nor displacement from its core territories.[28]

In the watershed decade that began in 1968, mutual tolerance gave
way to sectarian violence between Muslims and Christians and governmental inattention was replaced by state aggression toward Muslims.
Most datu politicians in Cotabato lost a great many of the capabilities
they had possessed to manage the Muslim populace, as they were confronted with new and severe political challenges, both internally from
a new Muslim counterelite and externally from the particular Christian
forces that controlled the state.

CHAPTER 7

Muslim Separatism and the Bangsamoro Rebellion

The year 1968 saw the onset of a decade of turmoil in Cotabato brought about by a convergence of tendencies that had been building since the founding of the Philippine republic. By that year, the social pressures generated in the postindependence period (especially as the result of Christian migration to the Muslim south) had begun to agitate the unsteady political status quo in Cotabato. Within a short while, the system of provincial governance constructed by Pendatun and Matalam disintegrated in the face of the rise of a Muslim counterelite and the onset of organized aggression by the Philippine state against its Muslim citizens. The declaration of martial law in 1972 by President Ferdinand Marcos ignited an armed separatist insurgency throughout the South directed by a new array of Muslim leaders. With few exceptions, the established datus of Cotabato denounced the rebellion and aligned themselves with the national state that had underwritten their local rule for more than seven decades.

THE EMERGENCE OF A MUSLIM COUNTERELITE

Two quite dissimilar education projects begun in the 1950s produced a distinct but variously composed Muslim counterelite by the late 1960s. The first project was a government program expressly designed to "integrate" Philippine Muslims into national life by providing a number of them with postsecondary educations in the national capital. The second effort was an externally funded Islamic education project designed to enhance Islamic faith and practice among Philippine Muslims by granting some of them the opportunity to study at Islamic centers in the Middle East. The graduates of these two scholarship programs constituted a new and differentially educated Muslim elite that was joined in Cotabato to an emergent Muslim commercial elite composed, for the most part, of former smugglers. These groups forged an alliance that provided the leadership for the separatist rebellion begun in 1972 and posed a direct challenge to the established postcolonial elite. We begin by considering these two education projects and their political consequences.

THE COMMISSION ON NATIONAL INTEGRATION AND THE GENERATION OF MUSLIM SEPARATISM

In 1954 the Philippine Congress, prompted by an intensification of Muslim "banditry" in Mindanao and Sulu, appointed a Special Committee to investigate what were by then the conspicuous economic disparities between Philippine Muslims and Christians generated by Christian migration to the Muslim South.[1] The committee, headed by Domocao Alonto, a prominent Muslim congressman from Lanao, selected a familiar object of study—"the Moro Problem"—and adopted the colonial discourse of Muslim backwardness and guided integration in its report. The Moro Problem was redefined to accord with the ideology of the postcolonial Philippine nation, referring now to "nothing less than the problem of integrating into the Philippine body politic the Muslim population of the country, and the problem of inculcating into their minds that they are Filipinos and that this Government is their own and that they are part of it" (Congress of the Philippines, House of Representatives, 1955, quoted in Gowing 1979, 208). The Congressional Report acknowledged the poverty plaguing Philippine Muslims but ignored the evidence linking the relative impoverishment of Muslims to Christian in-migration and blamed only Muslim culture for Muslim poverty: "In their ignorance and in their trend toward religious fanaticism, the Muslims are sadly wanting in the advantages of normal health and social factors and functions" (Congress of the Philippines, House of Representatives, 1955, quoted in Glang 1969, 35).[2]

The Special Committee recommended the creation of a Commission on National Integration (CNI). A 1957 act of Congress established the commission, authorizing it to "effectuate in a more rapid and complete manner the economic, social, moral and political advancement of the Non-Christian Filipinos" (Congress of the Philippines, House of Representatives, 1957, Republic Act 1888, quoted in Gowing 1979, 208). One of the few substantive accomplishments of the Commission on National Integration was to provide scholarships for a significant number of Muslim students to attend universities in Manila. Majul reports that the number of CNI scholars increased from 109 in 1958 to 1,210 in 1967 (1979, 191–92). While political maneuvering ensured that many of the CNI scholarships went to the children of datus, the scholarship program also represented the first opportunity for considerable numbers of non-elite Muslims to attend universities.

The total number of Muslim college graduates for the period between 1958 and 1967 was 1,391, many of whom received professional degrees. Although that number represents only about 16 percent of all CNI scholars, it is nonetheless a notable increase over the handful of Muslim students (probably never more than ten to fifteen per year) graduated from Manila universities during the late colonial and immediate postcolonial period. The CNI graduates, most of them from non-elite backgrounds, gradually constituted themselves as a new professional elite in their home communities. The shared experiences of the more than 8,000 Muslim CNI scholars studying in Manila between 1958 and 1967 also profoundly affected Muslim politics after 1968. Much of their political education was gained outside university lecture halls from observing and participating in campus political activism. They also experienced firsthand the magnitude of popular anti-Muslim bias in the national capital and, after the election of Ferdinand Marcos as president of the Philippines in 1965, witnessed an increasing antagonism toward Muslims by the same Christian-dominated state that had provided them scholarships.

In 1968 an event came to light that politically aroused the Muslim student community in Manila. In March of that year the newly elected Senator Benigno Aquino told the Senate of a report that Christian army officers had shot dead a number of Muslim recruits on the island of Corregidor in Manila Bay. According to a survivor who had told his story to Aquino, 180 Muslim trainees had been recruited in 1967 as part of a covert force connected with the Philippine Army and administered by the Civil Affairs Office. The trainees had reportedly protested the conditions of their training and demanded to be allowed to return to their homes. In reaction, at least 14 of them (and perhaps as many as 28) were executed without investigation or trial (George

1980; Majul 1985). Despite four separate congressional and military inquiries, and a great deal of press interest, the true purpose of the clandestine "Jabidah Project" and the reason for the execution of the Muslim recruits have never been made clear. The most widely repeated interpretation was that the project was part of a Marcos administration plan to invade the Malaysian state of Sabah on the island of Borneo by a force from Sulu that could not be directly linked with the Philippine Army.[3]

The so-called Jabidah Massacre had a galvanizing effect on the Muslim student community in Manila. Throughout the year, Muslim students demonstrated against the Jabidah killings. The Jabidah protests transformed one campus activist in particular into a Muslim separatist. Nur Misuari was a Tausug from Sulu and the son of a very poor family. Supported by a CNI scholarship, he had graduated from the University of the Philippines and by 1968 was teaching there in the Department of Political Science. Misuari had been active in progressive student politics for some time but, shortly before 1968, had begun to focus his efforts on issues specific to Philippine Muslims.[4] In 1967 he helped to found the Muslim Nationalist League and became editor of its official publication, the *Philippine Muslim News* (George 1980). Misuari has stated that it was the Jabidah protests that inspired his political career and motivated his rise to the leadership of the Muslim separatist movement (Majul 1985, 45). In a 1968 editorial in the official organ of the Muslim Nationalist League, he wrote: "Separatism is a costly and painful process and few ordinary mortals are prepared to pay the price. But this world has been a witness time and again to the division of certain countries into smaller ones. For, political division is a matter which is not fully within the control of men, nor yet a sole product of their whims and caprices. It is in fact mainly the creation of the actual conditions in which men find themselves. It is the creation of the system" (quoted in George 1980, 200). The rhetoric employed by Misuari here in one of his very first published statements on Muslim separatism borrows the language of revolutionary Marxism and reflects the political influences of the university-based activism of that period. Significantly, Misuari has redirected the revolutionary rhetoric of the Manila student movement (and of student movements elsewhere in that period) toward the goal of Muslim nationalism rather than adopting a specifically Islamic discourse.

That the assimilationist efforts of the Commission on National Integration should yield in ten years' time a Western-educated revolutionary poised to lead a Muslim nationalist rebellion against the Philippine state is as illuminating as it is ironic. It presents a characteristic instance of the genesis of ethnonationalism—a sweeping political phenomenon for which Brackette Williams has recently offered an innovative reading. According to Williams, any adequate analysis of ethnonationalism must treat ethnic differentiation as "an aspect of a total system of stratification"(1989, 421). In such a system, the most powerful members of any particular nation-state "determine who, among persons of different 'tribal pasts,' is trustworthy and loyal to the political unit" (1989, 419).

Following Williams's schema, in the new Philippine republic only Christian Filipinos were deemed entirely trustworthy and thereby considered "non-ethnic" despite the quite considerable ethnolinguistic diversity found among them. Non-Christian Filipinos (comprising Muslim-Filipinos and "Tribal-Filipinos"), deemed culturally suspect, were labeled "ethnic" (by assigning them hyphenated designators) and regarded as socially and morally substandard. Muslim-Filipinos, comprising the largest single category of non-Christians, were judged to be dangerously disloyal because of their long history of armed enmity toward Philippine Christians.

The distrust and devaluation of Muslims by the Christians who controlled the Philippine state is evidenced in the 1954 report of the Special Committee, which depicts Muslims as socially problematic by nature—mired in poverty as a result of their own ignorance and religious fanaticism. Official expenditures aimed at integrating them into the "body politic" were thought necessary precisely because Muslims were viewed as "holding the nation back" (B. Williams 1989, 435). It is worth noting that while the legislation establishing the Commission on National Integration authorized the commission to institute a broad spectrum of development programs and services ranging from irrigation projects to legal aid to road building, the only component to receive more than token funding was the scholarship program for higher education. In this respect, the postcolonial Philippine government continued the practice established during the American period of "developing" Philippine Muslims not by providing them the material resources of the West but by endeavoring to remove (by the selective provision of university educations) the cultural disabilities perceived to be impeding their advancement and, indirectly, that of the Philippine nation.

An unintended consequence of the CNI scholarships was the creation of a group of young Muslim intellectuals schooled in political activism and able to articulate the frustrations of a much larger group of Muslim students disaffected by their encounters with Christian cultural hegemony in Manila. Nur Misuari and other Western-educated leaders of the separatist movement that began to take form in 1968 had inherited an ethnicized Muslim-Filipino identity from their colonial-era predecessors and experienced its contradictions in their frustrated attempts at integration in the national capital. The Jabidah Massacre provided both provocation and metaphor. Philippine Muslims who had volunteered to serve the republic had been deceived, exploited, and treacherously murdered by Christian agents of the state. Efforts by Muslims to contribute to the Philippine nation as Muslims were repaid with abuse and betrayal. Misuari and other young Muslim activists saw only one proportionate response: Philippine Muslims had to "separate themselves from those against whom they [were] judged unfavorably and . . . in relation to whom they [were] materially disadvantaged"—they must proclaim themselves a "new people" (B. Williams 1989, 429). The separatist intellectuals rejected their ascribed hyphenated identities as Muslim-Filipinos (Muslim citizens of the Philippine nation) and proclaimed themselves "Moros." In a bold piece of semantic alchemy they appropriated and transfigured a colonial and Christian pejorative to denominate the citizens of their newly imagined nation. Henceforth, "Moro" would denote the descendants of those unsubjugated peoples whom the Spaniards and their colonized subjects feared and distrusted.

MIDDLE EASTERN EDUCATIONS AND THE FORMATION OF AN ISLAMIC COUNTERELITE

Before tracing further the path of Nur Misuari and his fellow Manila-based intellectuals toward Muslim separatism, the genesis of a second group of Philippine Muslim intellectuals needs exploring.

Between 1955 and 1978 the government of Egypt, as part of the pan-Islamic programs of Gamel Abdul Nasser, granted more than two hundred scholarships to young Philippine Muslims, the great majority of whom studied at al-Azhar University in Cairo (Mastura 1984; Majul 1979; George 1980). In the previous few years, some graduates of al-Azhar (mostly Indonesians) had been sent to teach in the Muslim Philippines, but it was only with Nasser's ascent to power in 1954 that significant numbers of Philippine Muslim students were able to undertake advanced studies at Islamic institutions in the Middle East.[5] A number of those students were scions of datu families, but many others were not, and the scholarships thus became another avenue for ordinary Muslim students to gain higher educations. Al-Azhar graduates returned to the Philippines after overseas stays averaging eight years, and most became religious teachers in their home provinces. While far fewer Philippine Muslims studied in Cairo than in Manila, the influence of Islamic graduates was out of proportion to their numbers. That influence initially took a political-symbolic form as al-Azhar graduates became involved in the leadership of the separatist movement. It was much later before the presence of indigenous Islamic teachers had a commensurate effect on popular Islamic consciousness in the Philippines. As in Manila, the Philippine Muslim student community in Cairo became a center for the development of activism in pursuit of social and political change in the Muslim Philippines, but, unlike that in Manila, student activism among Philippine Muslims in Cairo was explicitly and exclusively Islamic in character.[6]

One of the most politically inclined of the Cairo students was Hashim Salamat, a Magindanaon from Cotabato. Salamat, who left for Cairo in 1959, was related to Congressman Pendatun but his family was neither wealthy nor prominent. Salamat was a member of the fourth cohort of Cotabato Muslims to receive scholarships to al-Azhar. He returned to Cotabato in 1967 and obtained a position as provincial librarian. However, his real interest, as he stated in a 1977 interview, was to work to reform Muslim political and religious affairs in the province at least partly by participating in politics. Salamat and his al-Azhar cohort were frustrated in their attempts at political participation because, as he said, "the old Muslim traditional and political leaders wouldn't even allow us to get near them" (quoted in *Mindanao Cross*, February 12, 1977). Salamat eventually became associated with established Muslim politicians and, more consequentially, with Nur Misuari through a most unlikely intermediary, Datu Udtug Matalam, the recently retired governor of Cotabato and renowned champion of Muslim-Christian cooperation.[7]

DATU UDTUG MATALAM AND THE MUSLIM INDEPENDENCE MOVEMENT

In May of 1968 the establishment of the Muslim Independence Movement (MIM) was announced by its founder and chairman, the newly retired governor of Cotabato, Datu Udtug Matalam. The MIM had as its formal goals the secession of Muslims "from the Republic of the

Philippines in order to establish an Islamic State" (*MIM Manifesto* quoted in Glang 1969, 103). A contemporaneous editorial in the Cotabato City newspaper (*Mindanao Cross*, June 1, 1968) noted the irony in the fact that Datu Udtug, the former governor of the province and prominent advocate of Muslim-Christian political harmony in the region, had now founded a Muslim secessionist movement. The proximate cause for the sudden political transformation of Datu Udtug may be found in the circumstances of his retirement from the governor's office. In 1967, Datu Udtug became a political casualty of the national party politics about which he cared so little. Following the lead of his brother-in-law, Congressman Salipada Pendatun, Datu Udtug had been aligned for some years with the Liberalista Party. After an exceedingly bitter presidential election campaign in 1965, won by the Nacionalista Party challenger Ferdinand Marcos, Marcos led a Nacionalista push to unseat Liberalista officeholders in the 1967 local elections. One of the targeted provinces was Cotabato, previously considered the unassailable territory of Pendatun and Matalam. Marcos personally selected a Muslim Nacionalista candidate for the governorship of Cotabato, Datu Abdulla Sangki. Sangki was a member of the Ampatuan clan,[8] which was closely aligned with the Sinsuats, the persistent political rivals of Pendatun and Matalam. The Sinsuats and Ampatuans had, that year, affiliated en masse with the Nacionalistas.

Datu Udtug, who disdained electioneering, was unimpressed by this challenge, but Pendatun, a modern campaigner, took it quite seriously. Presumably, he was also aware that were a Nacionalista to attain the governorship of Cotabato, his own position as congressman for the province would become untenable. Pendatun persuaded the sixty-eight-year-old Udtug to withdraw from the election by offering to run for governor himself in his stead.[9] Pendatun chose Simeon Datumanong, a political protégé, as his running mate for vice-governor. Datumanong was a member of the Ampatuan clan and was chosen at least partly as a counterweight to the Nacionalista candidate. Pendatun won the governor's race by a slender margin but decided not to give up his seat in Congress after all. He never took the oath of office and Datumanong automatically became governor.

Datu Udtug thus found himself in 1968 involuntarily retired from public office and far from the reins of provincial power, which were now held by a youngster closely related to his political foes. He reportedly felt abused by his old comrade Pendatun and more disgusted than ever with national party politics. His resentment was intensified as the result of a separate incident. In August of 1967 his eldest son, Tuting, was shot and killed by an off-duty agent of the National Bureau of Investigation. Datu Udtug was anguished at this loss and then deeply offended when none of the newly elected provincial officials (with the exception of Pendatun) visited him to pay their condolences. The compounded frustration of Datu Udtug at his sudden powerlessness apparently led to his willingness to attempt a dramatic gesture to seek renewed respect and recognition. In his effort to be once again taken seriously he was successful beyond his expectations, at least in the short term.

Datu Udtug's MIM was never a popular secessionist movement. Its only public political actions were pronouncements in the form of manifestos and declarations of policy publicized in the national and international press and disseminated to politicians and Muslim leaders in the Philippines and abroad. There was little apparent public support for the secessionist goals of the movement among ordinary Muslims (George 1980, 152; McAmis 1974), and Datu Udtug himself eventually retreated publicly from his initial positions.[10] Nevertheless, the published statements of the Muslim Independence Movement were taken more seriously by Cotabato Christians, the national media, and the state than they were by Cotabato Muslims and, evidently, more seriously than intended by Datu Udtug. In the months following the initial manifesto, the national press carried headlines announcing that "War Brews in Cotabato." Christian settlers left some towns in anticipation of a Muslim uprising, and the national government transferred combat-ready troops to the province (George 1980, 135).[11]

The manifestos of the MIM also drew the prompt attention of those who controlled the state. President Marcos met with Datu Udtug publicly in October of 1968. Marcos acknowledged Datu Udtug's self-proclaimed role as "the leader of the more than four million Muslims in the Philippines," presented him with his gold watch as a token of friendship, and appointed him presidential adviser on Muslim affairs (*Mindanao News-Bulletin* October 25, 1968, quoted in Glang 1969, 28–29). The apprehension induced by Datu Udtug's essentially notional movement appears clearly related to its timing, coming just six weeks after the disclosure of the Jabidah Massacre. From the perspective of Manila, MIM appeared to be "a spontaneous southern backlash against the notorious Jabidah shooting" (George 1980, 133). Despite appearances, and notwithstanding Datu Udtug's implications to the contrary, the evidence suggests that the Jabidah Massacre was less an impetus for Datu Udtug's movement than were his own personal motivations. As George (1980) has argued, any provincial Muslim re-action to the Jabidah Massacre would have emanated first from Sulu, the home province of the recruits, rather than from Cotabato. By refer-ring to the incident, Datu Udtug was, in all likelihood, merely making use of media attention and Muslim anger generated by Jabidah, for personal ends.

The Muslim Independence Movement did, however, serve purposes and produce consequences quite apart from the intentions or actions of Datu Udtug. The MIM acted as a lightning rod, attracting mostly young, educated Muslims either disenchanted with or debarred from Muslim electoral politics. For a period of time Datu Udtug's home-stead at Pagalungan again became a center of political activity.[12] Udtug himself played a very limited role in MIM activities after his initial ef-forts. He appeared content with the recognition he had garnered by signing his name to manifestos and spent the rest of his life, until his death in 1983 at the age of eighty-four, farming his land.

While credible information on the covert political activities associ-ated with the Muslim Independence Movement is hard to come by, enough data are available to indicate how the MIM, though never a broad-based movement, became a vehicle for the convergence of old and new, established and antiestablishment, Muslim interests. In 1969, Hashim Salamat established an organization, Nurul Islam, to promote Islamic renewal in Cotabato. By 1970 Salamat had aligned himself and his organization with the MIM. Presumably, Salamat was attracted to the MIM by Datu Udtug's break with party politics, his call for an Is-lamic state, and his willingness to associate himself with young and idealistic men. It is known that by early 1969, Nur Misuari had also made the acquaintance of Datu Udtug and, more important, had made common cause with the two most prominent Liberalista Muslim politi-cians of the day, Salipada Pendatun of Cotabato and Rashid Lucman of Lanao. Misuari most likely had cemented his relationship with these men as a result of the Jabidah protests in Manila, which received sig-nificant support from opposition Muslim politicians.

Misuari became most closely associated with Rashid Lucman, a prominent Muslim congressman and Pendatun's counterpart in Lanao. Lucman was also closely acquainted with Tun Mustapha, the chief minister of the Malaysian federal state of Sabah. Mustapha had been angry with the Philippine government since it first announced a claim to Sabah. Mustapha was also an ethnic Tausug with many relatives living in Sulu and had become incensed both at the recruitment of Sulu Muslims to invade Sabah and at their subsequent treatment at the hands of Philippine agents (Noble 1983). The Jabidah Massacre served to confirm his worst suspicions of Philippine intentions. At some point in early 1969 a decision was made within this group to initiate a training program for Muslim guerrilla fighters. In late 1969, ninety young Muslim recruits, most of them Lucman's fellow Maranaos from Lanao—but also Magindanaons and Tausugs—began military training in the forests of Malaysia by professional instructors (Mercado 1984; Noble 1983). Nur Misuari was among the group, as was the son of Rashid Lucman and eight young Magindanaons. Although there is no evidence that Datu Udtug actively participated in the decision to train Muslim fighters, and although only a small percentage of the trainees were Magindanaon, this training has been referred to as an MIM program (see Mercado 1984; Noble 1983). The training was evidently financed as well as sanctioned by the government of Malaysia through the intercession of Tun Mustapha.

Misuari's intentions in taking part in (and probably initiating—see George 1980) the training program are rather easily discernible. It is apparent from his 1968 editorial quoted above that he had already accepted the inevitability of armed struggle to achieve Muslim secession. Given those convictions, Misuari's association with established Muslim politicians was pragmatic. With no resources of his own, and having disengaged himself from the campus-based Marxist nationalist opposition, he turned to those apparently sympathetic Muslims who had their own resources and, more important, access to potentially significant quantities of external resources.

The intentions of the Liberalista Congressmen, Pendatun and Lucman—both of whom publicly denied any association with the MIM or guerrilla training—are much less easy to discern. There is no evidence to suggest that their secret sponsorship of an armed force was a defensive response to any immediate threat to their persons, or even to their positions. It was more likely conceived as a new tactic in the evolving national party politics of the period. Both men found themselves in 1969 aligned as bitter foes of an increasingly aggressive national president who was actively strengthening (with money and arms) their Nacionalista Muslim rivals in their home provinces—in Cotabato, the Sinsuat-Ampatuan alliance; and in Lanao, Congressman Ali Dimaporo. Pendatun and Lucman most probably saw the creation of a well-trained armed force, whose instruction and supplies they did not have to finance and whose existence they could deny, as a useful new resource in a mixed political strategy.

The Magindanaon recruits returned from Malaysia to Cotabato to train additional young men and form part of the nucleus of the MIM youth section—the only dynamic segment of the MIM. The rest of the active core was composed of Hashim Salamat and some of his fellow al-Azhar graduates. Datu Udtug pledged to finance arms purchases but, according to Datu Adil, spent most of the allocated funds on farm improvements.

Although never a popular secessionist movement, the MIM did have political consequence as both a notion and a provocation. By articulating the idea of Muslim separatism at an opportune time it galvanized a new non-datu and antiestablishment group into political action while offering established Muslim politicians a novel weapon for opposing an unusually aggressive ruling party.

The focus thus far has been entirely on the formation of new Muslim political elites and their relation to the beginnings of a movement for political separation from the Philippine republic. To understand how ordinary Muslims became inclined toward armed separatism requires the investigation of an unprecedented string of violent incidents in Cotabato beginning in 1970.

SECTARIAN VIOLENCE IN COTABATO

The communal violence that swept across Cotabato in early 1970 was a diverse and complex phenomenon with multiple causes.[13] Written and oral reports of the violent incidents confirm that they were overwhelmingly sectarian in nature—that is, they consisted of attacks by armed Christian or Muslim gangs on (often unarmed) members of the opposite ethnoreligious category. Most commonly, Christian gangs assaulted Muslim farmers and burnt their houses, and Muslim gangs retaliated in kind against Christian farmers. Although the ethnoreligious strife never occurred on a provincewide scale—instead exploding in particular localities or municipalities for fairly specific reasons and usually for a limited duration—the scale of destruction was catastrophic. In one two-month stretch, the *Mindanao Cross* reported more than 137 people killed. A government report published in the *Mindanao Cross* (November 20, 1971) cited 305 Muslims and 269 Christians killed, and almost five hundred homes burned, in the period between January and October of 1971. The actual number was likely much higher as many incidents were not reported (McAmis 1974). By the end of 1971, the number of refugees within Mindanao forced from their home communities by the violence was estimated at more than 100,000 (Majul 1985; McAmis 1974).

While the preponderance of violent clashes was sectarian in appearance, the antagonisms that underlay them, when closely analyzed, were not solely (or even predominantly) ethnoreligious in nature. The three major lines of dissension in the region seem to have been principally class-based rather than ethnically motivated. These were, first, conflict between ordinary Christian settlers and Muslim elites; second, conflict between ordinary Muslims and Christian elites—often representatives of the state; and third, intra-elite conflict—usually, but not always, between Muslim and Christian elites. Although many, if not most, of the actual clashes occurred between ordinary Muslims and Christians, an exploration of four major outbreaks indicates that the antagonisms that motivated the violence were of one of the above three types, and that often those initiating the violence were in the employ of one or another elite group.

EPISODE 1: "TOOTHPICK" AND THE TIRURAY RESISTANCE

In March of 1970 in the small town of Upi in the Tiruray Highlands south of Cotabato City, an eruption of violence occurred that is generally regarded as having opened a two-year period of intense sectarian conflict in Cotabato (see, e.g., George 1980; McAmis 1974; Stewart 1977). The instigators in this case were an armed band of Tiruray led by Feliciano Luces, alias "Toothpick," a Christian Ilonggo settler.[14] They clashed initially with an armed Muslim gang led by Disumimba Rashid, an already notorious outlaw. Toothpick himself went on to attain quasi-legendary status as a ferocious and fanatical anti-Muslim (see, e.g., George 1980). It is impossible to assess the accuracy of this image, but it is important to note that, at the outset, newspaper reports indicate that Toothpick's attacks were neither simply anti-Muslim nor generally perceived that way.

Native Tiruray who had taken up plow farming and Ilocano farmers who had migrated to the Upi Valley in the 1920s had coexisted peacefully for some time. In the postwar period they were joined by Ilonggo homesteaders and, increasingly, by Magindanaons (Schlegel 1979). Since independence, the municipality of Upi had been under the political control of the Sinsuat family. By 1970, the tensions produced by postwar immigration to Upi were released in violent responses to perceived exploitation. Early newspaper accounts and letters to the editor portrayed Toothpick's armed exploits as those of a Robin Hood defending poor Tiruray, Christians, and Muslims from Muslim outlaws in the employ of wealthy and powerful men. Newspaper reports suggest two causes for the outbreak of violence in Upi: "landgrabbing" and extortions by elites. Influential Muslims and Christians had reportedly titled a good deal of occupied land in the area and were using Muslim outlaw bands to gain possession by scaring off the inhabitants. In addition, Muslim datus had been coercing tribute from Christian and Tiruray villagers. The Tiruray band led by Toothpick was originally organized as a response to both those provocations. Later, Toothpick apparently was employed by a Liberalista Christian politician in a violent but unsuccessful attempt to oust the Sinsuats from power in Upi. The anti-Muslim reputation of Toothpick seems to have derived from those efforts.

EPISODE 2: PROVINCIAL ELECTIONS, *ILAGA* TERROR, AND THE MANILI MASSACRE

The next outbreak of sectarian violence occurred in the Cotabato Valley proper in late 1970, and by mid-1971 had encompassed eighteen municipalities in its northeastern portion (McAmis 1974, 46).[15] This conflict was unrelated to that in Upi; it was also much more costly in lives and property damage, with scores of farms burned and farmers killed, and thousands made refugees. The violence was largely limited to new settlements in Christian majority areas. A newspaper editorial early in 1971 blamed the violence on "Ilonggo fanatics new to the area" (*Mindanao Cross,* February, 20, 1971). These were the so-called *Ilaga,* or "Rats"—armed bands of Christians, usually Ilonggos, that terrorized Muslims. The single most shocking act committed by the Ilaga—and the one that was to reverberate the farthest—was the massacre of sixty-five men, women, and children in a mosque in the village of Manili in June of 1971.

There has been a good deal of speculative writing pointing to a group of Ilonggo Christian politicians as the founders, masterminds, or sponsors of the Ilaga (see, e.g., George 1980; Majul 1985; Mercado 1984). These suppositions are beset by certain logical problems[16] as well as by an almost complete lack of reliable information. However, there is evidence to indicate that certain politicians gave some support, and reason to assume it would be in their interest to do so.

Local elections were held in 1971, with the governorship once more being contested. President Marcos again handpicked the Nacionalista candidate for governor—this time Carlos Cajelo, an officer in the Philippine Constabulary. Marcos had apparently come to the conclusion that no Muslim candidate could topple Pendatun's Liberalista machine in Cotabato, so he chose a Christian candidate, presumably aware that in order to win, Cajelo would need to draw virtually all Christian votes away from the incumbent, Simeon Datumanong.

Cajelo, who was still the active commander of the Philippine Constabulary of the province at the start of the campaign period, faced formidable problems in his bid. First, Datumanong was a moderately popular governor and Cotabato Christians were accustomed to voting for Muslim gubernatorial candidates. Second, Cajelo was a relative newcomer to the province and was not well known. Although an Ilonggo himself, he could not even automatically rely on Ilonggo support. A number of Ilonggo politicians and voters resented Cajelo as a presumptuous newcomer and had pledged their support to a popular veteran Ilonggo mayor who was running for governor as an independent Nacionalista candidate. Any development that moved Christians away from Muslims, consolidated Christian strongholds, and roused Christian interest in a strong law-and-order candidate was in the interest of Cajelo and those Nacionalista mayors who supported him (most, apparently, did not); and although as recent provincial commander of the Philippine Constabulary he had ample access to armed force, the existence of a deniable, freelance force able to expedite such a development would also have been in his interest.

No firm evidence exists to support the suggestion that the official Nacionalista candidate for governor encouraged or supported Ilaga terror. The Liberalista Congressman Pendatun was, however, clearly of that opinion when in an October 1971 speech he blamed the violence in the province on Christian politicians trying to "wrest control of the province from Muslims" and warned his audience that the Ilaga would disturb "bailiwicks of the Liberalista Party one week before the elections" (quoted in *Mindanao Cross*, October 30, 1971). It may also be noted that Carlos Cajelo won the governor's race by a comfortable margin, that some municipalities that had always supported a Muslim

for governor voted in favor of Cajelo,[17] and that Ilaga violence ended
suddenly soon after the election.

EPISODE 3: REPUDIATING THE AMPATUANS

In a series of incidents that began in mid-1971, the Ampatuans were
virtually driven out of most of their home municipality, Ampatuan, by
armed Christian bands. Although Nacionalistas and strong supporters
of Marcos, the Ampatuan clan suffered significant losses during this
period. The Ampatuan datus were widely regarded as the most abusive
toward Christian settlers. They reportedly sold a great deal of forested
land to Christian homesteaders, allowed them to clear it, then drove
them away. They were said to have extorted rice and money from
Christian farmers, ruling their municipality as a private fief. Muslim
farmers reportedly fared little better than their Christian counterparts
and were taxed and fined excessively. In 1971, Christian victims of the
Ampatuans retaliated. The Ampatuans responded in force and the municipality became a battle zone for some months. As in Northeast
Cotabato, however, it was the ordinary unarmed Muslims of Ampatuan municipality who suffered most at the hands of Christian bands.

EPISODE 4: "THE BATTLE OF BULDUN"

In August 1971, in the town of Buldun in the Iranun highlands to the
north of the Cotabato Valley, fighting broke out between the indigenous Muslim inhabitants and Christian loggers for reasons not made
clear in reports of the incident. After some Christian loggers were
killed in retaliation for the shooting death of a local Muslim official,
Buldun was fortified by local Muslims in expectation of a counterat-
tack. A detachment of the Philippine Constabulary advancing on the
town was fired upon and its commanding officer killed. The impression spread that those behind the barricades in Buldun were well
armed and well organized and thus members of the "Blackshirts," the
rumored military arm of the MIM. The Philippine Army arrived in
battalion strength and Buldun was bombarded by artillery for four
days, after which an ultimatum to surrender was issued to the towns-
people. By this time, however, the national media had relayed the story
of Buldun around the country, and public outcry forced the interven-
tion of President Marcos, who personally negotiated with the mayor of

Buldun and averted the almost certain destruction of the town (George 1980; Majul 1985; McAmis 1974).

THE AIMS AND CONSEQUENCES OF SECTARIAN VIOLENCE

These four episodes are meant to illustrate some notable aspects of the period of sectarian violence in Cotabato and throughout the southern Philippines.[18] While in all four episodes it was Christians who were the primary instigators of violence, in two of them—at Upi and Ampatuan—the initial targets of the attacks were specific Muslim datus aligned with the Marcos administration. In the other two episodes—at Manili and Buldun—the primary targets were ordinary Muslims. The dissimilar nature of this initial targeting suggests that the apparently sectarian violence was neither uniformly structured nor monocausal. The first type consisted of more or less spontaneous uprisings by ordinary Christian settlers (or Tiruray farmers) aimed at oppressive Muslim datus. By 1970, the Sinsuats and the Ampatuans were the two most powerful Muslim political families in Cotabato. That their close connections with the ruling national party did not deter the Christian attacks upon them suggests strongly that their attackers were not simply agents engaged in a Marcos administration master plan to control the province. The hundreds of ordinary Muslims who were spillover victims of these two episodes of violence certainly experienced the attacks as sectarian in nature but also, one may imagine, directed blame at the datus who drew the Christian fury down upon them.

The second form of sectarian violence consisted of organized assaults on Muslim communities. The episodes of violence in the Cotabato Valley and Buldun point to the conspicuously non-neutral attitudes and activities of representatives of the state. At no time during the sectarian conflict in Cotabato did the Philippine Constabulary or Army assault a Christian armed camp the way they did Buldun. Further, when Muslim noncombatants were attacked by Ilaga gangs, the Philippine constabulary was invariably slow in coming to their defense. Most distressing to Cotabato Muslims was the ample circumstantial evidence implicating the Philippine Constabulary in Ilaga terror. An often-cited example was the fact that Manili, where the Ilaga massacred scores of Muslim civilians, was under formal constabulary control at the time of the massacre. The incidents in Buldun occurred just two months after the Manili massacre, and it is understandable that the Muslim inhabitants of Buldun reacted to the arrival of the Philippine

Constabulary with armed apprehension. By the end of 1971, with the man who was commander of the provincial constabulary at the time of the Manili massacre and the battle of Buldun now the governor-elect, Cotabato Muslims had good cause for intense distrust of the provincial and national administrations.

No documentary evidence exists to suggest that the apparent collusion of agents of the state with armed Christian terrorists was part of a political strategy formulated by the Marcos government. Nevertheless, incidents such as the Manili massacre and the battle of Buldun left many with the impression that such a "genocidal" state policy existed. That impression was consequential in at least three ways. First, the perception of a government-endorsed anti-Muslim policy reached the international Muslim community and led to protests and other activities on behalf of Philippine Muslims. Most important for subsequent events, that impression was gained by Libyan Premier Muammar Kadaffi, who heard news of the Manili massacre from a BBC radio broadcast (Majul 1985). In the United Nations, Kadaffi charged the Philippine government with genocide and threatened to give aid to Philippine Muslims (George 1980; Noble 1976). Evidence suggests that Rashid Lucman was the principal link at this time with both Tun Mustapha and Muammar Kadaffi.[19]

Second, the perceived anti-Muslim strategy of the state also spurred the formation of the Moro National Liberation Front (MNLF), an underground organization founded by Nur Misuari. According to Mercado (1984), in mid-1971 Misuari held an organizational meeting in Zamboanga that was attended by the most committed of the ninety original Malaysia trainees. At that meeting, certain traditional leaders, such as Datu Udtug, were repudiated for their opportunism, and the MNLF was organized with Nur Misuari as its chairman. Its goal was the liberation of the homeland of Philippine Muslims from the Philippine state. Although the MIM under Datu Udtug was rejected at the meeting, some traditional leaders, most notably former congressman Rashid Lucman, were approved for leadership positions in the MNLF.

Finally, the biased and aggressive actions of the Philippine Constabulary and Army left the ordinary Muslims of Cotabato with the lasting impression that those who held state power not only had little interest in protecting them but actively meant them harm. Associated with this impression was the developing realization that datu officeholders were either unable or unwilling to protect them against the hostile forces of the state. That knowledge, and the consequent search for new protectors, conditioned the response of ordinary Muslims to the next major episode of state aggression.

MARTIAL LAW AND THE BANGSAMORO REBELLION

When President Ferdinand Marcos declared martial law on September 21, 1972, the principal reasons offered for its imposition were the existence of armed conflict between Muslims and Christians and a Muslim "secessionist movement" in the Philippine South (Marcos 1972). The information available from that period provides scant justification for such an emergency measure. Sectarian violence was on the wane, with no serious incidents reported in the previous six months. There had also been no public pronouncements or activities by Datu Udtug and the MIM for more than a year.[20] The imposition of martial law was, in fact, the proximate cause, not the consequence, of an armed Muslim insurgency against the Philippine state, and it led to an unprecedented level of violence and disruption in Cotabato and all of Muslim Mindanao. By 1977, the government estimated that there were as many as 1 million displaced civilians in the South and at least two hundred thousand additional refugees who had fled to Sabah (Mercado 1984, 162).

The martial law regime immediately moved to collect all unauthorized guns in the Philippines by ordering the surrender of civilian firearms. Three weeks after declaring martial law, President Marcos announced that he was prepared to commit an entire division of troops to the South to "annihilate" outlaws if all guns were not turned in by the 25th of October. A few days before the deadline, Marawi City, in the province of Lanao, was attacked by more than four hundred armed Maranaos. They held strategic positions in the city for three days until overpowered by superior army forces.[21] One week later, fighting began between Muslim rebels and government soldiers in Cotabato, and in mid-November Marcos sent thousands of troops to Mindanao (Mercado 1984). By late November, fierce clashes between government units and separatist rebels were occurring throughout the South (Schlegel 1978).

THE ACTIVATION OF THE MORO NATIONAL LIBERATION FRONT

Martial law, with its ban on political groups, caused the dissolution of such aboveground Muslim organizations as the MIM and Nurul Islam, and the activation of the underground Moro National Liberation

Front. By the end of 1972, the developing Muslim insurgency began to coalesce under its banner. The MNLF never controlled all of the rebels fighting the government and was, in fact, a loosely knit group, with the borders between those fighters who were members of, aligned with, or exterior to the MNLF never very clear. Nevertheless, the MNLF was the principal, and by far the most important, armed separatist organization, largely because it became the major supplier of arms and ideological support for the insurgency. One of the reasons for the loosely knit character of the MNLF was the fact that virtually its entire core leadership was, by 1973, operating from outside the country, far from local commanders. Nur Misuari, with a large reward offered for his capture, escaped from Manila to the South after martial law was declared, from there to Sabah, then on to Libya (George 1980; Majul 1985).

The MNLF was formally organized into two parallel structures: one political, the other military. The political wing was composed of a central committee, various bureaus, and a system of provincial and village committees. The military wing—the Bangsa Moro Army—had an overall field marshal, provincial field marshals, and zone commanders at the municipality level (Noble 1976). The chairman of the central committee, almost all of whose members were in Tripoli by 1974, was Nur Misuari. The vice-chairman, by 1974, was Hashim Salamat. In his 1977 interview, Salamat states that he and his companions were forced underground when, immediately after martial law, Datu Udtug signed an "affidavit" against them and turned it over to the Philippine Army (*Mindanao Cross,* February 12, 1977). A short while later, his group joined forces with Nur Misuari, and Salamat then made his way to Tripoli. Abulkhayr Alonto, member of a prominent Maranao family, was overall field commander of the Bangsa Moro Army and one of the few top leaders to remain in the Philippines. Although all estimates remain only rough guesses, the MNLF probably came to have between ten thousand and thirty thousand men in its military branch[22] (Noble 1976; Majul 1985). The authority over rebel fighters enjoyed by the MNLF derived at least partly from its access to critical resources, particularly weapons, from outside the Philippines. Before the removal from power of Tun Mustapha in late 1975, the primary conduit of weapons was by boat from Sabah (Noble 1976). The weapons arrived in Sabah from Libya and other Muslim nations. The MNLF also controlled political and military training, propaganda, and diplomatic contacts with Muslim, primarily Arab, states. Before considering the ideological and diplomatic strategies of the MNLF, a description of the armed struggle in Cotabato is in order.

THE INSURGENCY IN COTABATO

Cotabato was the site for some of the earliest and most extensive armed collisions between government troops and Muslim insurgents. Despite the defensive and seemingly spontaneous nature of the earliest clashes, the insurgency in Cotabato quickly took on the appearance of coordination and centralized planning. In early 1973, in a "blitz-like operation" rebels simultaneously attacked at least eight municipalities in Cotabato and controlled them for some time (Abat 1993, 37). Cotabato City and its airport complex were ringed by MNLF-controlled areas and Datu Adil remembers that for lack of traffic, "grass grew on the main highway" linking the city and airport. After recovering from their shock at these coordinated assaults, Philippine Army commanders began to retake rebel-held areas by making use of their superior weaponry. In some cases, army counteroffensives were particularly brutal—reminiscent of the slaughters committed by the American army seventy years earlier. In a two-month siege of Tran, a rebel mountain stronghold in the Tiruray Highlands, hundreds of Muslim civilians were reportedly killed in repeated air bombardments.[23]

Both rebel and Muslim civilian casualties were heavy throughout 1973 due to a lack of training on the part of rebels and their reliance on the traditional but questionable strategy of creating fixed bases and attempting to hold them with relatively large contingents of fighters (Ahmad 1982). As a consequence, the rebels conceded the advantage of mobility to the army, which moved its troops in helicopters and troop carriers. In Tran, Reina Regente, and elsewhere, the Philippine Army conducted siege operations that left the rebels outmaneuvered and outgunned (Abat 1993; Ahmad 1982). By early 1974, however, the rebels had switched to a war of mobility and surprise, using guerrilla tactics and taking advantage of their familiarity with local marshes and jungles. Philippine Army strategy gradually shifted in response. In January of 1974 the Pulangi River was closed to all civilian traffic to impede the movements of Muslim guerrillas, and two months later all of the waterways in the newly created Maguindanao Province were closed by the military.[24] The government also gradually increased the number of military personnel deployed in Cotabato, and it adopted such Vietnam War tactics as the creation of strategic hamlets, new sur-

7. Cotabato MNLF fighters in the field, circa 1975. Although the Philippine military closed all major rivers in Cotabato to civilian traffic in 1974 to impede guerrilla activities, MNLF fighters were able to move largely unhindered on the innumerable small waterways of the region. As pictured, MNLF fighters were typically quite young, and many wore their hair long in keeping with the fashion of the period. Photograph by Larry Johnson.

veillance techniques, and assassination squads (Ahmad 1982). The rebels, nonetheless, fared better than they had in 1973. Casualties lightened and morale increased. By February 1975 they were steadily harassing army positions at the edge of Cotabato City and shelling the city with mortars. Rice production in the region fell to less than 20 percent of normal yield (Kiefer 1987). Threatening the city, however, proved to be the maximum extent of rebel military capabilities, and by 1976 the war in Cotabato was stalemated, with neither side able to inflict a critical defeat on the other.

REBEL LEADERSHIP IN COTABATO

Precise information on the organizational structure of rebel resistance in Cotabato is unavailable, but it is possible to discern some general outlines. Rebel leadership revolved around the MNLF but there also existed some independent or mostly autonomous commanders. The top MNLF leadership in the province was overwhelmingly young, most of them college students or recent college graduates when they joined the rebellion. These were, for the most part, the former members of the MIM youth section, both al-Azhar–graduated clerics and college-educated students or professionals. A number of them attended classes at Notre Dame University in Cotabato City just prior to martial law. Some were members of prominent datu families, others were not.

Local rebel commanders were of two general types. Some were young and relatively well trained, having learned military skills in the army, the ROTC, or in the MNLF's Malaysian training camps. Others were former outlaws, possessing the two requisites for insurgency—guns and the inclination to use them against agents of the state—and finding common cause with the antigovernment stand of the MNLF. Two of the best-known rebel commanders in the province, Datu Ali Sansaluna and Disumimba Rashid (the same man who fought against the Tiruray), were outlaws as well as sons of nonprominent datu families before joining the MNLF. Both had acquired popular (if not entirely deserved) reputations as social bandits prior to becoming rebels. Datu Ali attained a high position in the provincial command of the MNLF but was assassinated as the result of an internal power struggle in 1974. Disumimba surrendered personally to President Marcos in 1980 for the promised sum of 1 million pesos (see chapter 8).

Support from elite noncombatants is also somewhat difficult to assess. Some established datus supported the rebels clandestinely, a few did so openly; most, as we shall see, did not support them. There was one new elite group that provided quite substantial financial, logistical, and even military support to the rebels. They were the former cigarette smugglers of the Cotabato coast. Those engaged in cigarette smuggling had generally prospered from the trade, and the most successful of them had shifted fairly easily to legal enterprises, investing in maritime transportation, fishing, urban real estate, or agricultural land. When the insurgency erupted, the former smugglers were positioned, as well as inclined, to aid the rebels. For one, they possessed the resources, skills, and contacts to smuggle arms from Sabah through Sulu to Cotabato. They were also well positioned to help rebel commanders in Cotabato coordinate activities with fellow rebel leaders in Sulu and those in self-imposed exile in Sabah. Very few of the former smugglers had been involved with national party politics and most were strongly opposed to the Philippine state, and to Ferdinand Marcos in particular, because of the forced curtailment of smuggling. In addition, they had no strong ties with the prominent datu families of the province, most of whom regarded them as parvenus. A number of the former smugglers provided very substantial support for the separatist rebellion in Cotabato in the form of supplies, shelter, transportation, and smuggling services. Many former smugglers and, more commonly, sons of smugglers also fought actively in the rebellion.

MAGINDANAON DATUS AND THE REBELLION

Individual members of prominent datu families were faced with severe political constraints during the rebellion. If they supported the martial law government they risked rebel retaliation and the loss of political legitimacy. If they supported the rebels, they invited government reprisals and the forfeiture of their political positions. Given those pressures, the established Muslim political elite of Cotabato responded to the insurgency in three general ways. One segment reacted by denouncing the rebels outright and pledging loyalty to the martial law state. This group was composed, first, of Nacionalista datus such as the Sinsuats and Ampatuans. At the first indication of insurgency in Cotabato in early 1973, the Sinsuat family issued a "manifesto" in which they denied any part in the rebellion, pledged their loyalty to President Marcos and the republic, and predicted the "ultimate triumph of the military forces" (*Mindanao Cross*, March 31, 1973). However, that sort of response was also publicly made by a number of their former Liberalista foes, including the two most prominent ones. Datu Udtug met with President Marcos in early January 1973, well before any concerted rebel activity in Cotabato, to pledge his cooperation with the martial law regime. A few months later, after the insurgency had intensified, Datu Udtug publicly denounced the rebels, expressed ignorance of their motives, and stated that he was "against them" because they did "not listen to and cooperate with the datus of Lanao, Sulu, and Cotabato" (quoted in *Mindanao Cross*, March 31, 1973). Udtug made similar public statements throughout the rebellion, charging the rebels as outlaws and condemning "unscrupulous" Islamic clerics associated with the rebellion.

While the response of Datu Udtug was motivated (at least in part) by his loss once again of influence and authority, the reaction of Salipada Pendatun illustrates the more ambivalent reaction of an opposition Muslim politician left suddenly with neither power nor a familiar forum. Pendatun remained in Manila (and spent some time in the United States) for two years after the declaration of martial law. In late 1973, in his one public statement on the rebellion published in Cotabato, he urged Muslim support for the martial law regime. In late

1974 he returned to Cotabato, he announced, in order to "get involved in the restoration of peace and order in Maguindanao" (quoted in *Mindanao Cross,* November 9, 1974). Pendatun arranged a series of meetings with city leaders soon after his arrival to try to stop the fighting, which had become quite intense and close to the city. The major result of those meetings was a joint statement calling for, among other things, the withdrawal of the military from Cotabato. A few weeks later, four grenades were thrown into the Pendatun compound in Cotabato City and a short time after that Pendatun left the country for the Middle East. There he joined with Rashid Lucman and together they offered their assistance to Nur Misuari, who created an advisory council for them to head (George 1980, 262). By 1977, however, the two former congressmen were attempting to take control of the MNLF away from Misuari. Not succeeding at that, they formed their own organization, the Bangsa Moro Liberation Organization (BMLO), based in Jeddah, Saudi Arabia. The BMLO took precedence over the MNLF, stated Pendatun and Lucman, because their early support of Misuari had been crucial for the formation of the MNLF. Notwithstanding their claims, the BMLO garnered little support in the Philippines and almost none in Arab capitals (Majul 1985). In 1980, Pendatun returned to the Philippines and publicly pledged his services to President Marcos and the martial law government. Within weeks he was back in Cotabato making speeches where he "reminded the Muslims of the many good things done for them by President Marcos" (*Mindanao Cross,* January 10, 1981).

A second group of datus, mostly young and educated at Manila universities, were less obviously but more actively compliant to the martial law regime. These individuals professed sympathy with many of the grievances of the rebels but rejected violence or secession as legitimate means to redress those wrongs. They accepted government money or took government positions and, as sponsored intellectuals or government officials, cooperated with the martial law state.

A third segment chose active rebellion. Those who initially chose this course were often the junior members of datu families, many the sons or younger brothers of those who followed the first two strategies. Some became local field commanders and others attained high positions in the Kutawato Revolutionary Committee, the provincial leadership body of the MNLF. The most notable feature of the traditional elite leadership of the rebellion in Cotabato was its rapid rate of defection. Datu commanders surrendered earlier and in greater num-

bers than any other rebel leaders. The defections of the most prominent datu commanders appear directly linked to the efforts of other
datus (often close relatives of the former) working with the martial law
regime. Datu Guiwan Mastura, the nominal leader of a segment of
the Tran insurgents and the former mayor of Lebak, was the first
prominent datu commander to surrender. In June of 1973, Datu Guiwan and twelve other ostensible rebels—all prominent datus—personally surrendered to President Marcos. Their surrender reportedly was
arranged by Simeon Datumanong, who, a few months later, was
appointed by Marcos as governor of the newly created province of
Maguindanao (Damaso 1983). In March 1975, Peping Candao, an
MNLF commander and son of a prominent Muslim politician in Cotabato City, surrendered with his men. One year following his return, his
brother, Zacaria Candao, was appointed governor of Maguindanao
Province to replace Datumanong who had taken a higher position with
the government. In January 1976, the director of the political bureau
of the Kutawato Revolutionary Committee defected to the government, and one month later his older brother became executive director
of the Regional Commission for the newly created Region 12, a multi-
province governmental division covering central Mindanao. By 1980,
virtually all members of the traditional elite had abandoned the rebellion. Most former outlaws had also surrendered for cash rewards, thus
leaving, in the words of a current rebel commander, "mostly the poor
remaining" to carry on the armed revolt.[25]

THE WAR OF REPRESENTATIONS

As noted above, the ideological and diplomatic strategies of the MNLF
were as important for directing the insurgency as were its military efforts. The diplomatic contest between the MNLF and the Marcos administration is the best-documented element of the war and has received prominent and comprehensive treatment in the literature on the
rebellion (see, e.g., Majul 1985; Noble 1983; George 1980). For that
reason, and because diplomatic maneuvers bore little direct relation to
events in Cotabato, I will treat them only superficially. The ideological
struggle of the rebellion, which impinged more immediately on the
course of the fighting in Cotabato, has received less careful attention.

Although specifically religious appeals in the form of calls for
Islamic renewal and jihad (struggle in defense of the faith) played an
instrumental role at various points in the Bangsamoro Rebellion

(especially in Cotabato, see below), the central theme employed by the MNLF was a cultural-historical appeal to the concept of Philippine Muslim nationalism. That theme was articulated by Nur Misuari in a 1977 speech given in Algeria: "In keeping with the desires of the broad masses of our people, the MNLF adopted a political programme which called for the complete liberation of our people and national homeland from all forms and vestiges of Filipino colonialism, to ensure our people's freedom and the preservation of our Islamic and indigenous culture and civilization" (quoted in Majul 1985, 139).

The rebellion as conceived by Misuari was a nationalist struggle that had as its goal the establishment of a single independent homeland for the three major and ten minor ethnolinguistic groups that comprise the Muslim peoples of the Philippines. It was therefore necessary to place primary emphasis on preexisting bases for political unity and political competence—foundations that transcended ethnolinguistic boundaries. The search for the fundament of a modern Philippine Muslim nation motivated the development of the myth of Moro-hood—the account of a concerted, persistent Muslim resistance to Spanish aggression. The term "Bangsamoro" ("Moro nation") was a distillation of the core nationalist theme.[26] "Bangsa," which may be glossed as "descent group," "tribe," or "race" as well as "nation" (Fleischman et al. 1981, 10), is a term connoting descent, corporateness, and shared heritage. "Moro" was, as we have seen, the term used by Spanish colonizers to refer to the local Muslim societies that resisted Spanish attempts to establish hegemony in the southern Philippines. That term survived as a pejorative among Christian Filipinos primarily through the cultural institution of the "moro-moro," a form of folk theater in which Christian heroes battled Moro villains, who were depicted as cruel and barbarous pirates. Rebel ideologues, led by Nur Misuari, transformed the epithet into a positive symbol of national identity. Moros were depicted as the first nationalists of the Philippines, an entity whose very name denotes a colonized people. "Moro not Filipino" became a slogan of the rebellion. Moro culture heroes such as Sultan Kudarat were rediscovered and the unity and continuity of the Moro anticolonial struggle reestablished. The Moro nation was imagined as a sovereign republic composed of the descendants of those freedom fighters and their supporters.[27]

A logical correlate of the Muslim nationalist appeal was renewed emphasis on traditional Philippine Muslim political institutions, particularly the long-defunct sultanates, which were, it was pointed out, the first indigenous states in the Philippines. Because their aim was to focus attention on a glorious past, rebel leaders were understandably ambivalent about the living descendants of the rulers who led past Moro resistance to alien domination. Although both Misuari and Salamat, in their pre-MNLF days, had held as a top priority the reform or elimination of datu leadership, the official ideology of the MNLF hardly addressed issues of internal social transformation. In official communiqués, contemporary datus were chided for slipping from the high standards of their heroic forefathers, but in the process their status as hereditary leaders was reaffirmed. The existence of aristocratic, autocratic leadership was retained, at least implicitly, as an intrinsic component of Moro political culture.

There were practical considerations in the hesitation to criticize the institution of datuship. First, the MNLF, especially in the early days, relied on the help of certain prominent traditional leaders and, even though relatively little assistance was forthcoming, could not afford to risk its loss through political condemnation. Second, strong criticism of traditional leadership might have alienated some ordinary Muslims, especially in areas, such as Lanao, where traditional datuship (in a form in which power was distributed much more diffusely than in Cotabato) was still very strong. Third, a call for the abolition of the datu system would have undercut the rebellion's symbolic claims to continuity with past anticolonial struggles and, moreover, would have sustained the critical opinions of Christians who advanced the view that the "datu system" was the single cause of Muslim underdevelopment.[28]

In the war of representations, the MNLF faced a formidable foe in Ferdinand Marcos, a consummate manipulator of political symbols. With the assistance of certain collaborating datus, Marcos quickly moved to ensure that the central symbols of the Bangsamoro Rebellion were dislodged from the exclusive control of the MNLF and employed for the purpose of advancing the legitimacy of the martial law regime among Muslims.

President Marcos realized fairly early on that an exclusively repressive response to the rebellion in the South was far too costly financially and politically. By 1975 he had committed the bulk of his armed forces to counter the rebellion and had three-fourths of the Philippine Army deployed in the South. The annual budget of the Armed Forces of the Philippines had increased fivefold, to approximately $325 million, since martial law was declared (Ahmad 1982; Noble 1976). Military casualties were estimated to exceed one hundred per month in periods of intense fighting. Most of the 1973 graduating class of the Philippine Military Academy was reportedly killed in the fighting (Noble 1976). There was a high level of dissension in the army and growing dissatisfaction with the military draft (Ahmad 1982; Noble 1976). Equally worrisome was the threatened suspension of oil deliveries to the Philippines from Arab oil producers should Philippine policy toward its Muslims not take a visibly more benevolent turn (Noble 1976).

Marcos quickly augmented the mailed fist with the outstretched hand of friendship to right-minded Muslims. He began a two-pronged campaign to convince Muslims in the Philippines and, more important, heads of Muslim states abroad, of his sincere desire to solve the "Moro problem." As one measure he began a highly publicized program of economic development for Muslim Mindanao. Plans included reconstruction projects to repair war damage, infrastructural improvements, relief and welfare projects, and the resettlement of refugees. The only projects actually implemented in Cotabato were airport, road, and harbor improvements—projects which, not incidentally, benefited the Philippine military more directly than ordinary Muslims (Noble 1976).

The second component of the government's public relations campaign was a concerted effort to symbolize its good intentions toward Muslims. A large mosque was built in the center of Manila, important Muslim holy days were officially recognized by the government, and President Marcos himself claimed Muslims as his ancestors (Majul 1985). With the assistance of cooperating Muslim scholars, an Islamic Studies Institute was established at the University of the Philippines and a code of Muslim personal laws was drafted and approved by the president, though never effectuated while he held power. As part of the symbolic initiatives of the government, Moro culture heroes, originally resurrected by Muslim separatists, were incorporated into the national pantheon. Statues were erected, streets renamed, and national holidays declared by the government in honor of the apical ancestors of Moro nationalism.

In line with these iconic endeavors, collaborating datus and the martial law regime cooperated to enhance one another's claims to legitimacy among the Muslim population through the symbolic trappings of datuship. The frequency of investitures of traditional titles increased steadily throughout the martial law period. In 1974, at the height of the armed rebellion, the Christian military commander of Central Mindanao, Brigadier General Fortunato Abat, was "adopted as a son in the Sultanate of Maguindanao" by the collaborating datus

of Cotabato (Abat 1993, 98). The culmination of this series of proclamations was the 1977 investiture of President Ferdinand Marcos himself as Sultan Tinamuman (the Sultan Who Has Fulfilled the Prophe-
cies) in a ceremony sponsored by the combined royal houses of Lanao.

Equivalent efforts were exerted by the government to delegitimize
the MNLF and its leaders. From the outset of the insurgency the government labeled MNLF rebels as communists and "Maoist Muslims"
(Imelda Marcos quoted in Schlegel 1978). Repeated efforts were made
to associate Nur Misuari with the Communist Party of the Philippines
in order to convince Muslims at home and abroad that he was a
Marxist-Leninist disguised as a Muslim (Majul 1985). A related strategy promoted returned rebel commanders as legitimate spokesmen not
only for Philippine Muslims in general but for the MNLF. These men,
many of them from datu families, had surrendered to the government
in exchange for incentives that included large cash payments, timber
concessions or other special export licenses, and government positions.
In July 1975, to counter MNLF advances on the diplomatic front, the
government convened a highly publicized "peace talks" conference in
Zamboanga. Two hundred or so "rebels," all of whom had already
come to terms with the regime, were invited. The participants rejected
Misuari as their leader and pledged loyalty to the government. A number of them were then ceremoniously sworn in as local officials or in-
ducted into the regular army (Majul 1985).

In 1977, partly as a result of this skillful orchestration of political il-
lusions, the martial law regime was able to gain and maintain the upper hand in the contest of international diplomacy. In the last weeks of
1976, representatives of the Philippine government and the MNLF met
in Tripoli, Libya, to negotiate an end to the war in the South. Those
meetings culminated with an agreement on a cease-fire and tentative
terms for a peace settlement (Noble 1983). That peace settlement,
known as the Tripoli Agreement, "provided the general principles for
Muslim autonomy in the Philippine South" (Majul 1985, 73).

The Tripoli Agreement was initially hailed as a breakthrough in the
Mindanao war by all sides—the government, the MNLF, the Islamic
Conference of Foreign Ministers, and Libya, the latter two having
jointly sponsored the Tripoli conference. The agreement seemed an
enormous diplomatic victory for the MNLF, for it implicitly recognized
the MNLF as the official representative of Philippine Muslims and accorded it belligerent state status. Further, the terms of the agreement
were quite favorable to MNLF demands. The cease-fire went into

effect in late January 1977 and was generally successful for about nine months. Talks were begun in February on the implementation of the peace settlement and very soon broke down over widely divergent interpretations of the key terms of the agreement. Marcos then proceeded to "implement" the Tripoli Agreement on his own terms, principally by creating two special "autonomous regions," one for Central Mindanao and the other for Sulu. The Marcos administration also benefited substantially from the signing of the Tripoli Agreement; it provided a much needed breathing spell from the economic drain of the war and eased the considerable diplomatic pressure for settlement coming from the Middle East. It is doubtful that President Marcos ever sincerely intended to implement the agreement as signed. The unilateral actions of the Marcos administration provoked angry responses from both the MNLF and the Islamic Conference (which still stopped short of imposing economic sanctions).

Although the cease-fire collapsed in much of the South before the year was out, the fighting never again approached the level of intensity experienced before 1976. After the signing of the agreement, the rate of defections from the MNLF accelerated, its support from foreign sources was reduced, and dissension intensified in its top ranks. The MNLF threat to the martial law state remained significant but was no longer an immediate one.

The "autonomous" regional governments devised by the Marcos administration in the South have been aptly described as "essentially hollow, and productive of cynicism, frustration, and resentment" (Noble 1983, 49). The governing bodies of the nominally autonomous regions were cosmetic creations with no real legislative authority and no independent operating budget. They were headed by martial law collaborators and rebel defectors, many of whom were datus and all of whom were absent from the province more often than not, usually in Manila pursuing separate careers or looking after business interests. By 1983, the regional governments had developed a layer of bureaucracy that employed a number of college-educated Muslims, but the great majority of Muslims were completely unaffected by the new regional administrations.

Despite the tremendous political upheaval of the 1970s, the structure of Muslim politics in 1980 looked remarkably similar to that in 1968: formal political power in Muslim Cotabato (now politically circumscribed as Maguindanao Province) remained in the hands of those most closely tied to the powers that controlled the central state. Those datus who had collaborated most energetically with the martial law regime had, for the most part, retained and in some cases enlarged their hold on Muslim politics in Cotabato. Appearances notwithstanding, Muslim politics in Cotabato, as well as political relations between the Philippine state and its Muslim minority, had been thoroughly transformed. A Muslim counterelite had emerged to condemn datu collaboration and defy state control. The separatist leaders had been outmaneuvered but not defeated in their war with the martial law government. The insurgents who supported them, though depleted by defections, remained under arms in considerable numbers in remote camps. Of equal significance, the actions of representatives of the Marcos regime before and during the war turned many ordinary Muslim civilians against the Philippine government and its datu collaborators and inclined them toward the separatists who claimed to be fighting on their behalf. The next chapter examines the Bangsamoro Rebellion from the perspective of its ordinary adherents. The chapter following chronicles the reemergence of a unified and reinvigorated Muslim counterelite to lead the unarmed struggle for Muslim autonomy and challenge directly the authority of datus to command Cotabato Muslims.

CHAPTER 8

Regarding the War from Campo Muslim

THE BANGSAMORO WAR AND THE MEANING OF CAMPO MUSLIM

The Bangsamoro Rebellion was waged as an intense armed struggle from late 1972 until early 1977. A negotiated cease-fire held for most of 1977, but by 1978 fighting had resumed, albeit at a somewhat reduced intensity. It was not until 1980 that armed clashes became infrequent and the separatist movement assumed a mostly unarmed form. This chapter returns us to the Cotabato City community known as Campo Muslim. As an urban poor community sheltering a large number of war refugees, Campo Muslim is an appropriate site from which to begin an investigation of the Bangsamoro Rebellion from the point of view of the rank-and-file insurgents and supporters who suffered the greatest losses of the war.

The term "Campo Muslim" denotes a bounded Muslim community in a city in which Christians predominate, thus signifying the accelerated marginalization of Cotabato's indigenous Muslims in their own traditional capital. The community's name also suggests a second significance. Campo Muslim is the site of a concentrated and self-consciously *Muslim* population. As such, it has always been viewed by separatist leaders as a vital resource for waging the Muslim nationalist struggle. There is yet another meaning to be found in Campo Muslim.

It is an urban poor community composed primarily of residents who are self-evidently impoverished not only in relation to the Christians who control the city but also by comparison to various other urban Muslims, including virtually all of those who seek their political support.

In this chapter and the two that follow, I examine the nature of rank-and-file participation in the Muslim separatist movement by exploring the interplay between these three meanings of Campo Muslim—as marginalized indigenous community, Muslim community, and urban poor community. In its every aspect, Campo Muslim provides the ideal setting to investigate contemporary Muslim politics (and especially Muslim nationalist politics) from the perspective of ordinary Muslims. Here I focus on the Bangsamoro Rebellion as experienced in and viewed from Campo Muslim. In particular, I argue (based on evidence collected in Campo Muslim) that ordinary fighters and followers of the separatist rebellion held views and produced symbols of the armed struggle that differed markedly from those promoted by movement leaders.

THE CONSTRUCTION OF CAMPO MUSLIM

A prominent datu politician, in a 1985 speech to support the reelection of Ferdinand Marcos, expressed the opinion of many of his fellow members of the Cotabato Muslim establishment when he stated that the most significant architectural accomplishment of the martial law period in Cotabato was the construction of the impressive Regional Autonomous Government (RAG) complex at the edge of the city. I was unable to find any poor Muslim resident of Cotabato City who shared that assessment. Most of those whom I asked had never been to the RAG Complex, for lack of travel fare or interest. Some of them referred to the complex bitterly as "the Graveyard of the Martyrs," inasmuch as it had been built on the site of a celebrated battlefield of the rebellion. In respect to most of its residents, it would be far more accurate to say that the construction of Campo Muslim was the most notable architectural consequence of martial law and the Bangsamoro Rebellion.

The story of the creation of Campo Muslim as a refuge for Muslims displaced from other communities because of political violence or economic loss is best introduced through the words and experiences of two early migrants to the community.

THE CASE OF KASAN KAMID

In 1986, Kasan Kamid was a thirty-five-year-old resident of Campo Muslim, married with four children. He supported his family by working as a middleman in the public market—buying coconuts or other produce from farmers or wholesalers at the river pier and selling them to retailers or retailing them himself at the nearby marketplace. A community organizer, he had established a residents' association in his Campo Muslim neighborhood to resist evictions, and organized Muslim street vendors to fight attempts by city authorities to remove them from the street fronting the public market.

Kasan is Iranun, and he was born in the city to a family of farmers originally from Nuling (now known as Sultan Kudarat), the coastal municipality just north of the city on the opposite side of the Pulangi River. His father owned three hectares of land in Nuling as part of a larger family holding but moved his family to Cotabato City in the 1950s, at a time when cigarette smuggling had begun to create economic opportunities for Muslims in the city. Kasan's parents operated a tiny stall in Matampay, a Muslim urban community on the river, where they sold nipa, vegetables, and bananas. His father often returned to Nuling to help his siblings harvest coconuts and rice.

In the early 1960s, Kasan's father purchased through installment payments ten hectares of land in a hilly region sixteen kilometers from the city near the main road running east. He relocated the family there and attempted to grow cash crops such as mongo beans and corn. In 1965 their water buffalo was stolen and the family, unable to replace it or to support themselves solely on the farm without it, moved back to the city. There, Kasan's mother again worked as a vendor while his father continued to work his land as best he could, traveling back and forth to the farm. In 1970 their house at the farm site was burned by the Ilaga.

That same year, Kasan began studies at the local college on a scholarship. At school he heard of secret military training for Muslim separatists in Malaysia. He planned to take part but could not afford the required travel expenses. In 1971 he eloped with a young woman from the city—a Christian who subsequently converted to Islam. His parents were at first bitterly opposed. They had a Muslim girl in mind for him, he knew, but he doubted he could ever afford the bridewealth payment.

The couple struggled their first year together. They lived in a Muslim community near the public market. While his wife worked sewing

buttons for a tailor, Kasan parlayed twelve pesos into seventy-five pesos of trading capital by selling first cigarettes and later chickens on
the street in front of the public market. With that stake he was able to
begin buying and selling vegetables. He also managed to attend college
until martial law was declared in late 1972.

Kasan did not join the fighters when the rebellion began a few
weeks later because he was by then a father. He did at one point use
his knowledge—acquired from two years of ROTC training—to assist
in the training of a contingent of rebels just outside the city. The rebellion, and the military occupation of the city, altered the character of
Muslim marketing in the city. After the army closed the river systems
to civilian traffic, Muslim farmers were unable to bring their products
to market or easily obtain city goods. They became willing to sell their
goods very cheaply or even barter them for such needed items as salt,
sugar, and cigarettes. City residents, on the other hand, were willing to
pay more for scarce produce, often not bothering even to bargain out
of the haste created by their concern to avoid the daily army patrols at
the public market. Good returns were thus available for those Muslims
willing to take great risks by disregarding the military's ban on river
travel in order to place upriver goods for sale in the city market. The
following is Kasan's account of those days: "When the military closed
the upriver areas to the city, we middlemen would have to sneak out of
the city to obtain goods, traveling by foot or in small boats. I would return to the city with as many as thirty chickens and ducks and three
goats. I was fired at by army helicopters patrolling the river. I would
leave the goods in the open and hide and come back for them. If you
were caught by military patrols they would beat you and steal your
goods. But it was the only way for middlemen to survive."

Kasan and his family moved to Campo Muslim in 1974, after much
of the neighborhood where they had been living near the public market
was destroyed in a single night by a fire started by military gunfire.
The public market neighborhood before the fire was divided into Muslim and Christian halves with a single barangay captain who was a
Christian.[1] In late 1973, a Civilian Home Defense Force (CHDF) detachment composed exclusively of Ilonggos was stationed at the public
market area,[2] and began to harass Muslim residents. On this particular
night, the CHDF detachment fired a single shot into the Muslim neighborhood. The regular army infantry battalion across the river, mistak-
enly believing that the shot was directed at them from the Muslim
neighborhood, opened fire on the neighborhood, a barrage that continued for most of the night. It took Kasan and his family five hours to

crawl two hundred meters to safety. The resulting fire destroyed a great number of houses in the Muslim neighborhood.

The military attack and fire had finally made life in the public market area unendurable for Muslim residents, and many of them, more than one hundred families, moved within the next few weeks to Campo Muslim, seeking a safer place to live. Those evacuees whose houses were still standing sold them "for pennies" to Christians. Campo Muslim was an undeveloped swamp far from their places of work but it was the only area in the city proper with a Muslim barangay captain, one who they hoped might be able to protect them from the deadly harassment of the Philippine military.

Kasan moved to Campo Muslim in the company of most of his neighbors. What they found was a marsh with water waist-high in parts. They used a convenient pile of garbage to begin to fill the swamp. Those who could afford them bought mollusk shells for additional landfill for their homesites. The evacuees brought wood salvaged from the destroyed houses in the public market community to build their first homes in Campo Muslim. They also began to pay land rent immediately to the owner of the property—five pesos (approximately U.S. twenty-five cents) per month.

THE CASE OF IMAM AKMAD

Imam Akmad is the chief imam (prayer leader) of the Campo Muslim mosque. A man of about fifty years of age in 1986, he and his wife are the parents of eight children. Imam Akmad was born in Kalanganan, just a few miles west of Campo Muslim.[3] He is also an Iranun speaker. Imam Akmad's father, whom he never knew, was a colorful character, and I was told many stories of his exploits as an aristocratic gambler and adventurer. The father of Imam Akmad was the first cousin of the Amirul Umra Sa Magindanao, the noble titleholder who ruled the district of Kalanganan.[4] Because of this kin relation, he possessed some tribute rights over land in Kalanganan and elsewhere. Imam Akmad related to me the following about his father: "I was told by my father's old friend, the Sultan sa Nunungan [in Lanao] that my father had more than twenty wives living along the shores of Ilana Bay from Bongo Island to Malabang, and others in Lanao and Sulu. My father would marry a woman, leave her with child and some means of support for a year or so, and move on. He returned once to my mother's house to claim me when I was three years old, but my mother hid me under a basket when she saw my father approaching." Akmad's father roamed throughout the South evading marital commitments and gambling debts. He fought and won numerous duels and performed many supernatural feats in his travels. "My father possessed many mystical powers. He was able to repel blades and bullets and could travel in mysterious ways. He would sometimes tell a companion to go ahead to a certain place and he would meet him there later. When the companion reached the appointed spot my father was already there and seated."

Imam Akmad's mother farmed her parents' land dressed like a man, wearing trousers and bolo (bush knife), to support her son. Akmad was also reared by his mother's brother, a guru, or traditional religious instructor. His uncle taught Akmad to recite the *Azan* (call to prayer) and to read the Qur'an. Akmad's vocation as an imam developed gradually. He farmed as a young man. After he married, he moved to Cotabato City to the house of his wife's father, a fairly prosperous smuggler, and went to work for him delivering cigarettes throughout Cotabato. He first served as an imam at the mosque in Katuli, a Muslim community directly across the river from Cotabato City. When the first mosque was built on Bird Island in 1968, he was asked to become the head imam there. After Bird Island was demolished in 1970, Akmad moved his family to Sulun, north of the city, to farm the land of his wife's mother.

In 1973, some of the earliest fighting of the rebellion in Cotabato broke out in Sulun, compelling Imam Akmad to move with his family to Campo Muslim. Campo Muslim was still rather sparsely settled in 1973, and Akmad was able to buy a small house close to the main road through the community—a road that had been built up with sand taken from Bird Island. They enlarged the house as the family grew. Akmad became head imam of the Campo Muslim mosque, a small concrete block structure with a tin roof. It was squat and unadorned but sturdier than most of the houses in the community.

PATTERNS OF IMMIGRATION TO CAMPO MUSLIM

The migration histories of the families of Kasan Kamid and Imam Akmad provide qualitative context for the quantitative census data I collected on migration to Campo Muslim. Nearly half (47.3 percent) of current Campo Muslim household heads moved to the community before 1976. The great majority of those arrived in the years between

1970 and 1976, the period when political violence was most pronounced in Cotabato. In contrast to Kasan Kamid and Imam Akmad, the majority of pre-1976 arrivals (63.8 percent) moved to Campo Muslim directly from their birthplaces. Of the eighty individuals who moved directly to Campo Muslim from birthplaces outside the city prior to 1976, thirty-four (42.5 percent) left their rural communities as refugees from either sectarian violence or the Bangsamoro war. Forty (50 percent) moved to the city for economic reasons. The great majority (89 percent) of all pre-1976 arrivals to Campo Muslim reported that they chose to reside in that community because they already had relatives living there (28 percent), or because it was the safest, most convenient, or only available place to live (61 percent). Census data indicate that Campo Muslim grew together from its edges. The areas nearest the two already established communities were occupied first, often before 1970. The swampier inner portions were then taken up by later arrivals.

Campo Muslim, then, has never been a community made up entirely—or even primarily—of war refugees. It is, nevertheless, an urban refugee community to the extent that the great majority of its pre-1976 arrivals (93 percent) migrated to the city to escape political or economic problems in the countryside. In particular, 63.3 percent of pre-1976 immigrants were farmers forced, for one reason or another, from the land. All the same, Campo Muslim is not a community of landless cultivators. Some 32 percent of pre-1976 arrivals reported that they "owned" agricultural land.[5] Thus, many Campo Muslim residents had rights in land but had (temporarily or permanently) abandoned that land either because they could not make a living from it or, as in the cases of Kasan Kamid and Imam Akmad, conditions became far too dangerous to continue to support themselves on it.

THE WAR IN CAMPO MUSLIM

This section relates how Campo Muslim residents endured the military occupation of their community during the Bangsamoro Rebellion. It is a story assembled from many days and nights spent recording reminiscences that were often animated and anguished in equal measure.

Many of the early migrants to Campo Muslim came in search of a safe haven from the depredations of the Ilaga or the abuses of the Philippine Army. On their arrival in the community, however, they found that those leaders who seemed likely sources for protection were either ineffective or uninterested. The barangay captain, Datu Kamsa, cooperated with the martial law regime and made no effort to shield community residents from the army. When army intimidation of community members intensified he left the city to visit his land in the countryside. Campo Muslim residents also remember him for humiliating and abusing new arrivals to the community, particularly war refugees from upriver.

Even had he been willing, it is unlikely that Datu Kamsa could have protected Campo Muslim residents from the army. The full military occupation of Cotabato City established in late 1973 stripped virtually all nonmilitary authorities, Muslim and Christian, of any effective power. The military ejected the Christian mayor of the city, Teodoro Juliano, from office and jailed him for three years for too strenuously protesting the usurpation of his mayoral powers. Local datus were quite fearful of the military and attempted to maintain low profiles. Even prominent datus such as the Sinsuats, closely aligned with the Marcos government, had little sway with military authorities; they bestowed honorary titles and awards on local commanders in an attempt to gain some influence with them. Campo Muslim residents remember that, at the time, datus did not wish to be called by that title in public, and hadjis (those who had made the pilgrimage to Mecca) no longer wore their distinctive white caps for fear of attracting persecution by soldiers. Islamic clerics in the city were particular targets of abuse because the Philippine military assumed them to be the instigators of the rebellion. They too could not publicly defend other Muslims.

While rebel units often prevailed in armed skirmishes with the Philippine military, they were usually not available to protect Muslim civilians. In a pattern typical of guerrilla warfare, the very success of the rebels at harassing and eluding government soldiers invited often severe army retaliations against Muslim civilians. Such reprisals led many rural Muslims to flee to the city only to face further repression at the hands of the army in the urban communities where they had resettled.

Active rebel fighters stayed in Campo Muslim during the rebellion but always in small numbers and on a temporary basis. The city was an exceedingly dangerous place for insurgents. They faced the continual risks of being stopped at a checkpoint or detained in one of the frequent military lineups. Identification by a government informant in such a lineup often resulted in summary execution at local military command posts. Consequently, rebels in the city more often relied on the protection of community residents than they provided protection to them.

By 1974, the section of the city that included Campo Muslim had come under direct military occupation. The army situated a military detachment on the riverside road in Lugay-lugay and established a checkpoint on the same road at Manday and another on the Manday bridge leading to the center of the city. In Campo Muslim itself, the army ordered signs to be posted on each house listing the names of all permanent residents. Visitors were required to register with the barangay captain. Community residents tell of being repeatedly accosted at the army checkpoints by soldiers who were often drunk and abusive. Because of the difficulty of traveling back and forth to the center of town after dark—and as an adaptation to the 10 P.M. to 4 A.M. military curfew—Campo Muslim residents started a night market in late 1974 where cooked food and other items could be purchased. When the barangay captain noticed the popularity of the market he built sturdier stalls on the lot, installed electricity, and began to charge rent to vendors.

The military occupation became more menacing for community residents following an incident early in 1975. Soldiers had apprehended two suspected rebels in the center of the city and were bringing them to the detachment at Lugay-lugay, apparently to execute them unofficially (described in the Philippine idiom as "salvaging"). Summary executions were reportedly common at the Lugay-lugay post. I was told that soldiers regularly shoved rebel suspects into the river, ordered them to swim and then shot them in the water. Such killings were officially reported as consequences of escape attempts. The two detainees, presumably aware of the fate that awaited them, struggled with their captors on the road in front of Campo Muslim, seized one of their guns and shot them before fleeing into the community. That night a platoon of soldiers entered Campo Muslim, firing into the air and at houses. The soldiers ordered the men of the community out of their houses then beat and abused them for most of the night. Residents still believe a massacre was avoided only because of the arrival of a Muslim army officer who took pity on the men and called off the soldiers.

On subsequent nights, and for months afterward, the military conducted regular "operations" in Campo Muslim. These sweeps usually occurred late at night but there were sometimes as many as three in a twenty-four-hour period, carried out by three different army units. In some of the operations the men of the community were made to file in front of an armored personnel carrier from which an unseen informer would view them, pointing out the rebels among them. Those identified as rebels were taken away and frequently not seen alive again. At other times, all the men in the community would be loaded onto trucks and taken to military headquarters on the other side of the city to be viewed by informers. Those released would then walk home. Occasionally, soldiers brought informers, their heads covered by masks, to the night market to point out rebels. Soldiers sometimes marked residents' hands with a rubber stamp if they had been cleared by an informer. The men of the community endeavored by various means to maintain those ink marks for as long as possible, even eating with spoons rather than with their hands in the usual manner.

Community residents received a respite from military raids when the rebel commander Peping Candao surrendered later that year with his fighters. In the last weeks of 1975, Candao's men were reconstituted into a CHDF unit and assigned to man the checkpoints in the Campo Muslim area, including the one at Manday Bridge controlling access to the community. Army units now required the cooperation of Candao's men to enter Campo Muslim. In this manner, the rebel defectors formed a protective buffer between the military and community residents.[6] Military operations were greatly reduced and daily molestations by soldiers in the area were virtually eliminated. In addition, the returnees patrolled the community, punishing thieves and disciplining anyone found drunk in public.

Prominent rebel defectors who acted as protectors of Muslims were found in other localities as well. Shortly after the surrender of Peping Candao, Commander Jack, a picaresque urban outlaw turned rebel, negotiated his own surrender and he and his men began defending Muslims in the public market neighborhood. Jack's surrender was notable for its terms. As he states them today, he and his men (more than three hundred of them surrendered) were allowed to keep all their weapons and occupy the public market neighborhood. The military in the area were to be confined to within ten meters of their barracks and any military operations in the area had to be coordinated with him. The only condition he recalls being placed on him was that he try to convince other rebels to surrender. For more than a year, Commander Jack and his men comprised an independent armed force in the center of the city, keeping the peace, protecting Muslim civilians and, on multiple occasions, openly battling government troops that attempted to regain control of their zone. In late 1976, Commander Jack was captured by ruse and imprisoned for eleven months.[7] In early 1976, another commander, Tocao Mastura, surrendered and received as compensation the mayorship of the municipality of Nuling, just north of the city. He maintained his own CHDF unit of rebel returnees that also effectively insulated Nuling residents from army incursions.

Residents recall that conditions in Campo Muslim and the city actually worsened somewhat after the cease-fire in early 1977 as a consequence of three factors. First, the number of rebel defectors in the city increased dramatically after the cease-fire. Almost all were armed and most had not received the allowances promised them. Payments anticipated by defectors were often never dispensed to them by the government, or, if disbursed, were either soon cut off or retained by their former commanders. Those more larcenous among the returnees took up extortion and kidnapping to earn money (some among them had left that sort of work to become rebels). Kidnappings of members of wealthy families became a regular occurrence in the city, sometimes instigated by Christians who hired returnees to carry them out. Poor Muslims, however, suffered most regularly from the extortions of the former rebels. Community residents tell the story of one notorious returnee who stood at a busy street corner in the Muslim quarter of the city with a half coconut shell at his feet and a pair of .45 caliber automatic pistols in his belt. Only when the shell was filled with money by passersby would he retire to a nearby beer hall. Another former rebel operated a protection racket exacting payments from Muslim pedicab drivers. A nonextortionary form of intimidation, but one equally disturbing to urban Muslims, was practiced by a certain returnee who accosted young Muslim women dressed in snug-fitting jeans at the public market and forced them at gunpoint to remove their jeans and proclaim themselves prostitutes for having worn them. Public outcry eventually ended these public humiliations, probably by means of a warning from active rebels.

Second, after the cease-fire was broken by the government in late 1977, the war took on a form that, while less intense, was more injurious for urban noncombatants. From 1978 till 1980, fighting centered on the city more than ever before, making the streets of the Muslim districts especially hazardous as urban assassins and terrorists took over the conduct of the war. The military had developed special intelligence units (known as "U2" units), composed mostly of recruited rebel defectors. These operated as murder squads—targeting other returnees who had turned to crime or, more typically, active rebels in the city who had been identified by informers. Urban rebels retaliated against informants and members of murder squads. The rise in urban violence was not limited to political killings. Old feuds were reactivated as private antagonists began to settle long-deferred private scores, and crime-related homicides increased as military control was eased somewhat in the city. The assailants in most of these killings attacked their targets on busy public streets, using automatic rifles or, occasionally, hand grenades. The victims left in their wake were as often accidental as intended. Urban terror bombings, which began in 1975 and continued well into the 1980s, added to the distress of the public assassinations. Grenades were thrown into movie theaters, parades, or public gatherings, and although they most often had the appearance of being the work of Muslim rebels, the majority of their victims were ordinary Muslims.[8]

Third, life in Campo Muslim itself became more difficult after the cease-fire agreement. Shortly after the start of the cease-fire, the men of Peping Candao were transferred from the Campo Muslim area and the checkpoints were again manned by regular army troops. The military resumed and intensified regular lineup operations in Campo Muslim. Soldiers again assembled, abused, and sometimes arrested male residents. Some measure of protection against this second wave of military harassment came from another unlikely source.

On August 17, 1976, a powerful earthquake struck Cotabato, damaging a number of buildings in the city and destroying many homes in Campo Muslim. The tsunami that followed devastated Muslim coastal communities and forced many evacuees to resettle temporarily in Campo Muslim. Shortly after the earthquake, two Filipino Catholic nuns, members of a religious order active in the province, settled in Campo Muslim in order to aid earthquake victims. With the permission of the barangay captain they built a small house in the center of the community and began distributing food and medicine. The sisters remained in the community even after the immediate needs of the evacuees were met, providing medicines and rudimentary health care to community members. They met a good deal of resistance from community members who were suspicious and resentful of the continuing presence of representatives of the Catholic Church in this Muslim community. One of the nuns, Sister Theresa, soon began to supplement her provision of health services by actively defending the young men in the community from military harassment. She used her special status and her ties to some army commanders to limit the number of raids and to protect the rights of the arrested. Through this work she gained the trust of a number of community members and began to train some of the young men, including Kasan Kamid, in community organizing. By 1979 she had established a growing community action program that included nutritional assessments, aid distribution, cooperative stores, and the monitoring of military detention cases. Through its sponsorship of Sister Theresa, the local Catholic diocese had become, by 1980, the principal provider of social and protective services in the community.

THE WAR FROM CAMPO MUSLIM

From my conversations with Campo Muslim residents I received, in addition to the picture of the war as it occurred in their community, a broad depiction of the Bangsamoro Rebellion as experienced by ordinary Muslims. The most recurrent image presented in these accounts was one of acute loss. When residents remembered the war, they rarely emphasized their personal afflictions, instead matter-of-factly cataloguing the damage wrought by the conflagration that swept over them. The composite story, however, was a chronicle of immense suffering and devastation. Nearly every resident I spoke with had lost a close relative and many mourned more than one family member killed in the fighting. Most had been driven from their land, often after their homes and livestock had been destroyed. In 1985 I met numerous farmers who had yet to replace draft animals shot or stolen during the war. I heard of other farmers who, having returned to farm their land after the cease-fire, were killed by roving bandits or, in some cases, by unexploded ordnance.

Almost all families had lost valuable family heirlooms (*pusaka*), most often gold jewelry, but also brass pieces, antique porcelain jars, decorated chests, swords, and fine textiles. These treasured items, many of which were important ritual items in traditional celebrations, were either stolen by the military or sold to meet the subsistence needs of war refugees. They had been held in families for generations but are now rarely seen among ordinary Muslims in Cotabato. In addition to losing homes and loved ones, many Campo Muslim residents were thus also culturally impoverished as a result of the war, having lost key heirloom items that served as material representations of cherished cultural traditions.

The severe losses described by Muslim noncombatants, together with the casualties suffered by rank-and-file rebels, provoke the questions addressed in this section: how did ordinary Muslims understand this costly struggle? What was their primary impetus for joining or supporting the rebels? To what extent were the key symbols and goals of Muslim nationalist ideologues shared by rank-and-file fighters and supporters? In what follows, I focus first on the experiences of rank-and-file insurgents and on the unofficial songs that expressed their sentiments about the rebellion. I then consider the understandings of ordinary Muslim civilians and especially the magical stories that voiced both their support for the rebellion as well as their dissent from official Muslim separatist rhetoric. Together, these unauthorized narratives demonstrate the remarkable degree to which the experiences, interpretations, and motivations of the ordinary fighters differed from those of movement leaders.

THE EXPERIENCES OF RANK-AND-FILE INSURGENTS

Among the Campo Muslim residents (and their friends and relatives) who spoke with me about the rebellion, a number were former or current insurgents. It became clear from our conversations that certain motivations and sentiments were strongly shared among all of them. Not surprisingly, all the fighters expressed enmity toward the martial law regime and a desire to be free of its rule. Virtually all of them reported that they had joined the rebellion to defend themselves and their families against the Philippine government. Some also expressed a desire to protect Philippine Muslims and the Islamic faith against attack. With five of the former combatants I also conducted detailed interviews concerning their wartime experiences. Four of them had joined the armed resistance in 1971 or 1972, before the declaration of martial law, in order to defend themselves and other Muslims against the Ilaga and the military. The following quotes from two of the former fighters are typical: "The rise of the Ilaga caused young Muslims such as me to join the front to defend the people as fighters, to protect the people and Islam": "I joined because of the violence created by the Ilaga; because there was no place safe during the trouble at that time." The fifth fighter, a local commander, joined the rebels immediately after the declaration of martial law for reasons somewhat more particular: "I was an enlisted man in the army in the late 1960s. When my enlistment was up I went to college. But when martial law was declared I was called up again—required to reenlist—even though I had been disqualified more than once because of illness. Still, they accused me of being AWOL, so I went to the mountains [and joined the rebels]."

Rebel fighters, in general, were very young, mostly fifteen to twenty-five year olds. Two of the fighters I interviewed enlisted as teenagers (fifteen and sixteen years old) and two others joined in their very early twenties. The last fighter, Nasser, was twelve years old when he joined the rebels in 1972. As he remembers, "I was the youngest in my squad. I wore short pants, even into combat."

Each of these fighters received some sort of formal training, those who joined earlier being trained multiple times. Nasser, who received the most training, was trained five separate times, gaining instruction in armed combat, jungle survival, and treatment of civilians, as well as political instruction in "strong resistance." Muslim clerics figured significantly in the armed separatist leadership in Cotabato in the 1980s and some had substantial roles during the war as well. The fighters I talked to had different amounts of contact with clerics, as suggested in the remembrances of two fighters: "There were no *ustadzes* [Islamic teachers] in our camp. The only ustadz I knew was Kudin, who was also a rebel but not a commander"; "The *ulama* [clerics] supported the rebels through education. They also joined the combatants. Ustadz Kusain was the chaplain of my zone. Ustadz Hassan was a member of the general staff. He was a commander and a companion of Hashim Salamat, a graduate of al-Azhar and a one-time military trainee in Syria." All the fighters interviewed reported receiving support from Muslim noncombatants: "The Muslim populace supported the rebels 100 percent. Often money given to the people by the government was given by them to us"; "We supported ourselves through contributions from civilians, including businessmen. This supplemented what we received from abroad." Each of the fighters, as recorded in the following five quotes, recalled the hardships and losses that they, their companions, and Cotabato Muslims in general suffered; they also remembered the exhilaration of struggling, and often prevailing, against great odds:

> Military operations in my zone started in 1973. There were air attacks and artillery. There were also tanks and napalm and helicopters. But many soldiers died. The army only controlled the areas within the poblacions [towns proper]. There were many abuses by soldiers: they raped and murdered civilians; they looted and destroyed houses, mosques, and schools. The army even declared Pagalungan and Carmen municipalities no-man's lands [free-fire zones].

I took part in three battles in Sulun. The first lasted one day, the second lasted seven days, and the third lasted twenty-nine days. There were only one hundred men against three battalions of the AFP (Armed Forces of the Philippines) with air and sea support. We had only seventy guns. Some were homemade. We had no M16s, only Garands and BARs [Browning automatic rifles]. My young fighters were very brave. They were angry if they couldn't fight. They regarded the war almost as if it were a game.

The second battle I took part in was in Biniruan, close to the city. The army used tanks and battalions of troops. We lost one dead and two wounded. Many soldiers were killed. Our commander waited until the soldiers were very close to us, not much more than five meters, until he gave the order to fire. That was to make sure we could kill the soldiers.

We suffered injuries and deaths at every fight. In my first battle we had thirty casualties because we were ambushed by the military while marching. We were on our way to reinforce our comrades in Midsayap when we were ambushed. The ambush was actually an accident because we were passing on parallel paths. We retreated into the forest. Two of my friends were killed. Many soldiers were killed in every encounter.

I fought at Tran in 1973. There were only thirty of us fighters, but many civilians. They had been abandoned by Datu Guiwan Mastura when he surrendered and went to Manila. He was not a true rebel. The government used jets against us and many civilians died. The army was only able to capture civilians there, and those they captured they abused . . . My father, brother and sister were killed by the army.

None of the five fighters I spoke with ever surrendered officially to the government. Two remained under arms in rebel encampments. The other three considered themselves inactive rebels, having returned from the hills and forests to civilian life but willing to take up arms again should the need arise. Each of the three returnees left the rebel ranks after the cease-fire. One returned home because his commander went home. Nasser, the youngest, went back to civilian life to attend high school. Those who remained under arms bore no ill will toward those who returned home. Instead, they considered them inactive reserves in the continuing struggle. They were even sparing in their criticism of those commanders and followers who surrendered early to the government and received compensation, remarking only that they "lacked determination." This remarkably tolerant stance toward early rebel defectors contrasts with official pronouncements by the separatist leadership and indicates both a divergence from official attitudes and an appreciation for the political (and moral) complexities of a largely defensive insurgency. Additional evidence for the independent perceptions of rank-and-file rebels is found in the unofficial songs composed and performed in rebel camps.

RANK-AND-FILE PERSPECTIVES:
REBEL SONGS IN CAMPO MUSLIM

A number of the political idioms that the rank-and-file fighters employed (in some cases self-consciously) in our conversations were identical to those advanced by rebel leaders. At the same time, it was striking to note how rarely any of the insurgents, in expressing their motivations for taking up arms or fighting on against great odds, made spontaneous mention of either the Moro nation (Bangsamoro) or Islamic renewal, the two central components of Muslim nationalist ideology.[9] Direct interviews were not my primary means for discovering rank-and-file perceptions of the ethnonational rebellion. A richer source of information was the songs and stories of the rebellion that community residents shared with one another and repeated to me. Those narratives reinforced the impressions gained from interviews that unofficial understandings of the rebellion were not congruent with its official ideology.

One night in Campo Muslim I happened upon a performance of rebel songs in the house of Kasan Kamid. His elder brother was visiting on a short leave from his overseas job in Saudi Arabia and had arranged to make a recording of a performance to take back with him. I added my tape recorder, and over two nights I recorded almost three hours of songs performed by a young man with a splendid voice and a battered guitar.

I later heard some of the same songs performed in a variety of public settings: at political rallies, on Muslim radio shows, and on jukeboxes in Muslim coffeehouses throughout the city. Most of the songs had been composed between 1973 and 1977 (the period of the armed rebellion) by three renowned singers. All three were rank-and-file insurgents from lower-class backgrounds. One of the three was killed during the fighting. The other two became well-known after the ceasefire in 1977, when they began to perform the songs in public. Before 1977, they were sung almost exclusively in rebel camps to fighters. The man whose performance I recorded is an illiterate dockworker. Too young to have fought in the armed rebellion, he is a second-generation singer who was taught the songs by the most active of the original composers.

Rebel songs comprise a new and distinct genre of Muslim popular music. The songs share Western harmonic features and a common topical content, with all lyrics addressing some aspect of the armed rebellion. While traditional phrasings are occasionally present, all the songs exhibit a modern lyrical style. Some, especially those songs concerned with forced separations or unrequited love, are variations on a novel song form popular in the years prior to the rebellion. From the mid-1950s, local singers had put Magindanaon lyrics to the melodies of popular Filipino love songs heard on the radio (whose original lyrics were in Tagalog, Visayan, or English).[10] These adaptations, especially popular among teenagers (Wein 1985), differed in lyrical style from traditional love ballads, which are distinguished by the obliquity of their metaphors. The new ballads are, by contrast, notable for their directness of expression. Rebel singers used these popular love songs as the basis for many of their ballads.

Other rebel songs, usually up-tempo, inspirational pieces, borrow motifs and melodies from contemporaneous Filipino or American popular music. The following song, "Mana Silan Cowboy" ("They Are Like Cowboys"), is sung to the melody of Glenn Campbell's 1975 American hit record "Rhinestone Cowboy."[11]

Nineteen seventy-one
taman ku seventy-nine,
entu ba su lagun mayaw
pan su rebolusyon
siya kanu embala-bala
a inged u mga Moro.
Guden makating-guma
su Paminasakan.

Natadin su mga manguda,
lu silan natimu u damakayu.
Mana silan cowboy,
di magilek masabil.
Mawasa, mamala;
ulanan a sinangan
kanu mga lalan.
Namba su paninindeg.

From nineteen seventy-one
until nineteen seventy-nine,
those were the years when the
revolution was raging
throughout all the different
communities of the Moros.

It was the time when the
Destroyer had come among us.

The young men at first were scattered, but they gathered together deep in
    the forest.
They are like cowboys,
unafraid to be martyred.
[They fight] wet or dry;
they are soaked by the rain and scorched by the sun along the way.
These are the revolutionaries.[12]

While putting Magindanaon lyrics to nonindigenous melodies is certainly not a new undertaking (it may be traced to the late American period), the combination of melodies, lyrics, and topics found in rebel
songs does constitute a distinct popular genre that offers a source of
grassroots expressions of support for the armed separatist struggle. As
noted above, the songs are of two types. The majority are ballads of
separation or loss, lamenting loved ones left behind by rebels gone to
fight in the forest. The rest, as with "Mana Silan Cowboy," are patri-
otic songs, glorifying the struggle and extolling the virtues of the fighters and their commanders. The following introductory stanzas from
two songs exemplify each type:

Song 1

Manguda a inendan sangat
I kamiskin nin.
Uway den u inendan
paninindeg ku inged,
Jihad pi Sabilillah.
Ayag tig i inendan,
sekami a paninindeg pimbulugan sa limu
na inenggan sa tademan.
Tademan di lipatan.

Uway den u inendan na
rasay rumasay kami
sa hadapan sa Kadenan
ka Jihad pi Sabilillah
taman den sa kapatay.
O seka papedtayan na
pamimikilan ka den.

The young man whom you rejected
was a poor man, it's true.
But now he's fighting for the homeland
and offering his life
in the struggle for the faith.

I whom you rejected say to you,
that we the fighters are shown mercy and are given recognition,
given recognition that will
never be forgotten.

Yes, you've refused me, it's true.
Yet we fighters suffer hardship
till we stand before our God;
we will sacrifice ourselves
for the sake of our religion
until the day we die.
Oh my beloved, please consider this.

Song 2

Aden maulad a lupa
a gadung a pedsandengen
na san bun ba i dalepa ni Hadji Murad.
Pagagayan, panandeng, ka pamagayanan nilan
i sundalo a pagukit ka di nilan kalininyan
madala su Agama.

Ka duwan nengka den, Marcos
ka di ka den makandatu ka inagawan
ka nilan ku bangku nengka matilak
bangunan sa Mindanao.

Behold in the distance
a wide green land.
That land is the abode
of Hadji Murad.
[The fighters] lie in wait
for the soldiers to approach,
for they never will allow
their religion to be lost.

Oh Marcos, you are pitiful
for you can no longer rule here.
They have seized from you
your splendid throne,
the realm of Mindanao.

These two sets of lyrics, typical of the discourse found in rebel songs, are revealing both for what they voice and do not voice about the objectives of the rebellion. Song 1 combines the themes of romantic redemption and religious struggle as a rejected suitor seeks to convince the woman for whom he yearns that the rebellion has introduced new standards of worthiness. It expresses in its opening lines a significant independent incentive for taking part in the rebellion: fighting as a perceived avenue for poor men of low status to improve their relative social standing. As nearly all rank-and-file insurgents were drawn from subordinate classes, the composer, in framing this ballad as a poor man's entreaty, gives voice to social resentments and aspirations broadly shared by his principal audience.

Two central concepts found in most of the rebel songs—"inged" (community or homeland) and "jihad" (struggle in defense of the faith)—are textually coupled in the first song.[13] The inged is the socio-cultural entity in need of defense. As a term referring to any sociopolit-ical collectivity larger than that found at a single residence site, "inged" is usually glossed as "settlement" or "community" but may also be used to refer more broadly to a "homeland." Though both terms reference political entities, "inged" and "bangsa" possess quite different connotative meanings. "Bangsa" may be glossed as "coun-try," "nation," "race," "ethnic group," or "tribe" (Fleischman et al. 1981, 10). As used in the term "Bangsamoro," "bangsa" describes an imagined community—an ethnic *nation*. "Inged," on the contrary, de-notes a familiar, territorially bounded, and, often, face-to-face commu-nity. In none of the rebel songs I recorded (some in multiple versions) did the terms "bangsa" or "Bangsamoro" ever occur. "Moro" appears only once, in the song "Mana Silan Cowboy" in conjunction with "inged" in a phrase referring to the geographical extent of the rebel-lion, which is said to be raging "siya kanu embala-bala a inged u mga Moro" (in all the different ingeds of the Philippine Muslims). While fighting for the inged is not alternative to fighting for the nation (bangsa), neither is it simply a subjacent goal. If it were, one would ex-pect at least an occasional reference to the "bangsa" that has sub-sumed the various ingeds. These are not found in the songs, nor were they heard to any measurable degree in the many private and public conversations I had with rank-and-file fighters or their civilian sup-porters. Fighting for the inged is a collateral goal—one conceptually distinct from the nationalist project but germane to it.

In song 1, "inged" and "jihad" are thematically linked: the commu-nity being defended is the indigenous community of the faithful. Song 2 extends this theme. There, the inged to be protected is the homeland of Cotabato Muslims.[14] In these lyrics, Cotabato is represented as the *dalepa,* or occupied territory, of Hadji Murad, the commander of the Cotabato rebels. The rebels have repulsed Ferdinand Marcos the in-vader (signified in the song "Mana Silan Cowboy" as "the Destroyer") and recovered from him his *bangunan,* the territory ruled by him in

Muslim Mindanao. The rebels are ready to repel all military counterattacks in order to preserve their religion. This second song expresses the fighters' particular notion of jihad—armed resistance to the specific aggressive actions of the martial law state, personified by Marcos. For rank-and-file rebels, struggle in defense of Islam was coincident with armed defense of cultural tradition, property, livelihood, and life. In this song as in the first, those sentiments are expressed in the language of locality and territoriality—"lupa" (land), "dalepa" (occupied territory), and "bangunan" (realm)—rather than in terms of nationality.

DIVINE MERCY AND DIVERGENT EVALUATIONS: THE REBELLION ACCORDING TO ITS ORDINARY ADHERENTS

What of the understandings of ordinary Muslim civilians, nearly all of whom supported the rebels during the insurgency in Cotabato? The official ideology of the Muslim separatist movement was not widely disseminated to non-elite Muslim civilians during the armed phase of the rebellion. Rebel ideologues were in self-imposed exile abroad, and Campo Muslim residents told me they possessed little or no knowledge of rebel leaders beyond the level of local commanders until after the first cease-fire in 1977. Even after the cease-fire, when key separatist symbols were more effectively presented to the Muslim populace, they did not readily take hold. The residents of Campo Muslim were generally familiar with the nationalist rhetoric of the rebellion, but even after years of appeals to Bangsamoro nationhood continued to denominate themselves either as "Muslims," which was also the term used by local Christians to refer to them, or by the name of their particular ethnolinguistic group, rather than identify themselves as "Moros."

Muslim civilians did identify strongly with rebel fighters during the insurgency, viewing them as their primary protectors from the murderous hostility of the military. A rebel commander remarked to me that early in the rebellion Muslim civilians provided little support to the insurgents but that the depredations of the Philippine military quickly gained adherents for the rebel cause.[15] He added that other factors intensified support for the insurgency: "The government caused the masses to support the rebels, especially after the Ilaga were formed into CHDF units. When the government realized the damaging effect of that decision, they organized Muslim CHDF units, but ten men would only receive two guns. Most datus, however, were afraid to support the rebels."

As the government's campaign against Muslim insurgents intensified, military attacks on Muslim civilians multiplied, further alienating
ordinary Muslims from the Philippine state and solidifying their identification with the rebellion.[16] Popular support for the rebels was expressed symbolically in popular narratives of the divine mercy shown
to rebels. In accord with cultural practices widespread in Southeast
Asian warfare, individual rebel fighters sought magical powers—especially invulnerability to blades and bullets—through the use of spells,
amulets, and other manifestations of esoteric knowledge (see Bowen
1993; Kiefer 1972; Reid 1988).[17] Distinguishable from these individual acquisitions of magical protection was the popular belief in divine mercy (*limu a Kadenan*) bestowed collectively on all rebel fighters
(expressed in the first verse of song 1 above).

Divine mercy was most often manifested as supernatural assistance
received from local spirits. Popular narratives relate how government
boats were overturned and attacking soldiers devoured by spirit crocodiles. These *pagali* (literally, relatives)—ancestor spirits who appear in
the form of crocodiles—were described for me by a Campo Muslim
resident in the following account: "The pagali are large crocodiles with
bands of yellow around their necks. In times past, people would place
food on the riverbanks as offerings to petition them for favors. These
stories are hundreds of years old, but we have proof that these spirit
crocodiles still exist because they assisted the fighters during the rebellion. Once, in fact, when a carnival came to Cotabato City during the
war, the government soldiers arrived and shot all the crocodiles on display there."

The most frequently reported instance of supernatural assistance
was that received from a class of spirits known as *tunggu a inged*, or
Guardians of the Inged. The tunggu a inged may appear as animals,
birds, or even insects but very often take the form of giants (*masela a
mama*—literally, large men) as described in the following narrative:

> The masela a mama are not always visible. They appear only to certain
> people at special times. They live in remote places and stand more than
> fifteen feet tall. Before the coming of Sarip Kabungsuwan [the man who
> brought Islam to Cotabato] they were always visible, but they became
> frightened of him. They said: "His voice is louder than ours." They as-
> sisted our forefathers long before the rebellion. The individual who saw
> one of them would know that something was about to happen—usually
> something bad—and prepare for it. The masela a mama aided the rebels
> during the conflict by guiding them through valleys at night. At other
> times they would create fog so the enemy could not see the rebels. One

day during the war, my uncle, a commander, was sleeping in camp after the midday meal when he woke to see one. He told his men, "We must leave this place." As soon as they had left, artillery shells began to fall on their camp.[18]

These and other unauthorized narratives illustrate how those deemed to be fighting for the inged were afforded divine mercy in the form of supernatural assistance from local spirits, most prominently from the supernatural guardians of the inged.[19]

Unofficial interpretations of the events of the rebellion were also vehicles for ordinary followers to express their approval or disapproval of its developments. For illustration, we may examine the operation of subordinate perspectives in regard to rebel commanders who defected from the separatist cause. Defections were a serious problem for the Cotabato rebel leadership. The martial law regime offered substantial economic and political incentives for rebel commanders to "return to the folds of the law." Stories told by Muslim subordinates recount how some of those defections provoked supernatural sanctions. The following narrative concerns the tribulations of one of the best-known rebel commanders, Disumimba Rashid, after he surrendered to the government for the promise of a large sum of money: "Disumimba was a notorious outlaw who joined the MNLF and became a famous fighter. He possessed the power to transform himself into grass or a tree or an animal. However, many misfortunes befell him after he surrendered: motors on military boats that carried him would fail and tires blew out on trucks in which he rode. He was finally killed a few years ago for unknown reasons." Disumimba's eventual violent death attested to the failure of his protective magic and the withdrawal of divine mercy.

Other prominent defections were evaluated quite differently by ordinary Muslims. The three well-known defecting commanders depicted above—Peping Candao, Commander Jack, and Tocao Mastura—surrendered to the government contemporaneously with Disumimba Rashid, yet none of the them was reported to have suffered any divine retribution and all three remained popular with Muslim subordinates long after their defections. Their contrasting fortunes relate to their postdefection activities. Each was instrumental in insulating poor Muslim communities from many of the daily predations of the Philippine military. Disumimba provided no comparable postdefection services and the popular assessment of his abandonment of the rebellion appears to reflect that fact. Although all four defections were identically injurious to the rebel cause, and the defectors equally condemned by rebel leaders, the estimations of Muslim subordinates centered on a separate set of considerations, most immediately a concern with securing protection from state aggression.

Perhaps the most poignant instance of unauthorized understandings by subordinate adherents concerns a special sort of divine mercy shown to *sabil*, or rebel martyrs, as described in the following account: "Previously, when the fighters were killed, their bodies did not smell bad or decompose, even for one entire week. The bodies exuded a pleasant fragrance. They had the scent of flowers. They were real *mujahideen* (those engaged in a struggle for the faith) who fought and died for Allah." As this passage suggests, these perceptions have a distinct periodicity. At one point in the rebellion this mercy ceased and rebel corpses decomposed just as those of government soldiers. The previous quote continues: "Later, if the rebels fought the soldiers or paramilitaries they would all smell bad; because now it was all just for politics." That perceptual shift on the part of followers demarcated the post-cease-fire period of late-1977 to 1980, a phase of the armed rebellion marked by the urbanization of the war, political infighting between rebel factions, and general confusion and disillusionment. Rebel actions had come to resemble "normal" political activity rather than jihad, and as a result divine mercy had been withdrawn.

The belief in the magical preservation of the corpses of slain rebels was widely shared among rebels and their supporters and was sanctioned by Islamic clerics. Ordinary followers, nonetheless, separately established clear limits to such divine evidence of participation in a righteous struggle. Despite rebel leaders' assertions of the integrity of both the armed struggle and the bodies of recently slain fighters, Muslim subordinates observed only deterioration. That withdrawal of blessing was an expression of their assessment, based on shared experience, of the "normal" political activity of Muslim leaders.

CONCLUSION

The marshbound community of Campo Muslim offers an analytical vantage ground from which to survey the understandings of the ordinary adherents of the Bangsamoro Rebellion. For the greatest part of the period of armed separatist struggle, popular support for the separatist insurgency was substantial in Campo Muslim and throughout Cotabato and was expressed unofficially in songs and stories. Those unauthorized narratives nevertheless reveal that ordinary Muslims' perceptions and representations of the war were often conspicuously independent of the ideological influences of any separatist leaders or, for that matter, of any elite group.

A close reading of the cultural work of the rank-and-file composers of the unofficial songs of the Bangsamoro Rebellion reveals significant variance from its official motives. Song 1 presents the voice of a self-consciously "poor man" who sings of social distance and social rejection before "horizontal comradeship" (Anderson 1983). The song's narrator—a failed suitor turned rebel—unabashedly pursues a separate reward of genuine social recognition (represented by his request for reconsideration by his beloved) in addition to the official cultural recognition as either victor or martyr offered to individual fighters.

The two key unofficial images found in the lyrics of both songs— those of "inged" (community, homeland) and "jihad"—are deeply resonant ones signaling fundamental understandings about community and religious identity. Those terms convey deeply held notions not at odds with those that separatist leaders wished to implicate in their nationalist appeals for the "complete liberation" of the Philippine Muslim "homeland" in order to ensure the preservation of its "Islamic and indigenous culture" (Misuari quoted in Majul 1985, 139). The wide use of "inged" and "jihad" in inspirational rebel songs reflects the power of those mythical concepts to motivate Muslim fighters. They expressed with particular force the fears (of the aggression of the Christian-controlled martial law state) and longings (for an end to domination by hostile outlanders) of ordinary Muslims and provided fuel for separatist military mobilization in Cotabato. Although the cultural knowledge imbedded in those two terms was widely shared, they could nevertheless possess quite different colorings for differentially situated Muslims. In Cotabato, most elite and non-elite adherents shared the view that the Bangsamoro Rebellion was a struggle to preserve the integrity of Muslim communities and defend against Christian hostility. Interpretations diverged, however, at the point of delineating the boundaries of the crucial community and the parameters of religious struggle.[20]

The most commonly endured experience of Muslim subordinates immediately prior to and during the rebellion was terror at the hands of the Philippine military. Their suffering generated a community-based "knowledge of the moment" (Rebel 1989, 362) that conditioned the responses of ordinary Muslims to the nationalist appeals of separatist leaders. The search for protection against external aggression was a powerful impetus for joining or supporting the separatist insurgents and was independently symbolized by subordinates in magical narratives of the bestowal of divine mercy. For Campo Muslim residents especially, effective protection was often not forthcoming because of the limited capabilities of the rebels in the city. When comparable protection became available for Muslim urban residents from rebel defectors, they accepted it unreservedly. Although the defectors had deserted the armed struggle for the officially imagined community (Bangsamoro), they had not abandoned their primary communities (ingeds), and divine mercy was permitted them. Today those defector-defenders remain heroes to community members who nonetheless express commitment to Moro nationalism.

Magical stories describing the condition of the corpses of slain rebels present another dramatic instance of contrary interpretations of key communal representations. By recognizing or denying the signs of martyrdom, storytellers either acknowledged or disputed official assertions of jihad. The increased difficulties and disillusionment experienced by ordinary noncombatants (especially urban residents) during the late stages of the armed rebellion prompted some of them to perceive the political landscape differently than separatist leaders and, eventually, to interpret central signs of the struggle in a manner that directly countered official versions—in effect, denying political legitimacy to certain officially sanctioned insurgent activities. The Muslim nationalist cause saw its lowest levels of popular support during this period. As described in the following chapters, substantial popular backing was only recovered some years later in a reconstituted form through the strenuous efforts of a coalition of Muslim clerics and politicians to build a broad-based political movement for Muslim autonomy. All the same, the independent motivations, perceptions, and assessments of ordinary Muslims have persisted in postrebellion politics in Cotabato City.

CHAPTER 9

Unarmed Struggle

The political configuration of Campo Muslim is uncommonly accordant with its physical arrangement. The community faces the Pulangi River and the riverside thoroughfare leading to the center of the city. On that road, directly opposite the main entrance to Campo Muslim, lies the large house of Datu Kamsa, the barangay captain (see map 4). Traditional and modern bureaucratic authority merge in the person of Datu Kamsa. Together with his barangay council, composed mostly of elder datus, he adjudicates community disputes in much the same manner as his precolonial predecessors. As a government functionary, he also implements state policies in the community (to the extent he is able) and coordinates the government assistance infrequently provided to Campo Muslim.

An unpaved main road bisects Campo Muslim, running perpendicular to the paved riverside road. The forepart of the community, that closest to the river and the barangay captain, is very densely populated. Here, behind the buildings lining either side of the main road, the crowded and partially flooded interior (sa lusud) residential areas are found. Farther down that road, houses become less tightly spaced, and small rice fields appear. By the section of road farthest from the Pulangi River, the community assumes a nearly rural appearance. Here, away from the immediate borders of the road, rice fields and coconut trees predominate, with houses thinly distributed among them. Electricity and city water taps are scarce this far from the city road, but

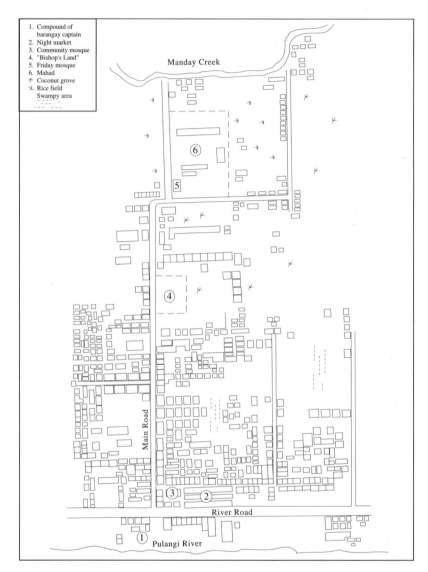

Map 4. Campo Muslim

the clamor and squalor of the forepart of the community are also mostly lacking. Here, at the end of the road, and at the edge of the community and city, lies the Mahad al-Ulum al-Islamia (known by community residents as "the Mahad"), the largest Islamic school (madrasah) in Cotabato.[1] The school was founded by Omar Pasigan, an Islamic teacher who graduated from al-Azhar University in Cairo. One of the first scholars (alim) hired to teach at the Mahad was Ustadz Ali Abdul Ajiz Naga,[2] also a graduate of al-Azhar, and a classmate of Hashim Salamat, one of the founders of the Moro National Liberation Front. Ustadz Ali spent much of the rebellion in Cotabato City and was arrested four times by the military. He taught Arabic, Qur'anic ex-egesis (tafsir), as well as other courses. At the Friday noon assembly prayer (Salatu'l-Jumah) he often gave the sermon (khutbah) at the mosque on the grounds of the Mahad. In those sermons he typically counseled community members to become "genuine Muslims" (tidtu-tidtu a Muslim) in their behavior and instructed them in the funda-mentals of Islamic equality and justice. Ustadz Ali also occasionally traveled "inside" (sa lusud), to the mountain headquarters of the Cota-bato rebels—a daylong round-trip journey—to attend meetings and seminars. His affinity with the rebel leadership derived from kinship and school ties with members of the "inside" ulama—those Islamic clerics who remained with the rebels in the hills or in exile abroad—as well as from his commitment to the goal of political autonomy for Philippine Muslims under Islamic governance.

The residence of the barangay captain and the Mahad demarcate the political as well as the territorial antipodes of Campo Muslim. The former is situated on the riverside road near the city center and nearby regional military headquarters, the sites of Christian ascendancy and state order. The latter sits at the edge of the community, far from the Christian core of the city and close to the place of escape; the wide, roadless floodlands lying south and west of the city proper that have sheltered so many Muslim rebels.

This chapter examines the mostly unarmed struggle waged in Cota-bato from 1980 until 1986 between the political alliances expressed spatially by these polar positions in Campo Muslim. It was a struggle between Muslim contenders fought almost entirely in cultural arenas but with the same final stakes as in the armed rebellion—the right to rule Muslim Cotabato. Unlike the armed rebellion in Cotabato, it was an aboveground ideological struggle over nothing less than the moral authority to command Cotabato Muslims. For the first time in the history of Cotabato, a consolidated Muslim counterelite challenged in public (though not traditionally political) arenas the political legitimacy of the datu establishment.

That cultural conflict is viewed here through the eyes of the Muslim subordinates who found themselves caught between the contending alliances (quite literally so in the case of Campo Muslim). While the struggle occurred to various degrees throughout Muslim Cotabato, Campo Muslim once again offers a convenient point of departure, especially insofar as the ideological contest was especially attuned to the Muslim urban masses. My main purpose in this chapter is to demonstrate the ways in which ordinary Muslims actively evaluated and responded to the ideological arguments of the two contending elite groups—arguments concerning the fundamental issues of Islamic authority and Muslim identity in Cotabato. I begin by considering a development significant for both community and regional politics: the emergence of an ulama independent of datu supervision.

THE RISE OF AN INDEPENDENT ULAMA AND ISLAMIC RENEWAL

I closed the previous chapter by noting that the Cotabato rebel leadership regained popular support in the early 1980s with the assistance of Islamic teachers, who had begun to play an increased public role. Here I trace the emergence of Islamic clerics in Cotabato whose religious and political views differed sharply from those of the datu establishment.

The history of the modern ulama in Cotabato dates from 1951. That was the year Maulana Mohamed Abdul Aleem Siddiqui, an Egyptian missionary, visited Cotabato City. According to Imam Akmad, the head imam at the Campo Muslim mosque, the Maulana was the first alim to have arrived in Cotabato in his lifetime. Imam Akmad and his wife vividly remember that short visit:

> The Maulana gave a speech in the city plaza during his visit. He spoke in Arabic, which was translated into English and then into Magindanaon.[3] During the speech there were rain clouds approaching, but the Maulana told the crowd not to worry about them. When he finished his speech he walked to his hotel and the rain clouds were right at his back. As soon as he entered the hotel rain began to fall in torrents, causing flooding in the city.
> The Maulana held a public debate with a Catholic priest in Buluan. After that debate the priest removed his crucifix and threw it in the river.

8. Photograph commemorating the 1951 visit of Maulana Mohammad Abdul Aleem Siddiqui (left) to Cotabato. The Maulana, the first Middle Eastern Muslim missionary to visit Cotabato in the modern era, is pictured here in the city plaza, accompanied by an unidentified Magindanaon datu.

The Maulana went from house to house in Muslim communities in the city to urge the men to come to Friday noon prayers. He was also the first person ever to instruct women to wear *hijab* [head coverings] in the mosque.

In 1952, the first resident Islamic missionary in local memory arrived. As Ustadz Ali recalled, "In 1952, a missionary from al-Azhar was sent here—Abdul Ghani Sindang, an Indonesian. He remained here in Cotabato for more than four years and was the first Islamic teacher ever to be called ustadz.'"[4] Ustadz Sindang arrived in the Philippines in 1950 along with another missionary from al-Azhar. Their first school in Malabang closed within a year and Sindang proceeded to Cotabato City (Muslim Association of the Philippines 1956, 106). He is almost certainly the same missionary referred to by Hunt in his brief account of Muslim religious education in Cotabato in the early 1950s: "In 1950, a formal Islamic school was set up in Cotabato, housed in a residence donated by a local datu and headed by a Muslim missionary sent by the Egyptian government. In addition to learning to read the Qur'an in Arabic, the students are taught to understand the language" ([1957] 1974, 205). Imam Akmad remembers the first ustadz born in Cotabato: "The first local ustadz was Ustadz Hadji Salik Badruddin. He returned from Saudi Arabia after World War II, in the 1950s. He founded the Nakdah [a madrasah] in Mabini."

As these accounts illustrate, the emergence of a new ulama in Cotabato resulted from the reestablishment of ties with Islamic religious centers after World War II, and an unprecedented intensification of ties with al-Azhar University in Egypt. The Islamic scholars who returned from al-Azhar were regarded collectively as a new species of religious specialists and were addressed by the new title "ustadz." Before the 1950s, religious teachers were usually referred to by the non-Islamic term (of Sanskrit origin) "guru." The aims of religious education also began to be altered with the growth of madrasahs headed by missionaries and, eventually, by local al-Azhar graduates. Prior to the development of madrasahs, religious education took place at the home of the guru and had as its goal the reading and memorization—but not the translation or interpretation—of the Holy Qur'an. This traditional Islamic education was widespread but very rudimentary; the great majority of students studied just two or three years, and those who studied longer were still rarely able to understand what they read.[5] The low level of religious education was reflected in Friday services. Passages read from the Qur'an were not typically translated and genuine *khutbah* (commentaries based on the passages read) were rarely given.

By contrast, the new madrasahs emphasized the understanding of Arabic and the textual exegesis of the Qur'an. Instruction at the secondary level has come to include courses in Islamic History, Exegesis (Tafsir), and Tradition of the Prophet (Hadith), all taught primarily in Arabic. The advancement of Islamic education altered contemporary religious services. Qur'anic passages are now almost always translated and regularly commented upon in khutbahs by ustadzes. The transformation of religious services eventually came to include changes in the political arrangements associated with community prayers. By tradition—one reinvigorated in the postwar economic boom in Cotabato—community mosques were endowed, sustained, and controlled by local datus. As we have seen (and as indicated in the passage from Hunt just quoted) datu sponsorship extended to religious schools as well (Hassoubah 1983). Under traditional arrangements, in place as recently as the late 1970s in some areas, Friday assembly prayers would not begin until the arrival of the datu or his representative. The imam (prayer leader) of the mosque paid his respects first to the datu, who sat at the very front of the congregation, before beginning the service. Imams were considered functionaries of the ruling datu and, in most cases, belonged to datu families.

The close association between nobility and religious leadership gradually began to weaken with the emergence of the ulama. For one, clerics used Friday sermons to advance an alternative, egalitarian ideology as part of their program for Islamic renewal.[6] The following passage from my field notes illustrates the use of Friday sermons to emphasize equality and social justice in Islam. The passage paraphrases the contents of a Friday sermon given by Ustadz Ali in Campo Muslim:

> The sermon given today by Ustadz Ali concerned the true meaning of being a Muslim. His talk was based on the *ayah* [Qur'anic verse] "Do not die until you become a Muslim." He stated that to become a Muslim one must *act* like a Muslim at all times. Behaving like a Muslim consists of much more than merely praying and fasting. It means practicing social justice.
>
> He related a story about Caliph Ali. Ali was involved in a legal dispute with a non-Muslim and both parties went before a *qadi* (Islamic jurist) to resolve the matter. When Ali entered the hearing room the qadi received him with lavish servility. When the non-Muslim arrived the qadi acknowledged him brusquely. Ali became quite angered at this behavior

and reminded the qadi of his duty to dispense justice and treat all men equally before the law.

Imam Akmad put such messages in perspective in the course of discussing changes in the office of imam: "The institution of imam has existed from the time of the Prophet. Here [in Cotabato] it was believed that the imam had to be from the datu class because he needed to be a strong man. If he did not belong to a datu family it was thought that there would be punishment from God. This changed when the ustadzes came. They said: 'There are no differences among people in the eyes of God.'"

In one of my conversations with Ustadz Ali, he commented on the claim of traditional elites to politico-religious leadership on the basis of descent from the Prophet Muhammad:

> The ustadzes do not like such claims. Muhammad did not appoint his successor. He did not believe in blood relatedness as the criterion for leadership. The blood relation of the caliphs to Muhammad was a distant one. What the ustadzes want to see are honorable leaders, trusted leaders, not leaders chosen solely on the basis of blood inheritance. We are not attempting to do away with the role of descent. We do not deny the tarsilas [genealogies]. But we do try to support the good datus. To attempt to remove the datus would create difficulties. The issue of noble inheritance is a problem we have long had. Good people with good minds have had little chance if they were not royal descendants. We cannot remove the problem of inheritance overnight. It must be a gradual process.

The ideological project of the ulama, advanced at Friday sermons and other public forums, did not directly challenge the myth of sanctified inequality as inscribed in the tarsilas. It did not deny the existence of a nobility, for such a frontal assault on the core element of the ideology of traditional rule would have alienated them from potential supporters (including, in some cases, their relatives) as well as invite the ire of powerful political figures. Instead, they disputed the claim that nobility was the single criterion for politico-religious leadership. This argument was presented in a gradual and indirect manner by emphasizing populist aspects of Islamic doctrine and by supporting "good datus"—those few who meet the ulama's criteria for Islamic leadership.

The connection between nobility and religious leadership has also been interrupted by the increasing availability of alternative sources of funding for religious purposes. External funds arrived first in the form of the scholarships from the government of Egypt in the 1950s, a flow that expanded rapidly in the 1970s and 1980s. Virtually all the later funding came about as a direct consequence of the armed struggle during the 1970s. As early as 1971, the Libyan government provided funds for mosque and madrasah construction, and in 1978 the Organization of the Islamic Conference of Foreign Ministers (OIC) dispensed funds for the building of thirteen new mosques in the South and the repair or expansion of a great number of mosques and madrasahs (Majul 1985). The Kingdom of Saudi Arabia also contributed (and continues to provide) financial support for various religious projects. Middle East governments have provided missionaries to the Muslim Philippines since the 1950s, and Egypt continues to send teachers for one- or two-year assignments in Cotabato. More significantly for the development of an independent local ulama, the governments of Libya and Saudi Arabia began to support a small percentage of local ulama as long-term missionaries. Ustadz Ali received a small salary from the government of Libya.

Since the late 1970s, significant additional funding has come from private institutions and individuals in the Middle East through contacts developed by both the Muslim separatist rebels and local ulama. The Mahad al-Ulum al-Islamia in Campo Muslim has been the beneficiary of such funding. The Mahad, when it was founded in late 1979, relied at first on local funds alone but soon obtained external financial support from private donors in Saudi Arabia. As a result, it rapidly expanded, even adding an English program.[7] Today the Mahad, with more than four hundred students in its Arabic program, is one of the largest Islamic schools in the Philippines and attracts students from all the southern provinces. With its well-constructed two-story buildings and its large cemented courtyard, it is far and away the most impressive establishment in Campo Muslim.

Before moving on, let me reemphasize a point made previously. While their origins may be traced to the early 1950s, it is not accurate to speak of the ulama as a significant religious force before 1980. Despite the accelerated construction of mosques and establishment of madrasahs in the 1950s and 1960s, there is reason to doubt claims (see, e.g., Bauzon 1991; Gowing 1979) for any substantial advancement in Islamic education or orthopraxy prior to that year. In an extensive survey conducted in Muslim Mindanao in 1980, Hassoubah found that "madrasah graduates [were] still unable to use the Arabic language with proficiency" (1983, 74).[8] In respect to religious orthopraxy, Islamic observance for the large majority of Cotabato Muslims prior to 1980 resembled, with local modifications, that described for ordinary Muslims in other parts of the southern Philippines and in much of the rest of Islamic Southeast Asia (see, e.g., Kiefer 1972; Fraser 1960; Djamour 1959). While there was strict compliance with certain aspects of Islamic doctrine, alcohol use and gambling were widespread, Arabic prayers seldom understood, beliefs in spirits common, Qur'anic education extremely rudimentary, and mosque attendance slight.

The principal reason for the absence of substantial Islamic renewal prior to the 1980s despite the presence of reform-minded clerics was a lack of opportunity. While numbers of Middle East–educated clerics returned to the Philippines in the late 1960s, they were almost immediately engulfed in the armed conflict of the 1970s. It was nearly 1980 before conditions existed that allowed local ustadzes to teach and preach unconstrained by datu influence or military harassment. When they finally spoke out publicly, they not only promoted an Islamic populism but strenuously championed the reform of particular cultural practices. As we shall see, those efforts at religious reform have been the source of some contention in Campo Muslim and throughout Cotabato.

In 1985–86, the ustadzes of the Mahad provided services to their host community that were for the most part limited to spiritual guidance and religious education. Although located in Campo Muslim, the Mahad was not altogether a part of it. The relative elegance of its structures contrasted with the plainness and poverty of the rest of the community. The Mahad was built in Campo Muslim but never primarily intended to serve community residents. While it was not unusually expensive, most families in Campo Muslim could not afford the tuition to send their children to the Mahad and, while I lived there, very few scholarships were available to community residents. An observer standing in the main road of the community could easily discern this in the busy two-way morning traffic, as students from relatively more affluent locales within and outside the city entered Campo Muslim to attend the Mahad, while most Campo Muslim children left the community to attend public, state-run schools.

The lack of engagement of the local ulama with the immediate and material problems of the community may be partly explained by limited resources. Unlike Christian educational and charitable organizations, the ulama possessed no linkages to international community development organizations. According to Ustadz Ali, the private overseas donations received by the Mahad carried spending restrictions that tied their use to narrowly defined religious purposes. A second factor was that most of the local ulama lacked experience with nonreligious community affairs and paid limited attention to the pressing economic problems of the community. Most had no education in, or practical experience with, community development. At least one influential ustadz expressed his awareness of this shortcoming. After certain of the local ulama accused Nur Miskin, a student activist, of being, alternatively, a *Shia*[9] or a communist, he went "inside" to talk with Ustadz Salim, the highest-ranking cleric in the Cotabato rebel leadership. On hearing of the accusations, Ustadz Salim commented, "Da pan ustadz siya" (There are no ustadzes here yet), by which he meant that local ustadzes had yet to attain the knowledge he thought an ustadz should have. Ustadz Salim added that many young ustadzes knew nothing about community problems and needed to be educated about those problems and their causes.

THE MILF AND THE NEW OPPOSITION ALLIANCE

A new Muslim separatist organization, the Moro Islamic Liberation Front (MILF) first announced its independent existence (as distinct from the MNLF) in 1984. The establishment of a rival Moro "liberation front" resulted from a political schism between Hashim Salamat and Nur Misuari, the chairman and vice-chairman respectively of the MNLF. The rift, which had been developing for some time, first became public in December 1977, after the collapse of the second round of talks in Tripoli, Libya, aimed at implementing the peace accord and cease-fire agreement. By 1980, the "New Leadership" (Salamat quoted in Mastura 1985, 16) faction of the MNLF had moved its headquarters to Lahore, Pakistan, and Salamat was having success promoting his leadership to international Islamic organizations and "moderate Arab states" (Mastura 1985, 15). Salamat's faction also engaged in talks with the Philippine government on reopening negotiations to implement the Tripoli Agreement. While the Misuari faction had become intransigent after the failure of the 1977 Tripoli negotiations, reverting to a separatist stance after having previously agreed to a negotiated autonomy within the framework of the Philippine republic, the Salamat faction maintained a conciliatory posture, endorsing "a peaceful resolution of differences on the issue of autonomy" (Salamat quoted in Mastura 1985, 15).

In early 1980, Salamat's group suffered a stunning political blow. Amelil Malaguiok (alias "Commander Ronnie"), the chairman of the Kutawatu Revolutionary Committee (KRC), defected to the government with a number of his field commanders and received as his prize the premier position in the newly formed regional autonomous government of Region 12, encompassing Central Mindanao. The Kutawatu Revolutionary Committee had been the largest regional unit in the MNLF, and the only one effectively controlled by the Salamat faction. Although it never recovered its momentum on the diplomatic front, the Salamat group did rebuild its command structure and regain its popular support in Cotabato. This success was due in part to the personal popularity of Hadji Murad, the man who assumed the chairmanship of the KRC (the name of which was changed at about this time to the Kutawatu Regional Committee). As we shall see, the revitalization of the KRC was also aided by the development of an aboveground political support structure. In mid-1984, six years after his "takeover" (Mastura 1985, 15) of the MNLF, Salamat officially changed the title of his organization to the "Moro Islamic Liberation Front" to "underscore Islam as the rallying point of the Bangsamoro struggle" (1985, 17). In a letter to the secretary general of the Organization of the Islamic Conference, Salamat elaborated: "All Mujahideen under the Moro Islamic Liberation Front (MILF) adopt Islam as their way of life. Their ultimate objective in their Jihad is to make supreme the WORD of ALLAH and establish Islam in the Bangsamoro homeland" (emphases in the original; 1985, 18). Salamat's principal aim of establishing Islam in Muslim Mindanao varied markedly from that of his rival, Misuari, who sought first the creation of a separate state in the Moro homeland. It is doubtful, however, whether the stated objective of the newly formed MILF was really different from the goals formulated by Salamat and the al-Azhar group twenty years earlier. The name change of the Salamat faction represented less an alteration of goals and more a recognition that, after six years of challenges to his leadership of the MNLF, Nur Misuari retained a tenacious grip as chairman. Salamat's only option was to relinquish his claim to sole leadership of the original front and develop another organization. Here it was politic to choose a name that best emphasized the differences between his new front and the original Moro *National* Liberation Front.

When I began my field research in 1985, the members and supporters of the Cotabato MILF faced arrest and detention without trial as participants in an illegal armed organization. Because of that political reality, I did not question Campo Muslim residents about the activities of the MILF, nor did I seek interviews with its current members. Even so, community residents volunteered a good deal of information about the MILF and I engaged in informal and often unexpected conversations with active rebels. Nevertheless, as a result of my approach, and because the MILF operates as an underground organization, I know less about the MILF than I do about other political associations.

In 1984, the Salamat faction had undergone a reorganization before taking on a new name. In the letter quoted above, Salamat also explained that reorganization, and included the following passage: "The MILF operates as a parallel government vis-à-vis the enemy government within its area of responsibility and exercises influence extensively among the Bangsamoro masses in a degree more effective and binding than that of the enemy administration" (quoted in Mastura 1985, 18). An MILF "shadow" government did exist in Campo Muslim. A clandestine MILF barangay committee paralleled the one headed by Datu Kamsa. While I lack specifics of its day-to-day operation or influence, my impression is that, as with many other Philippine political associations, it functioned in an ad hoc and informal manner. In addition to shadow-governing offices, there were also "invisible" MILF workers, active agents who operated secretly in the city (or elsewhere away from rebel-held areas). Invisible workers kept track of developments in their areas of operation and performed other assignments, which almost certainly included the selective use of intimidation. The Kutawatu Regional Committee published a local underground news sheet, *Tantawan*[10] —a mimeographed bulletin written in English with some Tagalog, which appeared monthly or bimonthly. It carried editorials and reports of local incidents—particularly of armed clashes between MILF units and the military.

Although it is difficult to determine with any precision how "effective and binding" was the influence exercised by the MILF in Campo Muslim, the MILF was more influential in most matters than the "enemy administration." No collective political activities (e.g., rallies or demonstrations) were undertaken without at least the implicit approval of the MILF, and few individual decisions that had political implications were made without consideration of the likely reaction of the MILF. Those community members summoned to MILF headquarters always endeavored to respond promptly and in person. During my stay in Campo Muslim, a number of these summonses concerned the politically volatile issue of the conspicuous operation of a Christian charitable organization in Campo Muslim.

CHILD SPONSORSHIP AND CHRISTIAN
HEGEMONY IN CAMPO MUSLIM

The efforts of Sister Theresa to aid victims of the 1976 earthquake first brought representatives of the Catholic diocese to Campo Muslim. Their presence continued in a more institutionalized form after her departure in 1981 (it was widely rumored that the new bishop had removed the popular Sister Theresa because he disliked her independent manner). In 1983, Reconciliation House, the community service program established by Sister Theresa, was expanded and redesignated as "the Reconciliation Center." The new bishop secured external funding for the expanded community program from the Christian Children's Fund (CCF).

By 1986, the Reconciliation Center program supported 165 students in Campo Muslim, or one child each from just less than one-fourth of the households in the community. Operating with a monthly budget of fifteen hundred dollars, the program was intended to educate children, develop community leaders, train local health workers, and provide parental education in child care, nutrition, and home economics. As articulated by its director, the program guided recipient households in value formation and social responsibility. The principal form of assistance provided to recipient families was educational support for one child per household. CCF "scholars" received the equivalent of five to ten dollars a month in tuition fees (often for Catholic schools), clothing, and school supplies. Overseas funds were generated by means of individual sponsorship arrangements. Participating children received letters from their American sponsors and were required to respond to them with the assistance of program staff members. School clothing and supplies were purchased with vouchers at the Reconciliation Center store. Parents of supported children could also receive small loans and free instruction on topics such as money management and herbal medicine.

Although this support represented more material assistance than provided by any other agency or association in Campo Muslim, the tangible results of the program as of 1986 were questionable, even perverse.[11] CCF-sponsored children did tend to be members of some of

the poorest families in the community, but after three years of participation in the program, the average monthly household income of CCF
members remained well below the community average.[12] Child sponsorship arrangements had also generated new tensions and dependencies in the community.

The often ambivalent attitudes of recipients toward the CCF program were revealed most clearly to me in a conversation I had with a
couple living in the very poorest interior portion of Campo Muslim.
When I arrived at their house seeking census information, Andig, a laborer caring for his four-month-old son while his wife was away, invited me in. While we were talking, his wife, Taya, returned from
bathing. She wrapped her wet hair in a piece of cloth, then sat and began to breast-feed her baby. As the baby nursed, Taya took a small
packet of tobacco from underneath her malong (skirt), sprinkled some
tobacco on a strip of newspaper, and rolled a long thin cigarette. She
joined the conversation, supplementing her husband's often hesitant responses with animated comments.

She told me, "I have borne seven children but only three survive. I
have my own work as a *labandera* [washerwoman]. I earn as much in
a day as my husband." When I asked her about CCF, Taya complained
about the program and brought letters and pictures from her child's
sponsor to show me. I translated the letters for her and she had questions: "Is it true, as some of the ustadzes say, that children in the CCF
program are sometimes sold to foreigners"? I told her I didn't think
that was true. "Is it true that the Sisters change the children's names to
Christian names in their letters to their sponsors"? I told her I did not
know whether that happened but that many of the sponsors were not
aware that the children they sponsored were Muslims, or even that
they lived with their families. "What is the real reason that the sponsors' names are torn off the envelopes before their letters are given to
the children?" she asked. I said that I thought it was because the CCF
wanted to be able to control the correspondence between sponsors and
recipient families. "You know," she said, "the sponsor of the daughter
of Babu Amina visited them a few months ago. She was an old woman
from America. After that woman left, Amina and her husband enlarged their house. I heard she was given one hundred dollars by the
sponsor. Tell me, how can I invite the sponsor of my child to visit?" I
had no answer.

Program recipients viewed themselves as clients receiving resources
from mysterious and powerful outsiders. They reciprocated with the

deference, obedience, and attendance required to maintain the relationship. They complained about their powerless position vis-à-vis the program workers above them and the foreign sponsors beyond their reach, but they also defended the program against those who would remove it from the community. As it was the only source of external funding available to them, recipient families expressed a strong material interest in its continuation.

The physical as well as fiscal presence of the Catholic diocese in Campo Muslim was a political affront to the MILF and the ulama. They were unable, however, to provide comparable resources to community residents. Disapproval of the CCF program by the MILF was a cause of some considerable anxiety among its participants. Two entries from my field notes provide illustration:

> Nur [my research assistant] and I went to zone four this morning to interview a man who lived there. He was not at home so we left a message with his daughter. Nur told her vaguely that we wanted to talk to him, and we made an appointment for the next morning. We then went off to another interview and returned one hour later to our house. An older woman, somewhat agitated, arrived soon after and asked for Nur. She was the wife of the first man we had intended to interview. Her daughter told her we had been asking for her husband and had described us. She recognized Nur from the description and knew that he was active in rallies connected to the "inside" (she thought I was "an Arab"). Her daughter is a CCF scholar, and she knew that there were problems concerning the "inside" and the Reconciliation Center. She thought we had come from the MILF and was worried, so came looking for Nur to see what the problem was. We explained to her the purpose of the research. I hadn't anticipated that I would be mistaken for an MILF official.[13]

> [Kasan] told me that he was tired and had broken his [Ramadan] fast early today because he had made a long hard trip to Bumbaran to talk with the vice-chairman of the Kutawatu Political Office of the MILF. The vice-chairman had sent him a typed letter in Magindanaon [four days earlier] asking him to come to talk about the CCF program in Campo Muslim. Kasan left very early in the morning. He went first to Parang, then took another long jeep ride east, then rode in a pedicab into the mountains to the "liberated area." At their meeting, the vice-chairman simply asked him for an "update" on the CCF program. Kasan gave him that and added his opinion that it would put great hardship on recipient families to remove the program. The vice-chairman replied that "it is best to be practical now," which Kasan took to mean that he thought that the CCF program should remain for the time being. Kasan also received an endorsement from him in the form of a signed, dated letter stating that they had met.

The most frequent services provided by the MILF involved adjudication. MILF courts heard cases on topics from homicide to land disputes to adultery. One outgrowth of the MILF's adjudication services was its registration of marriage contracts. Philippine Muslims very seldom registered births or marriages with governmental agencies. Muslim children became officially known to state authorities only when registered at public schools. Beginning in 1983 or so, the MILF provided a marriage contract form that asked for the names of the bride and groom and witnesses and the amount of the bridewealth. One copy of the contract was left with the bride and the other sent "inside" to the Kutawatu Regional Committee. Such MILF services, it may be noted, involved the direct participation of the ulama. All MILF adjudication was conducted by "inside" ulama, using *Sharia* (Islamic) law in a more stringent (although still locally modified) manner than it was traditionally applied. MILF marriage contract forms were provided to local ustadzes, who presided at most marriages.

THE COUNTERELITE CONSOLIDATED: THE MILF-ULAMA-PROFESSIONAL COALITION

Crucial to the MILF recovery in Cotabato in the 1980s was an alliance of ulama and pro-MILF professionals working aboveground to advance its interests. The reason for the cooperation of the new ulama with the MILF is easy to discern. Most al-Azhar–educated ustadzes in Cotabato were, like Ustadz Ali, connected to their underground ulama colleagues by kinship links, cohort ties, and shared convictions. Although the underground ulama—who preached only at mosques in the countryside—spoke much more radically than the aboveground clerics, the latter tended to support the position of the MILF and were generally viewed as public spokesmen for the MILF.

Less obvious is the reason for the coalescence of interests between the MILF, the independent ulama, and a number of Manila-educated Cotabato professionals. While their affinity may be traced ultimately to their shared antagonisms toward the Marcos regime and its (primarily) datu collaborators in Cotabato, those shared interests were forged into a political coalition through the catalyzing efforts of a single individual. As a former political appointee of the martial law regime and the son of a datu, Zacaria Candao seemed an improbable candidate to organize an alliance of the Cotabato counterelite. At the same time, his

professional training, political experience, and kin connections furnished him with a political tool kit possessed by few other public figures in Cotabato, Muslim or Christian. Candao was a native of Cotabato City and member of a prominent city family. His father, Datu
Liwa Candao, served for many years as vice-mayor of the city. Candao
graduated from a Manila law school in the late 1960s, and in 1976, in
the midst of the Bangsamoro Rebellion, was appointed governor of
Maguindanao Province by Ferdinand Marcos on the recommendation
of Simeon Datumanong, whom he replaced. Less than one year later
he resigned the governorship to join the MNLF cease-fire negotiating
panel in Tripoli. As he relates it, in 1977 he was asked by Nur Misuari
to act as a technical advisor to the MNLF for negotiations concerning
the details of the Tripoli Agreement that had been signed in December
of 1976. Four months of intensive negotiations produced only stalemate, and the talks were abandoned. December of 1977 brought the
split in the MNLF leadership. Candao supported the Salamat "takeover" and remained with Salamat in Cairo for one year. In 1979, Candao led a team from the Salamat faction that held exploratory talks
with the Philippine government aimed at reopening formal negotiations. Those talks collapsed with the surrender of the chairman of the
Kutawatu Revolutionary Committee, Amelil Malaguiok, to the government. Soon after, Candao returned to Cotabato as legal advisor to
the Central Committee of the MNLF.

One of the few concrete results of the Tripoli talks was the establishment of official committees to monitor the cease-fire: one each
from the government and MNLF in each region of the South. By 1978
the cease-fire arrangement had disintegrated and the original function
of the committees was rendered moot. Nevertheless, Salamat decided
to maintain the Cotabato cease-fire committee to document "military
atrocities" in the region. Yearly reports were submitted to the Organization of the Islamic Conference. Two of the most prominent aboveground Islamic clerics in Cotabato—Ustadz Yahiya and Ustadz Pasigan, the founder of the Mahad al-Ulum al-Islamia—led the Cotabato
cease-fire committee. Zacaria Candao worked closely with these men
after his return and together they became the first entirely public and
aboveground spokesmen for the MNLF (soon to be the MILF) in
Cotabato. They also formed the core of a coalition being developed
quietly but energetically by Candao.

Candao forged wider links with the Cotabato ulama by organizing
and sponsoring large *da'wah* (call to faith) conferences. At the confer-

ence I attended in 1985, religious and regional political issues were intermingled, and copies of the official organ of the MILF Central Committee were included in every attendee's information packet. One important offshoot of the conferences was the establishment of a popular
nightly da'wah radio program that provided religious and political information to listeners.

Candao also had close kinship and friendship ties with the new
Muslim commercial and professional elites of Cotabato City and its
environs—those who had provided so much support in the past to the
Muslim rebels. He encouraged the formation of Islamic-oriented
family organizations among these friends and relatives. With the help
of the local ulama, he also began to build a base of support among the
Muslim urban poor, particularly in Campo Muslim. A major accomplishment of the new opposition alliance organized by Zacaria Candao
was the introduction of a new potent political vocabulary into Muslim
politics in Cotabato. "Islamic Unity" became a catchphrase for the local opposition, and, for the first time, Islamic phraseology began to be
used in everyday political discourse in Muslim Cotabato. The aboveground coalition combined an Islamic message with well-developed
kinship and economic ties among two rising elite groups—the ulama
and the professionals and entrepreneurs, who were, in many cases, the
sons of successful smugglers. Joined with the underground MILF, the
alliance presented a new and formidable challenge to the collaborative
traditionalism of the datus who monopolized formal political posts in
Muslim Cotabato in the early 1980s.

An extraordinary event that occurred in conjunction with the 1985
"Da'wah Conference" illustrates the Muslim opposition's unprecedented use of Islamic renewal as a cultural frame for public political
protest against the martial law regime and the datu establishment. The
organizers of the conference staged a large parade through the city to
celebrate its opening. As many as ten thousand madrasah students
from throughout the province marched from the Mahad in Campo
Muslim, through the city plaza to the parade ground of the Central Elementary School, where they were reviewed by a number of dignitaries
including the Muslim military commander of the region and the Muslim governor of the province.

As the very first event of its kind in Cotabato, the parade was remarkable in itself, displaying the exceptional growth in Islamic education in the province in the previous five years. However, it also included a political demonstration by Muslim college students that had

been planned weeks earlier at the Mahad in Campo Muslim. At that meeting, representatives from various Muslim student organizations at local colleges were addressed by Ustadz Ali, who spoke about the courage required to demonstrate publicly and told stories of his days as a student in Cairo demonstrating against Nasser. The students gathered again at the Mahad on the day before the parade to prepare placards and banners. Some of those carried messages (in English), such as "Allah Hates Oppressors" and "We support the Mujahideen in Afghanistan," and a few had quotations in Arabic from the Qur'an. Others held slogans that pointedly though obliquely protested the martial law regime ("Muslims and Christians Have a Common Enemy"), while still others voiced explicit criticism ("Military Out of Mindanao"). The most directly confrontational slogan stated: "MMA = Ministry of Munafiq Affairs." This message denounced the Ministry of Muslim Affairs, a new government agency created as part of the Marcos regime's unilateral implementation of the Tripoli Agreement, as a hypocritical, anti-Islamic (*munafiq*) institution. Zacaria Candao arrived at the Mahad later in the day and reviewed the banners. He asked that the four most controversial not be carried in the parade but approved their display at the school ground afterward. While it is not clear that Zacaria Candao or Ustadz Ali actually initiated the student demonstration, they clearly approved and facilitated it. With the addition of the student demonstrators, the parade represented not only the largest Islamic event ever held in the province but also the very first mass political action engaged in by Cotabato Muslims.[14]

TRADITIONAL ELITES AND THE POST-REBELLION ESTABLISHMENT

By 1980, with the end of the active rebellion and the relaxation of stringent military rule, the datus of Cotabato had reestablished themselves to a remarkable degree in positions of political power. Members of datu families long allied with President Marcos held positions as minister of Muslim Affairs (a recently created cabinet-level post), representative to the Batasang Pambansa (or National Congress, created in 1978 by presidential decree), and governor of the province. Members of datu families more recently affiliated with the Marcos regime (i.e., since the declaration of martial law) held positions as provincial board member, regional assemblyman, and chairman of the Philippine

Amanah Bank (a government development bank operated on Islamic guidelines), and as vice-mayor and city council member of Cotabato City. Additionally, rebel returnees who were members of datu families held prominent positions in the regional autonomous government. In all, six of eight regional assemblymen from Maguindanao Province were members of prominent datu families,[15] and six of the seven officers of the provincial committee of the ruling party, the KBL (Kilusang Bagong Lipunan, or New Society Movement), were traditional elites. Of seventeen municipalities in Maguindanao Province, twelve were headed by datus. On the whole, traditional elites appeared to have survived martial law and the Bangsamoro Rebellion with little permanent damage to their political capabilities. With effective one-party rule and an increase in development funds channeled from the central government to Cotabato, the political positions of many collaborating datus were, in fact, more secure and potentially more profitable than before martial law.

Datu Ali Dimaporo, the Maranao governor of the neighboring province of Lanao Del Sur, anchored the government-datu alliance throughout Muslim Mindanao. Dimaporo's ties with President Marcos had made him both enormously wealthy (his holdings reportedly included apartment buildings in Los Angeles) and a national political figure. He ruled his province as a traditional domain and maintained a sizable private army. By the early 1980s, Ali Dimaporo was widely acknowledged to be the most powerful politician in Mindanao. He not only had a direct line to the presidential palace (he was, it was said, the only Muslim whom President Marcos really trusted) but maintained a warm relationship with the Philippine military. He flew on military airplanes, gave his blessings to military operations against Muslim rebels, and reportedly engaged in mutually beneficial business deals with high military officers. He was the leader of the KBL in Mindanao and the sole gatekeeper between the Marcos regime and Mindanao Muslims. All successful petitions by Muslims to the Marcos administration were said to pass through him.

In August 1982, Ferdinand Marcos appointed Dimaporo as the only Muslim member of the National Executive Committee—a body that served in a special advisory role to the president (McAmis 1983). Later in the year Dimaporo—whose genealogical claims to nobility were equivocal at best—arranged to have his preeminent political role in Mindanao traditionally validated. He had himself "enthroned" as "His Royal Highness, the Sultan of Masiu" (in some accounts, as the

Sultan of all the Sultans) in a lavish ceremony attended by President
and Mrs. Marcos and much of the traditional nobility of Muslim Mindanao (McAmis 1983).[16] The self-proclamation of Ali Dimaporo is
credited with encouraging a series of similar proclamations in Cotabato. Old titles were resurrected and new "royal descendants" organizations sprang up at a rapid rate between 1982 and 1986.

The collaborating datus of Cotabato and the administration they
served provided few, if any, discernible services to ordinary Muslims
between 1980 and 1986. The Regional Autonomous Government had
no power of taxation and little government money to spend. Most of
what budget it had was spent on itself. The expansive RAG complex at
the edge of the city included, among other things, a bowling alley and
tennis courts for the use of representatives and employees. Because the
RAG had no real power or funds to implement projects, it was viewed
by many as simply an "unnecessary, expensive bottleneck to getting
projects approved and implemented" (McAmis 1983, 37). The agency
established by the martial law administration to manage economic development in the Muslim South—the Southern Philippines Development Authority—was, by 1980, officially headed by Imelda Marcos.
Its only recognizable accomplishment in Cotabato City was a large
housing development located just south of the city, not far from the
RAG complex. The prices of homes built there were far beyond the
economic capabilities of low-income families. Virtually all were owned
by middle-income government employees.

Government assistance to residents of Campo Muslim was scarce
and irregular. A number of government projects had been promised
over the years in the community, and some had even been initiated, but
none was ever fully implemented. The only governmental material assistance I witnessed in Campo Muslim occurred during the 1986 presidential election campaign when a KBL campaign van arrived in
Campo Muslim to distribute free medicine. A large crowd of residents
gathered and signed their names on KBL lists in order to receive medicines marked prominently with labels that read: "For government use,
not for sale." I heard stories of other assistance provided during election campaigns by certain local officeholders seeking reelection who
installed streetlights or water pumps in the community. The only regular service provided by Datu Kamsa, the barangay captain, was adjudication. During the time I lived in Campo Muslim, Datu Kamsa began
to charge money for his adjudication services, ostensibly to discourage
frivolous claims.

The opposed political coalitions I have just described did not constitute neatly delineated camps. They were, for one, thoroughly crosscut
by kin connections. The complex political attachments among Zacaria
Candao—the leader of the opposition alliance—and his datu relatives
(some of whom live in or near Campo Muslim) provide illustration.
Candao and Datu Kamsa—the barangay captain of Campo Muslim
and a Marcos loyalist—were second cousins. Datu Kamsa was opposed in the 1980 election for barangay captain by Datu Mokamad,
his first cousin who was also the first cousin and close ally of Zacaria
Candao. The election was fiercely contested, with community observers remarking that had the two candidates not been so closely related there would surely have been bloodshed. The brother of Datu
Mokamad, Datu Simeon, had joined the KBL and occupied a high
provincial office. Another brother, Datu Monib, fought with the rebels
and still actively supported the MILF. As a direct descendent of the
Umarmaya sa Magindanao, one of the highest officeholders of the
Magindanao Sultanate, Zacaria Candao possessed a closer descent relationship to the Magindanao core nobility than any of his datu
cousins, yet he had chosen not to call himself "datu."

Such tangled relationships demonstrate that political loyalties did
not divide cleanly along family lines, with the result that close relatives
were sometimes aligned with bitterly opposed political factions. While
I found no direct evidence that such alignments were the outcome of
family-based strategies to spread political risk, the presence of close
relatives among one's political antagonists did undoubtedly facilitate
not only interfactional communication but also personal political re-
alignment under changed conditions. The one clearly discernible kin-
based political pattern in post-rebellion Cotabato was found among
members of the most powerful and well-established datu families in
the province, who tended overwhelmingly to align with the government-datu coalition.

THE STRUGGLE FOR MORAL
AUTHORITY IN COTABATO

With the political arena so narrowly circumscribed by the authoritar-
ian state regime in the early 1980s, the counterelite alliance confronted
the datu establishment in cultural arenas, disputing their right to exercise moral authority over Cotabato's Muslims. The challenge to traditional moral authority was extended incrementally by the newly active

ulama in the form of recommended alterations to accepted local practices. Recognizing that the proposed reforms were an attempt to undermine the core of the myth of sanctified inequality—the axiom that
as direct descendants of the Prophet Muhammad moral authority was
constituted only in them—datus countered with an intensified traditionalism. While this ideological struggle was waged over the right to
command the faithful, voices from Campo Muslim reveal that Muslim
subordinates often held independent opinions and acted upon them.

In Campo Muslim, contestations occurred in three cultural arenas:
religious ritual, popular culture, and adjudication; disputes in the first
two arenas concerned ritual and celebratory activities surrounding two
very important life crises: weddings and funerals. In Campo Muslim in
1985, I found that certain core Islamic practices—fasting during the
month of Ramadan, strict abstention from pork, ritual circumcision of
males, and the virtual absence of apostasy—had existed prior to the
emergence of the ustadzes and were little affected by them. Other areas
of religious practice and personal behavior had undergone appreciable
change that community members agreed was entirely positive. In the
estimation of residents, the attendance of male community members at
Friday congregational worship had increased and a greater number of
individuals were attentive to daily prayers. Incidents of public drinking
and gambling by community residents had apparently declined. Certain other beliefs and practices—particularly those concerning spirits
and magic—had yet to be addressed by religious reformers.

But some aspects of the cultural life of Campo Muslim were
strongly (though not always loudly) contested. These were cherished
(and usually well-established) practices that the ulama wanted to modify or eliminate. One contested area concerned traditional mortuary
rituals. As with other Islamic peoples in Southeast Asia (see, e.g.,
Bowen 1993), Muslims in Cotabato have added local accretions—involving additional prayers, the use of incense, and ritual ablutions at
the grave site—to the conventional Islamic burial service. The ustadzes
strongly disapproved of these practices as adulterations. More highly
contested were the extended death commemoration rituals—the most
important funerary ceremonies in the community. In common with a
number of other Southeast Asian societies—both Islamic and non-
Islamic—traditional belief requires propitiation ceremonies for the deceased at intervals of 3, 7, 40, 100, and 365 days after death. In Cotabato, these ceremonies take the form of ritual meals (*kanduli*) at which
prayers (*duwa*; in Arabic, *du'a*) are recited for the deceased.[17] In the

most traditional form of the kanduli, ritual specialists (*panditas*) chant the prayers in a version of the Sufi *tahlil,* or prayer litany (Reid 1984), in which the first words of the confession of faith, "La ilaha illa Allah" (There is no god but God), are recited repeatedly at various tempos accompanied by the swaying of the body from side to side. The rhythmic voices and movement produce a peaceful, entrancing effect in participants and listeners.

After initially objecting to all such propitiation ceremonies for the deceased, the ustadzes later modified their position and condoned the third day (*telu a gay*) death commemoration ceremony. They have nonetheless strongly criticized further ceremonies as ritually improper and wasteful of resources and disapprove of the traditional Sufic content of the kanduli. The economic argument of the ulama, that extended death commemorations were unduly expensive, pertained to customary ritual practice prior to 1972. Ritual feasts before that time involved very substantial costs for the relatives of the deceased, and it was not unusual for individuals to incur major debts as a consequence of sponsoring such feasts. Since 1972 the expenses associated with death commemorations had been substantially reduced (without a concomitant reduction in the number of commemorations) as the result of moderations in the scale of ceremonies necessitated by the calamitous economic losses of that period.

The ustadzes' strong disapproval of extended death rituals distressed many ordinary Muslims, who worried about losing the means to ensure that the spirits of their dead relatives were at peace. One community elder expressed the general uneasiness of many residents at the pronouncements of the ustadzes: "First they said that traditional [religious] practices would remain. Then they announced that they would all be removed, then that only some would be kept. People are confused." Trading on this unease, traditional elites took the lead in defending traditional practices as integral aspects of Magindanaon culture and accused the ulama of extremism in their efforts at religious reform. The comments of Datu Adil are representative of their assertions:

> Our elders had a saying: "Amayngka madakel niya a ulama nakauma, a magkapir tanu [When many clerics come among us we will become unbelievers]." Before [the emergence of the ulama], I didn't know what this meant, but now I do. It means that the ulama cause trouble. If one hundred clerics return to the Philippines [from studying in the Middle East], one hundred different translations of Islam will develop.[18]

>The ulama are trying to destroy our culture. They are influenced by Saudi Arabia, and the Saudi government is controlled by Wahhabis.[19] Wahhabis are not Sunnis [the major sect of Islam, to which belong virtually all the Muslims of Southeast Asia] . . . According to the ustadzes, the death commemoration is not allowed, but it is a beautiful practice . . . What has happened now is that, on the seventh day after a death, people report that they hear the voice of the deceased crying; "I am hungry, give me food." I have been told about one case where the ghost of the deceased appeared, and ran after an ustadz.

Despite the misgivings of ordinary Muslims and the active resistance of datus, the number of extended death rituals beyond seven days after a death seems to be declining. Of the ten or twelve death rituals I attended or was told about during my stay in Cotabato City, only two occurred later than seven days following a death—one at one hundred days and the other at one year. Both were held by datu families, and both included traditional tahlil chanting, which is also becoming less common. At most of the kandulis I attended, traditional chanting did not occur. In general, only relatively wealthy datu families—those most anxious to counter the influence of the ustadzes and best able to afford the expense—continued to hold the full range of traditional death celebrations. It is an ironic development, though not a surprising one in light of the history of Cotabato datus in the modern period, that those who have most energetically defended traditional religious ceremonies have also been the most thoroughly Westernized.

Implicit in the assertions of traditional elites about the religious reforms of the clerics is that they deprive local Muslims not only of cherished cultural meanings but of occasions for celebration. That implication seems justified when the range of attempted reforms is examined. The traditional celebrations (common throughout Muslim Southeast Asia) associated with two holy days—Maulid en Nabi (the birthday of the Prophet—Arabic Maulidu'n-Nabi) and the Layatul Kadir (the Night of Power—Arabic Lailatu'l-Qadr) have been de-emphasized or simplified due to the influence of the ustadzes. They have also discouraged elaborate celebrations for those returning from the pilgrimage to Mecca (Hajj). Additionally, clerics strongly disapproved of at least three indigenous cultural activities that were particularly enjoyed by young people. One concerns the death vigil traditionally kept by family, friends, and neighbors for seven nights after the death of a community member. Although the body (in accord with standard Islamic practice) is normally buried within twenty-four hours, it is believed that the spirit of the deceased remains at the family house for seven days and requires company. The vigil was an important social occasion for adolescent girls and boys, who stayed awake the entire night playing cards, mah-jongg, and other group games, occasionally even gambling for money stakes. A passage from my field notes describes one such vigil: "Tonight I attended a vigil for Kasan's mother. About twenty young people, most of them boys, played cards for pieces of candy. Two separate card games were in progress and the noise level was quite high. Kasan's brother-in-law had to hush them twice because of the Qur'an reading going on in the back room. There three imams read separate sections of the Qur'an simultaneously. The goal is to have the Qur'an recited completely once, and ideally twice, during the seven-day vigil."

The second activity, known as *panguyaw*, occurred on a wedding night. It was a postwedding parlor game in which the groom playfully pursued the bride around a sitting room to the noisy encouragement of the unmarried female friends of the bride. On the occasion I witnessed, the unmarried friends of the bride and groom gathered after the wedding ceremony at the house where the bridal chamber was located. As photographs were being taken, the young female friends of the bride encouraged the groom to show affection to his new wife by putting his arm around her, holding her hand, or kissing her on the cheek. The young spectators would shriek with glee when he complied with their requests. These popular practices have by no means been eliminated by the objections of the ustadzes, but clerical disapproval has clearly decreased their incidence and social intensity.

The third offending activity was an innovative form of indigenous popular entertainment first developed during the rebellion. The dayunday ("song duel") is an exceedingly popular form of public entertainment most often found in association with wedding celebrations. It is a modern adaptation of a traditional song form using Western instruments (guitar) and some aspects of Western showmanship, yet is still unmistakably an indigenous non-Western entertainment.[20] The dayunday involves a song contest between a man and a woman, or more commonly a three-way competition between two women and one man (or vice versa), with the singers trading off extemporaneous verses of romantic repartee. Dayunday singers are professional entertainers hired most commonly to perform at wedding celebrations. Ordinary Muslims would walk miles to attend dayunday performances that typically continued throughout the night.

9. A wedding procession near Campo Muslim. The bride, with head bowed as prescribed by custom, is accompanied by female attendants holding decorated umbrellas.

The ustadzes were offended by the dayunday and campaigned without success to ban it. They objected to men and women performing together and singing openly about love and romance. They claimed that dayunday performances encouraged unlawful sexual relations and elopements. Dayunday lyrics express sexual attraction indirectly, employing deep metaphors and archaic language.[21] Stage gestures—winks, nods, and nudges—depict flirtatiousness without being sexually suggestive. The overt sexual content found in the Western movies and music so pervasive in Cotabato City is entirely absent in dayunday performances. The ustadzes nevertheless attacked the dayunday more frequently and vehemently than they objected to Western entertainments because they viewed the dayunday as a pernicious cultural departure. It represented a revitalization (and, to some extent, a Westernization) of traditional popular culture at a time when the ulama were attempting to refashion social behavior to conform with the tenets of Islam. As an indigenous development it was more troubling than fully external influences because it represented a cultural drift directly away from the politico-religious project of the ulama. When it became clear that their denunciations had done nothing to lessen the popularity of

10. A 1988 dayunday performance in Campo Muslim. This public performance, given by three professional dayunday singers in conjunction with a wedding celebration, lasted from dusk till dawn and was attended by hundreds of community residents.

the dayunday, many ustadzes simply refused to attend weddings where the dayunday was performed. As clerics condemned dayundays, datus embraced them. Traditional elites sponsored every one of the dayundays I attended and, with the resumption of electoral politics in 1985, they became the most popular way to ensure large crowds at political rallies.

Another major area of cultural contention between clerics and traditional elites was adjudication. Datus pointed to instances of the austere application of Islamic law by certain clerics as evidence for ulama judicial extremism, as opposed to the more flexible penalties associated with traditional Magindanaon jurisprudence, where religious and social transgressions were "cured" by fines. During the latter part of the rebellion and in the years following the cease-fire, corpses (most often of females) would regularly be found floating down the Pulangi River from areas under rebel control. During my stay in Cotabato City fishermen still occasionally retrieved corpses from the river. It was widely accepted that these were the bodies of individuals punished for unlawful sexual relations by particularly strict ustadzes operating with the rebel forces. Many Muslims were troubled by this evidence of severe

compliance with the dictates of Sharia law, because it represented a serious escalation from the fines and forced marriages or beatings traditionally imposed for such transgressions. A story told by Datu Adil
about one of his acts of adjudication illustrates the differences between
traditional customs and the presumed adjudication practices of the
MILF:

> A man who was married with four children eloped with a woman to
> Davao. A party with guns was sent after him. The couple came to me in
> the middle of the night and asked me to help them. The man said: "I am
> a traveling insurance salesman, and while I was traveling I met this
> young woman and fell in love and we eloped." She was related to the
> Nuling datus, and ten years younger than the man. Her father was my
> friend. That was why they came to me.
>
> When the parents of the woman heard of my involvement they asked
> that the distribution of the bantingan [bridewealth] be held at my house
> and the wedding at their place. The bridewealth was seven hundred pe-
> sos. I fined the man three hundred pesos. I could have taken the whole
> fine for myself but I distributed most of it. They were in trouble when
> they came to me. The girl's parents had contacted Hadji Murad and the
> MILF was looking for them. The man would probably have been killed.

Despite stories such as these, and the clear evidence of a certain number of incidents of harsh punishments meted out by members of the
"inside" ulama, the majority of MILF adjudicators reportedly did not
dispense legal decisions resulting in penalties that were significantly
different from those traditionally imposed. The reason most often
given for their leniency was that local Muslims were not yet genuine
Muslims and so did not deserve strict Islamic sanctions.

POPULAR OPINIONS AND PRAGMATIC RESPONSES

Ordinary urban Muslims were not passive recipients of the cultural assertions of competing elite groups. On the contrary, they had distinct
views of their own and responded with a good deal of pragmatic resistance to the moral imperatives of the ulama or the traditional appeals
of the datus.

SCRUTINIZING THE INDEPENDENT ULAMA

As I walked with Nur Miskin one day along the busy river road con-
necting Campo Muslim with the rest of the city, we happened to pass a
prominent ustadz walking toward the community. The sight of the us-

tadz unaccompanied and on foot prompted Nur to remark, "See there, he is not like the datus, who travel only in cars and with bodyguards."

The residents of Campo Muslim found much that was appealing about the new ulama. As with Nur, they often expressed their approval to me in the form of a negative comparison: ustadzes are unlike datus. Residents also respected the ustadzes for the Islamic learning they had acquired, and they appreciated the social messages contained in some of the Friday sermons at the Mahad mosque.[22] Their admiration for the ulama notwithstanding, community members were, on the whole, quite resistant to ulama attempts to purify ritual practice or restrict popular celebration. The various proposed reforms caused confusion and apprehension as individuals were torn between abandoning identity-affirming rituals and practices and engaging in what the us-tadzes had characterized as un-Islamic behavior.

The mediator in many of these cultural disputes in the community was Imam Akmad, the head imam of the Campo Muslim mosque. The imam maintained close relationships with local ustadzes and had been much influenced by their teachings. At the same time, he identified with community members who were confused by the changes pro-moted by the ustadzes. In counseling community members, Imam Ak-mad distinguished between behavior that is un-Islamic and that which is anti-Islamic, and he suggested that there was nothing anti-Islamic in traditional rituals. He also expressed the sentiments of many commu-nity members by drawing a distinction between Islamization and Ara-bization. He advised members of his congregation that they were obliged to follow the injunctions of the Qur'an but not the practices of the people of the Middle East, and that the ustadzes sometimes con-fused these two. I once heard him comment that Allah revealed himself to the Arabs precisely because their behavior was so wicked. On bal-ance, the imam sincerely respected the ustadzes and counseled others to listen to their teachings. Yet he did not urge community members to change traditional practices, noting that the ustadzes were still young and lacking in practical knowledge. He himself had not ceased per-forming the "emergency" marriages traditionally required for unmar-ried women who had become pregnant. The ulama had disallowed these, declaring that what is *haram* (forbidden) cannot be made *halal* (permissible) by means of post-hoc authorization.[23] Imam Akmad was sympathetic to the principle guiding the ustadzes' pronouncement but was also well aware that strict compliance with their prohibi-tion would be impractical—even injurious—insofar as emergency marriages were most often arranged to avert violent retribution for the grave offense to the honor of the family of a pregnant but unmarried girl. The imam, a man possessed of considerable spiritual potency, had made his own compromise with the new ritual order by choosing not to exercise his supernatural powers lest doing so be construed as a form of the sin of *shirk*, or attempted partnership with the divinity.[24]

The one-quarter of community households with children who were CCF recipients also quietly but firmly resisted two attempts by the local ulama to force the removal of the program from the community. Community ustadzes were understandably threatened by a large and well-funded program that promoted (intentionally or not) Christian cultural hegemony in a Muslim community. Community recipients held some similar feelings but recognized as well that most of the ustadzes neither shared their poverty nor seemed concerned to alleviate it. Although many of the parents of CCF recipient children were acutely anxious at being associated with activities that had been characterized as anti-Islamic by the community ulama and the MILF, they nevertheless made known to the ustadzes that they would not cooperate in the program's removal unless another could be provided in its place.[25]

As teachers rather than ritual specialists, the ustadzes did not play an especially active role in the daily religious life of the community. The effect of their disapproval of so many activities associated with marriage and funeral ceremonies was to diminish their participation at ritual events they might otherwise have attended. Consequently, although the ustadzes were acknowledged as the most prominent religious figures in the community, they were not viewed by residents as specifically "community" leaders, nor indeed were they regarded as integral to community life. That fact was dramatically illustrated at the single most important community religious service of the year—the assembly prayers to celebrate Idul Fitr, the holy day marking the end of the Ramadan fast. The service was conducted in the community mosque rather than the Friday mosque at the Mahad and without the participation of a single ustadz.

Although I did not directly solicit community sentiments about the MILF, a number of community residents volunteered their opinions. From them I received the impression that there was a great deal of community support for the leaders of the Cotabato MILF forces who, despite their popularity, remained somewhat shadowy figures. I also sensed concern among community members to avoid offending (intentionally or unintentionally) representatives of a powerful armed underground organization. The only open (though quietly expressed) resentment I heard regarding MILF policies concerned the appropriation of community *pitra* (Arabic: *fitrah, zakat al-fitr*) contributions by the local MILF. Pitra payments, made at the end of the Ramadan fast, consisted in Cotabato of a quantity of polished rice equal to about two quarts (or its cash equivalent) per person in a household. One interpretation of the Islamic notion of *zakat* (almsgiving), of which pitra payments are a part, is that the giving of alms is obligatory and those alms should flow directly to mujahideen (those who struggle in defense of Islam) in periods of active conflict with nonbelievers.[26] On that basis, MILF representatives had, each year since the beginning of the Bangsamoro Rebellion, claimed the largest portion of the pitra payments collected by local imams, who were required by the MILF to keep a list of contributing households. Some Campo Muslim residents commented that the continued appropriation was unfair because many of the people in the community had greater economic needs than the rebels, who grew food for themselves in their rural camps. They also disputed the MILF-ulama interpretation of the contemporary situation, noting that the faithful were only obliged to support the mujahideen when they were actively fighting, and the war in Cotabato had been inactive for some time.[27]

DISREGARDING TRADITIONAL AUTHORITY

Despite their hesitancy about the reform program of the ulama, ordinary Muslims were not enthusiastic about the various appeals to shared tradition made by the datu elite. As mentioned above, I found little community regard for the traditional nobility, and some vocal disregard. Younger community residents, in particular, gave little heed to what they often referred to as "datu business." Some young people openly mocked the flowery speech of the elderly Sultan sa Magindanao when he occasionally gave speeches on the radio. Others hastened to point out to me that the paired words "*da*"and "*tu*"(meaning "absence" and "to grow") amounted to "no growth." Even community elders expressed their dislike of behavior they referred to as *datu-datu*— the social posing and status competition associated with traditional elites.

Opinions gathered from structured interviews provide a revealing pattern of attitudes concerning traditional elites. When asked to name the most powerful datu they knew of, 36 percent of community respondents could cite no one. Another 24 percent cited Zacaria

Candao, who at the time of the interviews had just been appointed governor of the province by the newly elected Corazon Aquino. Candao, as I have noted, neither referred to himself as a datu nor identified himself with the traditional nobility. Eighteen percent of respondents cited Datu Kamsa, the barangay captain. These responses indicate that a significant number of community residents no longer associated datus with political power (about 10 percent of respondents cited datus, such as Datu Udtug, who were no longer living), and that many of those who did continued to understand the term "datu" pragmatically, as one who rules.[28]

While a majority of Campo Muslim respondents (59.8 percent) reported that they would seek adjudication from Datu Kamsa, the barangay captain, in the event of a dispute with their neighbors, I also found that individuals brought different varieties of minor disputes to a range of adjudicators that included Imam Akmad, Kasan Kamid (in his capacity as formal leader of an organization of Campo Muslim neighbors), and other influential community members. For more consequential legal cases, residents relied on various forums, including both the Philippine legal system and the MILF courts. It was not, in fact, unusual for an individual to present a single claim successively in more than one forum in an attempt to receive a single favorable ruling. One community resident (an unusually litigious individual) became involved in a land conflict and first argued his case in the local provincial court where he received an unfavorable ruling. He then brought his claim "inside" to the MILF courts, where the decision again went against him. Subsequently, he presented his case before the government Sharia Court, a body of the regional autonomous government that applied a special law code loosely based on Sharia law. The Sharia Court had been labeled a "fake Islamic court" by the MILF and, at the time this case was brought before it, was very little used by Cotabato Muslims (the government Sharia Court also denied the man's claim).

The limited nature of the direct political influence exercised by either Datu Kamsa (and, by implication, other collaborating datus) or the MILF over community residents is indicated by the results of two elections. Mayoral elections were held in 1980, at a time when military control was still quite strong and the KBL, the party of the martial law regime, was at the peak of its power in Cotabato. Although the MNLF recommended nonparticipation in the election, the great majority of Campo Muslim household heads (88 percent) cast their votes. Of those household heads who cast their ballots in the city elections, 32 percent voted for the Chinese-Muslim KBL candidate, who was strongly supported by Datu Kamsa. Almost 25 percent voted for his opponent, Datu Mando Sinsuat, the former mayor. A great number of the votes for Datu Mando came from Iranun speakers who hailed originally from Kalanganan, a rural area lying within the city limits and the headquarters of the former smuggling economy. The former mayor had long had warm relations with the people from Kalanganan, while their relations with the barangay captain had been strained for some time. Most intriguingly, 13 percent of household heads voted for Teodoro Juliano, the former mayor who had recently spent three years in a military prison for daring to challenge military control of the city during the armed rebellion. The only Christian mayoral candidate, he had not been recommended by any Muslim community leader. Those who voted for him tended to be the poorest members of the community. Their electoral support was most likely acquired as the result of a specific method he had developed for obtaining Muslim votes. The Christian former mayor owned a lumberyard in the Muslim quarter and is said to have provided community members with wood for home-building free of charge. In exchange he required them to swear on a copy of the Qur'an that they would cast their vote for him.

In the last election of the Marcos period—that between President Marcos and Corazon Aquino—community members also voted in large numbers despite the fact that the MILF again took a nonparticipatory stance.[29] Those who participated voted overwhelmingly in favor of Corazon Aquino (by more than a three-to-one margin), in spite of Datu Kamsa's intensive campaigning for President Marcos.

CONCLUSION

In the years between the expiration of the armed rebellion in 1979 and the overthrow of the martial law regime in 1986, Campo Muslim residents found themselves situated, materially and metaphorically, between two contending Muslim elites. While neither group was integral to the community, both were intent on exercising authority there. Both were also able to apply considerable coercive force to enforce their claims, but there the resemblance ends.

The datu establishment was concerned with Campo Muslim only insofar as activities there posed a threat to their continued control of the province. Datu officeholders under the martial law regime made few direct attempts, in Campo Muslim or elsewhere, to seek legitimation for their rule from ordinary Muslims. The revitalization of the myth of sanctified inequality, as seen by the spate of royal proclamations during this period, seems not to have been aimed primarily at non-elite Muslims. It was associated instead with the Marcos regime's effort to legitimize the unilaterally established regional autonomous government (and thus delegitimize the MNLF and MILF) in the eyes of foreign observers, particularly Arab states.

The Muslim counterelite, composed of an aboveground coalition of ulama and professionals supporting (and supported by) an armed underground organization (the MILF), viewed Campo Muslim quite differently.[30] Intent on augmenting the separatist struggle (now reformulated as a struggle for genuine Muslim autonomy) with unarmed efforts, the counterelite regarded the people of Campo Muslim (and by extension all the ordinary Muslims of Cotabato) as an important political resource. As religious speech remained one of the few forms of public discourse permissible under martial law, members of the aboveground ulama quickly became important spokespersons for the Muslim opposition. While the ustadzes promoted Islamic renewal in order to perfect religious belief and practice in Cotabato, their reform project had direct political implications as well, most pointedly in its explicit challenge to the Islamic authority of the traditional nobility.

Zacaria Candao, the organizer of the aboveground opposition, proved exceptionally adept at employing Islamic renewal as a cultural frame for political activity under martial law. He organized Islamic conferences, established an Islamic radio program, and encouraged the formation of "Islamic family organizations." The da'wah parade and demonstration he coordinated combined Islamic rhetoric, political protest, and popular participation and became the model for subsequent mass actions in the post-Marcos period.

During the years of the armed rebellion, Campo Muslim residents (and ordinary Muslims in general) received little of the official ideology disseminated by leaders of the Muslim separatist movement. I have noted that, as one consequence, they constructed their own representations of the rebellion based on understandings that sometimes differed markedly from that of the rebel leadership. Beginning in 1980, when the al-Azhar–trained ulama began to speak out in mosques and Islamic schools in Cotabato City, Campo Muslim residents heard at last the Islamic core of the official separatist message. Some of that message appealed immediately, particularly when the ustadzes proclaimed political equality and economic justice to be essential aspects of Islam. The ustadzes also seemed altogether more admirable authority figures than most datus. Yet other pronouncements provoked considerable resistance from community residents. Calls by ustadzes to forsake therapeutic rituals and gratifying celebrations disheartened many.[31] Rumors of harsh applications of Sharia law in "liberated areas" of the province caused apprehension. Attempts by the ustadzes to remove the only social welfare program in Campo Muslim without providing a replacement generated resentment among its poorest residents.

With the assistance of such cultural mediators as Imam Akmad, community residents quietly but firmly opposed many of the changes promoted by the ulama without embracing the brand of traditionalism advocated by local datus. On the whole, Campo Muslim residents remained remarkably self-sufficient in terms of both ritual and political practice. Some looked to the Mahad (and by extension to the MILF) for political instruction or services, and others to the barangay captain (representing the government), and a number maneuvered in either direction depending on circumstances. For the most part, however, they lived their lives in between, and independent of, the opposed political camps.[32] The following chapter examines the termination of martial law in Cotabato and the nature of popular participation in the dramatically altered Muslim nationalist politics of the post-Marcos era.

CHAPTER 10

Muslim Nationalism after Marcos

The years between 1981 and 1986 saw the gradual reconstitution of the Muslim nationalist movement in Cotabato. While it lacked the strength for sustained armed engagements with the Philippine military, the MILF, with hundreds of armed fighters in secure mountain camps, remained a threat to the martial law government. On the basis of that continued threat its leaders pushed for the full implementation of the agreement signed in Tripoli. The MILF's diplomatic and publicity efforts were aided by a steadily developing aboveground alliance of Muslim professionals and clerics led by Zacaria Candao. During the same period, the Philippine Army gradually withdrew from the Muslim South to fight a communist-led armed insurgency that, by 1984, effectively controlled the rural hinterlands in large portions of the country.[1]

Muslim establishment elites (most of them datus), also took advantage of the loosening of military rule in Cotabato to reestablish local power bases. Establishment elites cooperated with the Marcos regime in attempting to convince external observers and (to a much lesser extent) local subordinates, that the rebellion was over, Muslim autonomy had been achieved, and the gains of that autonomy were being channeled to the Muslims of Cotabato. As described in the previous chapter, the cultural-political activities of both alliances in the first half of the decade reflected a gradual awareness—much more fully comprehended by the opposition alliance—that popular support was likely to become a decisive factor for those who wished to rule Muslim Cotabato.

The collapse of the Marcos regime in early 1986 brought a quickening of political activity in Cotabato. Most Muslim establishment figures lost their government positions, although a few held on to them or, improbably, acquired new ones.[2] Members of the datu establishment hurried to form local chapters of new or revived national parties to prepare for promised congressional and provincial elections. For its part, the Muslim opposition alliance found itself instantly propelled into the official political arena when its organizer, Zacaria Candao, was concurrently appointed governor of the province and chairman of the regional autonomous government. The MILF's goal of genuine autonomy for Philippine Muslims also seemed suddenly close at hand. The prospects for the full implementation of the Tripoli Agreement were significantly enhanced when Corazon Aquino, the widow of the Christian politician who had been the most strongly supportive of Muslim aspirations for self-determination, assumed the presidency of the Philippine republic.

In this chapter I draw together the themes presented in the previous two in order to present a detailed account of Muslim politics in post-Marcos Cotabato. I proceed by considering four political events: two mass rallies held in 1986 and two election campaigns—one for provincial governor and the other for city offices—conducted in 1988. Two new political features intersect in these events. First, each of the four political events included the active participation of the Muslim urban poor. That participation was diversely motivated and varied in form. Politicians made appeals to them, and made use of them, but in one event at least, the actions of poor Muslims surprised the Muslim elites who sought their cooperation. Second, three of the four events featured the unprecedented use of Islamic rhetoric (often voiced by Islamic clerics) in direct political appeals. It is the interplay between those two novel features of Muslim nationalist politics in the post-martial-law period that focuses this chapter.

THE *TAGUMPAY NG BAYAN* RALLY: POPULAR PROTEST AND THE ASCENDANCY OF THE MUSLIM COUNTERELITE

The Tagumpay ng Bayan (People's Victory) Rally was the first major political event of the post-Marcos period in Cotabato City. The rally, which took place in the Cotabato City plaza on February 26, 1986, was similar to many political gatherings held throughout the Philippines that day. It had been planned as a popular protest against the apparent theft of the presidential election by Ferdinand Marcos but was quickly transformed into a victory celebration after the so-called people power coup earlier that week induced the flight of Marcos to the United States on the twenty-fifth, the day before the scheduled protest rally. As a result, Corazon Aquino, his electoral opponent, assumed the presidency, ending the fourteen-year Marcos dictatorship.

The rally capped an exhilarating month for Cotabateños, including the residents of Campo Muslim. Even those community members who had most vocally professed disinterest in the 1986 "snap" presidential election were swept up in the contagious excitement of election day, February 7, and its aftermath. Local observers remarked on the unusual level of enthusiasm in the city for a presidential election, comparable to that generated by a local election. One reason for the high excitement was that the 1986 voting represented the first genuinely contested presidential election in seventeen years, the last having occurred in 1969, prior to the declaration of martial law.[3]

At the polling place closest to Campo Muslim the mood was festive. Children played while parents searched for their names on voting lists and cast their ballots. Young adults, most of whom had never voted in a national election, excitedly shared information. Elders lounged beneath trees drinking coffee and discussing politics. Later in the evening, after the polls had closed, Campo Muslim residents gathered in clusters on the main road to discuss the local results, exchange rumors, and listen to reports on the radio.

In Cotabato City, the challenger, Corazon Aquino, won in the polls by more than a two-to-one margin, while in the rest of Maguindanao Province Ferdinand Marcos led by an even greater, three to one, margin. The election in the city proceeded peacefully and without obvious irregularities or alleged incidents of voter fraud. The problem-free city polling was due in great measure to the work of volunteer poll-watchers from the provincial chapter of the National Citizen's Movement for Free Elections (NAMFREL), a nongovernmental organization established to monitor elections. NAMFREL first appeared in the Philippines in the early 1950s but was dissolved with the enactment of martial law in 1972. It reformed after the assassination of Benigno Aquino in 1983, with the assistance of unacknowledged American funding (Bonner 1987), and fielded an unusually effective nationwide force of volunteers in 1986 to monitor the presidential election in every province in the country. The NAMFREL volunteers at the large polling place near Campo Muslim consisted entirely of young Campo Muslim residents recruited by Kasan Kamid, a community organizer. They helped ensure that the 1986 election was conducted more freely than any other in the memory of Campo Muslim residents.

Election day conditions in the rest of the province differed dramatically from those in the city, in part because NAMFREL managed to place poll-watchers at only a small percentage of precincts. For most municipalities in the province, the 1986 election procedures differed little from those found in Muslim municipalities since the beginning of the republic. In a number of municipalities, polling places reported 100 percent voter turnouts with all ballots cast in favor of President Marcos. In some precincts Ferdinand Marcos received more votes than the number of registered voters. In at least one municipality—Barira—NAMFREL volunteers reported that all available ballots were cast the night before the election by barangay captains. In these municipalities, President Marcos led his opponent by margins as great as sixteen to one. In other municipalities voting went on with little interference, but local officials appropriated ballot boxes when they arrived at the municipal hall and conducted the vote count in secret. All seventeen municipalities in the province recorded that Ferdinand Marcos had received many more votes than Corazon Aquino.

This well-organized vóting fraud represented the last major endeavor of the KBL political machine in the province—part of a highly integrated national system for channeling significant amounts of money to political officials down to the barangay level to ensure a Marcos victory.[4] Despite the success of the machine in appropriating votes throughout the province, the 1986 election also saw the first significant challenges to the autocratic grip of traditional leaders on the election process. Those challenges most often came from young, urban-educated Muslims anxious for change. The following account presents the voice of Salik, a young member of a Muslim counterelite family, who returned to his birthplace from the city to monitor the election there for the opposition coalition, United Nationalist Democratic Organizations (UNIDO—see below). It is typical of three or four similar stories I heard following the election: "I was the UNIDO representative in my home barangay in Sulun. I spoke strongly there. The barangay captain almost cried when I opposed him. He told me: 'If we let people decide for themselves this year, Marcos will receive no votes and I'll be in trouble. Let's negotiate and make the results an even split.' I agreed to the 50–50 arrangement because the barangay captain is my relative. At the counting, the barangay captain wanted the results to show that Marcos had won by three votes but I insisted that there be an exactly even distribution as we had agreed."

A major impetus behind these new challenges was Zacaria Candao, the provincial chairman—for Maguindanao Province and Cotabato City—of UNIDO, the national opposition coalition that backed the candidacy of Corazon Aquino. Candao approached that difficult job with alacrity, relishing a direct electoral confrontation with establishment elites. He successfully associated the UNIDO platform with Muslim aspirations, even reconciling the nonparticipatory stand of the MILF—with whom he remained closely associated—with his own obvious electoral activism. He also arranged the defection to UNIDO of some Muslim KBL politicians, adding to the momentum of the UNIDO campaign in the city and province. Candao drew on his aboveground support network, as well as some assistance from the officially neutral MILF, to counter coercive moves by the KBL and to reduce somewhat the incidence of election fraud in the province.

Aquino supporters in the city and province watched intensely the unfolding post-election drama in Manila, expressing first hope, then frustration, and finally outrage, as Aquino, who had outpolled Marcos by a large margin in Cotabato City and a number of other provincial urban areas, was unaccountably falling behind in the official tallying in Manila. The three main political groups active in Aquino's Cotabato City victory met to organize a mass rally, coordinated with similar events nationwide, to protest the regime's increasingly conspicuous efforts to thwart the popular will by tampering with the national vote tabulation. The provincial chapter of UNIDO was composed largely of the Muslim counterelite under the leadership of Zacaria Candao. Members of the local chapter of Lakas ng Bayan (LABAN), the People's Power Party—a component of the UNIDO coalition and the specific party of Corazon Aquino—were almost entirely Christian and middle class, many of the most active of them women. There was also the Cotabato affiliate of Bagong Alyansang Makabayan (BAYAN), the New Nationalist Alliance—a federation of aboveground progressive nationalist organizations. Although BAYAN officially boycotted the presidential election, the (mostly Christian) members of its local chapter were active in the local NAMFREL chapter and almost all them had volunteered as NAMFREL poll-watchers or coordinators.

Although the rally as originally planned was to have equal participation from each of the three groups, it acquired a very different structure with the news of Marcos's departure. Anger gave way to exhilaration as citizens celebrated the toppling of the dictatorship. The rally transformed itself into a victory ceremony for the Muslim counterelite and an occasion to acclaim its leader, Zacaria Candao: a man who, overnight, had become the most powerful political figure—Muslim or Christian—in the province.

Although Muslims comprised less than half of the registered voters in Cotabato City, they formed the large majority of the crowd of more than fifteen thousand that overflowed the city plaza. Zacaria Candao, the featured speaker at the rally, addressed the crowd in untranslated Magindanaon—a language understood by almost none of the Christians present.[5] He spoke first of the new hope for the genuine implementation of the Tripoli Agreement under the Aquino government. He called for continued cooperation between Muslims and Christians, and for reconciliation, as well as wholehearted support for the new president. Among the numerous other speakers was a prominent ustadz, who may have been the first independent Muslim cleric ever to have spoken at a political rally from the stage of the city plaza.

Kasan Kamid and a group of Campo Muslim residents also shared the plaza stage with Zacaria Candao and other newly important politicians. They had marched to the rally with Candao at his request and stood on the stage that, just two weeks before, had been occupied by Sultan Ali Dimaporo and the leading Muslim KBL politicians of Mindanao. The world as viewed from that platform for a few exhilarating minutes seemed indeed to have been turned upside down.

While it is not clear to what extent Zacaria Candao planned his own sudden victory celebration, he did organize the highly symbolic march that preceded it. The plan for the original rally called for participants to march from different parts of the city to the central plaza. Candao chose to march from Campo Muslim. Early on the day before the rally he contacted Kasan Kamid as well as two young Islamic activists from the community who had helped to organize the student demonstration at the da'wah parade in 1985. He asked them to gather their "people" to participate in the march and rally. It was decided that one of the Islamic activists would give a speech at the rally representing the "Muslim Youth," and that Kasan would speak on behalf of the "Urban Poor."

The next day, thirty or so Campo Muslim marchers, more than a third of them women, assembled in the main road of the community. They wore yellow or green headbands—the colors of Corazon

Aquino's campaign and Islam, respectively—and carried banners and placards, some of them recycled from the da'wah parade. One of the new banners read in translation: "Forget the Old Politics and Confront the [Economic] Crisis."[6] When assembled, the Campo Muslim contingent filed to the intersection of the main community road and the riverside road. There they were joined by groups from the neighboring Muslim areas of Lugay-lugay and Kalanganan. When Candao arrived with his bodyguard, the parade commenced and streamed jubilantly through the city streets to the sound of drums and shouted slogans and the cheers of onlookers. It was the largest and most joyous of all the processions to the plaza.

When Zacaria Candao mounted the stairs to the large stage in the center of the Plaza, a number of his fellow paraders from Campo Muslim climbed with him. As the afternoon's speeches continued one after the other, however, a surprisingly familiar pattern emerged. The microphone was dominated by establishment politicians, almost all of them datus and many of them KBL stalwarts one or two months earlier. The podium was given over, time and again, to datu politicians who were recent defectors from the KBL to UNIDO. In a uniform fashion they called for genuine autonomy for Philippine Muslims, congratulated themselves for having been part of the UNIDO opposition, and attempted to excuse or obscure their activities during the rebellion. As the rally wore on, and the crowd waited for Candao to speak, the Campo Muslim group drifted down from the stage. When I rejoined them they were sitting off to the side, in the shade. I asked them why they had moved down and they grumbled that they were tired and it was hot up above. It was clear from their faces, however (an impression confirmed in later conversations), that they had also begun to feel discouraged and out of place, and so left the stage. The rally ended before either Kasan or Nur Miskin, the Islamic activist, was able to deliver his speech. By the end of the day it was unmistakably evident to the Campo Muslim marchers that many in the new UNIDO ascendancy had not forgotten "the old politics."

The favoring of recently defected datus over ordinary urban supporters suggests that as the purpose of the rally changed from protest to victory proclamation, Candao's political needs shifted accordingly. The rally, as originally conceived, was to have been the first mass protest in a series of urban actions—including general strikes—called by the national opposition to denounce the theft of the election. Candao needed to mobilize his mass urban base to carry out such popular protests, and had done so. When it was learned that the objective had been achieved, the protest became a victory rally and an occasion for Candao to begin to repay his datu allies.

In a conversation with him a short while after the victory rally, Candao indicated the reason for his reliance on the support of formerly establishment datus: "There is a problem finding new political leaders. My contemporaries all joined the KBL. In the election campaign I had a difficult time recruiting municipal UNIDO campaign chairmen. I was not afraid myself because I had the support of the MILF, but I cannot really blame others for hesitating. Other than the powerful families there were no organizations to protect people." Although there was ample political support for UNIDO in the city, for the difficult and dangerous electoral campaign in the countryside there were few available political allies other than those traditional elite politicians who took calculated risks based on personal political ambition and switched their allegiance from the KBL to UNIDO. As a result, the first public manifestation of the new, post-Marcos politics in the province was difficult to distinguish from the old.

Notwithstanding the remarkable persistence of datu politicians in Cotabato, there were to be two very significant innovations in Muslim politics—both prefigured in Candao's victory rally—in the post-Marcos period. The first was the self-conscious political use made of ordinary Muslims (and especially the "urban poor"), and the second was the introduction, for the first time in the modern era, of specifically Islamic elements—from green headbands to speechmaking by ustadzes—in public political discourse. Those two new features were combined in a most original form in the next major political event in Cotabato.

MUSLIM MASS ACTION: THE MILF "PRAYER RALLY"

By the end of March 1986, Zacaria Candao had attained unprecedented authority in the region. He had been designated by the new national administration as both acting governor of the province of Maguindanao and acting chairman of the Executive Council of the Regional Autonomous Government for Central Mindanao. The MILF, in contrast, had, by late March, been repeatedly frustrated in its efforts at national-level recognition as a result of the nearly exclusive attention paid by the Philippine government and national media to the original MNLF under Nur Misuari. Misuari had shown no inclination to reunite the separate rebel factions under one banner to present a united negotiating front and, for its part, the government of Corazon Aquino appeared willing to reopen formal talks with Misuari's group alone on regional autonomy as outlined in the Tripoli Agreement.

In the competition for government recognition as the legitimate representative of the Bangsamoro insurgents—and, by extension, of the "Bangsamoro people"—Misuari's MNLF held a number of advantages. Misuari was a signatory to the Tripoli accord while Salamat was not. Misuari had also met for a series of talks with Benigno Aquino in Damascus in 1981, and later, after Aquino's assassination in 1983, with his younger brother, Agapito, in Madrid. He was therefore more familiar to President Aquino and her advisors. In addition, as a result of a long history of media coverage, Misuari and the MNLF were both more familiar to Philippine Christians and more skilled in the techniques of obtaining media access than were Salamat and the MILF.[7]

By late March 1986, the MILF in Cotabato had decided to demonstrate to the Aquino administration exactly why it should be given due consideration. In self-conscious imitation of the Manila "people power" demonstrations that forced the flight of Ferdinand Marcos and brought Corazon Aquino to power, the MILF chose to stage a mass rally. As portrayed by Zacaria Candao in our interview, the MILF rally was conceived as an "exercise to determine if [the MILF] still had the support of the masses." As the MILF remained, at least formally, an illegal organization, its preparations for what became known as the "prayer rally" were carried out through the public leadership of the aboveground ulama.[8] The chairman of the organizing committee for the rally, like the rest of its official organizers, was a prominent aboveground ustadz. It was nevertheless clear to all concerned that it was the MILF leadership initiating and sponsoring the rally.

Campo Muslim residents were among those who participated in the preparations for the MILF rally. In the last week of March, an organizational meeting for the heads of Muslim student and community organizations was held at the public market mosque, attended by more than fifty people including Kasan Kamid and the two Islamic activists from Campo Muslim, Nur Miskin and Zamin Unti. Most of those in attendance had received letters inviting them to a meeting sponsored by "the Bangsamoro People."

One week later, about thirty of those attending the previous meeting were invited "inside" to the MILF camp in the mountains north of the city. They rode jeeps or pedicabs to the end of the road and walked three kilometers uphill to reach the camp. Some five hundred people attended that meeting, including community leaders and ustadzes from throughout Cotabato. The "facilitator" for the meeting was Hadji Murad, the commander of the Cotabato MILF forces. His minister of information was also present. They presented the formal objectives of the rally and described the form it would take. The participants, arriving from all parts of Cotabato, would march to the city plaza from different directions. Various areas of origin were identified by zone numbers corresponding to the zones of operation enumerated by the rebels during the armed insurgency. Ustadz Omar Pasigan, the founder of the Mahad in Campo Muslim and the finance chairman for the rally, noted that the expenses for the rally would total about seventy-five thousand pesos (approximately four thousand dollars), and he assessed individual organizations (mostly madrasahs) various sums to finance transportation, food, medicine, and placards. Those organizations would in turn collect contributions of goods and services from individuals.

Organizers began announcing the rally on Magindanaon-language radio programs just one week before it was scheduled to take place. Broadcast messages tended to be quite vague, announcing only that there would be "activities" (*pedsuwan-suwan*) in the city of Cotabato beginning on April 13. Announcers neither reported the purpose of the rally nor the fact that it was sponsored by the MILF, but did name the ustadzes involved in its organization. More precise news of the rally spread rapidly by word of mouth in Campo Muslim. Although there was never a formal announcement of the rally during Friday congregational prayers in the mosque, community residents quickly became aware that this was an MILF rally in support of Hashim Salamat and the full implementation of the Tripoli Agreement. I included a question about the prayer rally on a formal instrument I administered later to a random sample of community household heads. Of 122 interviewees, 93 (76.2 percent) reported that they had attended the rally. Another 8 (6.6 percent) replied that they were unable to attend but had contributed goods or services to rally organizers.

The gathering they attended was indeed an impressive display of organizational capability. With between fifty thousand and one hundred thousand people attending the prayer rally on each of its three days, it was by far the largest, and longest, mass demonstration ever staged in Cotabato City.[9] MILF supporters poured into the center of the city, preventing most businesses on or near the plaza from operating normally for two of the three days. Some 750 marshals appointed to control traffic and patrol the ranks of the rallyists effectively policed the entire central city for the duration of the rally. Marshals established checkpoints at the eight points of entry to the rally site and inspected parcels and conducted body searches of all individuals—participants or nonparticipants—entering the center of the city. Participants arrived from provinces as far away as South Cotabato and Davao Del Sur, but the majority of those present were reported to be from Maguindanao Province and Cotabato City. Most of the participants came at their own expense, carrying enough food for three or more days. From their headquarters at the Mahad in Campo Muslim, rally organizers arranged the stage program and managed the logistics of supervising a massive group of demonstrators.

On the opening day of the rally, the "mass media chairman"—also an ustadz—stated the objectives of the rally as follows:

1. To show the public, the government, and the world that the Bangsamoro people—Muslims, Christians, and the tribal Filipinos—support Hashim Salamat.

2. To respond to the peace and reconciliation leadership of President Corazon C. Aquino.

3. To push for the immediate and full implementation of the Tripoli Agreement of 1976 as the only sound and just political solution to the Mindanao problem.

4. To make known that before any implementation of the Tripoli Agreement there should first be negotiations between the MILF and the Philippine government.

5. Before these can be brought about, there should first be a strengthening of the cease-fire agreement (*Mindanao Cross*, April 19, 1986).

On the plaza stage, successive speakers—almost all of them ustadzes—called on the Aquino government to resume negotiations immediately with MILF leaders for the full implementation of the Tripoli accord under the auspices of the Organization of the Islamic Conference. Some speakers vowed that the rallyists would remain in the plaza until President Aquino responded to their demands. Between speeches, and in the evenings, demonstrators were entertained by singers performing rebel and religious songs, but not dayunday. On the last day of the rally, the demonstrators stood without complaint in the rain to listen to Zacaria Candao. Performing a dual role unique in the history of the Philippine republic, he both spoke in support of Hashim Salamat and the MILF and, in his capacity as government representative, accepted the manifesto of the rallyists for presentation to President Aquino.

Despite its impressive scale and coordination, the MILF rally drew almost no national media attention; only one Manila daily newspaper carried as much as a single short article on the mass demonstration. That lack of national notice was partly due to the extraordinarily Manila-centric focus of the national media but was also a consequence of the inexperience of the rally's organizers in attracting media attention. The rally also failed to prompt a specific response from the Aquino administration.

Unable to communicate effectively to the government or the Philippine public (let alone "the world") the extent of popular support in Cotabato for Salamat and the MILF, the prayer rally did not accomplish any of its stated objectives. Nevertheless, as an experiment to gauge the ability of its sponsors and organizers to mobilize Cotabato Muslims, it proved a tremendous success and doubtless influenced the next phase of Muslim nationalist politics in the region—the formation of an Islamic political party. To gain the attention of the national government and media, the MILF soon reverted to a well-practiced method and produced more favorable results.

ISLAM, POPULISM, AND ELECTORAL POLITICS: THE 1988 PROVINCIAL ELECTIONS

I left Cotabato City in September 1986, and returned in January 1988 to observe the political campaigns for the provincial and municipal elections held in February. A number of important political events occurred in the intervening fifteen months, two of which deserve mention.

By January 1987, the MILF saw its interests directly threatened by two moves of the national government. The first involved a number of provisions in an article of the draft constitution to be voted on in early February 1987. The provisions concerned the formation of an autonomous region for "Muslim Mindanao." They stated that the proposed autonomous region would only become effective when approved by a majority of the votes cast in a special plebiscite called for that purpose, thus ensuring that only provinces and cities voting favorably would be included in the autonomous region. In an "Official Declaration" in late December 1986, the MILF announced its rejection of the relevant article of the draft constitution because its provisions were not in keeping with the "true spirit of the Tripoli Agreement" and would not result in a "meaningful and genuine autonomy as envisioned in the duly-signed accord" (*Mindanao Cross*, December 20, 1986).

Second, the Aquino administration signaled that it had decided to resume formal negotiations with the MNLF, implicitly recognizing Misuari's group as the sole legitimate representative of the separatist movement. President Aquino had met personally with Nur Misuari in Sulu in September and, by early January, government representatives and MNLF negotiators were convening in Jeddah, Saudi Arabia. Governor Candao noted, in a January 3 newspaper report, that the MILF had been "driven to the corner" by its exclusion from the talks and by persistent government disregard of its proposals for a dialogue (*Mindanao Cross*, January 3, 1987). When the Jeddah negotiations produced a cease-fire agreement, Hadji Murad, the MILF chief of staff, warned of trouble should the Aquino government continue to deny the MILF the dialogue it had been asking for peacefully.

The following week, a few days before a scheduled trip by President Aquino to Cotabato, the MILF attacked, striking government targets in Cotabato City and other parts of Central Mindanao. Mortar shells fell in sections of the city and rebels burned the provincial capital building in Maganoy. Elsewhere in the region, power lines were cut, bridges burned, and police and army garrisons attacked. Twenty-five persons were reported killed in the fighting. President Aquino called an emergency cabinet meeting but decided not to cancel her trip to Mindanao. In Cotabato she met with Hadji Murad, and her chief negotiator arranged a temporary cease-fire with the MILF. The editor of the local newspaper remarked later in an interview with me that there would almost certainly have been more destruction in the city from the MILF attacks had not Zacaria Candao been in position as acting governor.

THE ISLAMIC PARTY OF THE PHILIPPINES

A second notable political event—one more consequential in the long term—was the formation of a new political party, the Islamic Party of the Philippines (IPP). Despite its expansive title it was a provincial party without formal ties to a national party apparatus or, for that matter, to any Islamic organizations in other parts of the Muslim South. The Islamic Party of the Philippines was organized in early 1987 at a meeting of the ulama of Cotabato called by Zacaria Candao. The published "program of government" of the IPP included the establishment of a meaningful autonomy in the "Bangsamoro Homeland," the eradication of "all forms of evil in the government and society," and the equitable distribution of wealth by preventing the "concentration of wealth in a privileged few hands." The program also contained a statement of belief that "Islam offers a complete basis for the solution of all human problems including socio-economic ones" (*Mindanao Cross,* April 11, 1987). Lanang Ali, the secretary-general of the party, was also legal counsel for the MILF, having succeeded Candao in that position.

Elections for the new Philippine Congress—the first opportunity to elect political representatives since the establishment of the new government—were held in May of 1987. The IPP contested the congressional elections and surprised the traditional Muslim elite when the politically unknown non-datu candidate they put forward for the congressional district that included Cotabato City outpolled a number of established datu politicians to place a close second behind the winning candidate. The winner, Datú Michael Mastura, was a member of the traditional core nobility and a nationally known figure who ran as the Aquino administration's candidate. A political moderate who had held various government positions throughout the armed rebellion, he had just concluded an assignment for the new administration as chairman of a presidential task force to examine the question of autonomy for Muslim Mindanao. He was well-known by most of the residents of Cotabato City—both Muslims and Christians—and well regarded by many of them. Nevertheless, he narrowly escaped defeat by a young political novice fielded by the IPP.

The strong showing of the IPP prompted the major datu families— including some who had been bitter enemies—to unite to an unprecedented degree to defeat Candao and the IPP in the January 1988 provincial elections. All concerned realized that the stakes were especially high. The overwhelmingly Muslim population of Maguindanao Province guaranteed that the province would be included in any Muslim autonomous region. Control of an autonomous province would depend on electoral support, so incumbents were sure to have an advantage. The political benefits that would accrue to the winner of the

1988 gubernatorial election provided a powerful inducement for cooperation within both the datu elite and counterelite coalitions. The
threat to traditional elite interests represented by the IPP also caused
Candao to lose many of the datu allies he had gained during his rise to
political prominence in early 1986—including the Mastura family.
The contest for the governorship set Candao, the appointed governor
and administration (as well as IPP) candidate against Datu Simeon Datumanong, member of a prominent datu family, former governor, and
onetime political mentor of Zacaria Candao. In at least three of its features, the 1988 electoral campaign for governor of Maguindanao
Province was without precedent in Cotabato. It was the first electoral
struggle between two clearly distinguished and ideologically opposed
Muslim elite groups for the leadership of the province. Also, for the
first time ever, Islamic discourse figured prominently in political appeals made to voters. As a consequence, religious disputes, such as that
about the proper role of the ulama, were finally contested in public political debates. And third, because of the new national political atmosphere and the loss of exclusive control of the province by the datu
elite, it was, in all likelihood, the most genuinely democratic election
ever conducted in Muslim Cotabato.[10]

ISLAMIC ARGUMENTS IN THE RADIO CAMPAIGN

Both electoral campaigns relied on radio speeches in Magindanaon as
a primary means to present their views. Campo Muslim residents lis-
tened to many of those speeches with great interest. In addition to
Candao himself and the members of his slate, the IPP campaign utilized two types of radio commentators: ustadzes and holders of traditional aristocratic titles. The traditional commentators for the IPP were
acquired to balance the use of the same sort of commentators by the
datu coalition. Traditional commentators for both candidates were
holders of long-defunct hereditary offices of the Cotabato sultanates.
They were authorities on taritib, the protocol governing relations
within the aristocracy and among the traditional estates. They survived
as dignitaries, old men with neither power nor real authority and a
good deal less public influence than the ulama. They were, however,
able to provide traditional legitimation as official spokesmen for the
old ways. The traditional commentators for the datu coalition recited
in detail the bloodlines of Datumanong and his slate. Those employed
by the IPP, although not endorsing the leadership of the ulama, praised

Candao and referred to him as "datu"—a term that, as I have noted, he never used for himself.

While the ustadz commentators on the da'wah radio program emphasized that Candao was the choice of the ulama because he served the people, much of their radio time was spent responding to the sharp attacks of the datu coalition. The IPP was repeatedly criticized for injecting Islam into electoral politics—a practice their opponents characterized as Shi'a-inspired heterodoxy.[11] Congressman Mastura, campaigning actively against the candidate endorsed by his own party, most cogently presented the objections of the datu coalition when he stated in his radio speech:

> It is a Shi'a principle that the ulama participate directly in government. IPP, do not use Islam for politics. This is a Shi'a policy. In Iran, the ulama want to be political leaders. I am not suggesting that in Islam the ulama cannot participate in politics. However, if the ulama comprise the political leadership, there will be no one to preach. The ustadzes have no need to be elected. They already have positions. They are already persons of authority because they have much knowledge . . . We do not want to create ayatollahs or mullahs here in the Philippines. If we did, we would be diverting from the Sunna [the divinely inspired precedents of the Prophet] related by Imam Shafii [the founder of the school of Sunni law predominant throughout Southeast Asia]. We must follow the straight path.[12]

An ustadz commentator offered the IPP response to those who, like Congressman Mastura, criticized the participation of the ulama in politics: "The right people to hold all political positions are people who fear God. Ulama participation in politics should not be criticized because such activity is their duty—to encourage those who do good, and discourage those who do evil. We have to determine who destroys us, who destroys Islam. We must determine who are our enemies. The principal duty of a Muslim is to correct mistakes, not by force but by one's words, one's heart." The ustadz also reminded voters that the IPP was a party of the many aligned against the advantaged few: "If you are weak by yourself, create an organization. Bring weak people together to resist a single powerful person who is doing wrong. We the weak people have grouped together to become strong. That is why we will vote for Candao because he represents the organization of the weak." The ustadz radio commentators also counterattacked by labeling Simeon Datumanong a "kafir" (unbeliever) because of his position as the Marcos-appointed governor of the province during the fiercest

fighting of the Bangsamoro Rebellion (conveniently overlooking the
fact that Zacaria Candao succeeded Datumanong in the same position). Datumanong was often pressured into quite defensive attitudes
when responding to these accusations, as illustrated by these excerpts
from one of his radio speeches:

> People have asked why, if I was with the government for twenty years, I
> could not achieve freedom for our people. I don't know what they mean
> by this statement, but if "freedom" means independence, I could not
> achieve that with my small government position. I am only an ordinary
> person. I did not have the authority to seek independence . . . My oppo-
> nent has accused me of being a kafir and charges that I was the master-
> mind of military operations here during the rebellion. But I think if you
> know me you cannot believe those statements. In regard to my being a
> kafir: how can that be? I've been to Mecca, I pray, I fast, I give zakat.
> God knows what I am. Concerning the [military] operations, I did not
> order them. I had no authority. During that time, if there was an opera-
> tion, I helped the evacuees. We provided medicine. We could not stop
> the operations. That was the character of the time. Do not blame me. It
> was a time of war. By blaming me you offend God.

The datu coalition attempted to deflect attention from Datumanong's
long history of cooperation with the martial law regime by pointing to
the potentially harmful consequences of Candao's close connections to
the IPP and the MILF. Congressman Mastura and his brother Tocao, a
municipal mayor, led the radio offensive:

> Candao and his party [the IPP] know nothing about government man-
> agement. These people do not know how to govern. They have joined
> the government to destroy it. This is because of their desire for revolu-
> tion. However, the "bomb" will fall on us . . . If we choose a strong man
> [referring to Simeon Datumanong], he could find the means for reconcil-
> iation [with the MILF]. But if we choose a leader whose mind is only on
> one side, and not on the welfare of all of the people [i.e., Zacaria Can-
> dao], then we cannot find peace in our region.
>   A few days ago [Candao] spoke in Darapanan [an MILF "liberated
> area"], and he told the people that those who support Simeon Datu-
> manong don't know what revolution is about. He said that revolution is
> different from governing. If that is his opinion of revolution, then he
> should not be in the government because revolution is opposed to the
> government. If you are in government, and work for revolution, you can
> be charged with treason and shot by a firing squad . . . I warn the people
> of my municipality [literally: my relatives] do not join the IPP poll-
> watchers because there will probably be picture-taking [by the military]
> of IPP poll-watchers to identify MILF cadres. If this happens to you, you
> should not blame me. I have already helped many people out of jail. You
> will have done it to yourself—I am not threatening you.

Zacaria Candao responded succinctly to these accusations and ad-monitions when, in one of his radio addresses, he spoke obliquely of the affinity between the program of the IPP and the earlier goal of Us-tadz Salamat to reform Muslim leadership: "If only those who were leaders twenty years ago had addressed the problems that were created in the previous twenty years, the Muslim people would have achieved real freedom. If they had led with the true governance of Islam, the struggles of the last twenty years would not have been necessary. But because they neglected those problems and abandoned the struggle, the young generation moved forward. Now the old politicians are schem-ing in order to recover the leadership again." He also replied pointedly to those who had referred to him as a misguided or disingenuous revo-lutionary:

> Regarding those who say that if I am a revolutionary I should stay in the jungle: they say this because they do not understand what is meant by revolution. It is true that we do not see the problems the same way. They do not know what it means to change our society. Revolutionaries do not just fight in the forest or use firearms. There are many ways to achieve our goals. It can also be done by speaking—telling the truth. If all a person knows is to work with the government to minimize the suf-fering of the people and help achieve change, this too could further our cause. A truly brave man confronts his enemy face to face—mind to mind. But my opponents think revolution only means to hide from one's enemy. When *they* met the enemy [referring to Ferdinand Marcos] they did not confront him, they became his friend. That is something I could not do.

It was evident from listening to the radio campaign—itself unexam-pled in Cotabato politics—that Simeon Datumanong and the com-mentators who spoke for him were uncomfortable with the new elec-tioneering style, one that required direct and extended appeals to a mass audience. Their discomfort with the new approach, and their ten-dency to revert to the political style of old, were evident in some of their speeches, as in this excerpt from one of Datumanong's:

> We [i.e., Datumanong and his slate] know how to govern, how to deal with people. We are all winners because all the datus, all the strong fam-ilies, all the *liders* [political brokers] are helping us. It is most obvious that the datus are helping us, especially the two congressmen [Datu Michael Mastura and Datu Guiamid Matalam, the son of Datu Udtug]. In regard to the ulama, they are helping us but are not doing so publicly because their support is in their hearts only. In our party are the most upright people. We believe in God. Even those powerful families who were fighting before are united behind me: the Masturas, the Sinsuats,

the Matalams. Because of that, after I am elected we will be able to develop peace and order.

Look at the former friends of Candao—individuals such as Guiamid
Matalam, Michael Mastura, Rajamuda sa Magindanao [a traditional titleholder and acting Sultan of Magindanao], Didagan Dilangalen [all
members of the traditional nobility]—and many of his own relatives. All
have left him [literally: stopped going to him]. Why did they do that? If
he were a good politician, his allies and relatives would not abandon him.

The radio speeches made it apparent that the definition of a "good
politician" was itself a topic of contention in the new Muslim electoral
politics of Cotabato.

ISLAMIC POPULISM AND CULTURAL PLURALISM

The populist Islamic appeals of Candao and the IPP were as alien to
the datu elite as they were threatening. Attempts by datu commentators to counter the IPP appeal in public speeches were often confused
and occasionally counterproductive. The populism of Candao's IPP
campaign—emphasizing justice for disadvantaged Muslims and "revolutionary" social change—echoed the Islamic messages advanced by
the ulama in Friday sermons since early in the decade, as well as the
public pronouncements of the MILF. But Candao's populist appeal was
not delimited by the ulama's program for Islamic renewal. In fact, IPP
campaign rallies were often surprisingly pluralistic as well as popular
events.

The plural and popular character of the IPP appeal was demonstrated in Governor Candao's final campaign rally. The rally for his
opponent, Simeon Datumanong, took place in the central plaza, a location that remained associated with traditional, establishment politics. Candao held his rally on the waterfront at the main riverside pier
in the Muslim quarter of the city. Candao sat in a chair on a hastily
constructed wooden stage flanked by Ustadz Yahiya and Ustadz Pasigan, his former comrades on the MILF cease-fire committee and the
cofounders, with him, of the IPP. Also seated on the podium were two
members of the core Magindanaon nobility—one of them a radio
commentator for Candao. At one point a young ustadz took the stage
with a group of young female madrasah students dressed in Middle
East–influenced gowns and head coverings and led them in a pledge to
support to the death Candao and the IPP. They were followed shortly
after by a young man and woman, both dressed in blue jeans and
T-shirts, who sang popular American songs to entertain the crowd.

The sometimes glaring juxtapositions on the waterfront stage illustrate the complex composition of Candao's electoral appeal. Not only had Candao declined the use of the title "datu" for himself, he had stated (in an interview with me) in the heady early days of his ascension to office in 1986 that he saw "no place for traditional titles or leaders." Why then did he utilize datu commentators in his 1988 campaign, and why were traditional dignitaries seated with him on stage at the rally? While these Magindanaon aristocrats reminded voters of Candao's aristocratic bloodlines, that does not seem to have been the main purpose of their inclusion in his electoral campaign. As illustrated in the pointed radio exchanges of the campaign, the ideological battle lines between the datu coalition and the IPP were very sharply drawn, and Candao had little to gain by diluting his message merely to call attention to the noble blood that flowed in his veins. Candao's primary purpose in including traditional commentators was more likely a circuitously populist one. Authorities on taritib (aristocratic protocol) such as those who endorsed Candao were spokesmen for (and embodiments of) all of Magindanaon tradition, not just the formal observances of the high nobility but also the familiar rituals, beliefs, and practices embraced by ordinary Muslims. The presence of traditional cultural authorities (in the persons of the aristocratic dignitaries) thus balanced that of the ustadzes, those who had called for the elimination of many identity-affirming traditional practices. As part of his popular appeal to voters, Candao wanted to signal ordinary Muslims that a vote for him would not be a vote to abolish all of local tradition but only its autocratic and abusive elements.

Equally incongruous was the cultural disjunction between the Islamic intensity of the madrasah students and the pop music fervor of the T-shirted couple that followed them to the stage. The ulama had long before made clear their disapproval of young Muslim men and women performing together on stage and singing about erotic love. Even so, the two most prominent ustadzes in Cotabato (as well as the female madrasah students) were among the audience for this performance. Nor was this the first such entertainment at a public appearance by Zacaria Candao. On one previous occasion he and his audience were entertained by a "Muslim fashion show" in which young Muslim women demonstrated various ways to wear the malong, a long tube skirt. At another event, a modern, and very sensual, version of a "traditional" Muslim dance was performed by a young woman. These two entertainments, unlike the rather straightforward Western entertainment at the waterfront rally, were forms of invented tradition. They presented generically "Muslim" versions of fashion shows and folk dance performances popular among Christian Filipinos. They were aspects of an ethnicized Philippine Muslim identity and tended to be organized and performed by members of the Westernizing Muslim elite, composed of the wealthiest and (usually) the most self-consciously aristocratic families. They were self-regarding artistic endeavors in a way that the dayunday—a genuinely popular entertainment—was not.

What all these artistic performances held in common was their potential for entertaining large Muslim audiences, and that clearly was the reason for their inclusion at mass political meetings even though the messages such entertainments sent seemed to contradict the teachings of the ulama. Zacaria Candao pragmatically included such entertainments (as another type of political resource) to draw large numbers of Muslim voters to his rallies and hold their attention. His need to provide Western (or Westernized) amusements in addition to Islamic presentations reveals something about the limited success of the Islamic renewal efforts of the ulama in the previous eight years.

The campaign message of Zacaria Candao and the Islamic Party of the Philippines was without precedent in Cotabato. Its proposal for a new politics based on ideal Islamic principles had broad appeal. One datu candidate in the provincial elections complained that he had lost even the votes of his relatives because of the attraction of the IPP. At the same time, the message presented in IPP electioneering differed from that offered by the ustadzes when they began to teach openly eight years earlier. The IPP appeal was less concerned with the purification of religious practice and the rejection of Western culture. Its radio messages utilized traditional as well as Islamic appeals, and its campaign rallies included traditional spokesmen and Western entertainments. This relaxation of some of the strictures of the Islamic renewal program represented a shift from a religious concern with Islamic purism to a political emphasis on Islamic-related populism. The IPP portrayed itself as the organization of the weak rather than the righteous, and it stressed Islamic entitlements rather than Islamic obligations. It offered a populist message—an inclusive and alternative Muslim nationalist appeal that emphasized ethical leadership and egalitarianism. That more eclectic message evidently appealed to Cotabato voters, who elected Zacaria Candao to the governor's office by a two-to-one margin.

MUNICIPAL ELECTIONS IN COTABATO CITY:
THE LIMITS TO ISLAMIC UNITY

The 1988 elections for municipal offices in Cotabato City differed notably in character and outcome from those held at the provincial level.
For one, the city elections were held among an electorate fairly evenly
divided between Muslims and Christians while the provincial electorate was overwhelmingly Muslim.[13] Second, while the provincial
elections were, for all practical purposes, quite narrowly focused on
two principal candidates, two parties, and two opposed political ideologies, the city elections were remarkably unconfined in the number
of variously affiliated candidates running for office. Twenty candidates
ran for city mayor and 133 candidates competed for ten city council
seats—an unprecedented array of contenders and parties reflecting a
complete reopening of the political process after years of effective one-
party rule under martial law.

Muslims comprised about half of those running for office: 8 of the
20 mayoral candidates, 6 of 11 vice-mayoral candidates, and somewhat less than 50 percent of the huge field of city council candidates.
They represented an exceedingly wide range of political opinion and
experience. Mayoral aspirants ranged from the former vice-mayor
Angka Biruar—a member of the Muslim counterelite and an experienced politician—to Zamin Unti, one of the young Islamic activists in
Campo Muslim, who was poor and unemployed, made his own campaign handbills, and ran on an independent Islamic platform. Between
them were contenders such as Peping Candao, the brother of Governor
Candao and the man who as a rebel defector protected the people of
Campo Muslim from the army during the rebellion; and Bai Fatima
Sinsuat, the head of the Progressive Labor Union, which controlled laborers on the main city pier.

The two leading Muslim candidates for mayor were Angka Biruar
and Peping Candao. While both could count themselves among the
Muslim counterelite, in their attributes and personal histories they differed markedly, both from one another and from Zacaria Candao, the
consolidator of that counterelite. Angka Biruar embodied the indistinct
boundaries between the old and new Muslim elite of Cotabato. He
was a prominent member of the foremost family of the coastal smuggler elite. The Biruars had operated (and some said still ran) the most
successful smuggling operation on the Cotabato coast. They had become quite wealthy from it—sufficiently wealthy to purchase from its

Christian owners a coconut plantation covering most of Bongo Island. They had also diversified into politics, sea transportation, and commercial fishing and had done well at all three. In addition, the Biruars were widely known for their concentrated efforts to purchase maratabat (status honor). Purchasing maratabat (in Magindanaon, *pamasa sa maratabat*) entails offering large amounts of bridewealth in exchange for access through marriage to traditional status honor. The amount of bridewealth paid by their father to acquire aristocratic wives for Angka Biruar and his brothers was said by some to be single-handedly responsible for much of the bridewealth inflation that had occurred in Cotabato since the 1950s. In age and political inclination, Angka Biruar was closer to the generation of Zacaria Candao's father, Datu Liwa, than to Candao himself. Like Datu Liwa, he had previously served in city government as a city councilor and vice-mayor. The Biruar family had controlled the coastal municipality of Parang for twenty-five years. As an Iranun, a member of the smuggler elite, and a (low-profile) supporter of the Bangsamoro Rebellion, Angka Biruar qualified as a member of the Muslim counterelite. As a former government official and member of a wealthy and politically powerful family concerned with traditional status-honor, he also resembled the members of the datu elite. Biruar was quite popular among certain Muslim voters (mostly Iranun), but he campaigned in a traditional style and lacked the charisma and clearly articulated political message of Zacaria Candao.

Peping Candao would seem to have had a ready-made advantage in his mayoral bid because of his kin connection to the most popular political figure in the province. Also in his favor was his personal history as a protector of city Muslims during the rebellion. Working against him, however, was his ten-year absence from the city. Peping had left Cotabato City in 1977, shortly after the start of the cease-fire, to pursue a career in the Philippine Army. By 1988, he was in many ways a stranger to the Muslims of the city, even to the residents of Campo Muslim. He in fact received a surprisingly small number of votes from the urban community that had once viewed him as a savior.

Radio messages also played an important role in the city campaigns, but because of the great size of the field and the character of the electioneering, radio messages consisted almost exclusively of short paid advertisements rather than speeches or debates. The 1988 campaign period was notable for the tremendous number of jingles, slogans, and pronouncements in Magindanaon, Tagalog, and English asserting that a particular candidate was the "representative," "voice," "friend," or "hope" of the "urban poor." As noted above, 1988 saw unparalleled attention paid to the urban poor electorate.[14] As the great majority of poor people in the city were Muslims, many appeals were made directly to the Muslim urban poor by both Muslim and Christian candidates. One Muslim city council candidate hired a popular rebel singer to write and perform a song for him in Magindanaon that proclaimed in part: "Prepare yourselves because the savior of the people has arrived. It is none other than the son of Attorni Paki [referring to the father of the young candidate, a well-known former provincial office-holder] . . . He is here to help the poor of the city."

An especially enterprising Christian city council candidate established an organization of poor people, the Kilusang ng Urban Poor (Urban Poor Movement), as part of his campaign.[15] He promised prospective members land and houses, the funding for which, he claimed publicly, would come from his "friends" abroad. He distributed membership cards for his organization in the public market neighborhood. The cards could be had for a one-peso fee to defray "office expenses." Poor city residents reportedly bought the membership cards as they would lottery tickets. The newfound concern by political candidates for the urban poor likely stemmed from two factors: the populist example set by Governor Candao since prior to his assumption of power in 1986, and the emergence in the previous few years of a number of genuine organizations of urban poor established by community organizers such as Kasan Kamid.

Despite its very impressive showing in the congressional and provincial elections, and the fact that IPP candidates captured a number of mayoral and other offices in municipalities throughout Maguindanao Province, the IPP was unexpectedly ineffective as a political force in the city polling. Their best showing was a third-place finish by their vice-mayoral candidate. None of the ten IPP candidates for the city council won seats, and only two placed among the top thirty finishers. Various factors may explain the IPP's poor performance in the city election. One very likely reason was that, unlike virtually every other participating political party, the IPP failed to field a mayoral candidate. As a consequence, the party was unable to present a complete slate to voters, and IPP city council candidates lacked a central popular figure with whom they could associate themselves. The IPP did not officially endorse a candidate for mayor because no name was offered that the IPP nomination panel could agree upon. Peping Candao presented the

most probable choice, but he chose to run as an independent candidate
for mayor as part of a slate that included Muslim and Christian candidates. IPP representatives explained that he did so for fear of alienating
potential Christian votes by his identification with an "Islamic" party.
At least two other widely known political figures and supporters of
Zacaria Candao—individuals who would also have been probable IPP
candidates—chose, apparently for the same reason, not to run as official candidates of the IPP. The IPP was left with candidates most of
whom were neither widely known nor politically experienced. On the
whole, they exhibited no special "Islamic" characteristics, though almost all were members of counterelite families. Two of the IPP's city
council candidates lived in Campo Muslim. One was a fish wholesaler
and the other a provincial livestock inspector.

A second, more general cause for the lack of success of the IPP in
city elections—one glimpsed already in the political calculations of
Peping Candao—was the problem of divided loyalties and conflicting
interests among Muslim candidates in the city. Knowledgeable political
observers in the city—both Muslims and Christians—agreed before
election day that Muslims had a unique opportunity to recapture the
mayor's office for the first time since 1967 and to win a significant
share of city council seats as well. This assessment was based on an assumption and a surmise. Observers shared the assumption that Muslim
voters would vote for Muslim candidates. One zealous IPP campaign
worker went farther and informed me that it was "compulsory" for
Muslims to vote for the IPP or, at the very least, for Muslim candidates, noting that it was their "religious obligation." Most observers,
however, simply expected that, because of personal ties, Muslim nationalist ideals, or ethnoreligious affinities, Muslims would choose to
elect Muslims to city office. The surmise stemmed from the fact that
the city electorate was fairly evenly divided between Muslims and
Christians. It held that, because there were four strong Christian candidates for mayor and only two dominant Muslim candidates, the leading Muslim candidate, Angka Biruar, had a strong chance of winning
if, as expected and rumored, the other Muslim candidates would
"throw their votes" to him at some point before election day.

Contrary to expectations, Muslims not only failed to regain the
mayor's office but did quite poorly in the city council race as well. In
that contest, the top ten vote-getters gained city council seats. The only
Muslim to be elected—an incumbent who ran and won in 1980—re-

ceived the least number of votes of the winning candidates. Neither of
the suppositions of political observers proved true. For one, Muslim
candidates did not unite at the last moment to consolidate candidacies
and outpoll divided Christian opponents. The only point at which
Muslim mayoral candidates united to any extent was after the election,
to protest their loss and accuse the winning Christian candidate of
massive cheating.[16] The city election campaign engendered not unity
but predictable divisiveness among contending Muslim candidates and
their supporters. That disunity extended to the ranks of the ulama.
During the campaign, a meeting was called at the Mahad in Campo
Muslim to decide which of the mayoral candidates should be supported. It was attended by ustadzes, imams, elders, community leaders,
and supporters of the IPP. Those in attendance were divided in their allegiances to various candidates, and a consensus was never reached.
The fact that the ustadzes were not unified in their political choices
was widely known and commented upon in Campo Muslim. When it
was announced at a seminar held for imams that Ustadz Pasigan, the
founder of the Mahad, favored the candidacy of Peping Candao for
mayor, the assembled imams paid little heed because it was common
knowledge that the founder's second in command, Ustadz Ali Abdul
Ajiz Naga, supported Angka Biruar.

That the city elections prompted competition rather than cooperation among Muslim politicians and their elite supporters is not a surprising fact. Nevertheless, the very poor showing of Muslim candidates
on the whole during a period when Muslim political awareness in
Cotabato seemed to be peaking was rather astonishing. As illustration,
in the race for mayor, Christian mayoral candidates gained over 71
percent of the vote although Christians comprised only about 52 percent of the city electorate. Voter turnout was relatively low, with less
than 59 percent of registered voters casting their ballots; and it is not
likely that Muslim turnout was much more than 10 percent below that
of Christians.[17] This suggests that at least some Muslims contradicted
the assumptions of Muslim and Christian political observers and voted
for Christian candidates. Vote tallies obtained from six Muslim
precincts appear to confirm that suspicion. Some Muslim politicians
took the fact that Christian politicians received votes in Muslim
precincts as prima facie evidence for ballot box tampering on the part
of certain Christian politicians. My evidence suggests, to the contrary,
that these were genuine votes. To understand this voting behavior it is

necessary to observe the city elections from the perspective of poor Muslims, focusing particularly on the economics of vote-buying and-selling.

LOCAL ELECTIONS AND THE MUSLIM URBAN POOR

For the poor Muslims of Cotabato City, many of whom could rarely afford the six-peso (thirty-cent) price of admission to a movie theater, the 1988 elections were a marvelous source of free entertainment. The unusually large field of candidates ensured that during the six-week campaign period, marches and rallies by various candidates and parties were held almost daily. Many, if not most of the rallies included dayunday performances. In the four weeks I spent in Campo Muslim prior to the election, three campaign rallies took place there, all with day-undays—the same number of public performances that might otherwise be held in a six- to eight-month period in the community. Audiences at the Campo Muslim rallies shouted for the dayunday to begin when they determined that the speeches of the candidates (all Muslims) had continued for too long. For their part, Christian candidates in advertising their campaign rallies, routinely announced the inclusion of dayunday performances "for our Muslim brothers." In addition to (or in lieu of) dayundays there were often other forms of entertainment, usually one or more singers performing popular tunes. The candidates themselves would sometimes sing as well after some playful badgering from the audience. The rallies and their associated parades, as well as the special nightly radio programs related above and the general air of excitement associated with political campaigning, combined to create a rare festive atmosphere for the city's poor.

Election campaigns generated more than just free entertainment. They were also a potential source of material resources, especially for those who actively sought them—usually younger males. Resources gained directly or indirectly from candidates took various forms. The most rudimentary sorts of benefits were those obtained by youngsters—usually young men—who marched (or sometimes rode) in the parades around the city held by various candidates. After watching one of these cavalcades pass by, with pedicabs and jeeps filled with riders and more than two hundred young people marching, I asked a friend who was with me how the candidate—who was not very widely known—acquired so many young supporters. He replied that *bata-*

bata (youngsters or young followers) such as those in the parade were easily obtained: "It is easy to find young unmarried men [*mga binata*] to join a campaign caravan. They are standbys [unemployed or under-employed school leavers]—they have nothing to do. They enjoy riding around the city in a truck and are happy to parade in exchange for *meryenda* [a snack]." He also noted that the young men marching in that particular parade were probably organized by their friends and also paid a small amount of cash each from "gas money" given to the organizers by the candidate.

More substantial material benefits were also available from candidates. These were sometimes directly solicited from candidates by individuals who might offer just their own vote—often euphemized as "assistance" (*tabang*)—but more commonly also the votes of others they claimed to represent. Two entries from my field notes illustrate this sort of solicitation. The first entry records the words of Zamin Unti, the Islamic activist from Campo Muslim who ran for mayor:

> A *kapatas* [labor foreman] offered me more than two hundred votes. He said, "I and my men will vote for you if you give us electricity." He knew that I did electrical work and he wanted me to provide the electricity first, before the election. A karate teacher with many students also came to me with a problem. He had a relative who needed an operation. He offered votes in return for my assistance. He did not ask me for money. He knew that I had worked with Zacaria Candao. He wanted a letter of introduction to Candao. He felt that Candao was the one person who could help him. I accepted neither of these offers.

The second excerpt concerns a story told to me by a Campo Muslim resident about the endeavors of some young men in Kalanganan, the rural area to the west of Campo Muslim:

> The elders in Bokhana [a *purok*, or small community, in Kalanganan] had decided to support Angka Biruar for mayor. Some young men from Bokhana went to Angka Biruar to "assist" him. The candidate said he had already given money to their purok leader [a member of the barangay council who represents a purok] and they should see him to obtain the money. The money was never forthcoming from the purok leader so they went to other candidates to offer their votes. They received money from a Christian candidate and voted for him because he had paid them, but also to defy their purok leader. When the purok leader, embarrassed to find that votes had been cast for a Christian candidate in his precinct, confronted the young men, they cited him a proverb: "If the hen obtains food but keeps it all to herself, her chicks will find food elsewhere."

Both excerpts point to the fairly common phenomenon of small-scale, freelance liders, or vote brokers.[18] These individuals approach various candidates claiming to have followers of some sort and offering votes in return for favors, not always in the form of money. Some very small-time liders taken on by a candidate will work for cigarettes, meryenda, and the promise of a job if the candidate wins.

Most transactions involving the exchange of votes for material benefits do not, however, occur as the result of freelance approaches from below. The greatest amount of vote buying and selling takes place within multilayered social networks that may long predate the campaign period. Such networks are important primarily as a means to assure that money channeled from the candidate will have the greatest likelihood of returning votes in his or her favor. Because voting is conducted secretly, this may be accomplished only indirectly, through personal ties and the desire of individuals to protect their reputations. Nur Miskin was the informal leader of a number of young men in Campo Muslim. He told me that he had been approached by two Muslim liders—both of them working for Christian candidates—and been offered money to provide votes. He expressed his view of the ethics and etiquette of vote-selling: "It is better not to accept money in exchange for votes, but if you take the money you should, as a Muslim, vote for the candidate whose money you were given . . . If I had taken money from [a certain lider] I would have told my followers to vote and at least have voted for his candidate myself because my reputation could be destroyed if the candidate received no votes in my precinct. His [the lider's] reputation would not be destroyed, but mine would. That is, of course, only if the candidate himself had met me or knew who I was."

Approaches to those with direct access to votes were usually made by the principal lider of a particular candidate. Targeted individuals—who would become subliders if they accepted the offer—tended to be those who possessed both influence and a good reputation in a particular community. Ideally, but by no means always, they also had some preexisting personal connection to the lider. Several such approaches were made to prominent community figures in Campo Muslim. The Muslim lider of a Christian mayoral candidate offered a popular purok leader in Campo Muslim one thousand pesos for his initial support and ten pesos for every vote he was able to recruit at fifty pesos apiece.[19] Nur Miskin was offered a significant amount of money by the Muslim lider of another Christian candidate for mayor in exchange for "gathering his men" and displaying them to the candidate.[20] Even the municipal chairman of the MILF shadow government was rumored to be operating as a lider for a Christian mayoral candidate and distributing one hundred–peso notes to Campo Muslim residents connected with the shadow government as a token of the candidate's "sincerity."[21]

Vote-buying networks could nevertheless malfunction in a number of ways, most likely at their lowest levels. As evidenced in the story from Kalanganan, money intended to purchase votes may never be distributed by subliders overconfident of their ability to recruit sufficient votes without direct payments.[22] On the other hand, money was occasionally distributed by subliders to voters without any clear instructions given for voting. That sort of breakdown was to be expected under circumstances such as those found in the 1988 elections, where a great many candidates were seeking to obtain votes with money, and vote-buying networks were hurriedly constructed and often weakly connected. I witnessed an example of this sort of vote-buying malfunction in Campo Muslim. One evening shortly before the election, Kasan Kamid was requested by the wife of a local purok leader to gather his relatives and followers from his neighborhood for a distribution of free rice given by a candidate. The woman was a sublider and had been given a fifty-kilo sack of rice to be distributed to registered voters. She informed Kasan because she was aware that he knew many people. The lider who recruited her and provided her the rice, was a Muslim middle-level government employee living in Campo Muslim. He worked for a Christian candidate and may have been a sublider himself. Kasan quickly relayed news of the distribution to his relatives and neighbors who hurried to the distribution site with plastic bags. Fifty one-kilo bags of rice were soon disbursed, with the name of each recipient relayed by Kasan and carefully recorded by the sublider. At no time during the distribution were recipients told whom to vote for or even informed which candidate had provided the rice. The list of recipients merely documented that the rice had actually been distributed; the list was delivered to the Campo Muslim lider immediately after the giveaway was completed. Some recipients approached Kasan the following day to ask which candidate had donated the rice. He told them that they were free to vote for whomever they wished.

The most efficient vote-buying networks were those that were well integrated from top to bottom. One such network conducted part of its operations in Campo Muslim. It existed to support the Christian candidate who eventually won the mayorship. The primary lider in the network was a prominent and well-regarded Muslim businessman in the city. This lider had a secondary lider—his first cousin—who was also well-respected, with numerous ties to Campo Muslim. The secondary lider contacted an individual in Campo Muslim to act as a community-level lider. This tertiary lider had, until recently, been underground as a Muslim separatist insurgent. He possessed a number of followers in the community and elsewhere and a wide reputation based on stories of his exploits as a rebel fighter. The three liders were also tied together by *utang na loob,* or debts of gratitude (literally, debts of the inner self). The two subliders had fought together in the armed rebellion. The primary lider had provided support to both of these men for some time. He had supplied them with guns and money while they were fighting, and had arranged to have his cousin, the secondary lider, freed from prison after the cousin had served two years of a much longer murder sentence. The Campo Muslim lider had been working to organize his followers since his return from "inside" in late 1986. On election day he stationed himself at the polling place used by most of his followers and quietly paid them after they had voted. The vote-buying network to which he belonged incorporated all of the features required by a candidate seeking to convert material resources into votes; its members were distinguished by their mutual trust, their competence, and their confidentiality.

Table 2 shows the votes gained by each of the eight mayoral candidates who garnered the most votes in the six precincts at the polling place used by most Campo Muslim voters. Checks of voter registration lists indicated that these precincts were used almost exclusively by Muslims. The table is incomplete in that it neither lists all the precincts used by Campo Muslim voters nor all the mayoral candidates. It does, however, give a general indication of the extent to which Christian candidates were able to capture the votes of poor Muslims. Candidates are listed only by ethnoreligious affiliation. Three Christians finished among the top eight candidates, garnering more than 19 percent of the votes cast for the leading vote-getters.[23] In one of the precincts (number 4) they received almost 30 percent of the votes cast for the leading candidates. All three of the top-finishing Christian candidates had liders operating in Campo Muslim. It should be noted that none of the precincts listed in table 2 were located at the polling place targeted by the efficient Campo Muslim lider described above. For various rea-

TABLE 2

TOP EIGHT VOTE-GETTERS FOR MAYOR
IN SIX CAMPO MUSLIM PRECINCTS,
1988 MUNICIPAL ELECTION

Candidate	Precinct number						Total votes
	1	2	3	4	5	6	
1. Muslim	34	62	38	34	33	34	235
2. Muslim	39	31	40	26	19	51	206
3. Muslim	27	21	26	10	8	14	106
4. Christian	11	9	10	13	7	6	56
5. Christian	11	3	9	8	8	12	51
6. Christian	5	1	4	15	7	4	36
7. Muslim	1	4	2	13	4	10	34
8. Muslim	7	2	2	2	3	6	22
Total	135	133	131	121	89	137	746

Cotabato City Registrar of Voters

sons, Campo Muslim residents who migrated to the community from rural areas within the city limits tend to register at their places of birth. As most of the followers of this lider hailed from Kalanganan, he stationed himself at that polling place on election day. There is reason to believe, therefore, that the percentage of votes garnered by Christian candidates from Campo Muslim residents at the Kalanganan polling place (which also had multiple precincts) was just as great, if not greater than that recorded for the precincts in table 2.

Qualitative data, gathered mostly in Campo Muslim, indicate that vote-buying conducted on behalf of candidates in poor Muslim communities was fairly widespread. They also indicate that Christian candidates relied more heavily on vote-buying to capture Muslim votes than did their Muslim counterparts. Most of the Muslim candidates for city office had far smaller resource bases for campaign expenditures than did the leading Christian candidates. It is also likely that, as with so many other observers of the political scene in the city, Muslim candidates assumed that Muslims would not vote for non-Muslim candidates and so spent too few resources to counter that possibility. In the absence of the clearly defined issues and charismatic candidate found in the provincial race, some of the Muslim urban poor ignored the vague promises and ethnic presumptions of Muslim candidates and responded to concrete offers for their votes, whatever their source.

Very often, the proximate sources of those offers were other, well-respected Muslims, most of them not so poor, who had, for their own reasons, decided that they preferred individual economic or political gain to whatever shared political benefits might accrue to them from a Muslim political reascension in Cotabato City.

CONCLUSION

As the post-Marcos era opened, the two mass rallies in the Cotabato City plaza demonstrated the promise of a popular-based Muslim nationalism led by a newly ascendant counterelite under the Islamic guidance of an independent and politically active ulama. Ordinary Muslims (and especially poor urban Muslims) were readily mobilized for collective action in support of Muslim autonomy—action that did not, to be sure, involve significant costs for ordinary participants. The MILF "prayer rally," in particular, demonstrated the considerable political influence and organizational abilities of the ulama acting on behalf of the MILF, notwithstanding the failure of the organizers to achieve their stated goals.

The gubernatorial election marked a watershed in Cotabato electoral politics. The winning candidate, Zacaria Candao, received virtually no local support from traditional elites and very little effective assistance from a national party but nevertheless defeated his datu opponent handily. An important factor in his success was the novel form of the electoral campaign itself—a structure, based on extended direct appeals to ordinary voters, that Candao had earlier cultivated and now used to his advantage in the more hospitable post-Marcos environment. The radio campaigning in the governor's race amounted to an extended broadcast debate between the two candidates over ideological as well as practical and personal issues. Almost everyone in Campo Muslim (as well as most of the Muslims in the province) has access to a radio, and the nightly arguments in that debate were followed carefully by many Campo Muslim residents. For quite possibly the first time in the history of electoral politics in Muslim Cotabato, direct ideological appeals (featuring Islam as a political language) reached mass audiences and became key considerations in the electoral choices of a great number of Cotabato Muslims.

Of equal significance was the design and content of the IPP appeal itself. The contest between the IPP and the datu coalition in the election for governor was on one level an ideological struggle, unparalleled in Cotabato, between those who endorsed the proposition that Islam is all-inclusive and cannot be separated from politics and those who believed that religion, including Islam, should be relegated to a private domain. However, as witnessed in Candao's final campaign rally, two key elements of the Islamic renewal program of the ulama (and high MILF leadership)—doctrinal purification and the rejection of Western cultural influence—did not receive emphasis in the IPP's electoral appeal. The Islamic message of the IPP was much more populist than puritan. With the need to win the hearts of ordinary voters firmly in mind, the electoral appeal of Candao and the IPP took careful consideration of the prior responses of ordinary Muslims to the ulama's program for Islamic renewal. The IPP message reflected a praxis based on years of implicit negotiations. It emerged out of the everyday interplay between incremental pressures for religious reform and small but significant resistances, and was as much the result of the pragmatic dissidence of non-elite Muslims as of the moral authority of the ulama.

The IPP campaign utilized aspects of traditional culture because much of that culture was identity-affirming for Muslim voters. It allowed Western (or Westernized) amusements because, although most Muslim voters favored political independence from Western rule as represented by the Philippine state, they appreciated many aspects of Western culture and did not endorse its wholesale rejection. Islamic populism was underscored in the IPP appeal because it coincided with the Islamic consciousness of the poor Muslims who comprised most of the Muslim electorate.

While the mass rallies and provincial elections demonstrated the promise of popular Muslim nationalism, the city elections revealed its limitations. The pragmatically modified IPP message of Islamic populism and separatism that proved so effective in the provincial elections was overcome in the municipal elections by more narrowly defined political and economic interests. The "Islamic unity" advocated by the IPP was nowhere evidenced in that election. Competitive Muslim candidates, concerned not to alienate city Christians, shunned the IPP precisely because of its Islamic appellation.[24] Members of the aboveground ulama, and even underground MILF operatives, actively supported separate candidates on the basis of kin or other particularistic loyalties. For their part, poor urban Muslims, in the absence of substantive campaign messages or charismatic candidates, approached the city elections primarily as an occasion to enjoy the various favors offered to attract the suddenly prized political resources they possessed.

That a good number of Campo Muslim residents provided their votes to Christian candidates in exchange for material gratuities suggests only that many poor Muslims were no less astute at obtaining particular benefits from collective political processes than were the Muslim vote-brokers and politicians with whom they transacted.

CHAPTER 11

Resistance and Rule in Cotabato

From the expressions of majesty of the precolonial sultans to the rhetoric of the first post-Marcos provincial election, power relations in Cotabato have been encoded in the language of Islamic authority and identity. Here I consider how power in Muslim Cotabato has been both enunciated by rulers and interrogated by those subjected to it. This study has addressed four key problems corresponding to four configurations of culture and power in Cotabato. First is the nature of "traditional" Islamic rule in Cotabato. To what degree did the myth of sanctified inequality accomplish the ideological incorporation of Muslim subordinates? This question has its ethnographic corollary: how are we to explain the fact that the same Campo Muslim narrators who disregarded dominant cultural productions justifying datu rule often told imaginative stories that justified the prepotency of those rulers?

The second problem concerns the derivation and prevalence of a transcendent Philippine Muslim (Moro) identity. How did American colonial efforts to rule Philippine Muslims spark the development of a transcendent Philippine Muslim identity? What was the nature of that identity and how widely did it diffuse among Cotabato Muslims? Third is the problem of rank-and-file mobilization for the Bangsamoro Rebellion. Why should the separatist rebellion have received so much popular support when its central message was transmitted ineffectively or not at all? What prompted the mobilization of armed force if not the resonant nationalist appeals of separatist leaders? Finally there is

the problem of the responses of ordinary Muslims to the postinsur-
gency movement for Islamic renewal—a project central to the continuation of the separatist struggle in unarmed form. How may we recon-
cile the popular admiration expressed for the independent ulama with
the widespread rejection of most of the elements of their renewal project?

The answers made to these questions challenge prevailing anthropological analyses of ethnonationalism and, more expansively, of the relation of political culture to collective action. They are, in the end, responses to one and the same problem—that of comprehending at once
the imaginative and strategic endeavors of subaltern actors and gaug-
ing their cumulative political consequence.

RULING IDEAS AND THE POPULAR IMAGINATION

To explore the message of the Cotabato case for theories of cultural
domination let me return first to the precolonial order in Cotabato.
The myth of sanctified inequality entitled an aristocracy to rule Cotabato Muslims based on its members' ancestral ties to the Prophet
Muhammad. Written genealogies—the tarsilas—served as ideological
instruments providing "proofs of legitimacy" for the ruling elite (Majul 1973, 3). The core principle of this dominant ideology of sacred ancestry was maratabat (status honor) and its primary dynamic was rank
competition within the aristocracy itself.

Ethnohistorical accounts suggest that the myth of sanctified inequality, and the struggle for status it generated, operated primarily to incorporate the precolonial ruling class, penetrating to a much lesser extent
among members of the underclasses (compare Abercrombie et al.
1980). Moreover, those aspects of the dominant ideology directed
squarely at Muslim subordinates, the legal codes (Luwaran) and the
assertion that subjects (*sakup*) were under the protection of the aristocracy, seem to have been routinely penetrated by Muslim subordinates.
Their direct experience of arbitrary punishments and the predations of
datus confuted the official transcript of social relations between rulers
and subjects. That experiential knowledge remained unspoken (and is
only hesitatingly related even today) because of the mortal dangers
risked by its telling. Awareness of the existence of hidden transcripts of
power relations in precolonial Cotabato (as well as in contemporary
Southeast Asia—Scott 1985) challenges those depictions of the precolonial polities of Southeast Asia that rely solely upon official texts or

aristocratic memories for the interpretation of traditional rule (see, e.g., Geertz 1980; Wolters 1982; Milner 1982; Errington 1989). What of the more fundamentally hegemonic qualities of premodern rule, those taken-for-granted features of the system of subjection that, in the conceptual scheme of Comaroff and Comaroff (1992) and others, would have been far removed from the public proclamations of the dominant ideology of sanctified inequality? Various candidates present themselves, among them the correlation drawn between communities (ingeds) and datus, such that it was difficult (though not impossible) to imagine a community without a ruling datu. Another was the social distinction drawn between slaves (ulipun or banyaga) and nonslave commoners (endatuan), or that between Muslim and non-Muslim subjects. To what extent did such cultural meanings and practices reproduce domination by naturalizing it? Undoubtedly some, but attempting to sort out the incorporative effects of those meanings from the material constraints of armed coercion and legal insecurity (manifested in the ever-present threat of expropriation or reduction to slavery) seems an impossible task given the paucity of historical evidence.

There may also be found in traditional Cotabato a distinct set of imaginative representations of rule emanating from below that appear to have had hegemonic effects. These are the symbolizations of power independently generated by Muslim subordinates. They include, most prominently, the monstrous aspect of Datu Utu and marvelous abilities of Datu Piang, but they also include stories of fantastic powers possessed by various contemporary datus. The endogenous character of these popular images of rule is strikingly illustrated in Campo Muslim. There poor Muslims routinely disregarded and often disparaged the ideological assertions of the Magindanaon aristocracy while simultaneously relishing and retelling stories of the supernatural potency of various datus, living and dead.

While both critics and proponents of the concept of hegemony have noted that subordinates routinely reinterpret components of dominant ideologies, anthropologists in particular have scarcely discussed the theoretical implications of independently generated popular imagings of rule.[1] Among other social analysts, Jon Elster especially has pointed to "endogenous preference formation" as an important phenomenon in social life (1985, 21). He is referring here to the cognitive process whereby "subjects invent their own mystification" by producing beliefs that justify their subjugation (1993, 65). The psychic mechanism that generates such beliefs is, according to Elster, the tendency to "reduce cognitive dissonance" (1985, 466) or to attempt to attain peace of mind. Following Elster's schema, the belief of Cotabato subordinates in the supernatural attributes of ruling datus reduced dissonance by placing power out of reach for those with only normal human properties, and thus served as a form of consolation. There are, however, other significances of independent belief formation by political subordinates insufficiently addressed by Elster. Popular imagings of rule such as those found among Muslim subordinates in Cotabato should be seen as creative responses to the direct experience of domination. They do not rely on the representations or even the language of ruling elites. Neither do they simply refract the dominant ideology or naturalize a set of social conditions. Instead, they denaturalize social power by portraying it as depending upon profoundly unequal allotments of supernatural attributes. While such beliefs may, as Elster proposes, serve to reproduce structures of domination, they are, in the Cotabato case, also directly counterhegemonic. For one, they explicitly contradict the dominant myth of sanctified inequality by endowing only certain manifestly forceful members of the Cotabato nobility with extraordinary traits. Additionally, insofar as these endowments (unlike the persuasions of the dominant culture) are independently conferred by subordinates, they may also be unilaterally withdrawn.

COLONIAL SUBJECTION AND THE
CONSTITUTION OF PHILIPPINE MUSLIM IDENTITY

We turn next to another arena of cultural domination to review the consequences of American colonial rule for Muslim identity in Cotabato. Various anthropologists have in recent years considered the complex connections between colonial domination and identity formation in postcolonial societies (see, e.g., Fox 1985, 1989; Kahn 1993; Kapferer 1988; Spencer 1990; B. Williams 1991). A brief review of the work of two of these writers will serve to bracket the case at hand.

Two books by Richard Fox (1985, 1989) examining the colonial construction of indigenous identities in India have furnished critical analytical insights into the articulated nature of identity formation and resistance under colonial rule. In his more recent work (1989) Fox has placed the colonial construction of identities in India in the context of a global process he describes as "a world-systemic orientalism"; a process whereby colonized populations "come to define their own culture according to the 'indigenations' asserted in Western Orientalism" (1989,

98, 92). According to Fox, "by the late nineteenth century, there was a world system of cultural domination—that is, a set of dominating cultural meanings constructing identity and self-perceptions in most corners of the globe" (1989, 98).

Applying a global perspective to the various "indigenations" associated with colonial situations allows comparison and the discovery of parallel processes. Indeed, Fox's earlier (1985) work on Sikh identity and resistance offers some rather striking parallels to that of Philippine Muslims under American rule.[2] The British colonial constitution of Sikh identity and its subsequent use as a basis from which to contest colonial domination provides an analog to the colonial origins of Moro identity in the Philippines. It also illustrates Fox's thesis, developed expressly in his later work (1989), that effective resistance to colonial domination emerges not from some unaffected or "untamed" sector of traditional culture but develops "within the Orientalist hegemony of the world system" (1989, 100). While this "unavoidable accommodation to hegemony" allows effective and sometimes successful cultural resistance against colonial domination, that resistance is unable to accomplish a complete escape from *cultural* domination because it accepts the "indigenations . . . encoded in the world system" (1989, 103).

Fox's thesis carries us quite far along in understanding the origins and uses of Moro identity in the Philippines but does not provide the analytical tools to make sense of the multiple layers of resistance witnessed in Cotabato. There is also a certain slippage in his usage of the notions of hegemony and cultural domination. At times Fox interprets hegemony as "attempted cultural domination" (1989, 92). More often, however, he follows Raymond Williams's conceptualization whereby hegemony references accomplished cultural domination—situations, that is, in which domination is "internalized and appears natural" (1989, 91). A second problem arises with the meaning of "cultural domination" itself. Surely, Fox does not mean to say that alternative cultural meanings and identities are necessarily extinguished as a result of "world-systemic orientalism," but only that cultural practices and definitions authorized by colonial powers become the most salient ones, especially for elite political actors. Yet there are also passages in his work that may be interpreted to suggest that "orientalist hegemony" paralyzes all definitions and identities other than those constructed by the world system of cultural domination (see, e.g., 1989, 99–100).

Another recent work on the colonial construction of local identities comes at the problem from a somewhat different angle and appears directly to challenge Fox's position. Joel Kahn (1993) traces the constitution of Minangkabau identity in colonial Indonesia. In doing so he launches a powerful critique of the notion, first formally introduced by Eric Hobsbawm and colleagues (1983), of "the invention of tradition," or the proposition that indigenous cultures in the postcolonial world are predominantly colonial constructs.[3] Kahn finds that argument problematic for various reasons, among them the following: "Traditions appear to be the sole inventions of westerners . . . What is often overlooked is that these very westerners were . . . ruling those peoples by means of the traditions they were inventing; that [colonized peoples] were creating their own traditions within those same colonial societies; that indigenous elites often constructed their traditions in conscious opposition to those of their colonial masters—in short, that a variety of groups and classes, usually in a cultural and hegemonic situation, were all 'inventing tradition' in the same social arena" (1993, 29).

Although not as severely contradictory as they first appear, the arguments of Fox and Kahn do present glaringly different perspectives on the generation of group identities in colonial situations. Fox accents the intensely constraining effects of a world system of dominating cultural meanings on identity formation among colonial subjects. Even indigenous resistance to colonial domination is overwhelmingly "secondary resistance" in that it "grows up within, and is compelled by, the world system of domination" (1989, 100–101). Joel Kahn underscores the strategic and creative capabilities of colonial subjects. The dominant cultural meanings and identities authorized by colonial authorities may constrain the cultural productions of subordinates in various ways but do not determine their content. Cultural forms, including forms of resistance, are created for different reasons by a wide range of actors and interrelate on the same social scape.

These cannot be mutually exclusive analytical stances. Both cultural domination and strategic cultural resistance are evident in virtually every colonial situation. The task is to sort them out and gauge their relative significance. Both elements were clearly at work in colonial Cotabato. The creation of a transcendent Philippine Muslim (Moro) identity during the American colonial period accords closely with Fox's orientalist hegemony thesis. The term "Moro" itself (with all its colonial connotations) exemplifies the process whereby members of a colonized population define themselves according to the "indigenations" advanced by their Western rulers. Key colonial agents (especially Najeeb Saleeby) sifted out the favorable attributes of "Moro" culture for administrative enhancement: Moros were uncivilized but not savages, fierce fighters though not religious fanatics, politically undeveloped yet not politically unsophisticated. American colonial practice (especially educational policies) encouraged the self-conscious development among certain Philippine Muslims of the Moro identity that had, until then, been only a Western ascription.

The American colonial promotion of Moro identity had a profound effect on the first generation of postcolonial Muslim leaders. They shared a rationalized and ethnicized identity as Muslim Filipinos—self-consciously Muslim citizens of the new Philippine republic. Their announced efforts to make Muslim Filipinos better citizens by making them better Muslims both acknowledged the legitimacy of the new Philippine state to rule Muslims and recapitulated the American colonial postulate that the principal cure for Muslim underdevelopment was Muslim self-improvement. The colonial notion of a single Moro identity had a dissimilar, yet equally profound, effect on the young, second-generation intellectuals who developed the movement for Muslim separatism. Those leaders manifestly rejected the underlying goal of American colonial policy toward Philippine Muslims—their integration into a unified, Christian-dominated, postcolonial state—yet embraced the idea of a transcendent Philippine Muslim identity as well as the term "Moro" itself. They made Morohood, and the presumed cultural essentials it referenced, the fundament of their political ideology. Those essentials included, most prominently, the recognition of the entitlements of a traditional aristocracy and the espousal of a glorious history of unified Muslim resistance to Western imperialists.

STRATEGIC MANEUVERS AND UNAUTHORIZED INVENTIONS

The unapproved activities of America's Moros at the St. Louis World's Fair provide a metaphorical reminder of how inaccurate it would be to regard the Muslim colonial elite as simply (or even primarily) objects of colonial manipulation. There were other cultural "inventions" by indigenous elites during the colonial period, by no means all of them authorized, or even noticed, by colonial agents. New datus constructed genealogies to link themselves to the precolonial nobility. Those cultural creations went hand in hand with actions that, if not intended to subvert colonial rule, certainly amounted to individual resistance to colonial supervision. We have seen that collaborating datus used their colonial offices to enrich themselves and fortify their local power bases at the expense of colonial coffers.

It is the strategic nature of the endeavors of the collaborating datus of the colonial period that appears most prominent. Members of the nouveau Cotabato nobility—Datu Sinsuat comes most readily to mind—managed to use American presumptions about the reverence felt by ordinary Muslims for their "traditional" leaders to strengthen their own political positions. They also sometimes used their new colonial posts to conduct "traditional" adjudications and collect "traditional" fines. Even the relatively more impressionable recipients of American educations—the Muslim elites born under American rule—did not routinely comply with American plans. Writing in 1941, Florence Horn reports that Princess Tarhata Kiram, who was sent by Colonial Governor Frank Carpenter to the United States for schooling, disappointed American authorities on her return: "Tarhata had such a fine time in the U.S. that for a while Carpenter was afraid she would never return to her own people. However, she did come back, apparently thoroughly Americanized, looking and behaving just like the short-skirted American girl of the twenties. The experiment seemed to have worked—until Tarhata left Manila and arrived in Jolo among her own people. She quickly reverted, put on Sulu clothes, filed her teeth, became one of the wives of a middle-aged Sulu datu, and with him, in 1927, fomented a minor uprising against the American Government" (1941, 155).[4]

The utilitarian aspect of the Muslim embrace of colonial meanings is no surprise when one remembers that Muslim elites were local rulers as well as colonial subjects. Colonial institutions were viewed by those rulers primarily as resources for power enhancement. Datus sent their slaves rather than their sons to American schools until convinced of the practical benefits of a Western education for continued local dominance.

It is unmistakable that American meanings powerfully influenced the self-awareness of numerous Philippine Muslims during (and after) the colonial era and permeated cultural resistance to Western domination, especially in the Muslim separatist movement. Just the same, it is important not to regard that process as either overpowering or entirely unidirectional. The "indigenations" of American colonialism may have constricted the political imaginations of Philippine Muslims but cannot be said to have paralyzed them.

It is left to ask about the cultural effects of American colonialism on non-elite Muslims. Joel Kahn (among others) reminds us that when juxtaposing local elite versus non-elite responses to colonial rule, it is a mistake simply to assume that precolonial meanings and identities—a "Little Tradition"—survived among subordinates while elites embraced (or were overcome by) "hegemonic modernist or orientalist discourse" (1993, 154). In Cotabato, despite significant legal transformations (in particular, the abolition of slavery and the introduction of private property in land), local relations of domination remained remarkably unaltered under American colonialism. Nevertheless, colonialism did occasion the creation or refashioning of cultural meanings and identities among non-elite Muslims.

Stories are still told today by ordinary Muslims of early encounters between Magindanaon notables and American colonizers. Imam Akmad told me about the first meeting between the Sultan of Magindanao and an American colonial official.

> The Sultan and his brother the Amirul were invited to the ship of the American. The American put on an exhibition for the Sultan. He said, "I will throw a bottle in the air and shoot it through the neck with my rifle. The bottle was thrown and the American fired and hit it just where he had promised. The sultan admired the shot and said, "I will do the same." When the bottle was thrown, the Sultan did not look at it but shot in the opposite direction. His bullet turned in midair and hit the bottle in the neck. When the American saw this he exclaimed, "You have bested me; I must give you a gift." He presented the sultan with a walking stick and a pair of golden slippers.

Such magical stories of the colonial era are clearly compensatory, relating how Cotabato Muslims answered American technical supremacy with magical prowess. They also speak more particularly to two colonial developments. First, such stories acknowledge symbolically that, despite the presence of a new and seemingly omnipotent external power, local rulers had retained their political potency. That was also the message expressed in the popular story of the magical finger of Datu Piang, which could call down the wrath of the colonizers on recalcitrant followers.

The stories also signify the development of an oppositional identity among ordinary Muslims. The full occupation of Cotabato by an alien power spurred the formation among Muslim subordinates of an identity bound up with the notion of an invaded homeland—an identity that drew a sharp distinction between indigenes and outlanders. They identified themselves as Muslims as opposed to outsiders, almost all of whom were non-Muslims. It was (and still is) an oppositional identity but one quite different from the self-conscious and objectified Muslim Filipino identity enunciated by most Philippine Muslim political leaders in the late colonial and postcolonial period. The unself-conscious cultural identity of ordinary Muslims has been illustrated by Patricia Horvatich's (1997) observation that the Sama (a Philippine Muslim population) "define almost everything they do [including gathering sea urchins] as Islamic because they are Muslim." The contrast between that sort of identity and the objectified Muslim identity of most Muslim elites is similar to the distinction made by Jonathan Friedman (1990) between two forms of Greek identity in a discussion of the phenomenon of Hellenism in the ancient world. In reference to Greek colonists in Asia he notes: "Colonists tend to develop a strong cultural identity, primarily as a means of distinction: 'I am Greek because I live like this, have these symbols, practice such-and-such a religion, etc.' But this kind of identity expresses a separation of the person from that which he identifies. The content of his social selfhood may become distanced from his immediate subjectivity: 'I am Greek because I do this, that and the other thing' does not imply the converse, i.e., 'I do this, that and the other thing because I am Greek'"(Friedman 1990, 26). Muslim colonial and postcolonial elites, with the assistance of American colonial agents, developed a self-regarding identity as Muslim Filipinos and engaged in rationalized Islamic activities (including most prominently the development of "Islamic" organizations) to demonstrate that identity to themselves and others. Ordinary Muslims, by contrast, continued to do what they had always done, with these activities now considered to be "Islamic" activities (rather than Sama or Magindanaon or Iranun activities) only because those engaged in them had begun to denominate themselves as "Muslims" to distinguish themselves from increasing numbers of non-Muslim outsiders.

POPULAR PARTICIPATION
IN THE BANGSAMORO REBELLION

Anthropological analyses of nationalist action have most often privileged the propulsive role of elite-generated ideas and images, especially as they engage individuals at a less-than-conscious level and articulate the unreflected anxieties and aspirations of everyday social life. In other words, they make use of various versions of the notion of cultural hegemony to account for the voluntary (and often enthusiastic) participation of members of subordinate classes in such movements.

Unofficial narratives of armed separatism from Cotabato suggest that ordinary adherents of armed nationalist movements are more discerning, and less ideologically incorporated, than anticipated by analyses keyed to the hegemonic effects of nationalist discourses. In Cotabato, Muslim nationalist ideological activity has not resulted in "the experiential starvation of the political imagination" of Muslim subordinates (Linger 1993, 18). Neither have subordinates become dependent upon the symbols issuing from "a nationalist ideological formation that has taken root in everyday life" to make sense of their experiences (Woost 1993, 516). To the contrary, many rank-and-file adherents of the armed separatist movement possessed both vigorous political imaginations and the words with which to exercise them. Ordinary Muslims expressed themselves in the unauthorized narratives of the armed rebellion. Rebel songs used a language notably independent of official separatist discourse to speak of social discontent as well as patriotism. While undeniably supportive of the rebellion, the songs also voiced distance from its official goals.

In the magical stories of the rebellion told by ordinary adherents, that distance begets resistance as storytellers "transform experience into agency" (Rebel 1989, 362). Here the critical assessments made of the rebellion by ordinary adherents questioned not only the claims and promises of movement leaders but also their fundamental aims and assumptions. While popular support for the separatist insurgency was substantial for most of the period of armed struggle and was expressed unofficially in songs and stories, at certain key junctures, most commonly where national interests collided with local concerns, some of those same narratives were used to voice resistance to official separatist rhetoric. Dissent was voiced obliquely (though unambiguously) through the absence of explicit agreement (some defecting rebel commanders did not suffer supernatural sanctions, some rebel corpses were not magically preserved). Those imaginative narratives were also charters for action. Divine decisions (to bestow or withdraw supernatural assistance) sanctioned popular choices to provide or withhold particular types of political support.

Although the concept of hegemony has been applied widely to explain the popular appeal of nationalisms, its analytical utility fails in the Cotabato case at the point where it is most needed—when one tries to understand the political actions of ordinary adherents of the

separatist movement. While leaders and followers of the separatist rebellion in Cotabato shared a common discursive framework, Muslim
subordinates evaluated the pronouncements of movement leaders
based on their separate shared experience. Those evaluations were au-
tonomously symbolized, and they led at times to actions that ran
athwart the official intentions of the separatist leadership. The independent expressions and efforts of rank-and-file adherents of the Muslim separatist movement remind us that the extent to which the "common sense" of subordinates has been reorganized by the workings of a
nationalist ideology—the degree to which subordinates have been incorporated into the "imagined community" of the nation—is an empirical question, and one that should not be settled prior to a thorough
search for unauthorized narratives. Analysts agree that cultural hegemony does most of its work not by defining what is legitimate but by
establishing what *is*. Popular narratives that denied divine mercy to
certain slain rebels or that declined divine retribution for certain rebel
defectors, amounted to refusals of official reality. Despite the discursive efforts of movement leaders, ordinary adherents elected a separate
reality, one that elevated local concerns above the Muslim nationalist
cause.

The Bangsamoro Rebellion had considerable success relative to
other separatist insurgencies despite the notable misalignment between
the official discourse of the rebellion and the language, perceptions,
and intentions of its ordinary adherents. While rank-and-file fighters
and supporters held certain beliefs and motivations in common with
movement leaders, they possessed others that were more situational—
more "practical"—than those enunciated in the authorized discourse
of Muslim nationalism. As long as the separate considerations of subordinate adherents were not contradicted by the official aims of movement leaders, popular mobilization was achieved. My interpretation of
the separatist insurgency waged in Cotabato suggests that anthropological analyses of armed separatism (and of ethnonationalist collective
action in general) could benefit from keener attention to the collateral
concerns of ordinary adherents and less energy invested in searching
for the hegemonic effects of nationalist ideas.

UNARMED STRUGGLE AND ISLAMIC RENEWAL

The Muslim separatist movement in Cotabato transformed itself into a
self-consciously Islamic movement in 1984 with the creation of the

Moro Islamic Liberation Front (MILF). While Islamic clerics had played key roles in the Cotabato movement from its beginnings, the launching of the MILF amounted to a formal declaration that, henceforth, the independent ulama (as well as ulama-led Islamic renewal) would predominate in the struggle for Muslim political autonomy.

The emergence of an independent, Middle East–educated ulama in Cotabato was an epochal event accomplished by means of international assistance and individual courage. Cotabato lies at the easternmost extremity of the Eurasian Islamic world. No significant Muslim populations of the Old World are further distanced from the central sites of Islamic ritual and instruction than are those of Mindanao. Islamic practice in the Cotabato sultanates for most of their history had reflected that extreme distance from Islamic centers. It was only as a result of the pan-Islamic initiatives of Nasser's Egyptian government that significant numbers of Philippine Muslims were, for the first time, able to pursue Islamic studies in the Muslim heartland. Those scholars returned to Cotabato after their long courses of study to encounter firm opposition from established Muslim elites and armed antagonism from agents of the Philippine government. With martial law, most were forced to flee underground or return abroad. Those who, like Ustadz Ali, remained visible suffered continual and sometimes brutal harassment at the hands of the Philippine military. None were able to speak out freely in public forums prior to about 1980. When finally free to speak they did so energetically, advocating the reordering of social and ritual as well as political life and garnering a great deal of attention from ordinary Muslims. That attention, however, was not entirely, or even primarily, approbative.

In what actual sense was the popular, aboveground, and ulama-led movement for Muslim political autonomy from 1980 onward an *Islamic* movement? To what degree, that is, was the collective political action of ordinary adherents motivated by Islamic imperatives and interpretations as enunciated by the ulama? At least two components of the Islamic appeals of the ulama resonated deeply with non-elite Muslims. There was first the notion of "Islamic unity." That concept is of course a universalistic one, referencing the establishment of a more uniform Islamic community in Cotabato, one encapsulated within a worldwide community of believers (the *umma*). For ordinary Muslims in Cotabato it was also a notion with very specific circumstantial connotations. "Islamic unity" was promoted by the ulama and the opposition alliance as the antithesis of familiar politics in Cotabato. The umma as political community offered the solution to internal divisions based on class, ethnicity, familism, and political factionalism in general. Islamic unity, it was said, would also accomplish what the armed rebellion had not—genuine political autonomy for Muslims—because a unified Islamic community could better withstand the divide-and-rule tactics of the Philippine government.

A second popular component of the ulama's message was the ideal of juridical equality for all Cotabato Muslims. The notion that datus and endatuan, rich and poor Muslims, ought to be judged equally by indigenous adjudicators was a radical one that greatly appealed to ordinary Muslims. There is a sense in which the ulama personified for non-elite Muslims the ideals of Islamic unity and juridical equality. Individual ustadzes had resisted co-optation by the Muslim establishment and the Philippine government. They lacked the usual accoutrements of authority—automobiles, armed escorts, and entourages—and those who hailed from powerful families did not conspicuously favor their relatives in their official pronouncements or activities.

On the whole, ordinary Muslims genuinely admired the ustadzes and those political leaders closely aligned with them. It was that admiration, more so than anxiety about applications of armed force by the MILF, that seems to have motivated much of the popular political support for the ulama-MILF coalition. The voluntary nature of that popular loyalty was illustrated by a 1986 incident recorded in my field notes—the arrest and subsequent release by government forces of Hadji Murad, the top military commander of the MILF.

> Hadji Murad and some of his companions were captured by the PC [Philippine Constabulary] on their way back from Marawi when their jeep broke down. They were taken to PC headquarters in Marawi City. Within a very short time many people ("thousands") had surrounded the PC camp, some with guns. The people gave an ultimatum that if Hadji Murad was not released by 10 P.M. they would storm the camp. Some women protesters did enter the camp. PC commander Gutang and Governor Zacaria Candao were told of the arrest and went to the camp. Governor Candao reportedly announced to the crowd that if Hadji Murad were not immediately released he would resign his post. General Gutang signed the release papers and Hadji Murad was freed that same night.

Just the same, non-elite Muslims also responded with argumentation and resistance to a number of the specific endeavors of the ulama. They objected to ulama attempts to reform ritual practice and made clear by their continued attendance that they opposed the ustadzes' denunciation of dayunday performances. While appreciative of moves toward juridical equality, they were intensely troubled at reports of severe applications of Islamic punishments by some nontraditional (i.e., ulama) adjudicators. In Campo Muslim, some of the disagreements were more expressly political. Many community members contested attempts by ustadzes to expel the CCF program without replacing it with comparable resources. They also disputed the continued characterization by the ulama and MILF in the 1980s of the separatist struggle as a jihad, because they resented making obligatory contributions to support mujahideen who were neither engaged in armed conflict nor experiencing economic conditions more difficult than their own.

Contemporary social analyses of Islam-in-place have emphasized the significance of the dynamic relationship between the ideal life prescribed for Muslims and the actual lives Muslims lead (Bowen 1993; Eickelman 1976; Ellen 1983; Kessler 1978; Roff 1985).[5] The expression of tensions between ideal and actual Islam in Campo Muslim highlights the two-sidedness of the dialogue between the "prescribers (ulama)" and those they perceived as backsliders (Roff 1985, 9). Among the independent ulama of Cotabato there had developed the notion that the Muslims of Cotabato had progressed partway toward the goal of becoming "genuine Muslims" (in Magindanaon, tidtu-tidtu a Muslim) and had to be gradually but firmly propelled farther along the path. An alternative opinion was evident among ordinary Muslims. As expressed by Imam Akmad of Campo Muslim, it turned the ulama's notion of incipience right around by maintaining that with time the ustadzes would obtain practical knowledge, relax their prohibitions, and accommodate certain local practices. The view expressed by Imam Akmad and other elders amounted to the assertion that there were two morally acceptable directions in which to move on the path of Islam: toward strict scriptural interpretation and toward local knowledge— what Roy Ellen (1983) has termed "practical Islam." Movement in the first direction was not invariably preferable, and movement in the second did not necessarily constitute backsliding.[6]

How then should the Islamic identity of ordinary Muslims in Cotabato be characterized? First of all, it is not, and probably never has been, predicated upon their holding their traditional nobility in "religious awe and adulation" (Glang 1969, 33). At the same time, as we have seen, most ordinary Muslims are not the sort of Muslims the independent ulama would have them be. They are Muslims who rely on magical charms and amulets and appease local spirits. They are Muslims whose religious practice exhibits a good deal of ritual impropriety, who may drink and gamble, neglect their prayers, and perform

religious rituals quite at variance with Islamic orthopraxy. They are
Muslims who embrace many ingredients of the highly Westernized culture of their Christian neighbors. While Muslim subordinates have, to
a significant degree, accepted the new source of moral authority represented by the independent ulama, they have done so despite its associated call for Islamic orthopraxy and the disenchantment of their
world, not because of it.

They are Muslims, they declare, because their forebears were Muslims, because they live in a Muslim homeland, and because they pro-
fess Islam. As we have seen, their "Muslimness" (Ellen 1983, 56) is an
oppositional identity but not one constructed for them by political
leaders. The ordinary Muslims of Cotabato have never uncritically embraced any of the dominant meanings of Islamic identity either ascribed or proposed to them. Their Muslimness is self-sufficient and has
resisted symbolic definition or moral supervision by either ulama or
datus. That is not to say that it is a fixed identity. Rather, it may be
said to represent "only the current state of play" (Bowen 1992, 668) in
three continuing and complexly intertwined dialogues: that between
ordinary Muslims and the independent ulama over styles of religiosity,
between traditional leaders and followers over the sources of political
legitimacy, and between Muslims and the Christian-controlled Philippine state over the parameters of regional self-determination.

As for the political potential of that Islamic identity, it is clear that
the ulama's message of Islamic unity and equality resonated far more
deeply with Muslim subordinates than the datu coalition's often awk-
ward appeals to traditional loyalties. The popular appeal of the political message of the ulama coalition allowed them to mobilize large
numbers of Muslims to support them in public demonstrations and
provincial elections (there were also, to be sure, some more practical
incentives for political mobilization, ranging from entertainment-
seeking to severe social pressure). In the municipal elections, however,
the ideal of Islamic unity ran directly up against the particularistic
goals of Muslim politicians and vote brokers and the practical economic considerations of Muslim voters.

CONCLUSION

What, finally, does the Cotabato case contribute to the broader debate
about cultural domination and resistance? On one hand, the evidence
from Cotabato provides superficial support to those who argue, contra

James Scott (1985, 1990), that domination and resistance should not be imagined as discrete categories nor should their cultural expressions be dichotomized into public versus hidden transcripts. Cultural domination in Cotabato has been embedded, to some extent, in everyday designations and distinctions as well as in the more formal assertions of power holders. Resistance has not only been found hidden away in private transcripts but also has been expressed, at least occasionally, in the public dialogue. These readily observable exceptions to the strict dichotomization of domination and resistance are joined in Cotabato by a less obvious one: the development of images of rule endogenous to Muslim subordinates, demonstrating that the private, unofficial transcript of power relations may serve to reproduce as well as express resistance to those relations.

On the other hand, important aspects of the Cotabato case do not sustain arguments for hegemony as a potent concept for the analysis of cultural order. For one, it offers no strong evidence for the political effects of the central ideological operation claimed for hegemony—the naturalization of the existing order. While some naturalization is indicated in that Muslim subordinates have tended to accept domination as a fact of life, it is far from clear that their acceptance of the inevitability of domination in general has played any significant role in maintaining particular social orders. As we have seen, endogenous collective representations of rule have actually denaturalized social power, an imaginative operation that exhibits counterhegemonic potential.

Neither is there much support to be found for the postulated correlate of naturalization, the "experiential starvation of the political imagination" of subordinates (Linger 1993, 18). Ordinary Muslims have been well able to imagine political realities alternative to those envisioned by their rulers. That such images have not resulted in a fully formed and publicly articulated vision of a social order that counters the predominant version does not diminish in the least their political significance. These independent cultural productions do demonstrate that Muslim subordinates have not been paralyzed (in imagination or action) by elite-generated political discourse.

The political imaginations of ordinary Muslims reflect their experiential knowledge. The daily life of political subordinates consists of more than ritual practices within taken-for-granted social configurations. It is also made up of historical events that test the core assumptions of the dominant culture. Subordinates' "experienced encounters with the limits of their own culture" and its sometimes savage incongruities create opportunities for insight and "the possibility of creative innovative practice" (Rebel 1989, 125).[7]

The materials from Cotabato suggest that those who depict hegemony as both vulnerable and imperishable have gotten it half right. Whether or not a particular array of dominant meanings has accomplished the ideological incorporation of a set of political subordinates is more properly an empirical question than an epistemological assumption. There is plentiful evidence from Cotabato of what may be termed failures of hegemony—"points of rupture, areas where a common discursive framework cannot be achieved" (Roseberry 1994, 366). Such ruptures are most apparent in the hegemonic project of the Muslim nationalist movement. There, rank-and-file adherents routinely resisted official interpretations of events, often by means of independent imaginative narratives that served as charters for political decisions directly at odds with the directions of movement leaders. Ordinary Muslims did not depend on elite-generated language and images to make sense of power relations. They were in no sense paralyzed by contradictory consciousness.

It is not at all difficult to find hegemony in the sense of *attempted* cultural domination at work in Cotabato. All who have sought to control Cotabato—both indigenous and external rulers—have had hegemonic projects. Such a project is most clearly evidenced, again, in the Muslim nationalist movement. Movement leaders articulated a coherent nationalist narrative intended to mobilize ordinary Muslims to rally to the separatist cause. While the separatist insurgents did gain a broad popular following, that successful mobilization had relatively little to do with the resonance of their nationalist message. A great number of factors motivated individual Muslims to fight for or otherwise support the armed separatist movement—self-defense, revenge, plunder, defense of local communities, social pressure, armed coercion, and personal ambition, among others. The idea of fighting for the Bangsamoro—for a nation of Philippine Muslims united by culture and history—was but one of those motivating factors and, if we use the popular songs and stories of the rebellion as indicators, not an especially potent one.

Those who observe the partial and often insignificant nature of everyday resistance and envision a web of cultural domination inexorably entrapping subordinates even as they attempt to resist provide a poetic but inapt metaphor. The weak, as James Scott (1985) reminds us, do not struggle helplessly but have their own weapons, among them the critical and imaginative faculties with which to cut through or dissolve the discursive snares of the powerful. Just the same—and despite hegemony proponents' useful reminders of the fragility of power—it must be remembered that the powerful do possess arsenals of their own with weapons quite capable of dispensing unambiguously deadly force. It is the difficulty of disentangling the effects of cultural domination from those of the more physical sort that has most vexed advocates of the hegemony concept (including Antonio Gramsci himself).

Derek Sayer has commented recently on the relationship between compliance and coercion in some remarks toward a reconceptualization of the notion of hegemony. He begins with an example drawn from Václav Havel—that of a Prague greengrocer who hangs a sign in his window saying "Workers of the World Unite."

> Havel's greengrocer had no interest in the fate of the international proletariat; he was merely participating in a ritual. But the "merely" is deceptive . . . We cannot infer from the greengrocer's likely nonbelief in what the sign says that his action is *meaningless*. For his displaying the sign— or more dramatically, failing to do so—sent out signals, clear to all . . . What displaying the sign signified was his willingness to conform, to participate in the established order as if its representations were reality. It also said, in a language all could read, that the greengrocer shared a real sociality with others, that of living the lie itself. (1994, 374)

Sayer observes further that while such "knowing complicity" does not constitute ideological incorporation (and is, in fact, "the exact opposite of 'false consciousness'"), these "ritual accommodations . . . disempower their participants, and the participants know this, too" (1994, 374). Hegemony, in Sayer's usage, resumes its inceptive Gramscian sense of consent to rule. Its power lies in the process of consenting itself. The act of publicly accepting the representations of rule as social reality diminishes individuals—by splitting public from private selves—and shapes social life by producing and reproducing "quite material forms of sociality" based on collective complicity (1994, 374). The source of hegemony's power, however, "is also exactly what is most fragile about [it], precisely because it does depend on people living what they much of the time know to be a lie" (1994, 377).

Sayer's thoughts on hegemony are both intriguing and unsatisfying. The cynicism displayed by Havel's greengrocer, while anticipated in a Stalinist panopticon, is probably not the most accurate exemplification of political subordinates on the whole. Nor does "living a lie" provide a complete description of the public selves of subordinates. As we have seen in Cotabato, subalterns may both invent their own mystification and engage in subtle negotiations with power-holders over the contours of social reality.[8]

All the same, Sayer has provided a critical insight into the hegemony concept—one pointedly illustrated by the material from Cotabato. For Sayer, the "moment of consent" that Gramsci termed "hegemony" is always a public moment. Hegemony references *public* consent to rule—consent expressed in public rituals. The power of hegemony lies not in its saturation of individual interiors but in the act of public accommodation to dominant representations. That power has two forms, one immediate and the other indirect. Public enactments of consent are directly useful for rulers in terms of the mobilization of bodies (if not minds) for particular purposes. They are also indirectly efficacious (and this is where Sayer proceeds beyond James Scott). Public accommodations to rule also reproduce domination insofar as the outward acceptance of dominant representations as social reality systematically disempowers subjects by making them collective (and conscious) accomplices in their own subjugation. Their public consent, however, is not the result of paralysis but of active (though very narrowly constrained) decisions.

With Sayer's comments in mind, there are at least three additional inferences to be drawn from the Cotabato case in respect to cultural domination and resistance. First, as Sayer observes, public acceptance of the representations of the dominant order stems from "everyday fear" (of ever-present coercions) but also from the promise of individual empowerments (Sayer 1994, 376). Ritual accommodations may be made either to avoid losses (of individual freedom or property) or to obtain access to various enabling resources. It follows that accommodations to ruling representations, whether by local elites to colonial control or by underclasses to local domination, are all of a kind and should be considered together. The accommodations to power observed in Cotabato—both of local elites to external rule and of Muslim subjects to indigenous leaders—comprised a single process operating at two levels. Cotabato Muslims have signaled their acquiescence to rule in manifold public rituals, displaying themselves as subjects of a sultan or as America's Moros or as citizens of the Bangsamoro. In every case, their acceptance of the social reality of the moment has been motivated less by the persuasiveness of the official discourse of the powerful than by other considerations. For Muslim elites, who had their presumed control of political subordinates with which to bargain, public submission to external rule was often exchanged for access to symbolic and material resources. The accommodations of ordinary Muslims stemmed more directly from the profoundly coercive nature of everyday life, and some of those coercions were not only explicitly recognized but also independently symbolized by subordinates. Yet for ordinary Muslims as well, public consent was also given to obtain access to resources: primarily protection but also economic resources and entertainment.

A second inference concerns everyday understandings, "practices and expectations" (Williams 1977, 110)—all of the more nondiscursive, taken-for-granted elements that occupy such an important place in various formulations of the hegemony concept. If, however, the focus is *public* consent and its consequences, then such everyday understandings are more straightforwardly theorized as aspects of material coercion, broadly conceived, rather than of hegemony. The organization of time and space within which individuals live their lives may have consequences that are profoundly coercive even if not fully recognized as such. "Power enforces the terms on which things must be done at the most everyday of levels" (Sayer 1994, 375). Muslim subordinates in Cotabato have found it difficult (though again, not impossible) to imagine a community (inged) not ruled by an autocratic datu because they have never been free of autocratic datus. They perceive an important social distinction between themselves and ordinary Christians at least in part because their treatment at the hands of the Philippine state has been so much worse than that of ordinary Christians. These examples constitute just the reverse of the "cultural shaping of experience" claimed for hegemony (Linger 1993, 4). On the contrary, the experiences of Muslim subjects have shaped their cultural perceptions.

Finally, a conception of hegemony stressing the distinction between public consent and private lives allows ample room for genuine resistance in spite of the disempowering effects of ritual accommodations. As we have seen, that resistance need not only be isolated but may, under certain circumstances be collectively expressed and acted upon. In Cotabato as in Havel's Czechoslovakia, the most politically consequential messages sent by subordinates were not those intended for official eyes and ears.

Notes

ABBREVIATIONS

CCF	Christian Children's Fund
CHDF	Civilian Home Defense Force
CNI	Commission on National Integration
IPP	Islamic Party of the Philippines
KBL	*Kilusang Bagong Lipunan* (The New Society Movement), the national political party created by Ferdinand Marcos after his imposition of martial law
MAP	Muslim Association of the Philippines
MILF	Moro Islamic Liberation Front
MNLF	Moro National Liberation Front
NAMFREL	National Movement for Free Elections
PC	Philippine Constabulary
UNIDO	United Nationalist Democratic Organizations, the national opposition coalition that backed the candidacy of Corazon Aquino in the 1986 presidential election

INTRODUCTION

1. My interviews in Cotabato were conducted primarily in Magindanaon, but also in Tagalog and, occasionally, in English. It was not uncommon for more than one language to be used in the course of a conversation.

2. A very important exception to that general trend is provided by a historian of the Philippines, Reynaldo Ileto, in his work *Pasyon and Revolution*. Ileto inquires of the Philippine Revolution begun in 1896, "how did the [lower classes] actually perceive, in terms of their own experience, the ideas of

nationalism" enunciated by their elite leaders (1979, 4)? It is the very same question I ask of the contemporary Muslim separatist movement in the Philippines. Ileto and I agree that the meaning of these movements was not the same for rank-and-file adherents and movement elites. There are parallels in this book as well with Ileto's focus on folk narratives, religion, and popular beliefs in preternatural powers. Our answers to the question about the perceptions and motivations of ordinary adherents do differ. Ileto launches his analysis from the position of wanting to know "how the traditional mind operates, particularly in relation to questions of change"(1979, 2). He tends to view the behavior of lower-class participants in the revolution as "attempts to restructure the world in terms of ideal social forms and modes of behavior" (1979, 8). Together with most contemporary anthropologists, I am quite skeptical of the existence of a "traditional mind" (of course, they and I have had the benefit of more than twenty years of hindsight since Ileto's initial writing). I also take a different view of the relationship between culture and collective action. I will argue that the independent perceptions and motivations of rank-and-file adherents of the Muslim separatist movement represent not only imaginative but strategic endeavors. That is to say, Muslim subordinates have exercised their political imaginations to envision a more perfect (though not always more "traditional") world, but also to voice their resistance to the official aims of movement leaders, especially when those goals seemed to contradict other, more local considerations.

3. The term "ordinary Muslims" is a problematic one (see Peletz 1997), and I need to define my particular usage before proceeding further. Throughout this work I use the phrase "ordinary Muslims" in three intermingled senses to reference three (near-perfectly) overlapping categories of persons. "Ordinary Muslims" refers first to those Cotabato Muslims (the great majority) who comprise the subordinate (or "lower") classes—those who occupy similarly disadvantaged positions in the regional system of resource distribution. In respect to relations of production almost all may be classified as peasants, low-skilled wage workers, or petty producers or service providers in the urban informal economy. Second, "ordinary Muslims" refers to those Cotabato Muslims who are not political elites. By my definition, political elites either occupy commanding positions at the head of a social grouping or are able to exert significant influence on those occupants as the result of their control of political and economic resources. In its third sense, "ordinary Muslims" refers to those Cotabato Muslims who possess neither a strongly self-conscious ethnic identity as Moros (Philippine Muslims), nor a highly objectified Islamic consciousness. The ethnoreligious consciousness of ordinary Muslims in Cotabato is discussed in detail farther on (see especially chapters 5 and 6). It should be assumed that, despite these similarities, significant differences in religious orientation and practice may be found among ordinary Muslims in Cotabato.

4. This notion of multidimensional "social fields of force" is taken from William Roseberry (1994, 357). Roseberry's own use of the metaphor is a reworking and extension of an image originally provided by E. P. Thompson (1978).

CHAPTER 1. THE POLITICS OF HERITAGE

1. The thrust of these efforts has shifted somewhat over time. Earlier works pointed out the contradictions and contestations contained within systems of domination (see, e.g., Abu-Lughod 1986; Comaroff 1985; Ong 1987; Stoler 1985). More recent treatments, responding to perceived simplifications in the literature on everyday resistance generated mostly from outside anthropology (see, e.g., Scott 1985, 1990; Willis 1981), have focused on "rethinking resistance" and its relation to domination (see, e.g., Abu-Lughod 1990; Kaplan and Kelly 1994; Kondo 1990; Lagos 1993; Linger 1993; Reed-Danahay 1993; Woost 1993).

2. This occurred earliest and most prominently in the work of Eugene Genovese (1974) on plantation slavery.

3. Perry Anderson notes, for example, that in some of his writings Gramsci contrasts the terms "hegemony" and "domination"—equating hegemony with "consent" and domination with "coercion." Elsewhere, however, "Gramsci speaks of hegemony, not as a pole of "consent" in contrast to another of "coercion," but as itself a synthesis of consent and coercion . . . This version cannot be reconciled with the preceding account, which remains the predominant one in the Notebooks" (1976, 24–25).

4. Raymond Williams's interpretation is also shared, in many of its general features, by such other analysts of the cultural politics of Western capitalism as Ernesto Laclau (1977) and Stuart Hall (1985).

5. In his 1977 work, Williams defines hegemony similarly as "a whole body of practices and expectations . . . a lived system of meanings and values—constitutive and constituting—which as they are experienced as practices appear as reciprocally confirming" (1977, 110). He notes also that hegemony "is continually resisted, limited, altered, challenged by pressures not at all its own" (112).

6. Williams seems to recognize this problem in his remark that "[t]he sources of any alternative hegemony are indeed difficult to define" (1977, 111).

7. Some of these anthropological usages display a similar internal inconsistency in speaking, on the one hand, of hegemony's power to shape the experience of subordinates and, on the other, of its susceptibility to challenge by those same subordinates. Comaroff and Comaroff argue that hegemony—"that order of signs and practices . . . that come to be taken-for-granted as the natural and received shape of the world"—is "habit forming" and so "is rarely contested directly" (1992, 23). At the same time they note that hegemony "is always intrinsically unstable, always vulnerable" (1991, 27). Michael Woost declares that hegemony comprises "both domination and resistance" and is best "understood as the *tendential* outcome of a struggle for order" (1993, 503). He also observes that "hegemony works behind the backs of those it dominates . . . in the sense that those who become the objects of the dominant ideological discourse are not freely formed subjects/individuals who deliberately decide whether or not to assign legitimacy to a social order" (1993, 516). Maria Lagos criticizes the tendency "to separate resistance from hegemony . . .

as if they were two different processes with different dynamics" (1993, 53). Daniel Linger defines hegemony as "the maintenance of a political structure through the cultural shaping of experience," while also declaring that "hegemony thrives on discontent" (1993, 4).

8. Numerous other anthropological treatments of nationalism have been produced. Some of these (see, e.g., Dominguez 1989; Handler 1988; Spencer 1990; Verdery 1991) have focused predominantly on the discursive productions of nationalist elites rather than on the popular reception of nationalist ideologies at the community level. Others have examined popular responses to national ideas without recourse to the notion of hegemony (see, e.g., Bendix 1992; Bowman 1993; Sluka 1989, 1995) or have applied it in a somewhat different manner than Raymond Williams (see, e.g., B. Williams 1991). Bruce Kapferer has developed the separate notion of "ontologies" (1988) to explain the motivational force of nationalist ideologies—a concept which, though clearly distinguishable from it, resembles hegemony in many respects.

9. Michael Woost faults Scott for failing to recognize the "shifting, uneven character of hegemony" (1993, 503). Deborah Reed-Danahay is troubled by a "disturbing simplification" in Scott's distinction between an official and a hidden transcript of power relations (1993, 223). Aihwa Ong, more specifically, accuses Scott of "misrepresent[ing] social realities in rural Malaysia as a simple dichotomy between a national hegemony and a resistant village subculture" (1995, 188).

10. A separate, ethnography-based critique has been recently leveled at Scott by Sherry Ortner (1995) and (in more detail) by Michael Peletz (1997). It is that by not considering ambivalence (mixed emotions) as a significant phenomenon among subordinates, Scott produces an "ethnographically thin" account of dominant-subordinate relations (Ortner 1995, 190). More generally, studies of domination and resistance that do not devote analytical attention to the problem of ambivalence run the risk of being "highly anemic with respect to their treatment of the cultural psychology of the social actors who are at the center of their inquiries"(Peletz 1997).

This critique may appear similar to one above but is quite separable. Ambivalence on the part of subordinates may arise from divided interests (stressed by Ortner) or as the result of moral constraints (emphasized by Peletz) or from various other sources, and may under certain circumstances produce political paralysis. But such paralysis is not brought about by the workings of hegemony. Ortner and Peletz seek primarily to "thicken" the ethnography of domination and resistance by adding the element of psychological ambivalence on the part of subordinates. See chapter 9 for a discussion of ambivalence as a factor influencing the behavior of Campo Muslim residents.

11. It has become increasingly commonplace to find in postcolonial situations mobilized peasants or urban workers fighting for or actively supporting armed ethnonationalist movements aimed at exchanging one set of state-level elites for another. Most of the armed secessionist struggles of recent occurrence have been carried out by populations exhibiting significant internal disparities in social power. Those struggles include, as a modest sample, armed movements for the creation of independent states or autonomous regions for Kurds,

Eritreans, Palestinians, Sikhs, Sri Lankan Tamils, Kashimiris, Basques, Shans, Ibos, Croatians, Abkhazians, Chechens, Sudanese Christians, and Philippine Muslims.

12. The distinction between nationalist killing and nationalist dying is not an unimportant one. There is, for one, a very great symbolic separation between the "giant exorcism" of the murderous Sinhalese rioting described by Kapferer (1988, 101) and the ritual self-sacrifice of Irish Republican Army's hunger strikers. In addition, the communal rioting provoked by nationalist passions that has erupted in India, Sri Lanka, and elsewhere is a far less dangerous undertaking for individual members of nationalist mobs than is rank-and-file participation in an armed separatist movement, even given that a fair proportion of the violent activity of separatist insurgents may be directed against unarmed civilians.

13. An ethical issue often accompanies the methodological problem. There is always the risk, even after an armed struggle has subsided, that eliciting and recording detailed narratives from non-elite adherents concerning their attitudes toward, or actions on behalf of, a separatist movement may endanger them in various ways.

14. For examples of such studies see Bowman (1993), Feldman (1991), Lan (1985), Mahmood (1996), Pettigrew (1995), Sluka (1989, 1990, 1995), Swedenburg (1990, 1991, 1995), and Zulaika (1988). Of these, the works by Bowman, Lan, and Sluka (1989) are principally focused on ordinary adherents and local communities. Those by Feldman and Zulaika take as their subject not nationalist struggles per se but political violence, specifically the ways in which violence is culturally constructed, ritually enacted, and reciprocally exchanged between political antagonists. Mahmood and Pettigrew have produced very different works, each of which focuses primary (though by no means exclusive) attention on the political and military leadership of the Sikh separatist movement. Swedenburg's work (1990, 1991) considers how popular memories of an earlier armed revolt have "undergone secondary revision for the sake of the [contemporary struggle for the Palestinian] nation" (1991, 177). David Lan's work, on nationalist guerrillas and peasants in Zimbabwe, is neither concerned with armed separatism nor, strictly speaking, with ethnonationalism. It is a study of a "popular" revolutionary struggle—one of the last of the twentieth century's "peasant wars" (Wolf 1969) of national liberation. It also remains one of the very best ground-level ethnographic accounts of an armed insurgency.

15. Similar observations have been made in theoretical form by Brackette Williams (1989) and ethnographically by Bowman (1993).

16. In a more recent work, Swedenburg provides more detailed depictions of the "popular" memories of Palestinian revolt he was able to elicit from informants—memories that "led a submerged existence in the everyday realm of private conversation rather than being expounded in the public arena" (1995, 27). He is more concerned, however, with how "popular memory and official Palestinian histories fused into a fairly unified picture" (1995, xxvi). Swedenburg defends his lack of interest in uncovering the "objective truth" of local resentments and rank-and-file dissension by noting that "solidarity requires us to

learn from and (to a certain extent) be tactically complicit with the silences . . . of the people with whom we live and study" (1995, xxviii).

While Swedenburg's stance may be an appropriate tactic in his particular circumstances, it represents a counterproductive strategy for the anthropological analysis of nationalism in general. By accepting public silence as genuine consent to the official versions of events and thereby ignoring the profound political tension between local concerns and nationalist goals, we achieve neither solidarity with, nor understanding of, those ordinary citizens caught up in nationalist movements, citizens who, like Slavenka Drakulic in Croatia, feel diminished by nationhood.

17. That refashioning may already be seen under way in various forms in the work of Hermann Rebel (1989) and William Roseberry (1989, 1991, 1994), as well as Derek Sayer (1994).

CHAPTER 2. PEOPLE AND TERRITORY IN COTABATO

1. Previous scholars have referred to the language and its speakers as Maguindanao (Mastura 1984; Stewart 1978), Magindanao (Beckett 1982; Ileto 1971; Mednick 1965), and Magindanaw (Llamzon 1978). I adopt the usage of Fleischman (1981b), who found in his linguistic research that Magindanaons "usually refer both to themselves and their language as /magindanawn/ and their land as /magindanaw/" (Fleischman 1981b, 57). The results of his survey of native speakers also showed an "overwhelming preference" for the spelling of their language as "Magindanaon." Informal data from my own fieldwork support Fleischman's findings.

2. The estimation of the Muslim population of the Philippines has involved a good deal of numerical uncertainty and political controversy. The figures used here, taken from the 1980 Philippine census figures as reported in *Ibon Facts and Figures* (see IBON Databank 1981), should be viewed as suggestive rather than definitive. For a discussion of the logistical and political problems associated with counting Philippine Muslims, see O'Shaughnessy (1975), "How Many Muslims Has the Philippines?" See also Majul (1979) for an alternative perspective. For examples of widely varying population estimates for Muslim ethnic groups compare the figures reported in Gowing (1979), Llamzon (1978), and Majul (1979).

3. Three other Magindanaon dialects are spoken outside the Cotabato River Basin by the descendants of settlers who emigrated from there. Taga-Biwangan ("from the left") is a place-name referring to those Magindanaon living to the south (or "left") of the Cotabato Basin along the long narrow seacoast that abuts the Tiruray Highlands. Taga-Kawanan ("from the right") is the term used for Magindanaons who have settled to the north on the northwest shore of Ilana Bay. Speakers of the Sibugay dialect are descendants of Magindanaon immigrants to Sibugay Bay on the Zamboanga Peninsula (Fleischman 1981b).

4. An intermediate dialect also exists, that of the Nagtaganen (or people in the middle) of the smaller Kabuntalan Sultanate, located where the Pulangi

splits into two branches. For our purposes, however, it may be subsumed under the Tau sa Ilud dialect.

5. There exists no complete ethnography and very little ethnographic description of the Magindanaon. Published ethnographic accounts of the Magindanaon are limited to an ethnomusicology study by Ernesto Maceda (1961) and an ethnographic appendix to a Ph.D. dissertation by James Stewart (1977). There is also a published proto-ethnographic account (in Spanish) by Blumentritt (1893). Jeremy Beckett (1993) has written on Magindanaon political culture. In folklore studies, Clement Wein (1984, 1985) has translated Magindanaon oral literature. Historical works on the Magindanaon are more abundant. Reynaldo Ileto (1971), Cesar Majul (1973), Michael Mastura (1984), and Ruurdje Laarhoven (1989) have written on the history of the Magindanaon sultanates. Ghislaine Loyre (1991) has contributed an ethnohistorical account of the institutions of the downriver (Magindanao) sultanate and Jeremy Beckett (1982, 1993) has focused on the Magindanaons under Spanish and American colonial rule. There is also a wealth of primary historical sources in the form of European reports from the seventeenth to the twentieth century in English, Spanish, French, and Dutch (see, e.g., Bernaldez 1857; Combes in Blair and Robertson 1903–19; Dampier 1906; Forrest 1969; Montano 1886; Nieto 1894).

6. Population estimates for the Iranun differ wildly. They range from the improbably high figure of 429,000 offered by Gowing (1979) to the impossibly low figure of 6,517 reported in the 1986 regional socioeconomic profile for Central Mindanao (National Economic Development Authority 1986) Both estimates apparently reflect substantial confusion in separating Iranun speakers from neighboring speakers of various dialects of Maranao. They also indicate that one of the capabilities that the Philippine state lacks is the capacity to enumerate, with any degree of accuracy, its peripheral populations. The range I offer may be taken as simply a rough guess.

7. Recent linguistic evidence has challenged prevailing assumptions that the Iranun are a dialectical subgroup of the Maranao and are relatively recent (circa 1765) migrants from Lake Lanao to the Cotabato coast (see, e.g., Ileto 1971; Kuder 1945; Mednick 1965; Warren 1981). After clearly establishing that Iranun is a language separate from Maranao, Fleischman (1981b) reports, based on measurements of cognate percentages, that the Iranun language is centrally located between Magindanaon and Maranao. This discovery lends strong support to the belief held by the Iranun themselves that their language is the original language from which the other two languages diverged (Fleischman 1981b, 70). Thus, when the divergence occurred, surely far earlier than 1765, it was the Maranao and Magindanaon who separated from the Iranun at the coast to move to the inlands and uplands, and not the opposite.

8. The propensity of the precolonial Iranun to travel long distances as maritime marauders, along with the fearsome reputations they gained as such, has led to the problem of distinguishing in historical records and oral traditions actual Iranun speakers from a variety of other sea raiders erroneously identified as "Iranun." The Tausug and other peoples of Sulu still use the term "Iranun"

to refer to all Muslims from Mindanao. And in the eighteenth and nineteenth centuries, the English used "Iranun" (or Illanun) to designate any "Sulu pirate" (Warren 1981).

9. For an ethnohistorical examination of Iranun defiance of external rule, see McKenna (1994). Few other studies of the Iranun exist. Eric Fleischman (1981a) has written a short account of traditional Iranun leadership, and Warren (1981) devotes a long and richly detailed chapter to Iranun raiding in the eighteenth and nineteenth centuries in his history of slave raiding and external trade in "the Sulu zone."

10. Tiruray women who married Muslim men usually became Muslims. In addition, Some Tiruray men recently have been converted to Islam.

11. Those four provinces are Maguindanao, Sultan Kudarat, North Cotabato, and South Cotabato. Of those four, only the first three lie within the Cotabato River Basin. General Santos City, a tertiary city on Sarangani Bay in South Cotabato, has grown rapidly as the extractive and plantation industries of South Cotabato—tuna, timber, and pineapples—have developed.

12. This approximate percentage is based on Philippine census figures for 1980 as reported in the 1986 regional socioeconomic profile for Central Mindanao (National Economic Development Authority 1986). As of 1980, Maguindanao Province had a population reported at 536,546 persons. Of this number, 396,400 (or 73.8 percent) were reported to be ethnic Muslims. In the region as a whole, there are reported to be 92,000 ethnic Tiruray. Almost all of these are located in Maguindanao Province.

13. For the purposes of statistical coverage, the Cotabato Basin may be defined as the area lying within the political boundaries of the three provinces of North Cotabato, Maguindanao, and Sultan Kudarat. Those provinces include large areas outside the Cotabato Basin, but most of their developed agricultural land lies within the basin itself.

14. As an example, in 1986 the basin produced more than 620,000 metric tons of rice on 182,480 hectares, a 15 percent increase over 1982 production, on a somewhat smaller harvest area (National Economic Development Authority 1986). These figures represent an average 1986 yield of 3.39 metric tons of unhusked rice per hectare—one of the highest in the country—and an increase from approximately 2.9 metric tons in 1982. It bears noting that the average yield for the predominantly Muslim Maguindanao Province, at 2.38 metric tons per hectare, was significantly lower than that for the two majority Christian provinces of North Cotabato and Sultan Kudarat, at 3.69 and 3.64 metric tons, respectively. While about 38 percent of the potential rice area in the latter two provinces (41,363 and 24,468 hectares, respectively) had been irrigated by 1984, less than 12 percent of the potential rice land in Maguindanao Province (14,358 hectares) was under irrigation by that year (National Economic Development Authority 1986).

15. More than one geographer has noted that Cotabato City's "eccentric" location on a low swampy interfluve between the two main distributaries of the Pulangi River has deterred its development into a major commercial center on a par with Davao or Zamboanga (Wernstedt and Spencer 1967, 554; Burley 1973, 216).

16. Four of the firms are engaged in timber extraction and processing. The remaining two produce cornstarch and corn oil. There are also a number of medium-size agribusiness operations—primarily fishponds and coconut plantations—in the vicinity of the city.

17. The considerable ethnic diversity found in Cotabato City was specifically addressed by Chester Hunt in a 1957 survey article entitled "Ethnic Stratification and Integration in Cotabato."

18. Hardly any Tiruray reside in Cotabato City.

19. In Davao, General Santos City, and Iligan, as well as in the cities of northern Mindanao, the language of public discourse is generally Visayan. In Zamboanga City, Tagalog is beginning to replace Chavacano as the language of commerce.

20. See, for example, the proceedings of the seminar on "The Mindanao Problem" published in the January 1987 issue of the Philippine journal of current affairs, *Solidarity* (Jose et al. 1987). See also Bauzon (1991), whose juxtaposition of "Islamic" and "Liberal" paradigms is simply a recasting of the oft-repeated argument that Muslim-Christian conflict in the Philippines is the consequence of clashing worldviews.

21. On more than one occasion, I witnessed Muslims with strongly separatist political sentiments standing to join in the singing of the national anthem of the Philippines at public meetings or seminars—a practice ingrained through education at state schools.

22. Muslim Chinese-mestizos have played prominent roles in Cotabato City in the present century as business entrepreneurs and politicians. See Hunt (1957) for a discussion of the changing character of the Chinese-mestizo community in Cotabato in the 1950s.

23. This information, and most of the quantitative data on the community that follows, was obtained by means of a household survey of Campo Muslim carried out to enumerate the population and obtain basic census information. Every household in the community was surveyed by myself and two research assistants who were also Campo Muslim residents. Information requested from household heads (self-identified) included age, birthplace, occupation, ethnolinguistic identity, length of stay in Campo Muslim, reason for migration to the city, number of occupants of the dwelling, and their relationship to the household head. Data were also collected by observation on house size and type and the presence or absence of water taps, electricity, toilets, radios, televisions, and refrigerators.

Delimiting Campo Muslim for census purposes was a fairly straightforward procedure. The community is bounded on two sides (front and back) by water, and its borders with the communities that adjoin it are clearly marked by roads or open spaces.

24. The terms "Babu" and "Bapa" (literally, "Aunt" and "Uncle") are used as terms of address and reference for community elders. The names Babu Imun and Bapa Akub, and most names used in this book, are pseudonyms.

25. Some years earlier, an enterprising Muslim owner of a dwelling overlooking the nearby Matampay River had constructed crude pay toilets, which were used primarily by Campo Muslim residents.

26. The *Mindanao Cross,* Cotabato City's weekly newspaper, would commonly conclude reports of armed robberies in the city by noting that "the suspects escaped into Campo Muslim." Community residents reject the characterization of Campo Muslim as a den of thieves, arguing that the robbers are not from Campo Muslim but that they actually flee through the community to reach the edge of the city and beyond.

CHAPTER 3. ISLAMIC RULE IN COTABATO

1. For examples of political ideologies in the Islamic world similarly based in sanctified inequality see Bujra (1971) and Combs-Schilling (1989). For a discussion of the doctrinal support for sanctified inequality in Islamic (and specifically Philippine Muslim) tradition, see Majul (1973, 3–6).

2. Two statements by Nur Misuari, founder and Central Committee chairman of the Moro National Liberation Front, may serve as illustration. In a 1975 policy paper entitled "The Rise and Fall of Moro Statehood," Misuari wrote, "[O]ne unalterable fact of history remains a cornerstone of the present revolutionary movement. This historical fact is inextricably linked to the Bangsa Moro people's inherent desire to be left free and sovereign having their own honoured place in the community of nations. Their national aspiration is nothing more than to enjoy *again* the prerogative of chartering their own national destiny with justice for all and to see the democratization of the wealth of their homeland" (emphasis mine; quoted in Mastura 1984, 111). In a 1977 speech titled "Cultural Genocide in the Philippines," he stated: "The Muslim people and homeland have 500 years of Islamic culture and civilization. They were once free, sovereign and an independent nation. As a matter of fact, they were once one of the strongest powers in Southeast Asia" (quoted in Majul 1985, 136).

3. I use the term "precolonial Cotabato" to refer to the entire period prior to the American colonial occupation of the region in 1899. Although the Spaniards had consolidated colonial control of the northern Philippines by about 1600, they never accomplished the complete political subjugation of the southern sultanates. Downstream Cotabato was occupied in 1861 and formally included as a Spanish possession, but Spanish colonial control never extended much beyond a rudimentary military occupation of strategic points on the Pulangi River (see chapter 4). Political and economic relations within Cotabato seem to have been only slightly affected by Spain's formal possession of Cotabato in the late nineteenth century. It is therefore not inaccurate to extend the "precolonial" period in Cotabato to the turn of the twentieth century.

4. This is a simplified compendium of the opinions of a number of public figures in Cotabato. For an example of this perception in written form, see Damaso (1983). For a rare dissenting opinion, see Lingga quoted in Gowing (1979, 241).

5. I employ the term "traditional" here not in any essentialist sense but as a shorthand reference to a host of local sociopolitical practices, beliefs, forms, and expectations, some of which are described in detail farther on. Some "tra-

ditional" arrangements in Muslim Cotabato are more ancient than others and not all are self-consciously or universally regarded as "traditional culture" (in Magindanaon, *adat betad*). They do, however, form a sociocultural domain largely uninfluenced by Western colonialism or the political domination of Christian Filipinos.

6. Datu Mohammad Adil had a long career in the Philippine Constabulary, and when I met him in 1986 he held the rank of lieutenant colonel (ret.). His followers referred to him as "Datu," and I use that honorific in these pages. Most Christians and members of the Muslim elite in Cotabato city referred to him as "Major Adil," referring to the rank he had held for a number of years. In 1992, he was invested with the title "Sultan sa Kutawatu" (Sultan of Cotabato) by the members of the high nobility of Cotabato.

7. Although the ethnographic material presented here reflects a broad range of positions and perspectives, it does present certain limitations. For one, it is somewhat removed, unavoidably, from the precolonial period; most narratives of past relations concern the very late precolonial or early colonial period. Another is that the voices of women, as well as detailed information on the social positions and political actions of women in the Cotabato sultanates, are mostly lacking here. There is somewhat more information on women available for the American colonial period, and I do attempt to make the voices of the women of Campo Muslim heard in the chapters concerning present-day Cotabato.

8. The term "bangsa," or "bansa," is found throughout the Malay world and has been used to refer to descent lines, descent groups, nations, castes, races, or estates. There seems to be some disagreement about its origin. Dewey (1962, 231) suggests that the term is Chinese in derivation. Milner (1982, xv) identifies "bangsa" as having a Sanskrit origin. This latter foreign derivation seems the more plausible one.

9. The term "sultanate" refers here to a political institution based on an Islamic legitimating ideology and headed by a sultan—a formally hereditary leader who possesses the authority to bestow titles and appoint individuals to specialized subordinate offices.

10. The diminution of the significance of local ancestry is by no means an automatic outcome of the introduction of a political system based on an Islamic model. Gullick (1958) and Mednick (1965) each describe systems where local ancestry was not devalued with the adoption of an Islamic political idiom. According to Mednick (1965), the Maranao, after the introduction of Islam, developed a single, complex status system based equally on local ancestry and descent from the prime Islamic ancestor (also Sarip Kabungsuwan). The Maranao sociopolitical system also remained relatively uncentralized. Gullick (1958) describes the ruling class of the Malay states, which were relatively more centralized than the Cotabato sultanates, as having two principal groups: members of the royal line, from which the sultan was chosen, and members of a number of nonroyal but noble local lineages that produced local officials (datus). The noble status of these local lineages was based not on their kinship links with the royal lineage but on their right to fill various chieftainships. This conferral of high status on particular lineages on the basis of ancient

agreements is paralleled in the special situation of one local descent line in Cotabato, the Tabunaway bangsa (see below).

11. Of the twenty tupus listed by Mastura (1984, 34) as having been under the administration of the Buayan Sultanate, only three are named after apical ancestors and two of these ancestors are immigrants who arrived after Sarip Kabungsuwan. Twelve of the tupus are named after their localities, one is not a descent line at all but a category for foreigners (*rafu*), and four represent caste-like groups of craft specialists who held a special dependent status under the sultan.

12. In a Maranao version of this myth, Sarip Kabungsuwan accidentally marries his long-lost sister, a more exact means for establishing an exogenous and unadulterated aristocratic lineage from a single apical ancestor (see Mednick 1965, 97). Similarly structured origin myths for sultanates are found throughout the Malay world. For illustrations from Perak and Maluku see, respectively, Sullivan (1982, 1) and L. Andaya (1993, 53).

13. The intermediate Kabuntalan Sultanate was established in the mid-eighteenth century by a branch of the Magindanao royal house (see Mastura 1984, 36).

14. I am grateful to John Bowen for pointing out the strong parallels between the political and status-ranking systems of the Magindanaon and those of the Bugis of Sulawesi. The Bugis system of rank gradation is quite similar to that found in Cotabato, especially in its assignment of intermediate descent-rank to children of unequally ranked parents (see below). Unlike in Cotabato, the central Bugis myth of noble descent is pre-Islamic, describing the Bugis nobility as descendants of "mysterious beings called "*tomanurung*" [in Bugis, literally, "One who descends"]" (Millar 1989, 43). For recent works in English on the Bugis see Millar (1989) and Pelras (1996).

15. This is the datu version of the original agreement between Sarip Kabungsuwan and Tabunaway. In the version told by present-day Tabunaway descendants (dumatus), the agreement included a clause declaring that the descendants of Sarip Kabungsuwan could not be proclaimed as sultans without the *consent* of the descendants of Tabunaway, and if this were not done the descendants of Tabunaway would have the authority to cancel the proclamation and take the leadership themselves. The datu version mentions only participation (implying ceremonial participation) in the investiture of the sultan. Mastura (1984, 5) notes that "dumatu" is the future tense of the verb "datu" (to lead) but does not offer an explanation for that designation. As the descendants of Tabunaway, the former ruler of Cotabato, the past tense of "datu" seems a more appropriate appellation. However, if Tabunaway is believed to have reserved the right to reassume the leadership of Cotabato under certain conditions, the term "dumatu" ("will lead") is descriptive.

16. Traditional Magindanaon status groups have been categorized by scholars in various ways. In general, analogies to classical or feudal European stratification systems have engendered more confusion than clarification. To cite an example, the endatuan have been described as "serfs" (Beckett 1982, 411), "freemen" (Stewart 1978, 244), and "commoners" (Mastura 1984, 33); the dumatu (see below) have been classified as "nobles" (Damaso 1983, 76),

"lesser nobles" (Stewart 1978, 244), and "commoners" (Beckett 1982, 411); and the ulipun have been mentioned as "vassals" (Mastura 1979), "servants" (Mastura 1984, 33), and "slaves" (Beckett 1982, 411). To avoid similar confusion, I endeavor to track as closely as possible the literal sense of the Magindanaon terms for these social categories.

17. Jeremy Beckett's (1982, 411) treatment of slave status in precolonial Cotabato differs from my own. He lists banyaga as occupying the fourth tier of the stratification system. He then suggests that since the status of an ulipun, at least in theory, could be changed with the clearance of his or her debt, that the ulipun do not constitute an estate. In support of my categorization I add to the reasons outlined above that the term "banyaga" has the literal meaning of "foreigner" or "alien." Gullick (1958, 104) employs a classification similar to mine for slave status in the Malay states. At the same time, it should be noted that actual social relations between ulipun and banyaga—and between those two unfree statuses and the other social strata—were more complex than the necessarily simplified description I present here. For comparison, see W. H. Scott's (1982) detailed account of the subtleties and complexities of the Tagalog slave system.

18. The conceptualization of maratabat among the neighboring Maranao is dramatically different from its use among the Magindanaon. Among the Maranao, maratabat primarily denotes rank honor and sensitivity about rank. It is a central and compelling social value that reflects pre-Islamic cultural traditions. Offended maratabat demands retribution that often takes the form of violent retaliation. The most distinctive aspect of Maranao maratabat is its relation to lineal descent and corporate kin responsibility. To defend one's maratabat is to uphold one's descent line. Both the responsibility for defending maratabat and the culpability for insulting it extend beyond the individuals involved in any particular incident of soiled maratabat. The pursuit of retribution for an offense to maratabat can last for generations. Individuals are socialized to seek revenge for long-past injuries to descent line honor by retaliating against a direct descendent generations removed from the original perpetrator. In a similar manner, badly soiled maratabat may be avenged immediately against a close kin of the offending party. In 1986, Manila newspapers luridly reported the murder of the seven-year-old daughter of a Magindanaon security guard at a Manila mosque by three young Maranao men whom he had publicly insulted the previous day. The reports did not explain the cultural logic behind the tragedy. The association between functioning local descent groups and the cultural intensification of maratabat (both lacking among the Magindanaon) is illustrated by a Maranao saying: "A man who has lost his bangsa has no maratabat" (Saber et al. 1974).

19. "Pamalung ka sa kaing sa saken na kundang aku na manik sa tulugan na entayn muna salegan u bulawan datumanung?"

20. Members of the ruling families of the three principal sultanates of the Cotabato Basin were linked by common descent and occasionally intermarried. Datu Kasim relates that those ties were recognized in the special three thousand–peso (or –dollar) bridewealth payment for marriages between two individuals of pulna rank. This represented one thousand pesos for each of the

three major royal houses of Cotabato. Compare Gullick's description of the "inner circle" of the Malay royal lineage (1958, 59–60).

21. The Cotabato sultanates had neither the number of offices of the Sulu Sultanate (see Majul 1973) nor the elaboration in ranked titles found among the Maranao (see Mednick 1965). Mastura (1984, 35) lists eleven offices (including that of sultan) arranged in three orders of rank for the Magindanao Sultanate.

22. Kinship links through males were, however, favored over those through females (Stewart 1977; Beckett 1982).

23. Those who received such "gift wives" (*tawakim*) were not required to provide bridewealth in return.

24. See Mednick (1965, 140–41) for a description of the use of a tarsila in the tracing of individual descent among the Maranao. For a fascinating, detailed illustration of written genealogies employed in a similar fashion elsewhere in the Islamic world, see Eickelman's (1976, 183–210) discussion of the uses made of silsila (name-chains) by the elite patrilineal descendants of a Moroccan marabout.

25. Similar mechanisms are found, for example, in the traditional political system of the Bugis. For men regarded as extraordinary achievers, the rule of female hypergamy may be suspended and noble ancestors rediscovered. Millar's observation about the Bugis holds equally well for Cotabato: "Given the Bugis assumption that descent-rank is correlated with character, it is natural that low-ranking people with exemplary achievements frequently are thought to have a high-ranking ancestor about whom people do not know. It is also natural that they use the strategy of 'marriage-up' to adjust for these achievement/descent-rank anomalies" (1989, 5).

26. Anthony Reid notes that for Southeast Asia in general in the sixteenth and seventeenth centuries, "state pageantry was the most effective way in which the citizenry was incorporated into the hierarchic state" (1988, 181). "For the majority of the population [royal and religious] festivals served three important purposes: participation in the majesty and hierarchy of the state; economic activity, such as marketing and rendering tribute; and entertainment" (ibid.).

27. The Bugis formally acknowledge the distinction between authority based on "proven superiority" (Millar 1989, 34) and that based in inherited nobility by recognizing a distinct category of individuals known as *tau matoa*, or "outstanding leaders" (1989, 6). That category crosscuts the status ranking system inasmuch as not all tau matoa are members of the high nobility. Many tau matoa do eventually obtain noble status for themselves or their descendants by means of the social mechanisms noted above.

28. Shelly Errington reports similar conceptions of highly potent individuals as inherently, and often unintentionally, dangerous in Luwu, South Sulawesi: "[T]he potent stinging energy of rulers and high nobles exists quite apart from their intention" (1989, 61).

Beliefs in the possession of special divine powers by rulers (in Malay, *daulat;* in Javanese, *wahyu*) that could be harnessed for the welfare of the community are found throughout Islamic Southeast Asia and have been shown to have pre-Islamic origins (see, e.g., B. Andaya 1975, 1979; L. Andaya 1975a, 1975b, 1993; Gullick 1958; Reid 1993).

Throughout the Malay world we find related belief in the punitive effect of such powers, with supernatural punishment (in Malay, *timpa daulat*) automatically befalling those who disobey or disrespect rulers (see, e.g., B. Andaya 1975, 1979; L. Andaya 1975; Gullick 1958). Such beliefs are also found beyond the Malay world. Errington reports them for Luwu, noting that "a person who failed to get off a horse or close an umbrella when passing in front of a high noble's house" would suffer supernaturally inflicted malady or misfortune (1989, 62). In other precolonial Islamic polities such beliefs seem to have been less developed (L. Andaya 1975) or nonexistent (L. Andaya 1993). I have found no explicit evidence for belief in supernatural sanctions for violations of rank honor in precolonial Cotabato.

29. Datu Adil, for example, tells of how as a boy he was sent by his father to a guru to learn the kamal arts.

30. In the preface to his work on Malay political culture on the eve of colonial rule, Milner (1982) describes his analytical goals—goals that seem representative of this interpretive approach as a whole: "I wanted to understand Malay political activity in Malay terms. In order to investigate the process of change during the colonial period, it was necessary to examine first not political institutions or the flow of "real power," but what Clifford Geertz has described as the "meaningful structures" by means of which Malays gave shape to their political experience. I needed to explore Malay political culture" (1982, viii).

31. The three most important informants cited by Geertz in his book *Negara* belonged to the traditional Balinese ruling class. Two of the three were members of the core nobility (1980, 142). For her work *Meaning and Power in a Southeast Asian Realm*, Shelly Errington relied on informants most of whom were the descendants of the former ruling family of the kingdom of Luwu in South Sulawesi (1989, 22).

32. Similar criticism has been made of those using an exclusively dyadic alliance perspective in examining modern political relations in the Philippines (see, e.g., W. Wolters 1984; Davis 1986; Kerkvliet 1990).

33. Beckett reports an oral tradition that the followers of Datu Utu, the last independent Sultan of Buayan, deserted him for his rival and former protégé, Datu Piang, because he refused to open his granaries to them during a time of famine (1982, 399). I suspect, however, that this is less an illustration of a norm of redistribution and the consequences of its violation, than of a typical response by followers to a critically weakened ruler who had lost most of his coercive power (see Ileto 1971, 95; and below).

34. Because an adjudicator's payment was most often taken as a percentage of the fine assessed, impartiality in the dispensation of justice was probably a practical impossibility (see Mednick 1974, 19–20).

35. Based on the ethnohistoric data she collected, Ghislaine Loyre notes that "[i]t would . . . seem that the [Luwaran] was hardly known and hardly used except by the legal specialists who advised the Sultans" (1991, 69). She also remarks that physical punishments, including executions, were very often

commuted to fines by adjudicators, citing for example the report of an eighteenth-century chronicler that "robbers could have a choice between having their hands cut off or paying three times the values of the stolen property" (1991, 47). While she explains such commutations as "intended to put a limit to violence" (1991, 46), it seems more probable that they reflected the political ecology of precolonial Southeast Asia—a region with plentiful land and relatively low populations in which local rulers competed for relatively scarce followers (see Reid 1988; and below).

36. Anthony Reid (1993, 268–69) provides several additional examples of arbitrary power from various precolonial Southeast Asian polities but notes that this form of political culture was not immutable: "[T]here were other times and places—Melaka around 1500, Banten and Patani around 1600, Aceh apparently in the 1580s and certainly in the 1650s, sixteenth-century Banda—when the great merchants were secure against arbitrary power and tended to build fortified compounds and brick warehouses" (1993, 269).

37. Forrest was a British East India captain who spent eight months at the capital of the Magindanao Sultanate in 1775–76, ninety years after Dampier's visit. His mission (ultimately unsuccessful) was to attempt to arrange the establishment of an English factory at the Magindanao Sultanate. His account of his visit is considered the best and most complete description of Cotabato during the eighteenth century.

38. Datu Adil recalled tales of how Utu's fierce and unpredictable nature made even his datu vassals fear for their lives: "Datu Utu would develop a craving for venison and send his datus out to hunt for him. The datus would encircle a valley, send in slaves as beaters, and shoot any deer they flushed. It was said that any datu who let a deer escape by missing his shot would immediately flee the territory rather than face the wrath of Datu Utu."

39. These accounts present a one-sided picture of class relations. Covert acts of resistance, such as those detailed in James Scott's *Weapons of the Weak* (1985), are absent in historical accounts and are not recounted in oral traditions. Subordinate behavior such as false compliance, foot dragging, and pilfering (see Scott 1985, 29) is conducted individually and ""offstage""(1985, 25) and is often not susceptible to public retelling. Of course "offstage" telling, such as relating the "secret" sins of particular datus, is itself a form of resistance. One of the few examples of overt resistance related to me was a story, told by Datu Adil, concerning the *melitan,* a castelike group of potters who were bound to the Sultan of Buayan. The sultan, at one time, had a member of the melitan put to death arbitrarily. In response, the melitan as a group refused to make any more pots and were able eventually to extract a promise from the sultan not to execute any more melitan without legal cause.

40. Like the janissaries of the Ottoman Empire, these bodyguards were Christians who were enslaved, trained, and formed into a military corps by a Muslim ruler. While the janissaries were acquired from the subjected Christian communities of the Balkans by means of the *devshirme,* a tribute of boys paid to the Ottoman sultan, the Cotabato bodyguards were taken in slave raids by Muslims on the Spanish-controlled Christian communities of the central Philippines.

CHAPTER 4. EUROPEAN IMPOSITIONS

1. Those sultanates most immediately affected by the fall of Melaka to the Portuguese include Patani, Aceh, Banten, Perak, Pahang, and Johor (Reid 1993).

2. The paired positions of tribute-taker and tribute-provider correspond generally with two classes that may be identified as nonproducers and direct producers. However, not all tribute-providers were direct producers. In addition, while the two class positions were mutually exclusive, the social positions were not, some individuals being both tribute-takers and tribute-providers.

3. As in the rest of the prehispanic Philippines and much of insular Southeast Asia, the division drawn between freemen and slaves often carried more social than economic significance (see, e.g., Warren 1981; W. H. Scott 1982, 1994). The economic positions of slaves and freemen were often indistinguishable, and, in the case of debt slavery, an individual might move from freeman to slave and back again more than once in his or her lifetime.

4. Wang Ta-yuan's *Tao I Chih Lueh* (*Summary Notices of the Barbarians of the Isles*), written in 1349, is the earliest recorded account that specifically mentions the Cotabato Basin. According to William Henry Scott, Wang describes "Mintolang" (Mindanao) "at the mouth of the Pulangi River in Cotabato [as] a strategic location with good communications to the sea and an abundance of rice and grain" (Scott 1984, 73). Cotabato at this time was exporting forest products such as sandalwood, ebony, and animal hides; and absorbing, in addition to a wide range of cloth and metal goods, such luxury items as gold, silk, and porcelain. In the Ming annals, begun in 1368, the rulers met in Mindanao were designated by the Chinese term for monarch (Wang) while overlords in Luzon in the northern Philippines were referred to as chieftains (W. H. Scott 1984, 78).

5. As noted in the previous chapter, the term "datu" refers both to hereditary members of a traditional nobility who claim the right to rule, and to actual leaders who command followers, and who are usually, but not always, members of the high nobility. Because of a system of cognatic kin reckoning, and various other sociopolitical factors, there are always more individuals able to claim membership in the traditional nobility than there are active leadership positions. Stewart (1977) distinguishes between these two meanings of "datu" by capitalizing the term when referring to positions of political leadership and using the lower case when speaking simply of the designation of rank. I have not systematized my references in that manner, and instead either modify "datu" with the term "ruling" when referring particularly to political leadership or assume the distinction is made clear from the context of the passage.

6. Forrest notes in reference to slaves being used as units of valuation in Cotabato: "Talking of the value of things here, and at Sooloo, they say such a house or prow [*prahu*, or ship], etc. is worth so many slaves; the old valuation being one slave for thirty kangans [or bolts of imported cloth]" (1969, 280).

7. For detailed descriptions of the politics and economics of debt-bondage in the Malay states see Gullick (1958) and Sullivan (1982). Although Sullivan is pointedly critical of Gullick's functionalist approach to the indigenous

Malay political system, his depiction of debt-bondage in Perak is in essential agreement with Gullick's overview.

8. In her *Triumph of Moro Diplomacy: The Maguindanao Sultanate in the 17th Century,* Ruurdje Laarhoven provides a vivid illustration of the practical limits on a sultan's political authority. She relates a Dutch account of the downfall of Sultan Kuday, who had succeeded to the Magindanao throne under a cloud of controversy in 1699: "[I]n January 1701, the sultan issued orders to completely close off the river at both ends of the [sultanate], and had it heavily guarded. The purpose was to have complete control over his subjects' movements, because he 'had introduced a new invention on how to raise money' "(1989, 103). It was reported to the Dutch ambassadors that the Sultan's scheme to require his subjects to purchase passes to travel into and out of the sultanate, and his threat to reduce any violators to debt-slaves, caused a massive defection of his datus and their followings. "As a result, Sultan Kuday was left only with 30 men, most of them slaves, in Simuay. The state council thus elected Anwar as the new king" (Laarhoven 1989, 103).

9. For a detailed account of the preferential access of seventeenth-century Magindanao sultans to external trade opportunities, see Laarhoven (1989).

10. It is tempting to view the two rival power centers on the Pulangi River as typifying van Leur's (1955) dichotomy between inland states and harbor principalities in the Malay world. The upriver sultanate was relatively inward-looking and drew resources from intensive rice cultivation, while the downriver sultanate was focused externally and founded on maritime trade. However, as Ileto (1971) notes, the downriver (Magindanao) sultanate also had an agricultural base in the delta and the upriver (Buayan) sultanate had other exits to the sea aside from the Pulangi River which allowed maritime trading and raiding.

11. Forrest uses the term "Haraforas" to refer to the Tirurays he describes. Dampier, writing a century earlier, employs a similar term—"Alfoores"—in reference to a distinct population "under the subjection of the Sultan of Mindanao" (1906, 333). These designations are undoubtedly related to the Molukan term "alifuru." As described by Leonard Andaya (1993), the alifuru were the interior inhabitants of Halmahera, distinguished from the *ngofagamu*—the common people (literally, "people of the land"). "Alifuru" was used generally to designate a number of distinct non-Muslim peoples of the interior highlands who were attached as client groups to various Muslim rulers. The reports of Dampier and Forrest suggest that the term was used in the same way in Cotabato. While the term "alifuru" apparently remains in use in Halmahera, I found no evidence for its continued use in Cotabato. For additional evidence for social and cultural linkages between Malukan and Mindanao in the sixteenth and seventeenth centuries, see Andaya (1993), Laarhoven (1989), and Majul (1973).

12. Beeswax was an especially desired item for external trade, particularly with Europeans. Most of the beeswax from Cotabato was shipped by Chinese junks to Manila for the candle-making industry (Wickberg 1965). It was also the primary export item in the Cotabato-Dutch trade (Laarhoven 1989). Also important at various times were gutta-percha and almaciga, two tree saps used

in insulation and varnishes, respectively, and traded via Sulu and Singapore to European markets.

13. Among the Chinese articles carried to Cotabato in the late eighteenth century, Forrest specifies "especially kangans [bolts of cloth], beads, gongs, china basons [sic] with red edges; deep brass plates, five in a set; deep saucers, three and four inches in diameter; brass wire, and iron" (1969, 281). Forrest also remarks on rates of exchange between the Tiruray and Magindanaons, most specifically in the following passage: "One day, near Tubuan, a Harafora [referring in this context to a Tiruray] brought down some paddy from the country: I wanted to purchase it; but the head man of the village, a Magindanoer, would not permit him to sell it to me. I did not dispute the point; but found afterwards, the poor Harafora had sold about three hundred pounds of paly [palay, or unhusked rice] for a prong, or chopping knife" (1969, 282).

14. Dampier also found goldsmiths, blacksmiths, and carpenters in the capital and a thriving shipbuilding industry (1906). When Forrest visited in 1775, he counted at least 370 buildings in the three settlements that made up the capital, as well as "many Magindanao mechanics, vessel builders, and merchants" (1969, 178–84).

15. Little information exists on the activities of the Iranun prior to the mid-eighteenth century. Laarhoven relates reports from Dutch visitors to the Magindanao Sultanate in 1700 that the Iranun were portrayed to them as dangerous rogues and "one of the least trusted and wildest groups in the territory of the sultanate" (1989, 111).

16. Some Iranun cruisers (mangayaw prahus) were as much as one hundred feet long, held three banks of oars, and carried close to two hundred men (Warren 1981, 179).

17. Most Filipino captives were sold initially at slave markets in Cotabato or Sulu. Before 1800, they were usually purchased by Bugis or Brunei merchants for transshipment to the Dutch port cities of Batavia, Malacca, Makassar, Palembang, or Banjarmasin. There they were resold to Dutch or Chinese households as servants, boatmen, laborers, and concubines. By 1800, however, Jolo Island, the capital of the Sulu Sultanate, had become the most important slave center in the entire region, absorbing the majority of Filipino captives brought there (Warren 1981).

18. Long-distance sea raiding carried out from Cotabato predated European penetration of the region and was probably very similar to that found elsewhere in the precontact Philippines. Raiding, or mangayaw, was a socially approved activity throughout the Philippines (and all of insular Southeast Asia) before the Spanish occupation. The primary objective of these (often reciprocal) raids was the acquisition of slaves for ransom, sale, or sacrifice (W. H. Scott 1982, 91). Seaborne raiding cannot be neatly separated from maritime trading. William Henry Scott, in fact, suggests the term "trade-raiding" (1982, 85) be applied to these activities because raiding victims were often former trading partners and captives were usually treated as commodities and sold as chattel slaves.

19. Laarhoven cites Dutch reports (again from 1700) to the effect that the Magindanao sultan did not have jurisdiction over the Iranun, "for they were in

the hands of their own chiefs" (1989, 112). The Dutch visitors did witness certain Iranun datus apparently rendering tribute to the Magindanao sultan. Laarhoven notes, however, that "no mention was ever made of the Iranun datus submitting to the obeisance ceremony" (1989, 111).

20. For a detailed account of the Chinese in seventeenth century Cotabato, see Laarhoven (1987).

21. In his description of Magindanaon laws, Forrest notes that the "Chinese seem to be excluded from the benefit of law: those in power often forcing *kangans* [bundles of trade cloth used as currency] upon them, and making them yearly pay heavy interest" (1969, 277).

22. Prior to the late nineteenth century, the Spaniards attempted only one additional full-scale military assault against Cotabato. Their 1639 campaign was thwarted by the downstream Sultan Kudarat (by every account an extraordinary military and political leader), with the assistance of the Iranun datus of the coast (Majul 1973; Laarhoven 1989). A principal tactic in Sultan Kudarat's anti-Spanish strategy was simply to withdraw his warriors and populace inland, thus forcing the Spaniards away from their coastal supply bases in order to pursue their attack (Laarhoven 1989).

23. See, e.g., the instructions given to Captain Esteban Rodriguez de Figueroa, who, in 1578, was commissioned to subdue the Moro sultanates of Sulu and Mindanao. They direct Rodriguez to promote trade with the Moros, explore their natural resources, Christianize them, and compel them to acknowledge Spanish sovereignty, in that order (Blair and Robertson 4: 174–81).

24. The only evidence I have seen from Cotabato is found in occasional references in the letters sent by Jesuit missionaries from the mission at Tamontaka. A typical passage, from January 1894 reads: "Three Sharifs [Islamic teachers] arrived with the mail boat [presumably from Jolo]. The same as always! When will they [referring to the Spanish colonial government] be convinced that they are those who oppose not only our ministry but also our dominion?" (letter of Mariano Suarez to the Mission Superior quoted in Arcilla 1990, 378).

25. In his impressive work, *The Sulu Zone 1768–1898,* James Warren (1981) examines and rejects the argument that Muslim raiding and slaving in the sixteenth to eighteenth centuries should be viewed within the framework of the "Moro Wars" as "retaliation against Spanish colonialism and religious incursion" (1985, xvi).

26. Laarhoven cites a late-seventeenth-century Dutch source who reports that "the trade with Manila never stops" (1989, 147). Dampier, who visited Cotabato in the same period, remarks of the Magindanaons that "their trading vessels they send chiefly to Manila" (1906, 340).

27. Cesar Majul's 1973 book, *Muslims in the Philippines,* is a Muslim nationalist history and is best evaluated in the context of the political environment in which it was written (see chapter 8). It compares favorably with Philippine nationalist histories, which virtually ignore the existence of Philippine Muslims (see Agoncillo 1969; Constantino 1975). Majul's corpus of work in general (see especially his 1985 work, *The Contemporary Muslim Movement in the Philippines*) is an impressive collection of carefully researched historical and political writings on Philippine Muslims.

CHAPTER 5. AMERICA'S MOROS

1. In addition to the materials cited below, see, e.g., Beckett (1982), who quotes a 1927 report from a colonial administrator entitled "Who's Who among the Datus (1982, 405). See also the chapter on "Moros" by former Governor General Forbes in his 1928 work entitled *The Philippine Islands.*

2. In his *Knowledge and Power in Morocco: The Education of a Twentieth-Century Notable,* Dale Eickelman offers a more general methodological justification for the use of "capsule social biographies," noting that they are a particularly useful means of "understanding wider social and political realities" in complex historical settings (1985, 14, 15).

3. Evaluating the events at Bud Dajo twenty-eight years later, Vic Hurley, a writer generally supportive of American military efforts in the Philippines, had the following to say: "By no stretch of the imagination could Bud Dajo be termed a 'battle' . . . There appears to be no justification for the intensity of the bombardment at Bud Dajo, and many Americans who witnessed the battle concur in this belief" (1936, 186).

4. In 1913, the last large-scale military action by American troops against Philippine Muslims took place, also in Sulu. At the battle of Bud Bagsak, approximately five hundred Muslim rebels (who were resisting an American disarmament policy) died after their fort was bombarded and stormed. American casualties were limited to fourteen killed and thirteen wounded (Gowing 1983, 240).

5. The short-lived tribal ward system seems to have been a compromise between the views of colonial administrators such as General Wood, who generally disdained Philippine Muslims and had little use for the traditional nobility, and those, like General George W. Davis, who in a 1901 report argued: "It seems to me that the worst misfortune that could befall a Moro community and the nation responsible for good order among the Moros would be to upset and destroy the patriarchal despotism of their chiefs, for it is all they have and all they are capable of understanding" (Report of Brigadier General George W. Davis to Luke E. Wright, Vice–Civil governor of the Philippine Islands, 4 December 1901, Bureau of Insular Affairs Records, file No. 5075–2, National Archives).

6. The "ama ni" form of reference is itself an honorific sometimes used as an alternative to the term "datu."

7. The very first armed challenge to American rule in the entire Muslim Philippines occurred in 1902 at Parang on the Cotabato coast, where Iranun fighters fired upon an American military patrol, killing one of them (Gowing 1983, 84). That initial attack was followed by a series of guerrilla-style raids over the next two years against U.S. forces (1983, 154). Sporadic Iranun armed resistance continued under various local leaders into the 1920s, meaning that Iranun insurgency began earlier and lasted longer than any other armed anti-American opposition in the Muslim Philippines. None of the Iranun efforts, however, attained the scale of Datu Ali's uprising or of other movements elsewhere in the South. American reports typically characterize Iranun armed defiance as "banditry" (see McKenna 1994).

8. Volkman (1985) reports very similar occurrences of elites substituting slave children for their own in colonial schools during the early years of the Dutch occupation of the Toraja highlands in South Sulawesi. Datu Adil informed me that certain of the slave children sent to American schools in Cotabato in the early colonial period went on to become some of the very first Magindanaon teachers and bureaucrats, and that their slave origins are a very closely kept secret.

Collaborating datus such as Balabaran also sent their slaves when asked to provide recruits for the Philippine Constabulary, a colonial police force with American officers, organized in Cotabato in 1904. The principal mission of the constabulary throughout the Philippines was to apprehend insurgents, identified officially only as "brigands" or "outlaws" after the inauguration of civil government in 1901 (White 1928).

9. A similar story is told that Sarip Kabungsuwan, the legendary founder of the Cotabato sultanates, could kill a man simply by pointing his finger at him. While Kabungsuwan ruled Cotabato on his own, Piang required external assistance. In the story about Piang, finger-pointing alone is not enough to kill a man. Also needed is an incantation (in Spanish) marking the intended victim as an enemy of the colonizers.

10. Letter of Joseph Ralston Hayden to Dr. Barr, September 21, 1926. Joseph Ralston Hayden Papers, Box 28, Folder 26, Michigan Historical Collections, Bentley Historical Library, University of Michigan, Ann Arbor. In the same letter, Hayden reports making the acquaintance of "Sunset" Cox, a colorful American colonial character—former American soldier, Philippine Constabulary officer, mercenary, and journalist—who had recently sold his services to Datu Piang as a publicist.

11. The Hayden Papers contain an unpublished manuscript on the life of Bai Bagungan by C. Montera (Box 27, Folder 30, Michigan Historical Collections, Bentley Historical Library, University of Michigan, Ann Arbor). While the prominent participation of Magindanaon women in economic and political life in the modern period is not an uncommon occurrence (see below), there is disappointingly little information available about the economic and political roles of Magindanaon women in the precolonial period. A Jesuit missionary writing in 1888 did offer the following intriguing comment about the wife of the Sultan of Barongis (a small upriver sultanate uncolonized at the time), giving indication that prominent public roles for women (aristocratic women at least) are not just a "modern" phenomenon: "The sultana is still young, very alert, and speaks with great self-assurance. She attends all the bicharas [political consultations] of some importance, and as a matter of fact, she is the one who wields the baton in the sultanate" (Ramon Bea to the Mission Superior, October 4, 1888, quoted in Arcilla 1990, 282).

12. While I have been unable to verify Datu Adil's account, it seems fairly certain that Datu Ortuoste was raised at the Jesuit mission in Tamontaka on the southern branch of the Pulangi River. That mission operated from 1862 until the end of the Spanish occupation of Cotabato. In 1872 the mission opened an orphanage for "ransomed slave children" (Arcilla 1990, xx). In that year a severe famine forced a number of Cotabato datus to sell their juvenile slaves. The mission continued the practice of purchasing children from Chinese

middlemen or directly from Muslims, usually in periods of epidemic or famine, for more than twenty years.

Datu Ortuoste's surname is of interest because it is identical to that of one of the most important officials of the Spanish colonial period in Cotabato, Don Pedro Ortuoste. Don Pedro was the official interpreter for the colonial government in Cotabato. While not an especially high-ranking office, the position carried a significant amount of actual power (Arcilla 1990). Don Pedro spoke Magindanaon and is reported to have been on very good terms with Cotabato Muslims (1990, 31), but it seems unlikely that he was the natural father of Datu Ignacio Ortuoste and there is no indication of any such connection. He was more likely a foster father or godfather. Missionary letters from Tamontaka note that the prominent Spanish families of Cotabato town sponsored "ransomed" children, acted as godparents at their baptisms, and provided them with both Christian names and Spanish surnames (Arcilla 1990).

13. An article in the *Philippine Herald* from September 11, 1933, describes in detail the funeral of Datu Piang and notes that Ignacio Ortuoste acted as "toastmaster" at Piang's "necrological service" at the burial ground (Bureau of Insular Affairs Records, File No. 5075 (post-1914), National Archives).

14. Datu Adil is referring here to spirit crocodiles (*mga pagali*); see chapter 8.

15. An early marriage was to the daughter of the Sultan of Kabuntalan (Beckett 1977).

16. An illustration of Datu Sinsuat's regional influence is found in a story told by Datu Adil of an event witnessed by his father circa 1930.

After the death of Sultan Mastura, all the leading datus of Cotabato gathered in the gambling house of Datu Sinsuat in Cotabato City to decide who the next Sultan of Magindanao should be. As established by tradition, a special panel of the nobility had been chosen to find the best hereditary candidate. The panel reported that they were undecided and asked Datu Sinsuat his opinion. Sinsuat pointed to a young man in the back of the room, Datu Esmael. He said, "Esmael is the most handsome and fair-skinned of all the candidates and he has sufficient blood ties. He should be sultan." The others agreed and Esmael was named Sulutan sa Magindanao

17. Quoted in Provincial Circular No. 98, January 15, 1935, by D. Guitterez, provincial governor of Cotabato. Joseph Ralston Hayden Papers, Box 27, Folder 30, File 1, Michigan Historical Collections, Bentley Library, University of Michigan, Ann Arbor. A letter from Cotabato Governor Guitterez to Director Guinguna (contained in the same file) notes that Datu Sinsuat was "apparently worried" about the directive. I have found no evidence, however, indicating that the directive substantially curtailed the incidence of traditional adjudications by Sinsuat or other Cotabato datus.

18. Datus Piang and Sinsuat each chose early on to collaborate with American authorities in order to gain an advantage over powerful and aristocratic competitors by allying with dominant outsiders.

19. Beckett states that it is "difficult to locate the source of this expansion," noting that there were very few Christian settlers in Cotabato until the

1930s, that tenancy rates were quite low, and that very few datus emerged as major landowners (1982, 403). He suggests, and I agree (see below), that the expansion of production must have taken place within the framework of traditional production relations.

20. Ileto (1971) suggests that the relative peace that existed between Datu Utu, the last independent Sultan of Buayan, and the Spaniards for roughly twenty years (ca. 1864–84) "was, to a great extent, due to the commercial rapport between them." After the Spaniards took control of the delta, commercial trade between sa laya and sa ilud went on much the same as before, with the Spaniards merely taking the place of the Magindanao Sultanate. Agricultural production was intensified upriver not only to supply Spanish garrisons but to compensate for the production shortfall in the delta caused by the migration of a great part of the delta's population upriver in advance of Spanish forces (1971, 30–31).

21. American colonial discourse on Philippine Muslims is peppered with such expressions as "Moroland," "Moro Policy," "the Moro Problem" (see below), "Moro country," and "Moro bandits." Specific Muslim ethnolinguistic groups were virtually always distinguished by their geographic location— as "Joloano Moros," "Lanao Moros," or "Cotabato Moros"—rather than by the names they called themselves (see Gowing 1983; Thomas 1971).

22. The use of this phraseology by representatives of the state to refer to various difficulties encountered in attempting to rule Philippine Muslims has exhibited remarkable longevity. Its first appearance in writing seems to have been as the title of Saleeby's 1913 essay. It was then used throughout the colonial and commonwealth period (see the various citations to the term in the index to Thomas 1971). In 1954, the Philippine Senate appointed a committee to study the "Moro Problem." The recommendations of that committee led to the creation of the Commission on National Integration in 1957 (Majul 1985; Tamano 1974).

23. Saleeby was certainly aware that Datu Piang, Datu Sinsuat, and others of the leading datus of Cotabato during his stay there had little in the way of blood ties to the high nobility of the Cotabato sultanates. Nevertheless, he seems to have been much taken with the idea of a traditional Muslim aristocracy in Cotabato. He spent a good deal of time with Datu (later Sultan) Mastura, who, while a prominent member of the high nobility of the Magindanao Sultanate and a direct descendent of Sultan Kudarat, was little more than a local dignitary. Saleeby describes Datu Mastura as "the best-informed datu of Magindanao" and declares that he possesses "the most reliable of the royal documents that have been preserved" (1905, 36). Mastura allowed Saleeby to copy those documents (most of them *tarsilas*), and they formed the basis of his 1905 *Studies in Moro History, Law, and Religion*.

24. Thomas remarks that "Saleeby's approach to governing and integrating the Muslims was referred to as the 'ideal' by others involved in Muslim policymaking, but few put it into practice" (1971, 15).

25. Carpenter to Secretary of the Interior Rafael Palma, January 27, 1919, Bureau of Insular Affairs Personal File—Tarhata Kiram, National Archives, Washington, D.C.

26. Memorandum submitted to Mr. Jorge Bocobo, August 19, 1935, p. 7, Joseph Ralston Hayden Papers, Box 29, Folder 24, Michigan Historical Collections, Bentley Historical Library, University of Michigan, Ann Arbor.

27. Ibid., p. 9. It should be noted that in contrast to Saleeby, who made his proposals to American colonial authorities, Kuder is here making an argument to Christian Filipino officials that it is in their self-interest to maintain and expand education programs among Philippine Muslims.

28. Salipada K. Pendatun to Vice-Governor General Joseph Ralston Hayden, August 15, 1935. Joseph Ralston Hayden Papers, Box 27, Folder 32, Michigan Historical Collections, Bentley Historical Library, University of Michigan, Ann Arbor.

29. Datu Adil told me that the initial "K" in Pendatun's name stood for Kuder, a middle name Pendatun had given himself to honor his former teacher.

CHAPTER 6. POSTCOLONIAL TRANSITIONS

1. Wolters reports a near-doubling of registered voters in the first fifteen years of independence, from 4.3 million in 1947 to 8.4 million in 1961 (1984, 143). A graph presented in Carl Lande's classic study of the structure of Philippine politics indicates a threefold increase in votes actually received by congressional candidates (from roughly 2.2 million to 6.5 million) within the same period (1965, 29). This expansion of the electorate in the postwar period (from 22 percent of the population in 1947 to 29 percent in 1959) was not due to a broadening of the criteria for inclusion—the poll tax and wealth requirement for voting were eliminated prior to the war—but apparently to an increase in voter registration in rural areas (Lande 1965; Wolters 1984).

2. For a comprehensive survey of immigration to Mindanao from other parts of the Philippines from the Spanish period onward see Wernstedt and Simkins (1965).

3. The seven agricultural colonies established by the Americans in Mindanao (six of them in Cotabato) included Muslims as well as Christian settlers. It was thought, in accord with the colonial "Moro Policy" outlined in the previous chapter, that Muslim farmers would learn more advanced methods (of both farming and family life) through imitation of their Christian neighbors (Pelzer 1945).

The agricultural colonies were relatively expensive to administer and had limited success. In 1918, colonial authorities instituted a new program that provided free transportation to selected prospective immigrants. Despite extensive advertising, this program also had disappointing results, primarily due to a shortage of immigrants willing to take up the offer of free land and free transportation (Wernstedt and Simkins 1965; Gowing 1979). One reason for their reluctance was undoubtedly the popular Filipino image of the untamed, bloodthirsty Moro. Advertising directed at prospective Christian homesteaders anticipated this problem by painting a very different picture of the indigenous inhabitants of Mindanao. The following passage (entitled "The Moro") from a brochure circa 1920 advertising immigration to Cotabato illustrates the attempt:

The Moro is first of all a farmer . . . Although entirely ignorant of the great world outside his rancheria he is a reasonable human being . . . Sometimes he evades the orders of the Government but when caught he meekly submits and considers it rather a joke on himself when punished . . . He welcomes the Christian Filipino colonist to his country, extends the hospitality of his home and table, and asks nothing but that his religion and tribal customs be not interfered with. (*Cotabato, Largest and Most Fertile Province in the Philippine Islands: Paradise of the Homeseeker from Over-crowded Luzon and Visayas*, Bureau of Insular Affairs Records, file no. 26741 (Post-1914), National Archives)

4. *Hukbalahap* is an acronym for the Tagalog phrase Hukbo ng Bayan laban sa Hapon, meaning the People's Army to Fight the Japanese.

5. The problem of titling already occupied land was aggravated by the acceleration of timber and pasture concessions granted by the Philippine government to corporations and individuals in the late 1960s to increase government revenues. Such leases were granted without apparent regard for the rights of prior inhabitants—usually Muslims or other ethnic minorities (George 1980).

6. Both Hunt (1957) and Mastura (1979) note that the descendants of the earliest Christian residents of the city, the families of soldiers and "presidios" from Zamboanga, still live in Manday, the majority Christian neighborhood that borders Campo Muslim.

7. This Muslim-Christian geographic alignment is another instance of the river-versus-road residency pattern found throughout Cotabato. It exists, I imagine, for the same reason found elsewhere: because the indigenous Muslims were the first to occupy the riversides and the immigrant Christians were the first to occupy (or file for legal ownership of) the roadsides. This seems a more plausible explanation than the one often repeated by Christians in the city: that Muslims simply "like to live by water."

8. It was reported in 1957 that a large part of the copra production of southern Mindanao and Sulu was being shipped to Borneo and exchanged for contraband goods, with American cigarettes the prime item of exchange (Hartendorp 1961). Trade figures from 1958 released by the Borneo government (Noble 1977, 67) show the Philippines ranking second only to Japan in its absorption of Bornean imports. According to Noble, that percentage was due primarily to the cigarettes and other items that left Borneo legally but entered the Philippines as contraband.

9. For an account of the establishment of quality cigarette production in the Philippines and its effect on the smuggling trade see Lewis Gleeck's (1989) *The Rise and Fall of Harry Stonehill in the Philippines*.

10. It was suggested by some that the mayor, who owned a fleet of cargo ships, may also have had a personal interest in the removal of Bird Island.

11. In 1967, Mando Sinsuat lost the mayorship to a Christian candidate in a race where he was also opposed by his half-brother, Datu Mama Sinsuat. The combined number of votes of the two Sinsuat brothers was greater than that of the Christian winner of the election.

12. The 1952 *Cotabato Guidebook* remarks of Datu Udtug's early career in his home municipality of Pagalungan that he "was very instrumental in helping the Christian settlers in getting homestead lots even if it was sometimes inimical to the interests of his brother Islams [*sic*]" (Millan 1952, 257).

13. Until the mid-1950s, Cotabato and the other majority Muslim provinces of the South were governed as "special provinces" and had their highest officials appointed by the central government in Manila (Gowing 1979, 186).

14. A front-page obituary for Datu Udtug in the *Mindanao Cross* (January 1, 1983) observes that under his governance "law and order was at its best in the province accented by close Christian-Muslim relation [*sic*]. Even in his official set up, his formula was: Muslim governor—Christian vice-governor—2 Christians to 1 Muslim in the 3-man provincial board."

15. The *Mindanao Cross* obituary of Datu Udtug just cited (January 1, 1983) continues by noting that "Kudin Dataya, his longtime private secretary and later executive secretary, remembers him as top in man-to-man diplomacy. He seldom delivered speeches. He approached people personally."

16. Numerous reports of the killing or wounding of members of prominent Muslim families in Cotabato may be found in issues of the *Mindanao Cross* from the 1950s and 1960s. Datu Adil related his personal involvement in a long, violent feud between his family and the Sinsuats beginning in 1949, in which his father was killed. For a vivid account of a similarly structured armed feud between the Masturas and Sinsuats in 1940, see Horn (1941, 166–68).

17. In his analysis of political relations in Central Luzon, Wolters notes that the central state resources flowing to (or through) local officeholders in exchange for their delivery of votes were actually of two types: "The transactions that occurred under these vertical alliances showed a mix of personal and more public aspects: personal in the exchange of votes for private gain such as credit, protection, prevention of audits, renewal of licenses, etc.; more public in the channeling of credit to the network of party followers; and generally public in the bestowal of pork-barrel funds for the whole community, e.g., the building of roads and bridges, the delivery of concrete, the erection of schools."

18. Autocratic rule at the local and provincial levels also removed much of the incentive to spend any significant proportion of the pork-barrel funds received for the benefit of the electorate, whose votes were, in most cases, simply appropriated from them. A story often told by ordinary Muslims in 1985 concerned a highway between Cotabato City and Marawi City that, according to official records, had been built three times but still did not exist in fact.

19. The political positions of Pendatun and Datu Udtug did occasionally diverge. In the 1963 Cotabato mayor's race, Pendatun supported Datu Mando Sinsuat, the son of Datu Sinsuat, who was the official candidate of Pendatun's political party. Although nominally a member of the same party, Datu Udtug refused to back a Sinsuat—the Sinsuats having always been his political foes—and endorsed Datu Mando's Christian opponent instead.

20. Philippine political parties date from the early American period. Only one of those early parties—the Nacionalistas—became a genuinely nationwide

entity. During the Commonwealth period it dominated electoral politics, but after independence in 1946 it was challenged by the Liberalistas, and a two-party political system developed, remaining in place until the declaration of martial law in 1972. In his well-known work on the Philippine two-party system, Lande (1965) finds it to be characterized by the extreme fluidity of party membership and weakness of intraparty solidarity; pronounced ideological similarities (including virtually identical official policies and internal structures) between the two major parties; and the virtual absence of any permanent rank-and-file party membership among the electorate.

21. Although Datu Pendatun was also the son of a sultan, he was not identified nearly as strongly with that cultural legacy as was Datu Udtug. One ready example is the very different terms of reference used for the two men. Salipada Pendatun is virtually always referred to as General or Congressman Pendatun, while the term of reference for Udtug Matalam is invariably the traditional one—Datu Udtug. Another indicator is that while I was told a number of stories about the magical powers possessed by Datu Udtug—including the report that he had a sixth finger on the palm of his right hand, which he used to perform marvelous feats—virtually no specific accounts were given of the supernatural abilities of Congressman Pendatun.

22. Similar combinations of relatively assimilated and relatively tradition-oriented datus may be found among all of the prominent Muslim political families of the province, particularly among the Sinsuats, Ampatuans, and Masturas.

23. The use of the term "Muslim Filipinos" to denote Philippine Muslim populations was also adopted by a number of scholars of the Muslim Philippines—see, e.g., the titles of the works by Gowing (1979), Gowing and McAmis (1974), and Mastura (1984). By contrast, Cesar Majul's 1973 Muslim nationalist history is conspicuously entitled *Muslims in the Philippines*.

24. *Hadji* (female: *hadja*) is the honorific title given to a Muslim who has made the pilgrimage to Mecca ("Hajj"). I use the English spelling usually seen in contemporary Cotabato. As the Magindanaon language lacks either an initial "h" or a "j" sound, the title was formerly rendered as *kagi* and that version is still often heard today.

25. The observations of Hunt about mosque attendance in Cotabato City in 1953 are relevant: "[O]nly a small percentage of the faithful attend group services with any degree of regularity ... The worshippers give every evidence of piety, but they cannot comprise more than fifteen percent of the Moros in town at the time. Leading datus do not seem to feel that their position demands regular attendance at public services" ([1958] 1974, 202–3).

26. Some of these, such as the "Knights of Mohammad," were clearly self-consciously Muslim versions of Philippine Christian voluntary organizations.

27. Datu Adil, who was present at the 1955 MAP conference, recalls that Edward Kuder was one of its principal organizers.

28. Datu Blah Sinsuat's introduction to the 1952 *Cotabato Guidebook* offers a narrative that illustrates some of the points discussed above. In that year, Datu Blah was serving as Cotabato's representative in the lower house of the Philippine Congress. A passage from his introduction demonstrates the manner

in which datu politicians presented themselves to Christians as both advocates for and supervisors of Cotabato Muslims.

I consider now the most opportune time to state that the unselfish Native who welcomed his Christian brother in years past should also receive the gratitude of the people of this province, all of whom are immensely enjoying the great opportunities here, the peace and quite [sic] that have been theirs since their coming. The harmonious relationship pervading among the populace of Cotabato is attributable only to the willingness of the Native to offer a little of his share of the natural wealth of his land of birth to his Christian brother so that both may not live in want.

Therefore, our Christian brothers who are more fortunate in having attained educational enlightenment should in reciprocation help to improve the lot of the Natives who are yet to learn the ways of the modern world. I urge this of my Christian brothers so that we may, in the end, secure the blessings of the one lasting peace and happiness here which even posterity may enjoy" (1952, vii).

In this single rather extraordinary passage, Congressman Sinsuat manages to reinforce Christian perceptions of Muslim cultural backwardness, to solicit resources to "improve" Muslim communities, and to insinuate that peace may not continue should his suggestions go unheeded.

CHAPTER 7. MUSLIM SEPARATISM

1. Outlaw activity commonly referred to as "banditry" was widespread in Cotabato and throughout the Muslim South in the 1950s. Much of it involved rather straightforward criminal activity, especially highway robbery and cattle rustling. Other incidents, however, have the appearance of social banditry and a few, including the famous "Kamlun Uprising" (Tan 1982, 68) of 1952 in Sulu, approached the level of genuine armed insurgency against the state. It was this latter episode of "banditry," along with a similar armed uprising in Kapatagan in Lanao, that prompted the formation of the Congressional Committee in 1954 (Tamano 1974).

2. Congressman Alonto was the keynote speaker at the First National Muslim Convention sponsored by the Muslim Association of the Philippines in 1955. In that speech he echoed the language of his committee's report, declaring to the delegates: "Let us purge ourselves of our defects," and proclaiming: "We need a thorough spiritual rejuvenation... If we are good Muslims we are automatically good citizens..." (Muslim Association of the Philippines (1956, 31).

3. The invasion, or infiltration, of Sabah apparently was to be made as part of the Philippine government's prosecution of its claim to Sabah. That claim was first announced by President Diosdado Macapagal in 1962 and was based on an 1878 transaction between the Sultan of Sulu and an Austrian businessman (Noble 1977).

4. George (1980, 197) reports that Misuari was "one of the founding fathers" of the Kabataang Makabayan (Nationalist Youth), the largest and most active leftist student organization of the pre-martial-law period. The Kabataang Makabayan was organized in 1964 by Jose Maria Sison, who in 1968 founded the Maoist Communist Party of the Philippines (CCP). Shortly thereafter, Sison organized the New People's Army and initiated a new armed communist insurgency against the Philippine state, one that eventually grew to be far more extensive and successful than the Huk Rebellion of the 1950s. A detailed account of the beginnings of this insurgency, including a description of radical student politics at the University of the Philippines in the 1960s, may be found in Chapman (1987).

5. Another featured speaker at the 1955 Muslim Filipino Conference was an Egyptian emissary, Sheikh Hassanal Baguri. In his speech, Sheikh Baguri announced the commitment of the Egyptian government to underwrite the advanced Islamic training of numbers of Philippine Muslims: "Our dear Muslim Filipino brothers, we are here declaring in the name of our government that we are ready to send you teachers for your schools and that we are even ready to establish an Islamic institution in the City of Manila for Islamic studies. We are ready to accept your sons and daughters to study in our universities and to give them all the facilities in our hands" (Muslim Association of the Philippines 1956, 40).

6. For an absorbing account of Islamic education and politics in Cairo in the mid-1960s see Gilsenan (1982).

7. The Muslim separatist movement was, to a significant degree, ignited by the aspirations engendered by both secular and Islamic higher education. The coalescence (at least for a time—see below) of Middle East– and Manila-educated activists in the MNLF leadership represents a distinctive variant of a pan-Islamic development recently analyzed by Dale Eickelman (1992): the relationship between mass higher education, political and religious activism, and transformations of religious authority.

8. The Ampatuans were descendants of Datu Ampatuan, a datu of the early colonial era who, like datus Ayunan and Balabaran had few blood ties to the precolonial high nobility of Cotabato. Datu Ampatuan, however, claimed Arab descent through his great-grandfather. He was a lieutenant of the anti-American Datu Ali but later allied with the pro-American Datu Piang. He succeeded to Datu Piang's seat on the Cotabato Provincial Board in 1917 (Beckett 1977, 1982).

The English term "clan" is widely used in the Philippines to refer to kin-based political factions, especially those with pronounced dynastic tendencies (see, e.g., Francia 1988). Its use in Cotabato has exactly the same meaning and is not intended to describe any actually existing corporate descent groups.

9. The *Mindanao Cross* reported on April 29, 1967, an announcement by Congressman Pendatun that he was running as the Liberalista candidate for governor because Datu Udtug was in "failing health."

10. By mid-1970, Datu Udtug had changed the name of the Muslim Independence Movement to the "Mindanao Independence Movement" in order to include Christians. Prior to this he had already modified his stand to one in favor of regional autonomy in a federal-state framework (see George 1980).

11. In an August 17, 1968, interview with the *Mindanao Cross,* Datu Ud-tug expressed puzzlement at the "war talk" creating anxiety in Christian settlers in North Cotabato and "causing many families to sell their property."

12. In 1966, after years of maneuvering, Datu Udtug succeeded in having the capital of the province moved to Pagalungan, his home territory, only to have it returned again to Cotabato City by Governor Datumanong immediately after his assumption of office.

13. Some writers (see, e.g., Gowing 1979; Majul 1985; Mercado 1984), in seeking a direct causal connection in the flow of events between 1968 and 1970, have suggested that the manifestos and activities of the Mindanao Independence Movement were principal precipitating factors for the wave of intense communal violence in Cotabato that began in 1970. There is little evidence for that proposal, however, and although the formation of the MIM may have marginally intensified Muslim-Christian tensions in the province, it was probably only a minor contributing factor. It is more productive, I believe, to view both the sectarian conflict and the formation of the MIM as effects of more fundamental political and economic pressures in the province.

14. "Ilonggo" is a term commonly used to refer to speakers of Hiligaynon (also called Ilonggo). Hiligaynon speakers originate from the provinces of Iloilo and Negros Occidental (on the islands of Panay and Negros) in the central Visaya region of the Philippines. In 1970, Ilonggos made up about 10 percent of the Philippine population. Ilonggos also composed a significant percentage of postwar migrants to Cotabato.

15. For a rare firsthand account of the sectarian conflict in the Cotabato Valley, especially as it occurred in and around Midsayap, see Stewart (1977, 254–61).

16. The Ilonggo politicians who, in these speculations, were supposed to have invented and supported the Ilaga were, in fact, themselves divided by separate political parties, aspirations, and interests. Not all were Nacionalistas, and those who were supported two different Ilonggo Nacionalista candidates for governor (see below). Also difficult to explain when considering these hypotheses is what sitting Ilonggo mayors, most of them ruling municipalities with large Christian majorities, would have to gain by initiating Ilaga terror within their areas of influence.

17. The experience of Doroy Palencia, a Christian Liberalista politician and longtime confederate of Datu Udtug, in the 1971 election is instructive. Palencia had been elected to serve on the three-person provincial board for every one of Datu Udtug's terms as governor and also under Simeon Datumanong. He stated in 1986 that he had been "strong" among Muslims during elections and that Christians also supported him. He failed in his bid for the first time in 1971, because, as he put it, the sectarian violence had caused both Muslims and Christians to mistrust him.

18. Although sectarian conflict did occur during this period in neighboring Lanao, and to the west across Ilana Bay in Zamboanga del Sur, by far the greatest number of violent incidents occurred in Cotabato.

19. Premier Kadaffi announced in 1972 that he would send "money, arms, and volunteers" to aid Muslims in the Philippines (quoted in Schlegel 1978, 48). There is also evidence from informants and elsewhere to suggest that

Kadaffi was already providing arms to Lucman, and through him to MIM, well before this announcement (Noble 1976).

20. Datu Udtug had, in fact, run for governor in the 1971 race as an independent Nacionalista candidate.

21. The Marawi uprising was, by most accounts, spontaneous and idiosyncratic. It reportedly took by surprise the MNLF leadership in Lanao Province, some of whom held high positions in the Marawi City government (see Mercado 1984; George 1980).

22. The Bangsa Moro Army has probably never had as many arms as men. A rebel commander informant noted in an interview that in his first armed encounter with the military, one hundred rebels shared seventy guns, some of them homemade.

23. An August 11, 1973, story in the *Mindanao Cross* reported 924 Muslim "surrenderees" from Tran, noting in passing that all of these were women, children, and elderly men.

24. In late 1973, what remained of the original province of Cotabato after the splitting off of South Cotabato in 1966 was subdivided by presidential decree into the three provinces of North Cotabato, Maguindanao, and Sultan Kudarat. The division coincided with the division of votes in the 1971 local elections. North Cotabato and Sultan Kudarat Provinces were 80 to 90 percent Christian and Maguindanao Province was 85 percent Muslim. All of the mayors in Maguindanao were Muslim, and virtually all in Sultan Kudarat and North Cotabato were Christian. The unusual shape of Maguindanao Province was the result of including pockets of Muslim population in areas such as Buldun, Buluan, and Pagalungan; and excluding the Christian communities of Pigcawayan, Pikit, and Esperanza (see map 3).

25. Iranun narrators are fond of pointing out that Iranun fighters are the only Muslim rebels who never surrendered to the Philippine government. While this exaggerates the facts, it is the case that Iranun commanders and their men were very disproportionately represented among those rebels who remained under arms as late as 1985. It may also be noted, in regard to Iranun armed involvement in the insurgency, that the mostly Iranun municipality of Subpangan on the coast north of Cotabato City was the site of some of the very first as well as the last armed engagements of the rebellion. Iranun commitment to the rebellion is, I believe, related both to their recent past as cigarette smugglers and to their long history of resistance to external domination (McKenna 1994).

26. The composite term "Bangsa Moro" has sometimes appeared in MNLF literature as one word and at other times as two. Current spokespersons for the Moro Liberation Front in Cotabato have stated a preference for "Bangsamoro" because of its emphasis on "bangsa," which they translate as "nation."

27. A policy statement from the first issue of *Maharlika*, an MNLF newsletter, clearly illustrates the national, rather than specifically ethnic or religious, character of the MNLF appeal:

> From this very moment there shall be no stressing the fact that one is a Tausug, a Samal, a Yakan, a Subanon, a Kalagan, a Maguindanao, a

Maranao, or a Badjao. He is only a Moro. Indeed, even those of other faith [*sic*] who have long established residence in the Bangsa Moro homeland and whose good-will and sympathy are with the Bangsa Moro Revolution shall, for purposes of national identification, be considered Moros. In other words, the term Moro is a national concept that must be understood as all embracing for all Bangsa Moro people within the length and breadth of our national boundaries. (Quoted in Noble 1976, 418)

28. In a 1975 lecture delivered at the National Defense College, Brigadier General Fortunato U. Abat, then commander of the Central Mindanao Command of the Philippine Armed Forces, expressed the widely held Christian viewpoint on the "datu system":

[T]here are irreconcilable features in the cultures of the Muslims and Christians. On the one hand, we have the Muslims and the Islamic religion, the datu system serving as their government, the lack of education and different customs and practices. While they arouse pity, they usually do not command the respect of the socially superior Christians . . .

Many blame [Muslim backwardness] on the absolute rule of the datus which has prevented their subjects from acquiring adequate, modern and respectable education. . . . [T]he landlessness of the majority of the Muslim masses . . . is due to datuism, the feudal form of the Muslim society and their way of life. (Abat 1993, 204–5)

CHAPTER 8. REGARDING THE WAR
FROM CAMPO MUSLIM

1. The barangay system was created by presidential decree on December 31, 1972, shortly after the imposition of martial law. Its purpose was to create basic political units—barangays—which could be used as instruments to further the objectives of martial law and at the same time provide controlled outlets for political participation.

The barangay is actually a very old precolonial political institution in the Philippines. It was a unit of thirty to one hundred houses under the authority of an autocratic headman (datu). The institution was adapted by Spanish colonial administrators to suit their needs (with the name "barangay" eventually changed to *barrio*). The term and institution were resurrected by the martial law regime as part of its attempt to equate nationalism with autocratic leadership. All barangay "captains" were, initially at least, appointed.

Modern barangays are intended as local-level political units and meant to be composed of a maximum of five hundred families. Cotabato City in 1985, however, contained only five barangays for its eighty thousand or so inhabitants. All were much larger than the ideal. Barangay Bagua, for example (the barangay in which Campo Muslim is located), contained four communities—Manday, Campo Muslim, Lugay-lugay, and Bagua—each with more than five hundred families. The reason for so few original barangays in the city is not clear. That more had not been created, despite widespread recognition of their need, was largely due to the strong opposition of the five current barangay captains. In around 1990, Cotabato City added a large number of new barangays but retained part of the former structure, designating the original five barangays as "Mother Barangays." Thus Campo Muslim is now its own barangay though still considered for some purposes a constituent unit of "Mother Barangay Bagua." For more information of the formation and functioning of the barangay system under the martial law regime, see Lapitan (1978).

2. The Civilian Home Defense Force was also created by presidential decree shortly after the declaration of martial law. CHDF units are paramilitary entities associated with particular barangays and under the formal direction of the barangay captain. CHDF members receive arms and a minimal stipend. During the rebellion, CHDF units were effectively controlled by the Philippine Army.

3. Kalanganan is the name for all of the area that lies between the Pulangi and Tamontaka Rivers and west of the city proper. Today it is included in the Cotabato City limits as the only entirely rural barangay.

4. Akmad's father, as a man of the coast, was almost certainly an Iranun speaker. That he was also a member of the Magindanaon aristocracy may be due partly to intermarriage. However, it also may be due to the fact, related by both Mastura (1984) and Ileto (1971), that in 1879 the Magindanaon title of Amirul Umra was conferred by the Sultan of Magindanao upon an Iranun datu from Malabang in an apparent effort to shore up the rapidly fading power and prestige of the downriver sultanate (see Ileto 1971, 42).

5. Questions on the interview schedule did not attempt to ascertain whether respondents held legal title to land. My principal concern was to find what percentage of residents held rights in agricultural land, regardless of whether those rights were legally recognized by the state. Qualitative research data suggest, however, that most respondents do hold legal title to the land in which they have indigenously recognized rights.

6. The members of Candao's CHDF unit apparently also saw their own role, to some degree, as protecting the community from army intrusions. Residents tell of one occasion in which the army brought an armored personnel carrier to the Manday bridge, intending to enter the community with it. Candao's men refused to let it pass, and when challenged entered the street with guns drawn to stop it. The standoff ended only when the military police arrived and negotiated a settlement.

7. As Commander Jack explains it today, "I was captured because the Tripoli Agreement had been signed, the cease-fire had started, and Hadji Murad [the Cotabato rebel commander] and his men had come down from the hills for peace talks. The military were afraid that we would join forces, so they detained me. Their official reason was that I was being detained for safekeeping."

8. The MNLF has never claimed responsibility for any of these terror bombings and none has ever been solved. There is a strongly held belief among some Christian as well as Muslim city residents that at least a portion of the bombings were the work of government agents attempting to discredit the MNLF.

9. Jeffrey Sluka reports responses from rank-and-file IRA members in Northern Ireland quite similar to those I found in Cotabato: "[T]he major reason [Republican guerrillas] give for why they turned to armed struggle is because they say that repression and state terror drove them to it. That is, when asked how they came to join the IRA, they do not usually refer to Republican ideology and goals, but rather they tell personal histories of their experience with repression and state terror" (Sluka 1995, 85).

10. In a recent illuminating discussion of musical code-switching, Mark Slobin employs the term "domestication" to refer to the sort of borrowing I have described—a process whereby "music is brought into the subculture from the superculture" (1993, 90). Slobin's musical "superculture" is conceived as a hegemonic system encompassing a music industry, governmental regulation, and "a set of standardized styles, repertoires, and performance practices" (1993, 33). Musical subcultures, or "micromusics," are "small musics in big systems" (1993, 11). The mass-marketed music of the Philippines, today overwhelmingly sung in English and largely produced in the United States and England, corresponds to Slobin's musical superculture, while Magindanaon music fits his definition of a "micromusic."

11. The English term "cowboy" is used by young men in Campo Muslim and throughout the Philippines to describe an individual (and occasionally an action) thought to be unusually rugged or reckless. That usage is derived from the Philippine-made Westerns that were extremely popular movie fare in the 1960s and 1970s.

12. This song, "Mana Silan Cowboy," is one of the few I recorded that dates itself fairly precisely. The time range indicated in the opening phrase (1971–79) indicates that this song was written after the 1977 cease-fire and intended primarily for public performance outside the rebel camps.

13. The early rhetoric of Muslim separatism did not emphasize jihad as a component of Bangsamoro ideology. Stress was placed instead on national identity. Only years later, after the cease-fire, did separatist leaders appeal to the concept of jihad, usually in the context of a broader Islamic renewal, as evidenced in the following passage from a 1985 declaration: "All Mujahideen . . . adopt Islam as their way of life. Their ultimate objective in their Jihad is to make supreme the WORD of ALLAH and establish Islam in the Bangsamoro homeland [emphases in the original]" (Salamat quoted in Mastura 1985, 17).

14. The "wide green land" of the first stanza of song 2 is a description of the Cotabato River Basin and a metaphorical reference to Cotabato as a whole. In his collection of Magindanaon folk songs, Clement Wein (1985) includes a song said to have been composed circa 1950 and sung to the melody of "Green Valley" which begins with the same couplet found in song 2 (1985, 117).

15. Compare Jeffrey Sluka's observation for Northern Ireland that "the British government and their Security Forces have applied military and judicial repression against the Catholic communities they believe support the Republican insurgency and . . . this has served to alienate the population and created and continuously reinforced popular support for the Republican movement" (1995, 76).

16. As late as the last month of 1977, one year after the cease-fire, a military air strafing killed fifteen Muslim civilians (six of them young children) and wounded many more in Kalanganan, within the Cotabato City limits (*Mindanao Cross,* December 17, 1977). As had happened on previous occasions, the military apparently mistook a wedding party for a gathering of rebels and opened fire on it.

17. Amulets (agimat) and especially *muntia*—rare stones with magical protective powers—were particularly popular with rebel fighters. Commander Jack possessed a muntia consisting of a petrified egg sac from a spider wrapped in a cloth and hung on a thong around his neck. Among its other powers it could detect and neutralize poisons placed in liquids.

18. Commander Jack recounts a very similar story from personal experience concerning assistance received from a tunggu a inged in another manifestation: "Once during the siege of Tran, I was eating ripe mango with my companion. I heard a bird call 'Awa, Awa' ['Awa' means 'leave' or 'get away' in Magindanaon]. I told my companion, 'Quick, we have to move.' He did not believe me. I jumped into our foxhole and just then a jet appeared overhead and dropped a bomb right where we were. My friend was blown to pieces."

19. Although these and other independent representations by Muslim followers accord with Islamic doctrine in that they are accounts of divine compassion shown for those fighting for Islam, their strongly folk-Islamic elements were disapproved of by Islamic clerics and discounted by some rebel leaders.

20. Although not given precedence in the authorized lexicon of the Muslim separatist movement, "inged" and "jihad" do have certain hegemonic connotations. As a term that describes a community but also a traditional political entity, "inged" suggests hierarchy and domination: a community ruled by an autocratic chieftain. Similarly, while "jihad" refers to the defense of the community against alien invaders, it also connotes armed mobilization at the behest of a local ruling elite. These terms, then, are part a "common meaningful framework . . . for talking about . . . domination" (Roseberry 1994, 361), yet may be given quite different emphases by subordinates and superordinates. More significantly for this case, ordinary adherents of the separatist movement have used these terms (or their particular colorings of them) to understand the rebellion, even though movement leaders have not employed them in official separatist rhetoric.

CHAPTER 9. UNARMED STRUGGLE

1. Madrasahs in the Muslim Philippines typically offer programs at the "elementary, preparatory and secondary levels of Arabic education." A madrasah that includes all three levels (a twelve-year program), or only the secondary program, is termed a *mahad* (in Arabic, *ma'ahad*) (Hassoubah 1983).

2. Alim is the Arabic term for a scholar who has mastered a specific branch of knowledge—a learned person, or savant. In the southern Philippines the term is used to refer to someone who has educational qualifications for, and is knowledgeable in, the teaching of Islam. The plural of alim is *ulama*. Ustadz

(from the Arabic *ustadh*, meaning "teacher") is the most usual term of address in the Muslim Philippines for an alim. (Glassé 1989; Hassoubah 1983).

3. This statement seems to suggest that in 1950 there was no Magindanaon speaker available in Cotabato who spoke Arabic well enough to translate directly for the Maulana.

4. Ustadz Abdul Gani Sindang arrived in the Philippines in 1950, along with another missionary from al-Azhar. Their first school in Malabang closed within a year and he proceeded to Cotabato City (Muslim Association of the Philippines 1956, 106). He is almost certainly the same missionary referred to by Hunt in his brief account of Muslim religious education in Cotabato in the early 1950s: "In 1950, a formal Islamic school was set up in Cotabato, housed in a residence donated by a local datu and headed by a Muslim missionary sent by the Egyptian government. In addition to learning to read the Qur'an in Arabic, the students are taught to understand the language" (1974, 205).

5. This traditional *maktab* system of Islamic education in Cotabato was quite similar to the *pondok* schools of Malaysia (see Nagata 1984) and the *pesantren* schools of Java (see Geertz 1968).

6. For an account of the politics of Islamic preaching elsewhere in the contemporary Islamic world, see Patrick Gaffney's (1994) ethnographically rich investigation of the complex connections between religious rhetoric (as expressed in Friday sermons) and political dissent in Upper Egypt.

7. Partial funding for the establishment of the English program was obtained from the Philippine government's Ministry of Muslim Affairs.

8. Hassoubah notes elsewhere that, despite the intensification of Islamic instruction in the Muslim Philippines, "the quality of education in the *madaris*, with very few exceptions, leaves much to be desired by way of being at par with standard schools in the Middle East or even compared to the quality of the Philippine public school system"(1983, 74).

9. In the context in which it was usually used, the term "Shia" was used pejoratively to mean a heretical Muslim radical influenced by the Shia Islamic government of Iran.

10. Tantawan is the Magindanaon name for the main hill of Cotabato City, commonly known as P.C. Hill because it had served as local headquarters of the Philippine Constabulary during the American colonial period.

11. For a detailed account of the operation of the Christian Children's Fund in Campo Muslim, including an analysis of the injurious effects of child sponsorship on the community, see McKenna (1988).

12. The mean estimated income of community households in 1985 was 1,333 pesos ($71.82) per month. That of CCF recipient families was about 900 pesos (less than $50.00) per month. Household income was calculated as the sum of the monthly earnings of the household head at his or her primary occupation, additional earnings of the household head (reported by just under 20 percent of respondents) from productive land, "sideline" jobs, or other sources, and monthly contributions from other household members (reported by slightly more than 60 percent of respondents). It is plainly a very inexact figure. Respondents often had no precise knowledge of contributions of other household members and, because of the high incidence of uncertainty in their

own economic endeavors, were sometimes able only very roughly to estimate their average daily income as well.

13. As this passage and the previous one suggest, it was most often women—the mothers of CCF recipients—who were forced to confront the pressures and contradictions involved in attempting to obtain CCF resources for their children. Their predicament illustrates what Sherry Ortner has recently referred to as the "multiplex identit[ies]" and "compounded powerlessness" of subaltern women—in this case as women, as poor, and as Philippine Muslims (1995, 184). By attempting to assist their children they placed themselves in an emotionally wrenching double bind, anguishing on the one hand about the imagined loss of their children to unseen and unreachable "sponsors," and on the other about the public disapproval of the ulama and MILF. At the same time, the responses they have made to their dilemma—seeking to contact sponsors directly to tell them the "true" stories of their families, insisting that those seeking to remove the CCF program provide another in its place (see below)—represent (as Ortner also notes) creative efforts on their part to "formulate projects and . . . enact them"(1995, 185).

14. As reported in the *Mindanao Cross*, Sandiale Sambolawan, the Muslim governor of the province (and a member of the Ampatuan clan), was disturbed by the student demonstration and enraged by the banner portraying the "Ministry of Munafiq Affairs" (*Mindanao Cross*, February 28, 1985).

15. Included among these six were the son of Datu Udtug Matalam, as well as two younger members of the Sinsuat and Ampatuan families.

16. A number of Magindanaon datus attended the ceremony, some of them traveling in the traditional manner on decorated boats to Lanao.

17. Similar ritual feasts (*kanduli, kenduri, kenduren, slametan*) held for various occasions by other Southeast Asian societies are described by Geertz (1960), Reid (1984), and Bowen (1992).

18. Datu Adil, fostered as a child by Edward Kuder, always preferred to speak to me in English. While strongly opposed to many of the efforts of the independent ulama, Datu Adil is also a vigorous proponent of Muslim autonomy and a very vocal critic of the martial law regime and its local supporters.

19. Wahhabism, an eighteenth-century Islamic reform movement in the Arabian peninsula begun by Muhammad ibn "Abd al-Wahhab, strenuously opposed Sufism and advocated puritanism in religious practice. Wahhabism played an important role in the creation of an Arabian state and remains the dominant variant of Islam practiced in the Kingdom of Saudi Arabia (Cole 1975; Eickelman and Piscatori 1996).

20. The lyrical form of the dayunday resembles that of the Magindanaon bayuk, a style of romantic poetry that almost certainly predates the arrival of Islam in Cotabato. The practice of romantic song duels between men and women was apparently found throughout the Philippines at one time. Anthony Reid, citing a seventeenth-century Spanish account, notes that spontaneous contests of romantic poetry and music (called *balak*) were "enormously popular in the central Philippines up to early Spanish times" (1988, 148).

21. Dayunday lyrics are customarily sung in an archaic form of Tau sa Laya (upriver) Magindanaon, the same form used for traditional ballads and

poetry. Downriver audiences typically find dayunday lyrics difficult to understand. At the performances I attended I found that I was able to make out only occasional words or phrases. My downriver companions reported that they understood, on average, about 25 percent of the lyrics. Difficulties with aural comprehension did not in the least hinder the enjoyment of downriver audiences. Campo Muslim residents advised me that the dayunday must be appreciated in its totality: the music, the showmanship of the performers, the costumes worn by the female performers, the nonverbal interactions among the singers, the repetitions of standard phrases—all combine to provide the entertainment experience so appreciated by ordinary Muslims.

22. Another of the Friday sermons of Ustadz Ali had as its theme the statement that "Allah will help the weak person to claim justice."

23. Clearly, a number of the behavioral reforms suggested by the independent ulama—their efforts to prohibit "emergency" marriages, the dayunday, and other entertainments—primarily reflected their concern with regulating the behavior of women. Those efforts did not, in 1986, extend to any specific attempts to prescribe either the proper dress or work activities for women.

24. Imam Akmad was by no means the only community elder to question the reform efforts of the independent ulama. A passage from my field notes relates another specific instance: "Bapa Hasan is a traditional healer. His cousin, Ustadz Murid (an important ustadz inside [in the MILF]), criticized him for these traditional beliefs, but Bapa Hasan showed the ustadz the passages in the Qur'an where it referred to such healing practices."

25. As suggested by the passage quoted above, the MILF acquiesced to community members on this issue, at least temporarily, for "practical" reasons.

26. Eickelman and Piscatori observe about varying Islamic interpretations of zakat:

> There is little agreement [about zakat] other than using it for humanitarian or charitable purposes: The Qur'an encourages Muslims to spend their *mal* (wealth) "out of love for Him, for your kin, for the needy, for the wayfarer, for those who ask, and for the ransom of slaves"(2:177). Some Muslims argue that it is a voluntary act of faith; others argue that it is obligatory . . . An indication of the degree to which doctrine is malleable is the specific political use of *zakat* in a resolution of the Organization of the Islamic Conference (1981, 699). It endorses collection of *zakat* to support the work of the Palestine Liberation Organization, rather than, for example, to support Palestinian widows, orphans, and refugees as might be expected. (1996, 16–17)

27. It may be noted in this context that the common term used to refer to the rebels—both current ones and those who fought during the active rebellion—was not "mujahideen" but the Spanish-derived "rebelde."

28. One respondent, in fact, cited the new president of the Philippines, Corazon Aquino, as the most powerful datu he knew.

29. It should be noted that the public position of the MILF in regard to voting in the 1986 presidential election was primarily one of indifference

rather than pointed opposition. As a (nominally) separatist organization, the MILF simply commented that it had no interest in elections of officials to a government that it considered illegal, with the implication that its supporters need have no interest as well. The following excerpt from an editorial carried in the January 1986 issue of *Tantawan,* the newsletter of the Kutawato Regional Committee of the MILF, illustrates official MILF attitudes toward electoral participation: "Many are asking this column whether the Moro Islamic Liberation Front (MILF) takes sides in the forthcoming election [for president] or any election in the future. Our answer to this is *solid NO!* The MILF does not believe in elections to correct injustices, oppression, exploitation, persecution and aggression in society" [emphasis in original].

30. The ulama and professionals who formed the aboveground component of the counterelite were able to acknowledge publicly their support for the MILF without fear of sharp reprisal only because of the formal cease-fire that still obtained between the MNLF and the Marcos government and the expressed interest of various Arab oil-supplying states in a continued dialogue between the government and the rebels on the issue of the full implementation of the Tripoli Agreement.

31. More than one Campo Muslim resident remarked on the main irony surrounding the ustadzes' adamant disapproval of dayunday performances. The dayunday first gained popularity during the period of the armed rebellion when military repression was most severe. Popular legend states that it was invented by an upriver rebel commander and his sweetheart. Dayunday performances were among the very few popular diversions available during those dark years when virtually all ordinary Muslims suffered as a result of the Bangsamoro Rebellion. Yet when the ustadzes, who were so closely associated with the leadership of the rebellion (and in many ways personified its aims), were able to speak openly after the cease-fire, one of their very first pronouncements was to denounce the dayunday.

32. In a recent work, Michael Peletz (1997), provides a fascinating discussion of the ambivalence of ordinary Muslims toward Islamic resurgence in contemporary Malaysia. While Campo Muslim residents expressed ambivalence toward Moro nationalism (both desiring and distrusting it), I did not find the same sort of responses in respect to the Islamic renewal efforts of the independent ulama. Instead, as I have noted, some aspects of the renewal program were accepted and others resisted, in some cases openly. The primary reason why the Cotabato case differs from that described by Peletz for Kelantan is that the independent ulama were openly opposed in Cotabato by established Muslim politicians who advanced an alternative ideology of moral authority. The existence of this powerful opposition allowed ordinary Muslims the opportunity for "fence sitting" and permitted potential mediators such as the community imam to explore the middle ground between the polar positions.

CHAPTER 10. MUSLIM NATIONALISM AFTER MARCOS

1. The Communist Party of the Philippines (CPP) was established in 1968 by a group of young intellectuals as a breakaway party from the older,

Moscow-oriented Partido Komunista ng Pilipinas. In 1969, the CPP formed the New People's Army as its military wing. In 1973, a revolutionary front, the National Democratic Front (NDF), was established by the CPP and other underground organizations, including the Christians for National Liberation. Observers agree that the NDF was effectively controlled by the Communist Party of the Philippines. The armed insurgency conducted by the New People's Army did not become active in more than a very few parts of the country until the end of the 1970s and was not considered a major threat by the government until the early 1980s (Schirmer and Shalom 1987).

2. For a detailed account of the extraordinary staying power of certain datu politicians in Cotabato, see McKenna (1992).

3. A presidential election was held in June of 1981, not long after the formal lifting of martial law. President Marcos ran for reelection unopposed by any meaningful opposition candidates. He won the election with about 86 percent of the vote (Bonner 1987).

4. Despite the KBL money distributed at the barangay level during the 1986 presidential campaign, I heard of not a single case of vote-buying in Maguindanao Province and of very few attempts among Muslims in the city. This was due to the absence of a tradition of vote-buying in Muslim Cotabato prior to martial law but also because of the coercive apparatuses available under martial law in Cotabato for repressing the popular vote.

5. This use of Magindanaon in a public speech by the soon-to-be appointed governor of the province was in itself unprecedented. English is the language of public political discourse in the Philippines. Every one of the speeches made at the KBL rally just two weeks earlier had been delivered in English (occasionally interspersed with Filipino, the other official national language). Even Datu Udtug Matalam, who spoke almost no English, endeavored to deliver his short and infrequent political speeches primarily in that language. Zacaria Candao's use of Magindanaon in his first public speech of the post-Marcos era—one delivered to Christians as well as Muslims—sent the clear message that, for the very first time, a Muslim nationalist had attained an official position of power in postcolonial Cotabato.

6. In Filipino, "Kalimutan ang Nakaraang Politika at Harapin ang Krisis."

7. Two additional factors may explain the special attention given to Nur Misuari and the MNLF by the media and central government. Misuari hailed from Sulu and his power base was there, particularly in Jolo. Philippine Christians (as reflected in the mainstream national media) know very little about Philippine Muslims. They do tend, however, to associate Muslims with seagoing people, colorful boats, and faraway islands. Tiny Sulu thus received a degree of media attention far out of proportion to the percentage of Philippine Muslims living there (less than one-third of the total).

The national government was also particularly concerned with Sulu because of its proximity to the very permeable national border with Sabah, Malaysia. Insofar as the islands of Sulu have overwhelmingly Muslim populations, are fairly easily defensible, and form the border between the Philippines and a powerful neighboring Muslim state, Muslim armed separatism in Sulu always posed the greatest immediate security threat to the territorial integrity of the

Philippines. For a comprehensive discussion of the unique position of Sulu Muslims see Kiefer (1987).

8. I was never able to determine the origin of the curious, and untranslated, English term "prayer rally" for the MILF's mass demonstration. The rally was not called in order to pray for divine assistance in achieving the full implementation of the Tripoli Agreement, or for any similar divine favor. Insofar as prayer (*salat*) in orthodox Islam consists solely of devotional worship, not supplication, it would have been quite surprising had that in fact been the goal of the rally. The term was likely borrowed from Roman Catholic practice and used with a Roman Catholic audience—the mainstream media and national administration—in mind. The "prayer rally" label accentuated the formal leadership of the rally by Muslim clerics and emphasized the religious character of the Muslim *Islamic* Liberation Front.

9. The previous record had been set just a few months earlier when more than thirty thousand people attended the Cotabato City campaign rally for Corazon Aquino on January 26. No one I spoke with at that time was able to remember a crowd as large as that ever having gathered in the city plaza.

10. I do not mean to suggest that the provincial voting resembled the North American ideal for democratic elections. Presumably there was a fair amount of vote-buying and other formally illegal activities (see below). However, it was the first-ever opportunity for individuals in a number of municipalities to cast their own ballots for freely chosen candidates without impediment from local authorities.

11. Such an attitude on the part of established Muslim political figures is certainly not unique to Cotabato. Eickelman and Piscatori provide examples from throughout the Islamic world of political leaders using various arguments against the mixing of religion and politics, including the rather extraordinary 1993 statement of King Hassan II that Moroccans should "render unto God that which is God's and unto Caesar (*Hiraql*) that which is Caesar's"(1996, 52).

12. Despite the implication in Congressman Mastura's speech of widespread ulama participation in political office-seeking, only one Cairo-educated cleric ran as an IPP candidate in either the provincial or city races. He won his race as the highest vote-getter of all candidates running for the eight-member provincial board. While many ustadzes were active IPP officers or members, no other ustadz ran for political office in Cotabato in 1988. I am not certain why this was so. A number of possible reasons come to mind, including the intention of the IPP to avoid just the sorts of charges leveled by Congressman Mastura.

13. There were some fifty-six thousand registered voters in Cotabato City in 1988—approximately twenty-nine thousand of them Christians and twenty-seven thousand Muslims. By contrast, Muslims comprise roughly three-quarters of the population of Maguindanao Province. Because of confusion over new rules promulgated by the National Commission on Elections after 1986, it was unclear until less than two weeks before the gubernatorial election whether or not Cotabato City residents would be able to vote in the provincial elections. They had never been allowed to before, and many Christian city residents, especially those associated with city government and the

Chamber of Commerce, preferred it that way. They felt threatened by provincial involvement in city affairs and did not want the economically independent city to become entangled in Muslim-dominated provincial politics. A Supreme Court decision shortly before the election exempted Cotabato City from the new rules, and city residents did not vote in the provincial elections.

14. Campo Muslim residents reported, and reviews of back issues of the local newspaper confirmed, that there was no attempt by any candidate in the 1980 city elections, or in three previous city elections, to appeal, in any specific fashion, to the urban poor.

15. The use of English here suggests that the term "urban poor" had become part of Philippine political vocabulary along with "poll-watcher," "people power," and "snap election."

16. After months of lawsuits and judicial hearings no substantial evidence of ballot box tampering or related voting fraud was established to support the charges made against any candidate, and the winners were officially proclaimed.

17. Voter turnout figures by precinct for the 1988 election were not available before I left Cotabato City. However, figures for the 1986 presidential election—which showed a similarly high level of preelection interest and a similarly low overall turnout (57.5 percent)—may be useful for illustration. Voter turnout in the seven precincts at which most Campo Muslim residents were registered was 54 percent. In seven similarly sized precincts in a middle-class Christian area of the city, 67 percent of registered voters cast their ballots.

18. Mary Hollnsteiner, in her 1963 book, *The Dynamics of Power in a Philippine Municipality*, provides a definition of the term "lider":

> The word "lider" though originating from the English word, "leader," has been incorporated into Tagalog speech . . . with a very precise connotation . . . [It] refers to the person with a large following in a barrio [barangay] who utilizes this support during political campaigns, where he pledges himself to campaign for a certain candidate or group of candidates. These candidates call him their "lider" referring to his dominance over his particular followers rather than to any superordinate position he holds in relation to the candidates. On the contrary, the "lider" . . . is a staunch *follower* of the candidate he is supporting. The "lider" has no official position as such but is repaid by candidates with favors which can in turn be distributed to his followers, reinforcing his position. (1963, 41, fn. 16)

As shall become apparent, Muslim liders in Cotabato City did not always exhibit all the attributes or behaviors included in Hollnsteiner's definition.

19. Fifty pesos (approximately $2.50) was reported to be the minimum cash price being paid for votes during the 1988 election. It was the equivalent of two day's wages for many of the residents of Campo Muslim.

20. Neither of these two individuals accepted the offers made to them. In my conversations with them, I was able to determine that their refusals were not based on any moral discomfort associated with brokering votes per se, or with brokering votes for Christian candidates. Instead they had to do with

concerns about their personal reputations. The purok leader planned to run for public office himself eventually and did not want to become indebted to, or associated with, that particular candidate. Nur Miskin, the Islamic activist, was attempting to build an organization and did not want it associated with "politics." He was also concerned with the potential problems associated with the sublider role. As he told both the lider and me: "If I took the money and distributed it all to my men, many would still say that I received much more. I would be considered just like Bapa Pantal [a well-known lider of Angka Biruar, the leading Muslim mayoral candidate]. Some of his followers are accusing him of taking money from Angka Biruar and not distributing it."

21. Although a Christian, this candidate was a member of a Chinese-mestizo Muslim family, had long-standing connections with certain prominent Muslim figures in the city, and was the "unofficial" IPP candidate for mayor. The IPP nomination panel had refused to endorse him, but some prominent IPP members apparently favored his candidacy.

22. It should be remembered in respect to this first sort of breakdown that while vote-buying was a long-established practice in multi-ethnic Cotabato City (as in the rest of the Christian Philippines), it was relatively rare in rural areas of Muslim Cotabato prior to 1986 insomuch as autocratic local rule usually made it unnecessary. In the 1988 elections, the incidents reported to me of subliders failing to distribute a candidate's funds invariably occurred in Muslim rural communities (such as Bokhana) within the city limits.

23. Votes gained by the eight leading candidates represented about 75 percent of the total votes cast in the six precincts.

24. It is doubtful that any of the Muslim candidates for mayor expected to attract significant numbers of Christian voters that would be alienated by the candidate's embracing the IPP. Their political calculus was more likely based on the knowledge that some Christian city residents had recently expressed anxiety at pronouncements of the IPP and MILF concerning their intention to have Cotabato City included in a Muslim autonomous region without holding a popular referendum on the issue. Given the level of Christian apprehension at the time, a candidate's affiliation with the IPP would be self-defeating in that it would certainly prompt a higher voter turnout among Christian city residents and might even provoke the leading Christian candidates to cooperate to prevent an IPP victory. As it happens, a government-sponsored referendum on the issue of autonomy did occur in November of 1989. Maguindanao Province was one of four Muslim-majority provinces in the Philippines that voted to form the Autonomous Region of Muslim Mindanao, while Cotabato City voted against inclusion in the autonomous region.

CHAPTER 11. RESISTANCE AND RULE IN COTABATO

1. See Chatterjee (1993), Comaroff and Comaroff (1992), Fox (1985, 1989), and Scott (1985, 1990) for examples of subordinates reinterpreting dominant representations.

2. Fox reports that the term "Sikh" refers to several cultural identities prevailing in the Punjab in the nineteenth century, identities that "subsumed a

range of quite different religious beliefs and social practices" (1985, 7). The British, however, regarded only one Sikh identity—the Singh variant—as the significant form and, in fact, believed the Singhs to be a separate race. In the early twentieth century, urban-based reformers "appropriated the Singh identity fostered by the British to launch an anticolonial protest" (1985, 12). In doing so they themselves merged the Sikh and Singh identities, promoted a single image of Sikh orthodoxy, and directly challenged Sikh collaborators with British rule.

3. Kahn is not alone in objecting to Hobsbawm's notion of "the invention of tradition." See Friedman (1992) and Kapferer (1988) for additional critiques.

4. For details on that armed uprising, which resulted in the deaths of thirty-five Muslim insurgents (Princess Tarhata and her husband escaped), see Thomas (1971, 73–76).

5. William Roff has described the source and consequence of that dynamism succinctly: "[T]he recognition of [the] non-congruence [between ideal and social reality] by both prescribers (*ulama*) and backsliders acts as a dynamic force within Islamic cultures, resulting in what can be seen as dialectic constantly engaged in translating synchronic tension (the aspect taken by the lack of fit at any given moment) into diachronic 'oscillation' (social, cultural, political, or ideational change in one direction or another)" (1985, 9).

6. For an engaging account of recent generational conflict among the Sama (a Philippine Muslim group of the Sulu archipelago) over "ways of knowing Islam," see Horvatich (1994).

7. William Roseberry presses a similar point in his writings on hegemony. Like Rebel, he proceeds from an explicit recognition of "differential experience in terms of . . . structures of inequality and domination" (1989, 48). The "common understandings and modes of interaction" that emerge across this differential experience "can never encompass" all of it. "Cultural production is not limited to those who control the means of cultural production. Experience constantly intrudes" (1989, 49).

8. Caution is required when assuming the widespread living of lies by political subordinates. The absence of ideological incorporation is just as much an empirical question as is its presence.

Glossary

ADAT   Customary law

AGIMAT   An amulet worn or carried to provide supernatural protection against blades or bullets or to otherwise protect an individual from his or her enemies

ALIM   (Plural, *ulama*) An Islamic scholar; an individual qualified to teach Islamic law

BANGSA   Nation, ethnic group, descent group

BANGSAMORO   The Philippine Muslim nation

BANTINGAN   Bridewealth

BANYAGA   Chattel slave

BARABANGSA   Royal lineage; the high nobility

BARANGAY   A political subunit of a municipality. Originally a precolonial political institution in the Philippines, the barangay was a unit of thirty to one hundred houses under the authority of an autocratic headman (datu). The institution was adapted by Spanish colonial administrators to suit their needs (with the name *barangay* eventually changed to *barrio*). The term and institution were resurrected by the martial law regime as part of its attempt to equate nationalism with autocratic leadership.

BAYUK   A ballad or chanted poem that relates a story, usually a love story

DATU   Ruler, leader, male member of the nobility

DA'WAH   Call to faith; the calling of people to the religion of Islam

DAYUNDAY   A romantic song duel between a man and woman, characterized by bayuk phrasings and incorporating extemporaneous verses

DUMATUS   The descendants of Tabunaway, a legendary Magindanaon chieftain who welcomed Sarip Kabungsuwan to Cotabato. The dumatus formed a special status group in the Magindanao Sultanate and were not obliged to pay tribute to any datu.

ENDATUAN   Those who are ruled; the subjects of datus

HADJI   (in Arabic, *hajji*) One who has made the pilgrimage to Mecca

ILAGA   Literally, "Rats." A term used to refer to armed bands of Christians, usually Ilonggos, that terrorized Cotabato Muslims in the late 1970s.

ILMU   Esoteric knowledge related to the acquisition of supernatural abilities

IMAM   A prayer leader; one who leads Muslims in a prayer service at a mosque

INGED   Community, locality, homeland

JIHAD   Struggle in defense of Islam

KAMAL   Power; supernatural power

KANDULI   A ritual feast held at funerals, weddings, or other special occasions

KARGADOR   (in Spanish, *cargador*) A waterfront laborer or cargo handler

KRIS   A finely made curved sword

KULINTANG   A musical instrument composed of seven small gongs arranged by size and played by beating

KUMPIT   A large motorized boat with a loading capacity of thirty tons

LIDER   A political broker; an individual who buys and sells votes in an election

LUWARAN   A set of written legal codes employed in the Cotabato sultanates that consisted of selections from the Shafi'i school of Islamic law combined with customary law

MADRASAH   (Plural, *madari*) An Islamic school

MARATABAT   Rank, or the honor due to rank

MORO   A term of Spanish origin used to refer to Philippine Muslims

PULNA   A social status designation for those individuals able to trace direct descent through both parents from Sarip Kabungsuwan, the founder of the Cotabato sultanates

PUSAKA   Heirlooms; pusaka usually have ritual as well as sentimental and intrinsic value

SABIL   A martyr; one sworn to fight to the death in defense of Islam

SHARIA   Islamic law, literally the "Way" or "Path" of Islam

TARITIB   The protocol governing relations between the sultan, datus, and subordinate classes

TARSILA   Written genealogy

TAU SA ILUD   Downriver People; a dialect of the Magindanaon language

TAU SA LAYA   Upriver People; a dialect of the Magindanaon language

TUPU   Descendant; local descent line

ULAMA   (Singular, *alim*) Islamic scholars; those qualified to teach Islamic law

ULIPUN   Debt-bondsmen

USTADZ   (in Arabic, *ustadh*) An Islamic teacher

Bibliography

Abat, Fortunato U., 1993, *The Day We Nearly Lost Mindanao: The CEM-COM Story.* Quezon City, Philippines: SBA Printers.

Abbahil, Abdulsiddik Asa, 1984, "Muslim Filipino Ethnic Groups." *Salsilah: A Journal of Philippine Ethnic Studies* 4(2):6–18.

Abercrombie, Nicholas, Stephen Hill, and Bryan S. Turner, 1980, *The Dominant Ideology Thesis.* London: George Allen and Unwin.

Abu-Lughod, Lila, 1986, *Veiled Sentiments: Honor and Poetry in a Bedouin Society.* Berkeley and Los Angeles: University of California Press.

Abu-Lughod, Lila, 1990, "The Romance of Resistance: Tracing Transformations of Power through Bedouin Women." *American Ethnologist* 17:41–55.

Adas, Michael, 1981, "From Avoidance to Confrontation: Peasant Protest in Precolonial and Colonial Southeast Asia." *Comparative Studies in Society and History* 23(2):217–47.

Adil, Mohammad, 1955, *Maguindanao before Piang.* Manuscript, Manila.

Agoncillo, Teodoro A., 1969, *A Short History of the Philippines.* New York: Mentor Books.

Ahmad, Aijaz, 1982, "Class and Colony in Mindanao." *Southeast Asia Chronicle,* no. 82:4–11.

Althusser, Louis, 1971, *Lenin and Philosophy, and Other Essays.* New York: Monthly Review Press.

Althusser, Louis, and Etienne Balibar, 1970, *Reading Capital.* London: New Left Books.

Amin, Samir, 1973, *Le Developpement Inegal.* Paris: Les Editions de Minuit.

Andaya, Barbara Watson, 1975, "The Nature of the State in 18th Century Perak." In *Pre-colonial State Systems in Southeast Asia.* Anthony Reid and Lance Castles, eds. *Monographs of the Malaysian Branch of the Royal Asiatic Society,* no. 6. Kuala Lumpur: MBRAS.

Andaya, Barbara Watson, 1979, *Perak, the Abode of Grace.* Kuala Lumpur: Oxford University Press.

Andaya, Leonard, 1975a, "The Nature of Kingship in Bone." In Anthony Reid and Lance Castles, eds., *Pre-colonial State Systems in Southeast Asia. Monographs of the Malaysian Branch of the Royal Asiatic Society,* no. 6. Kuala Lumpur: MBRAS.

Andaya, Leonard, 1975b, *The Kingdom of Johor: Economic and Political Developments.* Kuala Lumpur: Oxford University Press.

Andaya, Leonard, 1993, *The World of Maluku: Eastern Indonesia in the Early Modern Period.* Honolulu: University of Hawaii Press.

Anderson, Benedict R. O'G., 1983, *Imagined Communities: Reflections on the Origin and Spread of Nationalism.* London: Verso.

Anderson, Benedict R. O'G., 1987, "Introduction to Southeast Asian Tribal Groups and Ethnic Minorities: Prospects for the Eighties and Beyond." *Cultural Survival Report* 22. Cambridge: Cultural Survival.

Anderson, Perry, 1976, "The Antinomies of Antonio Gramsci." *New Left Review* 100:5–78.

Arcilla, Jose S., S. J., ed., 1990, "Jesuit Missionary Letters from Mindanao." *The Rio Grande Mission.* Publications of the Archives of the Philippine Province of the Society of Jesus, Volume 1. Quezon City, Philippines: Philippine Province Archives.

Bauzon, Kenneth E., 1991, *Liberalism and the Quest for Islamic Identity in the Philippines.* Durham, N.C.: Acorn Press.

Beckett, Jeremy, 1977, "The Datus of the Rio Grande de Cotabato under Colonial Rule." *Asian Studies* 5:46–64.

Beckett, Jeremy, 1982, "The Defiant and the Compliant: The Datus of Magindanao under Colonial Rule." In *Philippine Social History: Global Trade and Local Transformations.* Alfred W. McCoy and Ed C. deJesus, eds. Honolulu: University Press of Hawaii.

Beckett, Jeremy, 1993, "Political Families and Family Politics among the Muslim Maguindanaon of Cotabato." In *An Anarchy of Families: State and Family in the Philippines.* Alfred W. McCoy, ed. Madison: University of Wisconsin, Center for Southeast Asian Studies.

Bendix, Regina, 1992, "National Sentiment in the Enactment and Discourse of Swiss Political Ritual." *American Ethnologist* 19(4):768–90.

Bentley, G. Carter, 1986, "Indigenous States of Southeast Asia." *Annual Review of Anthropology* 15:275–305.

Bentley, G. Carter, 1987, "Ethnicity and Practice." *Comparative Studies in Society and History* 29(1):25–55.

Bernad, Miguel A., S. J., 1984, "The Jesuit Exploration of the Pulangi or Rio Grande de Mindanao, 1880–1890." *Kinaadman: A Journal of the Southern Philippines* 6(2):149–90.

Bernaldez, Emilio y Fernandez de Folgueras, 1857, *Resena Historica de la Guerra al Sur de Filipinas.* Madrid: n.p.

Blair, E. H., and J. A. Robertson, eds., 1903–19, *The Philippine Islands, 1493–1898.* 55 vols. Cleveland: A. H. Clark.

Blumentritt, Ferdinand, 1893, "Los Magindanaos, estudio etnografico." *Boletin de la Sociedad Geografica de Madrid* 35:267–85.

Bonner, Raymond, 1987, *Waltzing with a Dictator: The Marcoses and the Making of American Policy.* New York: Times Books.

Bourdieu, Pierre, 1977, *Outline of a Theory of Practice.* Cambridge: Cambridge University Press.

Bowen, John R., 1992, "On Scriptural Essentialism and Ritual Variation: Muslim Sacrifice in Sumatra and Morocco." *American Ethnologist* 19(4):656–71.

Bowen, John R., 1993, *Muslims through Discourse: Religion and Ritual in Gayo Society.* Princeton: Princeton University Press.

Bowman, Glenn, 1993, "Nationalizing the Sacred: Shrines and Shifting Identities in the Israeli-Occupied Territories." *Man* 28:431–60.

Brow, James, 1988, "In Pursuit of Hegemony: Representations of Authority and Justice in a Sri Lankan Village." *American Ethnologist* 15:311–27.

Brow, James, 1990, "Notes on Community, Hegemony, and the Uses of the Past." *Anthropological Quarterly* 63(1):1–6.

Bujra, Abdalla S., 1971, *The Politics of Stratification: A Study of Political Change in a South Arabian Town.* Oxford: Oxford University Press.

Bureau of Census and Statistics, 1965, *Facts and Figures about the Philippines, 1963.* Manila: Bureau of Census and Statistics, Republic of the Philippines.

Burley, T. M., 1973, *The Philippines: An Economic and Social Geography.* London: G. Bell and Sons.

Chapman, William, 1987, *Inside the Philippine Revolution.* New York: W. W. Norton.

Chatterjee, Partha, 1993, *The Nation and Its Fragments: Colonial and Postcolonial Histories.* Princeton: Princeton University Press.

Christie, Emerson Brewer, 1909, *The Subanuns of Sindangan Bay.* Manila: Bureau of Printing.

Cole, Donald Powell, 1975, *Nomads of the Nomads: The Al Murrah Bedouin of the Empty Quarter.* Arlington Heights, Ill.: AHM Publishing.

Comaroff, Jean, 1985, *Body of Power, Spirit of Resistance.* Chicago: University of Chicago Press.

Comaroff, John, and Jean Comaroff, 1992, "Of Totemism and Ethnicity." Chap. 2 in *Ethnography and the Historical Imagination.* Boulder, Colo.: Westview Press.

Combes, Francisco, S. J., 1903–19, "The Natives of the Southern Islands." In *The Philippine Islands, 1493–1898.* E. H. Blair and J. A. Robertson, eds. 55 vols. Cleveland: A. H. Clark.

Combs-Schilling, M. E., 1989, *Sacred Performances: Islam, Sexuality, and Sacrifice.* New York: Columbia University Press.

Constantino, Renato, 1975, *The Philippines: A Past Revisited.* Manila: By the author.

Contursi, Janet A., 1989, "Militant Hindus and Buddhist Dalits: Hegemony and Resistance in an Indian Slum." *American Ethnologist* 16:441–57.

Corrigan, Philip Richard D., and Derek Sayer, 1985, *The Great Arch: English State Formation as Cultural Revolution.* Oxford: Oxford University Press.

Crain, Mary, 1990, "The Social Construction of National Identity in Highland Ecuador." *Anthropological Quarterly* 63(1):43–59.

Damaso, Elena Joaquin, 1983, "Magindanaon Datuship." In *Filipino Muslims: Their Social Institutions and Cultural Achievements.* F. Landa Jocano, ed. Quezon City: Asian Center, University of the Philippines.

Dampier, William, [1697] 1968, *A New Voyage Round the World.* New York: Dover Publications.

Davis, William G., 1986, "Class, Political Constraints, and Entrepreneurial Strategies: Elites and Petty Market Traders in Northern Luzon." In *Entrepreneurship and Social Change: Monographs in Economic Anthropology, no. 2.* Sidney M. Greenfield and Arnold Strickon, eds. Lanham, Md.: University Press of America.

de la Costa, Horacio, S. J., 1961, *The Jesuits in the Philippines, 1581–1768.* Cambridge: Harvard University Press.

Denny, Frederick M., 1987, *Islam and the Muslim Community.* San Francisco: Harper Collins.

Dewey, Alice G., 1962, *Peasant Marketing in Java.* New York: Free Press of Glencoe.

Djamour, Judith, 1959, *Malay Kinship and Marriage in Singapore.* London: Athlone Press.

Dominguez, Virginia, 1989, *People as Subject, People as Object: Selfhood and Peoplehood in Contemporary Israel.* Madison: University of Wisconsin Press.

Drakulic, Slavenka, 1993, *The Balkan Express: Fragments from the Other Side of War.* New York: W. W. Norton.

Eickelman, Dale F., 1976, *Moroccan Islam: Tradition and Society in a Pilgrimage Center.* Austin and London: University of Texas Press.

Eickelman, Dale F., 1985, *Knowledge and Power in Morocco: The Education of a Twentieth-Century Notable.* Princeton: Princeton University Press.

Eickelman, Dale F., 1992, "Mass Higher Education and the Religious Imagination in Contemporary Arab Societies." *American Ethnologist* 4(19): 643–55.

Eickelman, Dale F., and James P. Piscatori, 1996, *Muslim Politics.*Princeton, N.J.: Princeton University Press.

Ellen, Roy F., 1983, "Social Theory, Ethnography, and the Understanding of Practical Islam in South-East Asia." In *Islam in South-East Asia.* M. B. Hooker, ed. Leiden: E. J. Brill.

Elster, Jon, 1985, *Making Sense of Marx.* Cambridge: Cambridge University Press.

Elster, Jon, 1993, *Political Psychology.* Cambridge: Cambridge University Press.

Errington, Shelly, 1979, "Some Comments on Style in the Meanings of the Past." *Journal of Asian Studies* 38(2):231–44.

Errington, Shelly, 1989, *Meaning and Power in a Southeast Asian Realm.* Princeton: Princeton University Press.

Feldman, Allen, 1991, *Formations of Violence: The Narrative of the Body and Political Terror in Northern Ireland.* Chicago: University of Chicago Press.

Fleischman, Eric, 1981a, "The Decline of Datuship in the Iranun Sultanate of Linek." *Dansalan Quarterly* 2(4):228–36.

Fleischman, Eric, 1981b, "The Danao Languages: Magindanaon, Iranun, Maranao, and Illanun." *Philippine Journal of Linguistics* 12(1):57–77.

Fleischman, Eric, 1981c, *Vocabulary: English-Pilipino-Magindanaon; Magindanaon-Pilipino-English; Pilipino-English-Magindanaon.* Manila: Summer Institute of Linguistics.

Forbes, W. Cameron, 1928, *The Philippine Islands.* Boston: Houghton Mifflin.

Forrest, Thomas, 1969, *A Voyage to New Guinea and the Moluccas, 1774–1776.* Kuala Lumpur: Oxford University Press.

Foster, Robert J., 1991, "Making National Cultures in the Global Ecumene." *Annual Review of Anthropology* 20:235–60.

Foucault, Michel, 1978, "The History of Sexuality." *An Introduction,* Vol. 1. New York: Random House.

Fox, Richard G., 1985, *Lions of the Punjab: Culture in the Making.* Berkeley and Los Angeles: University of California Press.

Fox, Richard G., 1989, *Gandhian Utopia: Experiments with Culture.* Boston: Beacon Press.

Fox, Richard G., 1990, "Introduction to Nationalist Ideologies and the Production of National Cultures." Richard G. Fox, ed. *American Ethnological Society Monograph Series,* no. 2. Washington, D.C.: American Anthropological Association.

Francia, Beatriz Romualdez, 1988, *Imelda and the Clans: A Story of the Philippines.* Manila: Solar Publishing.

Fraser, Thomas M., 1960, *Rusembilan: A Malay Fishing Village in Southern Thailand.* Ithaca: Cornell University Press.

Friedman, Jonathan, 1990, "Notes on Culture and Identity in Imperial Worlds." In *Religion and Religious Practice in the Seleucid Kingdom.* Per Bilde, Troels Engberg-Pedersen, Lise Hannestad, and Jan Zahle, eds. Aarhus, Denmark: Aarhus University Press.

Friedman, Jonathan, 1992, "The Past in the Future: History and the Politics of Identity." *American Anthropologist* 94(4):837–59.

Gaffney, Patrick D., 1994, *The Prophet's Pulpit: Islamic Preaching in Contemporary Egypt.* Berkeley and Los Angeles: University of California Press.

Geertz, Clifford, 1960, *The Religion of Java.* Glencoe: Free Press.

Geertz, Clifford, 1966, "Religion as a Cultural System." In *Anthropological Approaches to the Study of Religion.* Michael Banton, ed. ASA Monograph 3:1–46.

Geertz, Clifford, 1968, *Islam Observed: Religious Development in Morocco and Indonesia.* New Haven: Yale University Press.

Geertz, Clifford, 1980, *Negara: The Theatre State in Nineteenth-Century Bali.* Princeton: Princeton University Press.

Genovese, Eugene, 1974, *Roll Jordon Roll: The World the Slaves Made.* New York: Pantheon Books.

George, T. J. S., 1980, *Revolt in Mindanao: The Rise of Islam in Philippine Politics.* Kuala Lumpur: Oxford University Press.

Gilsenan, Michael, 1982, *Recognizing Islam: An Anthropologist's Introduction.* London: Croom Helm.

Glang, Alunan C. O., 1969, *Muslim Secession or Integration?* Quezon City: Alunan Glang.

Glassé, Cyril, 1989, *The Concise Encyclopedia of Islam.* London: Stacey International.

Gleeck, Lewis E., Jr., 1989, *The Rise and Fall of Harry Stonehill in the Philippines: An American Tragedy.* Makati, Metro Manila: Loyal Printing.

Golay, Frank H., 1961, *The Philippines: Public Policy and National Economic Development.* Ithaca: Cornell University Press.

Gowing, Peter Gordon, 1979, *Muslim Filipinos: Heritage and Horizon.* Quezon City: New Day Publishers.

Gowing, Peter Gordon, 1983, *Mandate in Moroland: The American Government of Muslim Filipinos, 1899–1920.* Quezon City: New Day Publishers.

Gowing, Peter G., and Robert D. McAmis, eds., 1974, *The Muslim Filipinos: Their History, Society and Contemporary Problems.* Manila: Solidaridad Publishing House.

Gramsci, Antonio, 1971, *Selections from the Prison Notebooks.* Ed. and trans. Quintin Hoare and Geoffrey Nowell Smith. New York: International Publishers.

Gullick, J. M., 1958, "Indigenous Political Systems of Western Malaya." *London School of Economics Monographs on Social Anthropology,* no. 17. London: Athlone Press.

Gullick, J.M., 1987, *Malay Society in the Late Nineteenth Century: The Beginnings of Change.* Singapore: Oxford University Press.

Hall, Stuart, 1985, "Signification, Representation, Ideology: Althusser and the Post-Structuralist Debate." *Critical Studies in Mass Communication* 22(1):13–29.

Handler, Richard, 1988, *Nationalism and the Politics of Culture in Quebec.* Madison: University of Wisconsin Press.

Harden, Edward W., 1898, *Report on the Financial and Industrial Conditions of the Philippine Islands.* Washington, D.C.: Gov. Printing Office.

Hartendorp, A. V. H., 1961, *History of Industry and Trade of the Philippines: The Magsaysay Administration.* Manila: Philippine Education Company.

Hassoubah, Ahmad Mohammad H., 1983, *Teaching Arabic as a Second Language in the Philippines.* Marawi City: University Research Center, Mindanao State University.

Hefner, Robert W., 1986, "Review of the Three Worlds of Bali, by J. Stephen Lansing." *American Anthropologist* 88(2):487–88.

Hobsbawm, Eric, and T. O. Ranger, eds., 1983, *The Invention of Tradition.* Cambridge: Cambridge University Press.

Hollnsteiner, Mary R., 1963, *The Dynamics of Power in a Philippine Municipality.* Manila: Ateneo University Press.

Hooker, M. B., 1983, "Muhhamadan Law and Islamic Law." In *Islam in Southeast Asia.* M. B. Hooker, ed. Leiden: E. J. Brill.

Horn, Florence, 1941, *Orphans of the Pacific: The Philippines.* New York: Reynal and Hitchcock.

Horvatich, Patricia, 1993, "Keeping Up with Hassans: Tradition, Change, and Rituals of Death in a Sama Community." *Pilipinas* 21:51–71.

Horvatich, Patricia, 1993, The *Parang Sabil* of Yusop Dais and the Politics of Identity in the southern Philippines. Unpublished paper. University of Hawaii.

Horvatich, Patricia, 1994, "Ways of Knowing Islam." *American Ethnologist* 21(4):811–26.

Hunt, Chester L., 1957, "Ethnic Stratification and Integration in Cotabato." *Philippine Sociological Review* 5(1):13–38.

Hunter, Shireen T., ed., 1988, *The Politics of Islamic Revivalism: Diversity and Unity.* Bloomington: Indiana University Press.

Hurley, Vic, 1936, "Swish of the Kris: The Story of the Moros." E. P. Dutton and Co. Reprinted *Filipiniana Reprint Series*, no. 10. Renato Constantino, ed. Manila: Cacho Hermanos, 1985.

Hurley, Vic, 1985, "Jungle Patrol: The Story of the Philippine Constabulary." *Filipiniana Reprint Series*, Vol. 4. Renato Constantino, ed. Manila: Cacho Hermanos. Original edition, New York: E. P. Dutton and Company, 1938.

IBON Databank, 1981, *IBON Facts and Figures, no. 76, 15 October 1981.* Manila: IBON Databank Philippines.

IBON Databank, 1985, *IBON Facts and Figures, no. 174, 15 November 1985.* Manila: IBON Databank Philippines.

IBON Databank, 1986, *IBON Facts and Figures, no. 181, 28 February 1986.* Manila: IBON Databank Philippines.

Ileto, Reynaldo C., 1971, *Magindanao: 1860–1888: The Career of Datu Uto of Buayan.* Cornell University Southeast Asia Program, data paper no. 82.

Ileto, Reynaldo C., 1979, *Pasyon and Revolution: Popular Movements in the Philippines, 1840–1910.* Manila: Ateneo de Manila University Press.

Jose, F. Sional, ed., 1987, "The Mindanao Problem." *Solidarity* 110:79–154.

Kahn, Joel S., 1993, *Constituting the Minangkabau: Peasants, Culture, and Modernity in Colonial Indonesia.* New York: Berg.

Kapferer, Bruce, 1988, *Legends of People, Myths of State.* Washington, D.C.: Smithsonian Institution Press.

Kapferer, Bruce, 1989, "Nationalist Ideology and a Comparative Anthropology." *Ethnos* 54(3–4):161–99.

Kapferer, Bruce, 1990, "Comments on Spencer's Writing Within: Anthropology, Nationalism, and Culture in Sri Lanka." *Current Anthropology* 31(3):291–94.

Kaplan, Martha, and John D. Kelly, 1994, "Rethinking Resistance: Dialogics of 'Disaffection' in Colonial Fiji." *American Ethnologist* 21(1):123–51.

Kerkvliet, Benedict J., 1977, *The Huk Rebellion: A Study of Peasant Revolt in the Philippines.* Berkeley and Los Angeles: University of California Press.

Kerkvliet, Benedict J., 1990, *Everyday Politics in the Philippines: Class and Status Relations in a Central Luzon Village.* Berkeley and Los Angeles: University of California Press.

Kessler, Clive S., 1978, *Islam and Politics in a Malay State: Kelantan, 1838–1969.* Ithaca: Cornell University Press.

Kiefer, Thomas M., 1972, *The Tausug: Violence and Law in a Philippine Moslem Society.* New York: Holt, Rinehart, and Winston.

Kiefer, Thomas M., 1987, "Resurgent Islam and Ethnic Minorities in the Philippines." In *Southeast Asian Tribal Groups and Ethnic Minorities: Prospects for the Eighties and Beyond.*" Cultural Survival Report 22. Cambridge: Cultural Survival.

Kirkup, James, 1967, *Filipinescas: Travels through the Philippine Islands.* London: Phoenix House.

Kondo, Dorinne, 1990, *Crafting Selves: Power, Gender, and Discourse of Identity in a Japanese Workplace.* Chicago: University of Chicago Press.

Kuder, Edward M., 1945, "The Moros in the Philippines." *Far Eastern Quarterly* 4(2):119–26.

Laarhoven, Ruurdje, 1987, "Chinese of Maguindanao in the Seventeenth Century from Dutch Sources." *Philippine Studies* 35:485–504.

Laarhoven, Ruurdje, 1989, *Triumph of Moro Diplomacy: The Maguindanao Sultanate in the 17th Century.* Quezon City, Philippines: New Day Publishers; distributed by The Cellar Book Shop, Detroit, Mich.

Laclau, Ernesto, 1977, *Politics and Ideology in Marxist Theory.* London: Verso.

Lagos, Maria L., 1993, "'We Have to Learn to Ask': Hegemony, Diverse Experiences, and Antagonistic Meanings in Bolivia." *American Ethnologist* 20(1):52–71.

Laitin, David C., 1985, "Hegemony and Religious Conflict." In *Bringing the State Back In.* Peter B. Evans, Dietrich Rueschemeyer, and Theda Skocpol, eds. Cambridge: Cambridge University Press.

Lan, David, 1985, *Guns and Rain: Guerrillas and Spirit Mediums in Zimbabwe.* Berkeley and Los Angeles: University of California Press.

Lande, Carl H., 1965, "Leaders, Factions, and Parties: The Structure of Philippine Politics." *Southeast Asia Studies,* monograph no. 6. New Haven: Yale University.

Lansing, J. Stephen, 1983, *The Three Worlds of Bali.* New York: Praeger.

Lapitan, Antonio E., 1978, "The Barangay System in the Philippines: A Historical Structure with New Functions." *Papers in Anthropology, University of Oklahoma* 19 (2):75–88).

Lazarus-Black, Mindie, and Susan F. Hirsch, 1994, "Performance and Paradox: Exploring Law's Role in Hegemony and Resistance." In *Contested States: Law, Hegemony, and Resistance.* Mindie Lazarus-Black and Susan F. Hirsch, eds. New York: Routledge.

Lears, T. J. Jackson, 1985, "The Concept of Cultural Hegemony: Problems and Possibilities." *American Historical Review* 90(3):567–93.

van Leur, Jacob Cornelis, 1955, *Indonesian Trade and Society: Essays in Asian Social and Economic History.* The Hague and Bandung: W. van Hoewe.

Linger, Daniel T., 1993, "The Hegemony of Discontent." *American Ethnologist* 20(1):3–24.

Llamzon, Teodoro A., 1978, *Handbook of Philippine Language Groups.*

Loyre, Ghislaine, 1991, "The Institutions of Maguindano." In *General History of the Philippines,* Part 6, Vol. 1. Manila: Historical Conservation Society.

Lynch, Frank, 1984, "Big and Little People: Social Class in the Rural Philippines." In *Philippine Society and the Individual: Selected Essays of Frank Lynch, 1949–1976.* Aram A. Yengoyan and Perla Makil, eds. Paper no. 24. Ann Arbor: University of Michigan, Center for South and Southeast Asian Studies.

Maceda, Jose, 1961, "Magindanao Music." *Philippine Studies* 9(4):666–71.

Madale, Nagasura T., 1986, "The Future of the Moro National Liberation Front (MNLF) as a Separatist Movement in the Southern Philippines." In *Armed Separatism in Southeast Asia.* Lim Joo-Jock and S. Vani, eds. Singapore: Institute of Southeast Asian Studies.

Mahmood, Cynthia Keppler, 1996, *Fighting for Faith and Nation: Dialogues with Sikh Militants.* Philadelphia: University of Pennsylvania Press.

Majul, Cesar Adib, 1973, *Muslims in the Philippines.* Manila: St. Mary's Publishing.

Majul, Cesar Adib, 1979, "Minorities in the Philippines: The Muslims." In *Trends in Ethnic Group Relations in Asia and Oceania.* Paris: UNESCO.

Majul, Cesar Adib, 1985, *The Contemporary Muslim Movement in the Philippines.* Berkeley: Mizan Press.

Marcos, Ferdinand, 1972, "Proclamation of Martial Law." *Philippine Sunday Express* 1(141):5–8.

Mastura, Datu Michael O., 1979, "A Short History of Cotabato City and Its Historic Places." In *Cotabato City Guidebook.* Simeon F. Millan, ed. General Santos City: Simeon F. Millan.

Mastura, Datu Michael O., 1984,"Muslim Filipino Experience: A Collection of Essays." *Philippine Islam Series,* no. 3. Manila: Ministry of Muslim Affairs.

Mastura, Datu Michael O., 1985, *The Crisis in the MNLF Leadership and the Dilemma of the Muslim Autonomy Movement. Collected Papers of the Conference on The Tripoli Agreement: Problems and Prospects,* September 13–14, 1985. Manila: International Studies Institute, University of the Philippines.

May, Glenn Anthony, 1987, *A Past Recovered.* Quezon City: New Day Publishers.

McAmis, Robert D., 1974, "Muslim Filipinos, 1970–1972." In *The Muslim Filipinos: Their History, Society, and Contemporary Problems.* Peter G. Gowing and Robert D. McAmis, eds. Manila: Solidaridad Publishing House.

McAmis, Robert D., 1983, "Muslim Filipinos in the 1980s." *Solidarity* 4:32–40.

McKenna, Thomas M., 1988, "Persistence of an Overthrown Paradigm: Modernization in a Philippine Muslim Shantytown." *Journal of Anthropological Research* 44(3):287–309.

McKenna, Thomas M., 1992, "Martial Law, Moro Nationalism, and Traditional Leadership in Cotabato." *Pilipinas* 18:1–17.

McKenna, Thomas M., 1994, "The Defiant Periphery: Routes of Iranun Resistance in the Philippines." *Social Analysis* 35:11–27.

Mednick, Melvin, 1965, *Encampment of the Lake: The Social Organization of a Moslem-Philippine (Moro) People.* Research series, no. 5. Chicago: Philippine Studies Program, Dept. of Anthropology, University of Chicago.

Mednick, Melvin, 1974, "Some Problems of Moro History and Political Organization." In *The Muslim Filipinos: Their History, Society, and Contemporary Problems.* Peter G. Gowing and Robert D. McAmis, eds. Manila: Solidaridad Publishing House.

Mercado, Elisio R., OMI, 1984, "Culture, Economics, and Revolt in Mindanao: The Origins of the MNLF and the Politics of Moro Separatism." In *Armed Separatism in Southeast Asia.* Lim Joo-Jock, ed. Singapore: Institute of Southeast Asian Studies.

Millan, Simeon F., ed., 1952, *Cotabato Guidebook.* Cotabato City: Simeon F. Millan.

Millar, Susan Bolyard, 1989, *Bugis Weddings: Rituals of Social Location in Modern Indonesia.* Center for South and Southeast Asia Studies, monograph no. 29. Berkeley: University of California.

Miller, Hugo H., 1913, *Economic Conditions in the Philippines.* Boston: Ginn and Company.

Milner, A. C., 1982, *Kerajaan: Malay Political Culture on the Eve of Colonial Rule.* Association for Asian Studies, monograph no. 40. Tucson: University of Arizona Press.

Molloy, Ivan, 1988, "The Decline of the Moro National Liberation Front in the Southern Philippines." *Journal of Contemporary Asia* 18(1):59–76.

Montano, Joseph, 1886, *Voyage aux Philippines et en Malaises.* Paris: n.p.

Muslim Association of the Philippines, 1956, *Proceedings of the First National Muslim Convention, Cotabato, June 8–12, 1955.* Manila: Muslim Association of the Philippines.

Nagata, Judith, 1984, *The Reflowering of Malaysian Islam: Modern Religious Radicals and Their Roots.* Vancouver: University of British Columbia Press.

Nairn, Tom, 1977, *The Breakup of Britain: Crisis and Neo-Nationalism.* London: New Left Books.

National Economic Development Authority, 1986, *Regional Socio-Economic Profile: Central Mindanao.* National Economic Development Authority, Region XII, Manila, Republic of the Philippines.

National Economic Development Authority, 1992, *Regional Statistical Compendium of Central Mindanao, 1986–1990.* Regional Development Council, National Economic Development Authority, Region XII, Manila, Republic of the Philippines.

Nieto Aguilar, Jose, 1894, *Mindanao, su Historia y Geografia.* Madrid: n.p.

Noble, Lela Gardner, 1976, "The Moro National Liberation Front in the Philippines." *Pacific Affairs* 49(3):405–24.

Noble, Lela Gardner, 1977, *Philippine Policy toward Sabah: A Claim to Independence.* Tucson: University of Arizona Press.

Noble, Lela Gardner, 1983, "Roots of the Bangsa Moro Revolution." *Solidarity* 4(97):41–50.

Ong, Aihwa, 1987, *Spirits of Resistance and Capitalist Discipline: Factory Women in Malaysia.* Albany: State University of New York Press.

Ortner, Sherry B., 1995, *Resistance and the Problem of Ethnographic Refusal.* Comparative Studies in Society and History, 37:173–93.

O'Shaughnessy, Thomas J., 1979, "How Many Muslims Has the Philippines?" In*Muslim Filipinos: Heritage and Horizon.* Peter Gordon Gowing, ed. Quezon City: New Day Publishers, 1979.

Patterson, Orlando, 1982, *Slavery and Social Death: A Comparative Study.* Cambridge: Harvard University Press.

Peletz, Michael G., 1996, *Reason and Passion: Representations of Gender in a Malay Society.* Berkeley and Los Angeles: University of California Press.

Peletz, Michael G., 1997, "'Ordinary Muslims' and Muslim Resurgents in Contemporary Malaysia: Notes on an Ambivalent Relationship." In *Islam in an Era of Nation States: Politics and Religious Renewal in Muslim Southeast Asia.* Patricia Horvatich and Robert Hefner, eds. Honolulu: University of Hawaii Press.

Pelras, Christian, 1996, *The Bugis.* Cambridge: Blackwell Publishers.

Pelzer, Karl J., 1945, *Pioneer Settlement in the Asiatic Tropics: Studies in Land Utilization and Agricultural Colonization in Southeastern Asia.* Special publication no. 29. New York: American Geographical Society.

Pettigrew, Joyce J. M., 1995, *The Sikhs of the Punjab: Unheard Voices of State and Guerrilla Violence.* London: Zed Books.

Rahman, Fazlur, 1966, *Islam.* New York: Holt, Rinehart, and Winston.

Ravenholt, Albert, 1956, "The Amir Mindalano: Profile of a Filipino Mohammedan Leader." *Southeast Asia Series,* Vol. 4, no. 10. New York: American Universities Field Staff.

Rebel, Hermann, 1988, "Why Not 'Old Marie' or Someone Very Much Like Her? A Reassessment of the Question about the Grimms' Contributors from a Social Historical Perspective." *Social History* 13(1):1–24.

Rebel, Hermann, 1989, "Cultural Hegemony and Class Experience: A Critical Reading of Recent Ethnological-Historical Approaches." Parts 1 and 2. *American Ethnologist* 16(1–2):117–36; 350–65.

Reed, Robert, 1963, "The Tobacco Economy." In *Shadows on the Land: An Economic Geography of the Philippines.* Manila: Bookmark.

Reed-Danahay, Deborah, 1993, "Talking about Resistance: Ethnography and Theory in Rural France." *Anthropological Quarterly* 66:221–29.

Reid, Anthony, 1984, "The Islamization of Southeast Asia." In *Historia. Essays in Commemoration of the 25th Anniversary of the Department of History, University of Malaya.* Muhammad Abu Bakar et al., eds. Kuala Lumpur: Malaysian Historical Society.

Reid, Anthony, 1988, "Southeast Asia in the Age of Commerce, 1450–1680." *The Lands below the Winds,* Vol. 1. New Haven: Yale University Press.

Reid, Anthony, 1993, "Southeast Asia in the Age of Commerce: 1450–1680." *Expansion and Crisis,* Vol. 2. New Haven: Yale University Press.

Roberts, D. S., 1981, *Islam, a Westerner's Guide.* London: Kogan Page.

Rodil, B. Rudy, 1986, "Reflections on the Moro Right to Self-Determination." *Moro Kurier* 1(3):7–14.

Roff, William R., 1985, "Islam Obscured? Some Reflections on Studies of Islam and Society in Southeast Asia." *Archipel* 29:7–34.

Roseberry, William, 1989, *Anthropologies and Histories: Essays in Culture, History, and Political Economy.* New Brunswick: Rutgers University Press.

Roseberry, William, 1994, "Hegemony and the Language of Contention." In *Everyday Forms of State Formation: Revolution and the Negotiation of Rule in Modern Mexico.* Gilbert M. Joseph and Daniel Nugent, eds. Durham: Duke University Press.

Roseberry, William, and Jay O'Brien, 1991, "Introduction." In *Golden Ages, Dark Ages: Imagining the Past in Anthropology and History.* Jay O'Brien and William Roseberry, eds. Berkeley and Los Angeles: University of California Press.

Rydell, Robert W., 1984, *All the World's a Fair: Visions of Empire at American International Expositions, 1876–1916.* Chicago: University of Chicago Press.

Saber, Mamitua, Mauyag M. Tamano, and Charles K. Warriner, 1974, "The Maratabat of the Maranao." In *The Muslim Filipinos: Their History, Society, and Contemporary Problems.* Peter G. Gowing and Robert D. McAmis, eds. Manila: Solidaridad Publishing House.

Saleeby, Najeeb M., 1905, *Studies in Moro History, Law, and Religion.* Dept. of the Interior, Ethnological Survey Publications, Vol. 4, no. 1. Manila: Bureau of Printing.

Saleeby, Najeeb M., 1908, *The History of Sulu.* Manila: Dept. of the Interior, Ethnological Survey Publications, Vol. 4, no. 2. Manila: Bureau of Printing.

Saleeby, Najeeb M., 1913, *The Moro Problem.* Manila: Bureau of Printing.

San Juan, E., ca. 1984, *Hypotheses toward Theorizing the Concept of the Bangsamoro Nation's Struggle for Self-Determination.* Manuscript, University of Connecticut.

Sarangani, Datumanong Di. A., 1974, "Islamic Penetration in Mindanao and Sulu." *Mindanao Journal* 1(1):49–73.

Sayer, Derek, 1994, "Everyday Forms of State Formation: Some Dissident Remarks on 'Hegemony'." In *Everyday Forms of State Formation: Revolution and the Negotiation of Rule in Modern Mexico.* Gilbert M. Joseph and Daniel Nugent, eds. Durham: Duke University Press.

Scaff, Alvin H., 1955, *The Philippine Answer to Communism.* Stanford: Stanford University Press.

Schirmer, Daniel B., and Stephen Rosskamm Shalom, eds., 1987, *The Philippines Reader: A History of Colonialism, Neocolonialism, Dictatorship, and Resistance.* Boston: South End Press.

Schlegel, Stuart A., 1970, *Tiruray Justice: Traditional Tiruray Law and Morality.* Berkeley and Los Angeles: University of California Press.

Schlegel, Stuart A., 1972, "Tiruray-Magindanaon Ethnic Relations: An Ethnohistorical Puzzle." *Solidarity* 7:25–30.

Schlegel, Stuart A., ca. 1977, *The Tiruray.* Manuscript, University of California at Santa Cruz.

Schlegel, Stuart A., 1978, "Muslim-Christian Conflict in the Philippine South." *Papers in Anthropology, University of Oklahoma* 19(2):39–54.

Schlegel, Stuart A., 1979, *Tiruray Subsistence: From Shifting Cultivation to Plow Agriculture*. Quezon City, Philippines: Ateneo de Manila University Press.

Scott, James C., 1985, *Weapons of the Weak: Everyday Forms of Peasant Resistance*. New Haven: Yale University Press.

Scott, James C., 1990, *Domination and the Arts of Resistance: Hidden Transcripts*. New Haven: Yale University Press.

Scott, James C., 1994, "Foreword." In *Everyday Forms of State Formation: Revolution and the Negotiation of Rule in Modern Mexico*. Gilbert M. Joseph and Daniel Nugent, eds. Durham: Duke University Press.

Scott, William Henry, 1982, *Cracks in the Parchment Curtain and Other Essays in Philippine History*. Quezon City: New Day Publishers.

Scott, William Henry, 1984, *Prehispanic Source Materials for the Study of Philippine History*. Rev. ed. Quezon City: New Day Publishers.

Scott, William Henry, 1994, *Barangay: Sixteenth-Century Philippine Culture and Society*. Manila: Ateneo de Manila University Press.

Shalom, Stephen R., 1977, "Counter-Insurgency in the Philippines." *Journal of Contemporary Asia* 7(2):153–72.

Siegel, James T., 1969, *The Rope of God*. Berkeley and Los Angeles: University of California Press.

Slobin, Mark, 1993, *Subcultural Sounds: Micromusics of the West*. Hanover, N.H.: University Press of New England.

Sluka, Jeffrey A., 1989, "Hearts and Minds, Water and Fish: Support for the IRA and INLA in a Northern Irish Ghetto." *Contemporary Ethnographic Studies*. London: JAI Press.

Sluka, Jeffrey A., 1990, "Participant Observation in Violent Social Contexts." *Human Organization* 49(2):114–26.

Sluka, Jeffrey A., 1995, "Domination, Resistance, and Political Culture in Northern Ireland's Catholic-Nationalist Ghettos." *Critique of Anthropology* 151:71–102.

Southall, Aidan, 1965, "A Critique of the Typology of States and Political Systems." In *Political Systems and the Distribution of Power*. Michael Banton, ed. Association of Social Anthropologists, *monograph no. 2*. London: American Tavistock.

Spencer, Jonathan, 1990, "Writing Within: Anthropology, Nationalism, and Culture in Sri Lanka." *Current Anthropology* 31(3):283–300.

Steinberg, David Joel, et al., eds., 1987, *In Search of Southeast Asia: A Modern History*. New York: Praeger Press.

Stewart, James C., 1977, *People of the Flood Plain*. Ph.D. dissertation, Department of Anthropology, University of Hawaii.

Stewart, James C., 1978, "The Maguindanao." In *Muslim Peoples: A World Ethnographic Survey*. Richard V. Weekes, ed. Westport, Conn.: Greenwood Press.

Stoler, Ann, 1985, *Capitalism and Confrontation in Sumatra's Plantation Belt, 1870–1979*. New Haven: Yale University Press.

Sullivan, Patrick, 1982, *Social Relations of Dependence in a Malay State: Nineteenth-Century Perak*. The Malaysian Branch of the Royal Asiatic Society, monograph no. 10. Kuala Lumpur: MBRAS.

Swedenburg, Ted, 1990, "The Palestinian Peasant as a National Signifier." *Anthropological Quarterly* 63(1):18–30.

Swedenburg, Ted, 1991, "Popular Memory and the Palestinian National Past." In *Golden Ages, Dark Ages: Imagining the Past in Anthropology and History*. Jay O'Brien and William Roseberry, eds. Berkeley and Los Angeles: University of California Press.

Swedenburg, Ted, 1995, *Memories of Revolt: The 1936–1939 Rebellion and the Palestinian National Past*. Minneapolis: University of Minnesota Press.

Tamano, Mamintal A., 1974, "Problems of the Muslims: A National Concern." In *The Muslim Filipinos: Their History, Society, and Contemporary Problems*. Peter G. Gowing and Robert D. McAmis, eds. Manila: Solidaridad Publishing House.

Tan, Eva Kimpo, 1974, "Pigcawayan, Cotabato." In *Changes in Rice Farming in Selected Areas of Asia*. Manila: International Rice Research Institute.

Tan, Samuel K., 1982, *Selected Essays on the Filipino Muslims*. Marawi City: University Research Center, Mindanao State University.

Thomas, Ralph Benjamin, 1971, *Muslim but Filipino: The Integration of Philippine Muslims, 1917–1946*. Ph.D. dissertation, Department of History, University of Pennsylvania.

Thompson, E. P., 1978, *The Poverty of Theory, and Other Essays*. New York: Monthly Review Press.

Toland, Judith, 1993, Introduction: Dialogue of Self and Other: Ethnicity and the Statehood Building Process." In *Ethnicity and the State*. Judith Toland, ed.New Brunswick, N.J.: Transaction Publishers.

Verdery, Katherine, 1991, *National Ideology under Socialism: Identity and Cultural Politics in Ceausescu's Romania*. Berkeley and Los Angeles: University of California Press.

Veyne, Paul, 1976, *Le Pain et Le Cirque*. Paris: Le Seuil.

Volkman, Toby, 1985, "Feasts of Honor: Ritual and Change in the Toraja Highlands." *Illinois Studies in Anthropology*, no. 16. Urbana and Chicago: University of Illinois Press.

Walton, John, 1984, *Reluctant Rebels: Comparative Studies of Revolution and Underdevelopment*. New York: Columbia University Press.

Warren, James F., 1981, *The Sulu Zone, 1768–1898: The Dynamics of External Trade, Slavery, and Ethnicity in the Transformation of a Southeast Asian Maritime State*. Singapore: Singapore University Press.

Warriner, Charles K., 1964, "Traditional Authority and the Modern State: The Case of the Maranao of the Philippines." *Philippine Sociological Review* 12(3 and 4):172–77.

Weekes, Richard V., ed., 1984, *Muslim Peoples: A World Ethnographic Survey*. Westport, Conn.: Greenwood Press.

Wein, Clement, SVD, 1984, *Raja of Mandaya: A Philippine Folk-Epic*. Cebu City, Philippines: University of San Carlos.

Wein, Clement SVD, 1985, *Songs of Life: Magindanao Folksongs*. Cebu City, Philippines: University of San Carlos.

Wernstedt, Frederick L., and Paul D. Simkins, 1965, "Migrations and the Settlement of Mindanao." *Journal of Asian Studies* 25(1):83–103.

Wernstedt, Frederick L., and J. E. Spencer, 1967, *The Philippine Island World: A Physical, Cultural, and Regional Geography*. Berkeley and Los Angeles: University of California Press.

White, John R., 1928, *Bullets and Bolos: Thirteen Years in the Philippine Islands*. New York: Century.

Wickberg, Edgar, 1965, *The Chinese in Philippine Life, 1850–1898*. New Haven: Yale University Press.

Williams, Brackette, 1989, "A Class Act: Anthropology and the Race to Nation across Ethnic Terrain." *Annual Review of Anthropology* 18:401–44.

Williams, Brackette, 1991, *Stains on My Name, War in My Veins: Guyana and the Politics of Cultural Struggle*. Durham, North Carolina: Duke University Press.

Williams, Raymond, 1977, *Marxism and Literature*. London: Oxford University Press.

Williams, Raymond, 1980, *Problems in Materialism and Culture*. London: Verso. First published as Base and Superstructure in Marxist Cultural Theory," *New Left Review* 82(1973).

Willis, Paul, 1981, *Learning to Labour: How Working Class Kids Get Working Class Jobs*. New York: Columbia University Press.

Wolf, Eric, 1969, *Peasant Wars of the Twentieth Century*. New York: Harper and Row.

Wolf, Eric, 1982, *Europe and the People without History*. Berkeley and Los Angeles: University of California Press.

Wolters, O. W., 1982, *History, Culture, and Region in Southeast Asian Perspectives*. Singapore: Institute of Southeast Asian Studies.

Wolters, Willem, 1984, *Politics, Patronage, and Class Conflict in Central Luzon*. Quezon City: New Day Publishers.

Woost, Michael, 1993, "Nationalizing the Local Past in Sri Lanka: Histories of Nation and Development in a Sinhalese Village." *American Ethnologist* 20(3):502–21.

World Bank, 1985, *The Philippines: Recent Trends in Poverty, Employment, and Wages*. Washington, D.C.: World Bank.

Wright, Patrick, 1985, *On Living in an Old Country: The National Past in Contemporary Britain*. London: Verso.

Zulaika, Joseba, 1988, *Basque Violence: Metaphor and Sacrament*. Reno: University of Nevada Press.

Index

Page numbers in italics refer to illustrations. Page numbers in bold refer to glossary definitions.

Abat, Brig. Gen. Fortunato U., *166*, 323n28
Abiden, Sarip Ali Zain-ul, 49
Adat (customary law), 62, 91, **337**
Adat betad (traditional culture), 300–301n5
Adil, Mohammad, 47, 62, 91, 96, 97, 98, 99, 108, 128, 130, 149, 158, 221–22, 226, 318n27
Adjudication practices: conflicts in, 225–26; loci of, 218, 230
Agimat (amulets), 192, 326n17, **337**
Akmad (imam of Campo Muslim), 174–77, 200, 202, 204, 227–28, 230, 233, 277, 283
Alah Valley: description of, 27; settlement of, *115*, 127
Alamada (Iranun insurgent), 97, 98
Alamada (village), settlement of, 116
Alcohol consumption, 36, 206, 220, 283
Ali (last independent ruler of Cotabato), 69, 94, 97
Alifuru (inhabitants of Halmahera), 308n11
Ali, Lanang, 247
Alonto, Abulkhayr, 157
Alonto, Domocao, 139
American colonialism. *See* United States

Amilbangsa, Ombra, 135
Ampatuan (datu), 320n8
Ampatuan clan, 145, 153
Anderson, Benedict, 14, 15, 16
Anti-Imperialist League, U.S., 89
Aquino, Agapito, 242
Aquino, Benigno, 140, 236, 242
Aquino, Corazon C., 230, 231, 235, 236, 238, 242, 244, 246, 332n9
Aristocracy, mythic (traditional), See *Datus*
Armed Forces of the Philippines (AFP), 165–66, 185
Asikin, Jusul, 49
Autonomous Region of Muslim Mindanao, 334n24
Ayunan, Datu, 98, 99, 100

Badruddin, Hadji Salik, 202
Bagong Alyansang Makabayan (BAYAN; New Nationalist Alliance), 238
Bagungan, Bai, 96
Baguri, Sheikh Hassanal, 320n5
Balabaran, Datu, 99
Balabaran, Sinsuat, 98–101, 102, 103, 110, 119, 276
Bangsa (descent groups), 47–48, 164, 190, 301n8, **337**

Bangsamoro ("Moro nation"), 81, 164, 186, 322n26, 337
Bangsa Moro Army, 157
Bangsa Moro Liberation Organization (BMLO), 162
Bangsamoro Rebellion: as armed struggle, 138–67, 170, 180–81; peace settlement for, 167–68, 170; political goals of, 14, 163–64; rank-and-file and civilian experience of, 183–94, 226–31, 278–80; as unarmed struggle, 170, 197–233, 280–84; unauthorized narratives of, 24, 192–95, 275–78; viewed from Campo Muslim, 170, 182–94. *See also* Muslim separatist movement
Bangun (wergild), 51
Bantingan (bridewealth), 51, 54, 62, 71, 129, 226, 256, 303–4n20, 337
Banyaga (chattel slaves), 51, 65–66, 71, 73, 102, 125, 271, 337
Barabangsa (royal lineage), 48, 49, 72, 337
Barangay system, 323–24n1, 337
Bates Agreement (1899), 90, 91
Bayuk (ballads or chanted poems), 53, 328n20, 337
Beckett, Jeremy, 57, 64, 65, 87, 92, 94, 97, 101
Bilaan ethnic group, *bangaya* slaves from, 73
Bird Island (*Punul*), 120–21, 123, 175
Biruar, Angka, 255–56, 258, 259, 261
"Blackshirts" (MIM), 153
Bliss, Gen. Tasker, 86, 96
Boka (Eid al-Fitr; Idul Fitr), 43–44, 228
Bongo Island, 32
Bourdieu, Pierre, 16, 60
British East India Company, 78–79
Buan, Rebecca D., 56
Buayan Sultanate, 29; founding of, 49–50; rivalry with Magindanao Sultanate, 70, 78, 83; sociopolitical structure of, 71; trade by, 72–74, 79
Bud Bagsak, battle of, 311n4
Bud Dajo, "battle" of, 89
Bugis ethnic group (Sulawesi), social organization of, 302n14, 304nn25, 27
Buisan, Datu, 82
Bukidnon-Lanao Highlands, 27
Bukidnon (or Bukidnon-Lanao) Plateau, 25, 32
Buldun: sectarian violence in, 153–54; settlement of, 116
Bureau of Lands, 117, 118

Cajelo, Carlos, 152–53
Campo Muslim: Bangsamoro Rebellion viewed from, 170, 182–94; boundaries of, 299n23; census of, 299n23; community solidarity in, 43; construction of, 124, 171–76; description of, 8, 39–44, 42, 170–71, 197–99; elections in, 236–37, 260–66; ethnic diversity of, 40–41; government assistance in, 218; "hidden transcripts" (of separatist discourse) in, 23–24; household income in, 211, 327–28n12; military occupation of, 176–82; political geography of, 197–99, 198; population size of, 39; resistance to dominant culture in, 43–44; sanitation in, 41–43; sounds of, 11–12, 43
Candao, Liwa, 214, 256
Candao, Peping, 163, 179, 181, 193, 255, 256, 257–58, 259
Candao, Zacaria, 163, 213–15, 216, 219, 229–30, 232, 234, 235, 238–42, 245, 246, 248–54, 266
Carpenter, Frank, 106–7, 114–15, 276
Catholic Church. *See* Roman Catholic Church
Cebuano ethnic group, 35
Cebuano language, 36
Celebes Sea, 27
Central Luzon, armed rebellion in, 115
Central Mindanao Highlands, 27
Central Mindanao, postcolonial settlement of, 116
Chavacano language, 299n19
China, trade relations with, 70, 73, 75–76, 77, 78–79, 83, 84
Chinese (immigrant) ethnic group: distribution of, 35, 120; expulsion of (1755), 75; Muslim Chinese-mestizos, 39; population of, 92; professions of, 36, 39, 75; trade by, 75–76, 79, 92, 95, 102
Christian Children's Fund (CCF), 210–12, 228, 283
Christianity: attempted conversion of Muslims to, 82
Christians for National Liberation, 330–31n1
Cigarette smugglers, 122–23, 160–61, 175
Civilian Home Defense Force (CHDF), 173, 179, 191
Clothing: Islamic (*hijab*), 202; traditional (of *datus*), 55; Westernized, 36
Comaroff, Jean, 271, 293–94n7
Comaroff, John, 271, 293–94n7
"Commander Jack," 179–80, 193, 326n18
Commission on National Integration, 139–43, 314n22

Communist Party of the Philippines (CCP), 167, 234, 330–31n1
"Communities, imagined," 14, 15, 16
Cotabato (Mindanao): American colonial policy in, 90, 93–97; *barangay* in, 323–24n1; Christian immigration to, 33, 35, 36–37, 113–19, 136–37; description of contemporary region and city, 32–39, 121; division of labor in, 35–36; earthquake in (1976), 181; economy of, 33–35, 121–23; elections in, 230–31, 236–38, 245–68; ethnic diversity of, 29–32, 35–39, 120; ethnographic descriptions of, 47, 57; fields of force in, 7; Islamic (precolonial, traditional) rule of, 45–68; "labor unions" in, 125–26; land (geographic description) of, 25–27, 26, 28; limits to Islamic unity in, 255–66, 267, 281; mass rallies in, 235–45, 266, 267; MILF attack on, 246; military occupation of, 177; moral authority in, 219–26; Muslim-Christian relations in, 36–39, 114–19, 120, 124–25, 136–37, 149–56; Muslim insurgency in, 3, 24, 158–59; Muslim postcolonial migration to Cotabato City, 119–24; Muslim rebel leadership in, 5, 6, 159–61; Muslim street vendors in, 37, 38, 172; naming of, 27; political economy of, 8, 69–80; population of, 29–32, 35, 120–21; postcolonial settlement of, 116–19; precolonial political relations in, 59–66; ranked status in, 50–51; sectarian violence in, 149–56; student demonstrations in, 215–16, 239; sultanates established in, 48; voter registration in, 264–65, 332–33n13
Cotabato River Basin: agricultural production in, 33; description of, 25–27, 26, 28, 32, 34; sectarian violence in, 151–53
Craft specialists, *tupus* of, 302n11
Crocodiles. *See* Spirit crocodiles
Cultural hegemony: accommodation to, 273, 288; and coercion, 18; critique of, 9, 18–19, 24, 279–80; definition of, 17–19; description of, 16–20; resistance to, 17, 18–20, 65, 271–72, 273, 277–78, 284–89
Cultural pluralism, 252–54

Dampier, William, 57, 64, 74, 75, 82
Datumanong, Simeon, 145, 152, 163, 214, 248–52
Datu Piang. *See* Piang, Datu ("Ama ni Mingka")

Datu Piang (Mindanao), population of, 29
Datus (aristocracy): acculturation of, 131–32; capriciousness of, 64, 67; clothing styles of, 55; collaboration with colonial authorities, 87–104, 106, 276; collaboration with Marcos government, 161, 162–63, 166–67, 168–69, 213, 231–32, 234; *dayunday* sponsored by, 225; definition of, 57–58, 230, 307n5, 337; legal protections by, 62–64; legitimacy of, 52, 270; and Bangsomoro rebellion, 161–63; naming of, 58; political relations of, 60–66, 71, 87–88; postcolonial rule by, 113–14, 124–32, 216–19, 231–32, 247–48, 250; in post-Marcos era, 234–68; public disregard of, 229–31; rank competition within, 50, 52–59, 229, 270; redistribution of goods by, 62, 67; ruling ideas of, 56–59, 66, 134, 270–72; sanctified inequality of, 45, 46, 50–51, 88, 103, 106, 204, 220, 232, 269, 270–72; supernatural abilities of, 58–59, 94–95, 127, 175, 271, 277, 318n21
Davao Gulf, 27
Davis, Gen. George W., 311n5
Da'wah (call to faith), 337
Da'wah (call to faith) conferences, 214–16, 232, 239
Dayunday ("song duels"), 223–25, 225, 260, 282, 330n31, 337
Death commemoration ceremonies, 220–23, 228
Death vigils, 222–23
Debt slavery, 51, 63, 71
Democratic Party, U.S., 89
Dilangalen, Didagan, 252
Dimaporo, Ali, 148, 217–18, 239
Divine mercy (*limu a Kadenan*), 192–94, 196, 279
Dominant cultures. *See* Cultural hegemony
Drakulic, Slavenka, 21–22
Dumatus (descendants of Tabunaway), 47, 50, 337
Dutch colonialism, 112
Dyadic alliances, 60, 72

Economic Development Corps (ED-COR), 115–16
Egypt: missionaries and teachers from, 200–202, 205; scholarships from, 143–44, 204–5, 281
Eickelman, Dale, 311n2
Elites. *See* Cultural hegemony; *Datus* (aristocracy); Subordinates

Ellen, Roy, 283
Elster, Jon, 271–72
Endatuan ("those who are ruled"): description of, 50, 338; obligations of, 71, 102, 271; protection of, 61
English language, 36, 37, 132, 331n5
Errington, Shelly, 59
Esteros River, 32
Ethnonationalism: definition of, 14, 142; homogenization of ideology in, 21–23; recent examples of, 294–95n11; revanchist or revitalistic spirit of, 46; willingness to fight and die for, 1, 15, 20
Experience, shared structures of, 59, 60

Filipino (Christian) ethnic group, as dominant culture, 36, 113–19
Forbes, Cameron, 96
Forrest, Thomas, 20, 64, 73, 75–76, 77, 78
Foucault, Michel, 16
Fox, Richard, 6, 272–73, 274
Friedman, Jonathan, 278
Fugate, James R., 107
Funerary rituals, traditional, 220–23, 228

Gainza, Francisco, 30–31
Gambling, 206, 220, 283
Geertz, Clifford, 59, 305n30
George, T. J. S., 147
Giants (*masela a mama;* "large men"), 192–93
Glang, Alunan, 56, 134
Gowing, Peter, 86, 87, 97
Gramsci, Antonio, 16, 17, 18, 287, 288
Gullick, J. M., 53
Gurus, religious education by, 202

Habeas corpus, suspension of, 2
Hadji status, 133, 177, 338
"Haraforas" ("Alfoores"), 308n11
Hasan, Bapa, 329n24
Hassoubah, Ahmad Mohammad H., 205
Havel, Václav, 287
Hayden, Joseph Ralston, 109, 110
Heritage, sharing of, 14
Hobsbawm, Eric, 274
Horn, Florence, 276
Horvatich, Patricia, 278
Hukbalahap (Hukbo ng Bayan laban sa Hapon) Rebellion, 115
Hunt, Chester, 119, 131, 202
Hypergamy, 53–54

Ilaga ("Rats"), sectarian violence by, 151–53, 154, 172, 183, 191, 338
Ilana Bay, 25, 30, 31, 33

Ileto, Reynaldo, 87, 93, 291–92n2
Illana Confederation, 30. *See also* Iranun ethnic group
Ilmu ("special knowledge"), 58, 338
Ilocano ethnic group, 35
Ilonggo ethnic group, 35, 321n14; in Civilian Home Defense Force (CHDF), 173; sectarian violence by, 151–53, 173
Ilonggo language, 36
Imams: definition of, 338; role of, 203, 204
Imperialism, self-liquidating, 89, 104
India, indigenous identities in, 272–73
Indios, definition of, 81
Indonesia: ethnic divisions in, 112; Minangkabau identity in, 274
Ingeds (localities): associated with ruling *datus,* 71, 72; connections between, 55; definition of, 338; mentioned in rebel songs, 190, 195; protection within, 62; related to *bangsa,* 47, 48, 190; residence of *endatuan* in, 50
IPP. *See* Islamic Party of the Philippines
Iranun ethnic group: anti-American insurgency among, 311n7; commitment to Muslim rebellion, 322n25; description of, 30–31; distribution of, 30–31, 41; population size of, 31, 35; professions of, 36, 75; trade by, 74–75, 78, 83, 122–23
Iranun language, 31
Islamic Conference of Foreign Ministers. *See* Organization of the Islamic Conference of Foreign Ministers (OIC)
Islamic Party of the Philippines (IPP): election campaigns by, 248–52, 257–58, 266–67; formation of, 246–48; populist and pluralistic character of, 252–54
Islamic populism, 252–54, 266, 267
Islamic renewal, 7, 186, 200–207, 232, 252, 267, 270, 280–84, 330n32
Islamic social identity. *See* Moro (Muslim ethnic) identity (Morohood); Muslim social identity
"Islamic Unity," 215, 281–82
Islam, spread of, 49

Jabidah Massacre, 140–41, 143, 146–47, 148
Jack. *See* "Commander Jack"
Jesuit missionaries, 79, 82, 97, 310n24
Jihad (holy war), 190–91, 195, 283, 338
Juliano, Teodoro, 177, 231

Kabungsuwan, Sarip: *pulna* status of descendants of, 53; as refugee from Por-

tuguese colonialism, 69; royal lineage established by, 48, 49, 50; spread of Islam by, 48–49; supernatural abilities of, 312n9; tracing descent from, 48, 50, 53
Kabuntalan Sultanate, 296–97n4, 302n13
Kadaffi, Muammar, 155
Kahn, Joel, 274, 277
Kalanganan *barangay,* 231, 261, 265, 324n3, 326n16
Kamal ("special power"), 58, 338
Kamid, Kasan, 172–74, 182, 186, 230, 237, 239, 240, 242, 257, 263
"Kamlun Uprising" (Sulu, 1952), 319n1
Kamsa (*barangay* captain in Campo Muslim), 177, 197, 209, 218, 219, 230, 231
Kanduli (ritual meals), 220–21, 222, 338
Kapatagan Basin, settlement of, 116
Kapferer, Bruce, 294n8
Kargador (dockworkers), 125–26, 126, 338
KBL. *See* Kilusang Bagong Lipunan (KBL, New Society Movement)
Kerkvliet, Benedict, 8
Kilusang Bagong Lipunan (KBL, New Society Movement), 217, 230–31, 237
Kilusang ng Urban Poor (Urban Poor Movement), 257
Kiram, Princess Tarhata, 106–7, 276
Knights of Mohammad, 318n26
Koronadal Valley, settlement of, 115, 127
Kris (sword), 338
Kudarat (sultan of Magindanao), 77, 82, 164, 310n22
Kuder, Edward M., 107–10, 111, 135–36
Kulintang, 338
Kumpits (motorized boats), in contraband trade, 122–23, 338
"Kuta Watu," 27. *See also* Cotabato (Mindanao)
Kutawatu Revolutionary (Regional) Committee (KRC), 162, 163, 208, 209, 214

Laarhoven, Ruurdje, 119, 308n8, 309–10n19
Lagos, Maria, 293–94n7
Lakas ng Bayan (LABAN, People's Power Party), 238
Lake Lanao Basin, 27
Lanao Plateau, 27, 31, 165
Layatul Kadir (the Night of Power), 222
Liberalista Party, 130, 145, 147–48, 317–18n20
Libungan Marsh, 27

Libya: foreign aid from, 205; missionaries and teachers from, 205; role in Tripoli Agreement talks, 167
Liguasan Marsh, 27
Linger, Daniel, 293–94n7
Loyre, Ghislaine, 305–6n35
Luces, Feliciano ("Toothpick"), 150–51, 155
Lucman, Rashid, 147, 148–49, 162
Lugay-lugay (community), 39, 178
Luwaran (written legal codes), 62–63, 104, 270, 338

Macapagal, Diosdado, 319n3
Madrasah (pl. *madari;* Islamic schools): in Cotabato, 199; curriculum of, 326n1; definition of, 338; establishment of, 133, 134, 135, 202–3, 205
Magindanaon ethnic group: collective identity of, 30; description of, 29–30; distribution of, 29–30, 41; ethnographic accounts of, 297n5; naming of, 27; population size of, 29, 35; professions of, 36; social organization of, 47–48
Magindanaon language: Christian speakers of, 36; dialects of, 29, 41; rally speech in, 239; rebel songs in, 11–12, 186–91, 195, 279
Maguindanao Province: boundaries of, 33, 322n24; elections in, 245–54, 266; population of, 298n12; waterways closed in, 158
Magindanao Sultanate, 27, 29; founding of, 49; peak of, 77; rivalry with Buayan Sultanate, 70, 78, 83; sociopolitical structure of, 71; trade by, 74–75, 77–78
Mahad al-Ulum al-Islamia (Campo Muslim), 199, 205, 206–7
Maharlika, 322–23n27
Majul, Cesar Adib, 49, 81–82, 140, 310n27
Makaalang, Sarip, 49
Makabalang (labor boss), 125
Malaguiok, Amelil ("Commander Ronnie"), 208, 214
Malaysia, Muslim separatist military training in, 148, 155, 160, 172
"Mana Silan Cowboy" ("They Are Like Cowboys"), 187–88, 190
Manday (village), 39, 178
Manday River, 32
Mangayaw (raiding), 309n.18
Manili Massacre, 151, 154, 155
Manobo ethnic group, *bangaya* slaves from, 73

Mantawil (sultan of Kabuntalan), 128
Maranao (Muslim) ethnic group: distribution of, 35, 41; impact of Islam on local ancestry of, 301–2n10; social organization of, 48; titleholders of, 304n21
Maratabat ("rank"), principles of, 51,
54, 101, 256, 270, 303n18, 338
Marawi City, attack on, 156
Marcos, Ferdinand: antismuggling activities of, 123, 160; candidates picked by,
152, 214; collapse of regime under,
235, 236–38; *datu* loyalty to, 161,
162–63, 166–67, 168–69, 213,
216–18, 231–32, 234; election of, 145;
fall of regime of, 3; martial law declared by, 3, 138, 156; and Muslim Independence Movement, 146; Muslim
nationalism after, 234–68; opposition
to, 160; opposition to Bangsamoro Rebellion, 165–66; reelection campaign
for, 171; and sectarian violence,
153–54, 155; as Sultan Tinamuman,
167; surrender of Muslims rebel leaders to, 160, 167, 168; as target of ethnic anger, 44; Tripoli Agreement implemented by, 168
Marcos, Imelda, 218
Marriage contracts, development of, 213
Mastura (sultan of Magindanao), 98,
313n16, 314n23
Mastura, Guiwan, 163, 185
Mastura, Michael, 56, 247, 249, 250,
251–52
Mastura, Tocao, 180, 193, 250
Matalam, Guiamid, 251–52
Matalam, Tuting, 146
Matalam, Udtug, 128–32, 137, 138,
144–49, 155, 156, 157, 161, 331n5
Matampay River: description of, 32; san-
itation along, 299n25
Maulid en Nabi (birthday of the
Prophet), 222
Mecca, pilgrimages to, 129–30, 133; cel-
ebrations on returning from, 222
Mednick, Melvin, 48, 63
Melaka, Portuguese colonialism in, 69, 80
Mercado, Elisio R., 155
MILF. *See* Moro Islamic Liberation Front
Milner, A. C., 60, 305n30
Mindalano (Maranao congressman), 134
Mindanao (Philippines): American colo-
nial settlement of, 90, 114–15; descrip-
tion of, 25, 26; Marcos-led develop-
ment of, 166; naming of, 27;
population of, 29–32
Mindanao and Sulu Mohammedan Stu-
dents' Association, 109

Mindanao Cross, 120, 129, 145, 149
Mindanao Independence Movement
(MIM), 320n10, 321n13
Ministry of Muslim Affairs (MMA): En-
glish-language education funded by,
327n7; opposition to, 216
Miskin, Nur, 207, 226, 240, 242, 262
Misuari, Nur, 141, 143, 144, 147, 148,
155, 157, 162, 164, 165, 167, 207–8,
214, 241–42, 246, 300n1
MNLF. *See* Moro National Liberation
Front
Moro Gulf, 27
Moro (Muslim ethnic) identity (Morohood): American colonial encouragement of, 87–88, 104–12, 132, 269,
272–78; definition of, 80–81, 143,
164, 338; development of, 5, 6, 69–85,
269, 272–78; as mythic, 45, 69, 80,
84–85, 164; postcolonial development
of, 132–37, 143, 275; practical,
283–84; among rank-and-file and civilian separatists, 4, 171, 183–94,
226–31; and reintegration programs,
139–43
Moro Islamic Liberation Front (MILF):
community support for, 228–29; counterelite coalition in, 213–16, 219, 232;
election nonparticipation advocated
by, 231; formation of, 207–10, 281; in
post-Marcos era, 234–68; "prayer
rally" organized by, 241–45, 266; services provided by, 212–13
"Moroland," 90
Moro-moro folk theater, 81, 164
Moro National Liberation Front
(MNLF): Aquino government recognition of, 241–42, 246; defections from,
160, 167, 168, 179–80, 185, 193–94,
196; election nonparticipation advocated by, 230; formation of, 155,
156–58; government opposition to,
167; ideological and diplomatic strategies of, 163–65, 167; leadership of,
159–60, 162; purpose of, 81, 155;
structure of, 157; terrorist activities attributed to, 181, 324n8
Moro Province, American colonial policy
in, 90–91
"Moro Wars," 81–82, 83
Mortuary rituals, traditional, 220–23, 228
Mosques: funding of, 205; Islamic renewal preached in, 203–4, 227,
232–33, 252, 267; transmission of
dominant ideology in, 57
Muhammad (the Prophet), tracing descent from, 49, 50, 52, 204, 220, 270

Muntia (magical stones), 326n17
Murad, Hadji, 208, 226, 243, 246, 282
Muslim Association of the Philippines
(MAP), 135–36
Muslim autonomous regions: created by
Marcos, 168; proposed, 3, 145, 164,
245–46; referendum on, 334n24
Muslim Filipino ethnic identity, 132–33,
275, 278
Muslim Independence Movement (MIM),
144–49, 156
Muslim Nationalist League, 141
Muslim separatist movement: ambivalence to, 294n10; development of,
138–69; factional infighting within, 3;
geographic distribution of, 2–3; as illegal, 2; imaginative narratives of, 19; Islamic renewal in, 7, 186, 200–207,
232, 252, 267, 270, 280–84, 330n32;
leadership of, 1, 6–7, 139; and new
Muslim social identity, 13; origin
myths of, 45; origins of, 3; post-Marcos era of, 234–68; rank-and-file and
civilian support for, 3, 4, 5, 7, 149,
171, 183–94, 226–31; reportage of, 1;
use of popular politics by, 3. *See also*
Bangsamoro Rebellion; Moro (Muslim
ethnic) identity (Morohood)
Muslim social identity: inclusivity of,
12–13; politicization of, 13. *See also*
Moro (Muslim ethnic) indentity (Morohood)
Muslims, ordinary: definition of, 292n3
Mustapha, Tun, 147–48, 155, 157

Nacionalista Party, 130, 145, 152, 161,
317–18n20, 321n16
Naga, Ali Abdul Ajiz, 199, 202, 203–4,
205, 206, 216, 259, 281
Nasser (rebel fighter), 184, 185
Nasser, Gamel Abdul, 143, 281
National Citizen's Movement for Free
Elections (NAMFREL), 236–37, 238
National Democratic Front (NDF),
330–31n1
National Executive Committee, 217
Nationalism: anthropological formula-
tion of, 14; and cultural hegemony, 16,
17–18, 20–24; ideologies of, 14; prolif-
eration of, 13–14; recourse to an imag-
ined past in, 46
National Land Settlement Administration
(NKSA), 115
Nations: definition of, 14; disparities in
social power in, 15; political goals of,
14
New People's Army, 330–31n1

New Society Movement. *See* Kilusang
Bagong Lipunan (KBL, New Society
Movement)
New Voyage Round the World
(Dampier), 57
Nobility, Muslim. See *Datus* (aristocracy)
North Cotabato Province, creation of,
127
Nurul Islam, 147, 156

OIC. *See* Organization of the Islamic
Conference of Foreign Ministers
Ong, Aihwa, 294n9
"Ontologies," concept of, 294n8
Organization of the Islamic Conference
of Foreign Ministers (OIC), 167, 168,
205, 208, 214, 244
Orientalism (orientalist hegemony),
272–73, 274
Ortner, Sherry, 294n10, 328n13
Ortuoste, Ignacio ("Datu sa Kutawatu"),
97–98, 102, 103
Ortuoste, Pedro, 312–13n12
Osmena, Sergio, 112, 126

Pagalungan: anti-Japanese activities in,
128–29; as provincial capital, 321n12
Palencia, Doroy, 321n17
Parang, battle of, 311n7
Partido Komunista ng Pilipinas,
330–31n1
Pasigan, Omar, 199, 214, 243, 252, 259
Patterson, Orlando, 61
Peletz, Michael, 294n10, 330n32
Pelzer, Karl J., 118
Pendatun, Salipada K., 109, 110–12,
111, 117, 120, 126–27, 128, 129, 130,
131–32, 135, 137, 138, 147, 152,
318n21; election to governorship, 145;
reaction to Muslim rebellion, 161–62;
relations with Muslim Independence
Movement, 148–49
Penguyaw (postwedding parlor game),
223
Philippine Constabulary, 118, 119, 125,
153, 154–55, 312n8
Philippine Muslim News, 141
Philippines: American colonial period in
(1899–1946), 3–4, 6, 69–70, 86–112,
300n3; census of, 29, 296n2; Christianization of, 82, 113–19; commonwealth established in (1935), 90, 110,
114–15; constitution of, 245–46; education in, 37–39, 94, 107–10, 133,
135–36, 138–44, 202–3, 205–6; elections in, 113, 130, 230–31, 236–38,
245–66; electorate of, 113, 130;

foreign aid to, 113, 121, 205; home-steading of, 90; Islamic "resurgence" in, 133–37, 147; Japanese invasion and occupation of, 110, 128–29; land speculation in, 118; martial law in (1972–1986), 3, 127, 138, 156, 231; Muslim population of, 2–3; national anthem of, 299n21; partial independence of, 108; plantation agriculture blocked in, 89–90; political clientelism in, 67; political economy of, 69–80; popular culture of, 12; postcolonial transitions in, 113–37; republic established in (1946), 6, 90, 108, 113–14, 124; Spanish colonial period in, 2, 5–6, 70, 76–84, 88, 92–93, 300n3; spread of Islam in, 49; tributary mode of production in, 70–72, 76; two-party political system in, 317–18n20

Piang, Datu ("Ama ni Mingka"), 91–97, 95, 99, 102, 103, 119, 131, 271, 277, 313n13

Piang, Gumbay, 103

Pigkawayan, postcolonial settlement of, 117

Pitra contributions, MILF appropriation of, 229

Polygyny, 54

Populism, Islamic, 252–54, 266, 267

Portuguese colonialism, 69, 80

Power, "personalistic idiom" of, 61

Progressive Labor Union (PLU), 125–26, 255

Pulangi River (Rio Grande de Mindanao): closed due to Muslim insurgency, 158, 173; description of, 25–27, 26, 30; sanitation along, 41; silting and dredging of, 120–21, 123; Spanish occupation of delta of, 119; transportation along, 32–33, 120

Pulna status, of sultans, 53, 338

Pusaka (family heirlooms), loss of, 182, 338

Putri, Rajah, 93

Quezon, Manuel, 100, 110

Quirino, Elpidio, 100, 127

Rafu (foreigners), 302n11

Rajamuda sa Magindanao, 252

Ramadan: puasa (fast) of, 43. See also Boka

Rashid, Disumimba, 150, 160, 193

Ravenholt, Albert, 134

Rebel camps: "prayer rally" meeting at, 242–43; reportage of, 2; ulama at, 199

Rebel songs, 11–12, 186–91, 195, 196, 279

Reconciliation House (Center) (Campo Muslim), 210

Redistribution, 62, 67

Reed-Danahay, Deborah, 294n9

Region 12, 163, 208

Regional Autonomous Government (RAG): role of, 218, 241

Regional Autonomous Government (RAG) Complex (Cotabato), 171, 218

Reid, Anthony, 304n26, 306n36, 328n20

Reina Regente, Spanish fort at, 92

Republican Party, U.S., 89

Resistance. See Cultural hegemony, resistance to

Rodriguez de Figueroa, Capt. Esteban, 310n23

Roff, William, 335n5

Roman Catholic Church, as relief provider in Campo Muslim, 181–82, 210–12, 228

Roseberry, William, 335n7

Sabah: Philippine refugees in, 156; proposed invasion of, 141, 147–48; weapons for Muslim rebels from, 157, 160

Sabil (rebel martyrs), 194, 196, 338

St. Louis World's Fair (1904), "Moros" at, 86, 275

Sakup ("those who are protected"), 61, 270

Salamat, Hashim, 144, 147, 149, 157, 165, 207–9, 214, 243, 244, 245

Saleeby, Najeeb, 27, 62, 92, 104–7, 134, 275

Sambolawan, Sandiale, 328n14

"Sanctified inequality," myth of, 45–46, 50–51, 88, 103, 106, 204, 220, 232, 269, 270–72

Sangki, Abdulla, 145

Sansaluna, Ali, 160

Santiago (Iranun insurgent), 97–98

Saudi Arabia: foreign aid from, 205; missionaries and teachers from, 205; opposition to religious control from, 222

Sayer, Derek, 287–88

Schlegel, Stuart, 32

Scott, James, 15, 18–19, 20, 23, 285, 286, 306n39

Scott, William Henry, 60–61, 62, 63, 64, 67, 307n4

Senate Committee on National Minorities, Philippine, 117

Separatist struggles: ethical issues of ethnography of, 295n13; methodological difficulties of ethnography of, 21–23; political goals of, 14; proliferation of, 13–14; remotivation for, 21. *See also* Muslim separatist movement

Shafi'i school of Islamic law, 62, 249

Sharia (Islamic law), 213, 225–26, 230, 233, 283, 338

Shi'a Muslims, 207, 249

Shirk, sin of, 228

Siddiqui, Maulana Mohamed Abdul Aleem, 200–202, *201*

Silsila (name-chains), 49, 304n24

Simeon (datu of Cotabatu), 219

Sindang, Abdul Ghani, 202

Sinsuat, Bai Fatima, 125, 126, 255

Sinsuat, Blah, 125, 126, 127, 318–19n28

Sinsuat, Duma, 127

Sinsuat, Mama, 316n11

Sinsuat, Mando, 124, 127, 231, 317n19

Slobin, Mark, 325n10

Sluka, Jeffrey, 325nn9, 15

Social disparity, theories of, 56

Social identity: description of, 12–13; politicization of, 13. *See also* Moro (Muslim ethnic) identity (Morohood; Muslim social identity

Social inequality, sanctification of, 45

Social justice, 203, 282

Society of the Indian Muslims, 135

South Cotabato Province, creation of, 127

Southern Philippines Development Authority, 218

Spanish colonialism, 2, 5–6, 70, 76–84, 88, 92–93, 300n3

Spells, 192

Spirit crocodiles (*mga pagali*), 99, 192

Status, precedence over wealth, 52–53

Steinberg, David, 89

Subordinates: "hidden transcripts" of, 18, 23, 270; resistance to cultural hegemony of elites, 17, 18–20, 65, 271–72, 273, 277–78, 284–89

Sufi *tahlil* (prayer litany), chanting of, 221, 222

Sultanates: definition of, 301n9; renewed emphasis on, 164–65

Sultans: allegiance to, 71–72; privileged access to external trading partners, 72; Sabbath observance by, 57; supernatural potency of, 58

Sulu Sultanate: American colonial policy in, 90, 91; American subjugation of, 88–89; debt slavery in, 51; expansion of, 77–78, 79; subordinates' position in, 61–62; titleholders of, 304n21; trade by, 78–79, 84

Swedenburg, Ted, 22–23

Tabunaway (legendary chieftain), 50

Tabunaway bangsa: status of, 301–2n10; *tarsilas* of, 52

Tagalog ethnic group, 35, 36

Tagalog language, 35, 36, 37

Tagumpay ng Bayan (People's Victory) Rally, 235–41

Tamontaka, Jesuit mission at, 97

Tamontaka River, 27

Tantawan, 209, 329–30n29

Tantawan Hill (Cotabato), 27

Tan, Tuya, 91

Tao I Chih Lueh (Summary Notices of the Barbarians of the Isles), 307n4

Taritib (oral protocols governing social relations), 52, 248, 253, 338

Tarsilas (written genealogies), 49, 50, 52, 54–55, 56–57, 104, 270, 338

Tau sa ilud (downriver people), 338

Tau sa laya (upriver people), 338

Tawakim ("gift wives"), 304n23

T'boli ethnic group, *bangaya* slaves from, 73

Tunggu a inged (Guardian of the Inged), 192–93

Thomas, Benjamin, 87

Timako Hill, 32

Tiruray ethnic group: description of, 31–32; distribution of, 299n18; exploitation of, 65; population size of, 298n12; productivity of, 73–74; trade relationships with sultanates, 73–74, 79–80

Tiruray Highlands: description of, 27, 31, 32; sectarian violence in, 150–51

Titles: colonial, 98; inheritance of, 53; in martial law period, 166–67, 177, 217–18; political clout of, 248–49; projection of personal power in, 58

"Trade-raiding," 309n.18

Traditional healers, 329n24

Traditionalism, 46. *See also* Cotabato (Mindanao), Islamic (precolonial, traditional) rule of

Tradition, invention of, 274

Tran, siege of, 158

Tributary modes of production, 70–72, 76

Tripoli Agreement, 167–68, 207, 214, 234, 235, 239, 242, 244

Tunina, Putri, 49

Tupus (local descent lines), 48, 338

Ulama (sing. *alim;* Islamic clerics and scholars): definition of, 337, 338;

description of, 184, 199, 200–207, 281, 326–27n2; opposition to traditional practices by, 219–26, 227, 233; political clout of, 248–50, 281, 282; popular scrutiny of, 226–29, 282–83; "prayer rally" organized by, 242–45

Ulipun ("disenfranchised" persons; debt-bondsmen): conversion of, 63, 71; description of, 51, 338; obligations of, 71, 102, 271

United Nationalist Democratic Organizations (UNIDO), 237, 238, 240, 241

United States: colonialism by, 3–4, 6, 69–70, 86–112, 269, 272–78, 300n3; foreign aid from, 236

Unti, Zamin, 242, 255, 261

Upi, sectarian violence in, 150–51

Ustadzes (Islamic teachers), 184, **338.** *See also Ulama*

Utang na loob (debts of gratitude), 264

Utu (sultan of Buayan), 64, 73, 79, 88, 91, 92, 93, 271, 305n33, 314n20

"U2" units (special intelligence units), 180

Visayan ethnic group, 36

Visayan language, 299n19

Vote brokering (lider), 261–64, 265–66, 268, 338

Wahhabism, 222, 328n19

Wang Ta-yuan, 307n4

Warren, James F., 51, 78, 310n25

"Watu na Ulu" (head of stone), 52

Weddings, 223, 224, 228

Wilkes, Charles, 61

Williams, Brackette, 142

Williams, Raymond, 16, 17, 273

Wolf, Eric, 76

Wolters, O.W., 60

Women: Islamic attempts to control, 329n23; as recipients of Catholic relief aid, 328n13

Wood, Gen. Leonard, 89, 90–91

Woost, Michael, 293–94n7, 294n9

Zakat (almsgiving), 229, 329n26

Zamboanga: "peace talks" conference in, 167; Spanish control of, 77, 83

[Handwritten annotations:]

FOREMOST HISTORIAN OF PHILIPPINES

1846 = STEAM-POWERED GUNBOATS STOPPED IRANUN RAIDING. 1861 = SPANISH FLAG OVER MAGINDANAO.

LATE 1700S = BRITISH COOPERATE W/ SULU SULTANATE AFTER DISCOVERING IMPT. TRADE LINK W/ CHINA + IT BECOMES IMPT. PORT FOR THEIR TRADE. SULU RAPIDLY EXPANDS + ITS NEED FOR LARGE LABOR FORCE HAD BEEN MET BY IRANUN SLAVING.

CHINESE TRADERS BECOME IMPT. MERCHANTS BASED IN COTABATO SUPPLYING MAGINDANAO SLAVES TO SULU, ONCE IRANUN SLAVING CURTAILED (79)

DATU ULU – LAST INDEP. SULTAN OF BUAYAN STARTS ENSLAVING NEARBY TIRURAY – SELLS TO CHINESE MERCHANTS. FORMER CLIENTS BECOME COMMODITIES (80)

ASIDE FROM PRIVATE RAIDS VS. SPANISH NORTH IT WAS MOSTLY A COLD WAR   1768–1846 ALMOST YEARLY

p?

CESAR

MAJUL — A NATIONALIST MORO HISTORIAN 1973

POSITS TRANSCENDENT MORO MUSLIM IDENTITY.

GEORGE, GOWING, MOLLOY + BAUZON HAVE AGREED
1980   1979   1988   1991

"MOROS HAVE FOUGHT SPANISH, AMERICANS + FILIPINOS"

DONT. CALL ALL MUSLIM POP.S. MOORS. SINCE   (80
MELAKA 1511.

SPANISH CALLED IRANUM (OR ILLANO) "MOORS"
                                        MOROS
    + NORTHERN PILLUP. "INDIOS".   (81

FOLK THEATRE FORM CALLED "MORO-MORO" DEPICTS
XIAN DEFEAT OF MUSLIMS PILLAGING VILLAINS. (81

MAJUL DISCUSSES "RELIGIOUS DIFFERENCE" WAS

CRITICAL TO SPANISH.

AIR + ROBERTSON 1903-19   + SALEEBY 1908   :

DESCRIBE SPANISH CAMPAIGNS FROM   1578 TO
LATE 1800S ATTACKING MOSQUES, SUPPRESSION
OF ISLAMIC TEACHING + COERCIVE CONVERSIONS
OF MUSLIMS TO XIANITY.   82.

- BUT ECON. MOTIVES ARE POWERFUL TRADE,
RESOURCES, TRIBUTE IN SAME TEXTS.

ISLAMIC CONSCIOUSNESS INTENSIFIED IN RESISTANCE
TO SPANISH =   LITTLE EVIDENCE ??   P82.

1603 ADDRESS — BY DATU BUISAN   FATHER OF

                                SULTAN KUDARAT

+

SULTAN

KUDARAT'S

ADDRESS TO

RANUN DATUS 1639 = NO REFERENCES TO ISLAM

JESUITS HEARD THEM.

Designer: Nola Burger
Indexer: Barbara E. Cohen
Compositor: Impressions Book
and Journal Services, Inc.
Text: 10/13 Sabon
Display: Sabon
Printer: Thomson-Shore, Inc.
Binder: Thomson-Shore, Inc.

TO LEYTE CHIEFS

SARIP KABUNGSAWAN — 1ST LEGENDARY FOUNDER OF COTABATO SULTANATE WAS REFUGEE FROM PORTG. CAPTURE OF MELAKA IN 1511.   (p69)

DATU ALI , LAST INDEP. RULER CAPTURED + KILLED BY U.S. 1905.   (69)

INDIG. POP-s = MAGINDANAON, IRANUN + TIRURAY USED PLUNDER OF PRIMARY PRODUCERS + COMMOD. PRODUCTION TO SURVIVE. — SLAVING TOO (70)
LOCAL OVERLORDS – "DATUS"

MAGINDANAO SULTANATE   +   BUAYAN SULTANATE
AT MOUTH OF PULANGI   UPSTREAM
                                                                    – FERTILE
RIVER   RICE PRODUCTION ↗   VALLEY

BOTH ENGAGED IN TRADE W/ MING CHINESE   p70

DATU UTO OF BUAYAN = MOST POWERFUL LEADER OF MID 1800s HAD 4-5000 SLAVES. p71 PROBABLY FROM NON-MUSLIM PHILP. LANDS.

CAPITAL SIMUAY OF MAGINDANAO WAS WEALTHIEST PLACE IN COTABATO + MALAY WAS SPOKEN THERE.— (NEAR COTABATO CITY)

IRANUM PIRATES RAIDED TO THE SOUTH (SULAWESI + BRUNEI.)
+ NORTH + OCCUPIED IMPT. NICHE.
INDEP., BUT ECON. LINKED TO MAGINDANAO SULT.
CHINESE THERE TOO — THROWN OUT 1755 BY
COLONIAL AUTHORITIES.

SPANISH OCCUPIED N. PHILIP. IN 1571 +
ALMOST IMMED. SOUGHT TO SUBDUE MUSLIM SOUTH
TRIED TO CONTROL ZAMBOANGA   (76)
PENN. TO CONTROL SEA LANES TO COTABATU.
+ BASILAN ISLAND   (77)
IT INVADED CHINESE - COTABATU TRADE.
NOT SUCCESSFUL IN STOPPING MARITIME RAIDING.

By MID-1700S. PHILIP. POP. WAS DISARMED.
+ IRANUN TOOK ADV. OF THIS FOR   (77)
RAIDING.

EARLY 1600S = COTABATU REACHED ITS HEIGHT
    UNDER SULTAN KUDARAT.
BUT BY 1775 - SPANISH INTERFERENCE W/
    CHINESE TRADE HAS IMPOVERISHED
    ~~MAGINDANAO~~ MAGINDANAO SULTANATE.   77

By 1800 = DECLINE BEGINS
    SULU SULTANATE RISES + CONTINUES SAME
        TYPE OF ECON. TRADE CENTER
    (SEVERAL TRADE ROUTES)
MAGINDANAO PROVIDES RICE TO SULU FOR
CHINESE GOODS. AFTER 1780 IRANUN
SHIFT ALLIANCE \ ALLEGIANCE TO SULU.   (78)

1605 + 1635 = SPANISH SIGNED TREATIES RECOGNIZING
    BUAYAN SULTAN AS PARAMOUNT RULER OF
MAGINDANAO.   1645 + 1719 = SIMILAR TREATIES
    W/ MAGINDANAO.
By 1837 = SPANISH PROTECTORATE (ALMOST).   78

LATE 1960S - STUDENTS + INTELLS BEGAN REBELLION (P3)

1970: SECTARIAN VIOLENCE IN COTABATO GAVE IT POPULAR
SUPPORT.

1972 MARCOS' DECL. OF MARTIAL LAW = IT BECOMES ARMED
SECESSIONIST FRONT

30,000 FOUGHT 9OUT TO STALEMATE

5% PHILP.
POP MUSLIM
3 MIL. TOTAL

1977 CEASE-FIRE + PEACE TREATY

"MUSLIM AUTONOMOUS REGION" NEVER MATERIALIZES

FIGHTING CONTINUES + DISARRAY.

BY 1980S = MASS-BASED ISLAMIC MOVEMENT LED
BY MUSLIM CLERICS.

1985 - MARCOS FALLS - ISLAMIC MOVEMENT USES
DEMOS TO PETITION GOVT. FOR AUTONOMY
ISLAMIC PARTY FORMS TO CONTEST ELECTIONS.

1972
1977
1ST
PHAS
OF
WAR

IT ORIGINATED DURING AMERICAN COLONIAL ERA
1899 - 1946 - NOT FROM 300 YR. RESISTANCE
TO SPANISH (P4)

IMAGE OF PHILIP. MUSLIM NATION "BANGSAMORO" HAD
VERY LITTLE RESONANCE AMONG RANK + FILE
ADHERENTS. (P4)

19:
ISLA
PAR
FOR
FOR
ELECTI

SPANISH CREATED 2 PEOPLES - CHRISTIANIZED +
COLONIZED IN THE NORTH + UNSUBJUGATED MUSLIMS
IN SOUTH. AMERICANS YOKED THESE 2 TOGETHER. (*)
S-6.

NO CONCERTED OPPOSITION EVER UNITED MUSLIM
PEOPLES OF THE SOUTH + ACCOMODATION WAS MOST (?)
FREQUENT RESPONSE TO SPANISH.

- THEY BECAME UNIFIED AS A RESULT OF AMERICAN (6)
"INDIGNATIONS" ASSERTED BY WESTERN ORIENTALISM